D1081682

Get the eBooks FREE!

(PDF, ePub, Kindle, and liveBook all included)

We believe that once you buy a book from us, you should be able to read it in any format we have available. To get electronic versions of this book at no additional cost to you, purchase and then register this book at the Manning website.

Go to https://www.manning.com/freebook and follow the instructions to complete your pBook registration.

That's it!
Thanks from Manning!

PRAISE FOR THE SECOND EDITION

The Quick Python Book

The Quick Python Book

THIRD EDITION

NAOMI CEDER
FOREWORD BY NICHOLAS TOLLERVEY

MANNING
SHELTER ISLAND

For online information and ordering of this and other Manning books, please visit
www.manning.com. The publisher offers discounts on this book when ordered in quantity.
For more information, please contact

    Special Sales Department
    Manning Publications Co.
    20 Baldwin Road
    PO Box 761
    Shelter Island, NY 11964
    Email: orders@manning.com

Manning Publications Co. 20 Baldwin Road PO Box 761 Shelter Island, NY 11964	Development editor: Christina Taylor Technical development editor: Scott Steinman Project Manager: Janet Vail Copyeditor Kathy Simpson Proofreader: Elizabeth Martin Technical proofreader: André Brito Typesetter and cover design: Marija Tudor

ISBN 9781617294037
Printed in the United States of America
1 2 3 4 5 6 7 8 9 10 – EBM – 23 22 21 20 19 18

The Quick Python Book

THIRD EDITION

NAOMI CEDER

FOREWORD BY NICHOLAS TOLLERVEY

MANNING

SHELTER ISLAND

For online information and ordering of this and other Manning books, please visit
www.manning.com. The publisher offers discounts on this book when ordered in quantity.
For more information, please contact

    Special Sales Department
    Manning Publications Co.
    20 Baldwin Road
    PO Box 761
    Shelter Island, NY 11964
    Email: orders@manning.com

Manning Publications Co.
20 Baldwin Road
PO Box 761
Shelter Island, NY 11964

Development editor:	Christina Taylor
Technical development editor:	Scott Steinman
Project Manager:	Janet Vail
Copyeditor	Kathy Simpson
Proofreader:	Elizabeth Martin
Technical proofreader:	André Brito
Typesetter and cover design:	Marija Tudor

ISBN 9781617294037
Printed in the United States of America
1 2 3 4 5 6 7 8 9 10 – EBM – 23 22 21 20 19 18

brief contents

v

contents

contents

foreword

I've known Naomi Ceder for many years, as a collaborator and a friend. She has a reputation in the Python community as an inspiring teacher, an expert coder, and a formidable community organizer. You would do well to listen to her wise words.

But don't just take my word for it! Naomi, in her role as a teacher, has helped innumerable people learn Python. Many members of the Python community, myself included, have benefitted from her work. Such extensive experience means she knows what aspects of the language are important for new Pythonistas to learn and which may require extra care and attention from the student. Such wisdom is skillfully distilled into the pages of this book.

Python is, famously, a "batteries included" language: there are many things you could do and areas of endeavor covered by Python's extensive ecosystem of modules. It's an exciting time to get involved with this powerful, easy to learn, and flourishing language.

That this is a "Quick" Python book reflects Naomi's concise teaching style and ensures you have the essentials of Python at your fingertips. Moreover, such essentials provide a firm foundation upon which to build your Python programming. Most important, by reading this book you will gain enough insight and context to act autonomously and effectively: you'll know what to do, where to look, and what to ask for when you inevitably encounter bumps in the road as you grow as a Python developer.

Naomi's book is the epitome of what it is to be "Pythonic": beautiful is better than ugly, simple is better than complex, and readability counts.

You have in your hands a wonderful guide for taking your first steps with Python. Best of luck for the journey ahead, and remember to enjoy the ride!

NICHOLAS TOLLERVEY
PYTHON SOFTWARE FOUNDATION FELLOW

preface

I've been coding in Python for 16 years now, far longer than in any other language I've ever used. I've used Python for system administration, for web applications, for database management, and for data analysis over those years, but most important, I've come to use Python just to help myself think about a problem more clearly.

Based on my earlier experience, I would have expected that by now I would have been lured away by some other language that was faster, cooler, sexier, whatever. I think there are two reasons that didn't happen. First, while other languages have come along, none has helped me do what I needed to do quite as effectively as Python. Even after all these years, the more I use Python and the more I understand it, the more I feel the quality of my programming improve and mature.

The second reason I'm still around is the Python community. It's one of the most welcoming, inclusive, active, and friendly communities I've seen, embracing scientists, quants, web developers, systems people, and data scientists on every continent. It's been a joy and honor to work with members of this community, and I encourage everyone to join in.

Writing this book has been a bit of a journey. While we're still on Python 3, today's Python 3 has evolved considerably from 3.1, and the ways people are using Python have also evolved. Although my goal has always been to keep the best bits of the previous edition, there have been a fair number of additions, deletions, and reorganizations that I hope make this edition both useful and timely. I've tried to keep the style clear and low-key without being stuffy.

For me, the aim of this book is to share the positive experiences I've gotten from coding in Python by introducing people to Python 3, the latest and, in my opinion, the greatest version of Python to date. May your journey be as satisfying as mine has been.

acknowledgments

I want to thank David Fugate of LaunchBooks for getting me into this book in the first place and for all of the support and advice he has provided over the years. I can't imagine having a better agent and friend. I also need to thank Michael Stephens of Manning for pushing the idea of doing a third edition of this book and supporting me in my efforts to make it as good as the first two. Also at Manning, many thanks to every person who worked on this project, with special thanks to Marjan Bace for his support, Christina Taylor for guidance in the development phases, Janet Vail for getting the book (and me) through the production process, Kathy Simpson for her patience in copy editing, and Elizabeth Martin for proofreading. Likewise, hearty thanks to the many reviewers whose insights and feedback were of immense help, including André Filipe de Assunção e Brito, the technical proofreader for this edition of the book, along with Aaron Jensen, Al Norman, Brooks Isoldi, Carlos Fernández Manzano, Christos Paisios, Eros Pedrini, Felipe Esteban Vildoso Castillo, Giuliano Latini, Ian Stirk, Negmat Mullodzhanov, Rick Oller, Robert Trausmuth, Ruslan Vidert, Shobha Iyer, and William E. Wheeler.

I have to thank the authors of the first edition, Daryl Harms and Kenneth MacDonald, for writing a book so sound that it has remained in print well beyond the average lifespan of most tech books, and for giving me a chance to update the second and now the third edition, as well as everyone who bought and gave positive reviews to the second edition. I hope this version carries on the successful and long-lived tradition of the first and second editions.

Thanks also go to Nicholas Tollervey for the kindness (not to mention speed) with which he wrote the foreword to this edition, as well as for our years of friendship and all that he has done for the Python community. I also owe thanks to the global Python community, an unfailing source of support, wisdom, friendship, and joy over the years. Thank you, my friends. Thanks also to my canine associate, Aeryn, who has faithfully kept me company and helped me keep my sense of perspective as I worked on this edition, just as she did for the second edition.

Most important, as always, thanks to my wife, Becky, who both encouraged me to take on this project and supported me through the entire process. I really couldn't have done it without you.

about this book

The Quick Python Book, Third Edition, is intended for people who already have experience in one or more programming languages and want to learn the basics of Python 3 as quickly and directly as possible. Although some basic concepts are covered, there's no attempt to teach fundamental programming skills in this book, and the basic concepts of flow control, OOP, file access, exception handling, and the like are assumed. This book may also be of use to users of earlier versions of Python who want a concise reference for Python 3.

How to use this book

Part 1 introduces Python and explains how to download and install it on your system. It also includes a very general survey of the language, which will be most useful for experienced programmers looking for a high-level view of Python.

Part 2 is the heart of the book. It covers the ingredients necessary for obtaining a working knowledge of Python as a general-purpose programming language. The chapters are designed to allow readers who are beginning to learn Python to work their way through sequentially, picking up knowledge of the key points of the language. These chapters also contain some more-advanced sections, allowing you to return to find in one place all the necessary information about a construct or topic.

Part 3 introduces advanced language features of Python—elements of the language that aren't essential to its use but that can certainly be a great help to a serious Python programmer.

Part 4 describes more-advanced or specialized topics that are beyond the strict syntax of the language. You may read these chapters or not, depending on your needs.

A suggested plan if you're new to Python programming is to start by reading chapter 3 to obtain an overall perspective and then work through the chapters in part 2 that are applicable. Enter in the interactive examples as they are introduced to immediately reinforce the concepts. You can also easily go beyond the examples in the text to answer questions about anything that may be unclear. This has the potential to amplify the speed of your learning and the level of your comprehension. If you aren't familiar with OOP or don't need it for your application, skip most of chapter 15.

Those who are familiar with Python should also start with chapter 3. It's a good review and introduces differences between Python 3 and what may be more familiar. It's also a reasonable test of whether you're ready to move on to the advanced chapters in parts 3 and 4 of this book.

It's possible that some readers, although new to Python, will have enough experience with other programming languages to be able to pick up the bulk of what they need to get going by reading chapter 3 and by browsing the Python standard library modules listed in chapter 19 and the *Python Library Reference* in the Python documentation.

Roadmap

Chapter 1 discusses the strengths and weaknesses of Python and shows why Python 3 is a good choice of programming language for many situations.

Chapter 2 covers downloading, installing, and starting up the Python interpreter and IDLE, its integrated development environment.

Chapter 3 is a short overview of the Python language. It provides a basic idea of the philosophy, syntax, semantics, and capabilities of the language.

Chapter 4 starts with the basics of Python. It introduces Python variables, expressions, strings, and numbers. It also introduces Python's block-structured syntax.

Chapters 5, 6, and 7 describe the five powerful built-in Python data types: lists, tuples, sets, strings, and dictionaries.

Chapter 8 introduces Python's control flow syntax and use (loops and `if-else` statements).

Chapter 9 describes function definition in Python along with its flexible parameter-passing capabilities.

Chapter 10 describes Python modules, which provide an easy mechanism for segmenting the program namespace.

Chapter 11 covers creating standalone Python programs, or scripts, and running them on Windows, macOS, and Linux platforms. The chapter also covers the support available for command-line options, arguments, and I/O redirection.

Chapter 12 describes how to work with and navigate through the files and directories of the filesystem. It shows how to write code that's as independent as possible of the actual operating system you're working on.

Chapter 13 introduces the mechanisms for reading and writing files in Python, including the basic capability to read and write strings (or byte streams), the mechanism available for reading binary records, and the ability to read and write arbitrary Python objects.

Chapter 14 discusses the use of exceptions, the error-handling mechanism used by Python. It doesn't assume that you have any previous knowledge of exceptions, although if you've previously used them in C++ or Java, you'll find them familiar.

Chapter 15 introduces Python's support for writing object-oriented programs.

Chapter 16 discusses the regular-expression capabilities available for Python.

Chapter 17 introduces more-advanced OOP techniques, including the use of Python's special method-attributes mechanism, metaclasses, and abstract base classes.

Chapter 18 introduces the package concept in Python for structuring the code of large projects.

Chapter 19 is a brief survey of the standard library. It also includes a discussion of where to find other modules and how to install them.

Chapter 20 dives deeper into manipulating files in Python.

Chapter 21 covers strategies for reading, cleaning, and writing various types of data files.

Chapter 22 surveys the process, issues, and tools involved in fetching data over the network.

Chapter 23 discusses how Python accesses relational and NoSQL databases.

Chapter 24 is a brief introduction to using Python, Jupyter notebook, and pandas to explore data sets.

The case study walks you through using Python to fetch data, clean it, and then graph it. The project combines several features of the language discussed in the chapters, and it gives you a chance to a see a project worked through from beginning to end.

Appendix A contains a guide to obtaining and accessing Python's full documentation, the Pythonic style guide, PEP 8, and "The Zen of Python," a slightly wry summary of the philosophy behind Python.

Appendix B has the answers to most of the exercises. In a few cases, the exercises ask you to experiment on your own. I don't attempt to provide answers for those exercises.

Code conventions

The code samples in this book, and their output, appear in a `fixed-width font` and are often accompanied by annotations. The code samples are deliberately kept as simple as possible, because they aren't intended to be reusable parts that can be plugged into your code. Instead, the code samples are stripped down so that you can focus on the principle being illustrated.

In keeping with the idea of simplicity, the code examples are presented as interactive shell sessions where possible; you should enter and experiment with these samples as much as you can. In interactive code samples, the commands that need to be entered are on lines that begin with the `>>>` prompt, and the visible results of that code (if any) are on the line below.

In some cases a longer code sample is needed, and these cases are identified in the text as file listings. You should save these listings as files with names matching those used in the text and run them as standalone scripts.

Exercises

Starting in chapter 4, this book provides three kinds of exercises. The Quick Check exercises are very brief questions that encourage you to pause and make sure you're clear on an idea just presented. The Try This exercises are a bit more demanding and usually suggest that you try your hand at some Python code. At the end of many chapters is a Lab, which gives you a chance to put the concepts of the current and previous chapters together for a complete script.

Exercise answers

Answers to most of the exercises are available in appendix B and are also included in a separate directory along with the book's source code. Keep in mind that the answers are not meant to be the *only* answers for the coding problems; there may be several other approaches. The best way to judge your answers is to understand what the suggested answer does and then decide whether your answer achieves the same end.

Source code downloads

The source code for the samples in this book is available from the publisher's website at www.manning.com/books/the-quick-python-book-third-edition.

System requirements

The samples and code in this book have been written with Windows (Windows 7 through 10), macOS, and Linux in mind. Because Python is a cross-platform language, the samples and code *should* work on other platforms for the most part, except for platform-specific issues, such as the handling of files, paths, and GUIs.

Software requirements

This book is based on Python 3.6, and all examples should work on any subsequent version of Python 3. (Most have been tested with a prerelease version of Python 3.7.) With a few exceptions, the examples also work on Python 3.5, but I strongly recommend using 3.6; there are no advantages to using the earlier version, and 3.6 has several subtle improvements. Note that Python 3 is *required* and that an earlier version of Python will not work with the code in this book.

Book forum

The purchase of *The Quick Python Book, Third Edition,* includes free access to a private web forum run by Manning Publications, where you can make comments about the book, ask technical questions, and receive help from the author and from other users.

To access the forum, go to https://forums.manning.com/forums/the-quick-python-book-third-edition. You can also learn more about Manning's forums and the rules of conduct at https://forums.manning.com/forums/about.

Manning's commitment to our readers is to provide a venue where a meaningful dialogue between individual readers and between readers and the author can take place. It's not a commitment to any specific amount of participation on the part of the author, whose contribution to the book's forum remains voluntary (and unpaid). We suggest that you try asking her some challenging questions, lest her interest stray!

The forum and the archives of previous discussions will be accessible from the publisher's website as long as the book is in print.

About the author

NAOMI CEDER, the author of this third edition, has been programming in various languages for nearly 30 years and has been a Linux system administrator, programming teacher, developer, and system architect. She started using Python in 2001, and since then has taught Python to users at all levels, from 12-year-olds to professionals. She gives talks on Python and the benefits of an inclusive community to whomever will listen. Naomi currently leads a development team for Dick Blick Art Materials and is the chair of the Python Software Foundation.

about the cover illustration

The illustration on the cover of *The Quick Python Book, Third Edition,* is taken from a late-eighteenth-century edition of Sylvain Maréchal's four-volume compendium of regional dress customs published in France. Each illustration is finely drawn and colored by hand. The rich variety of Maréchal's collection reminds us vividly of how culturally apart the world's towns and regions were just 200 years ago. Isolated from one another, people spoke different dialects and languages. In the streets or in the countryside, it was easy to identify where people lived and what their trades or stations in life were just by what they were wearing.

Dress codes have changed since then, and the diversity by region, so rich at the time, has faded away. It's now hard to tell apart the inhabitants of different continents, let alone different towns or regions. Perhaps we've traded cultural diversity for a more varied personal life—certainly for a more varied and fast-paced technological life.

At a time when it's hard to tell one computer book from another, Manning celebrates the inventiveness and initiative of the computer business with book covers based on the rich diversity of regional life of two centuries ago, brought back to life by Maréchal's pictures.

Part 1

Starting out

These first three chapters tell you a little bit about Python, its strengths and weaknesses, and why you should consider learning Python 3. In chapter 2 you see how to install Python on Windows, macOS, and Linux platforms and how to write a simple program. Chapter 3 is a quick, high-level survey of Python's syntax and features.

If you're looking for the quickest possible introduction to Python, start with chapter 3.

Part 1

Starting out

These first three chapters tell you a little bit about Python, its strengths and weaknesses, and why you should consider learning Python 3. In chapter 2 you see how to install Python on Windows, macOS, and Linux platforms and how to write a simple program. Chapter 3 is a quick, high-level survey of Python's syntax and features.

If you're looking for the quickest possible introduction to Python, start with chapter 3.

About Python 1

This chapter covers

- Why use Python?
- What Python does well
- What Python doesn't do as well
- Why learn Python 3?

Read this chapter if you want to know how Python compares to other languages and its place in the grand scheme of things. Skip ahead—go straight to chapter 3— if you want to start learning Python right away. The information in this chapter is a valid part of this book—but it's certainly not necessary for programming with Python.

1.1 *Why should I use Python?*

Hundreds of programming languages are available today, from mature languages like C and C++, to newer entries like Ruby, C#, and Lua, to enterprise juggernauts like Java. Choosing a language to learn is difficult. Although no one language is the right choice for every possible situation, I think that Python is a good choice for a large number of programming problems, and it's also a good choice if you're learning to program. Hundreds of thousands of programmers around the world use Python, and the number grows every year.

Python continues to attract new users for a variety of reasons. It's a true cross-platform language, running equally well on Windows, Linux/UNIX, and Macintosh platforms, as well as others, ranging from supercomputers to cell phones. It can be used to develop small applications and rapid prototypes, but it scales well to permit development of large programs. It comes with a powerful and easy-to-use graphical user interface (GUI) toolkit, web programming libraries, and more. *And* it's free.

1.2   *What Python does well*

Python is a modern programming language developed by Guido van Rossum in the 1990s (and named after a famous comedic troupe). Although Python isn't perfect for every application, its strengths make it a good choice for many situations.

1.2.1   *Python is easy to use*

Programmers familiar with traditional languages will find it easy to learn Python. All of the familiar constructs—loops, conditional statements, arrays, and so forth—are included, but many are easier to use in Python. Here are a few of the reasons why:

- *Types are associated with objects, not variables.* A variable can be assigned a value of any type, and a list can contain objects of many types. This also means that type casting usually isn't necessary and that your code isn't locked into the strait-jacket of predeclared types.
- *Python typically operates at a much higher level of abstraction.* This is partly the result of the way the language is built and partly the result of an extensive standard code library that comes with the Python distribution. A program to download a web page can be written in two or three lines!
- *Syntax rules are very simple.* Although becoming an expert Pythonista takes time and effort, even beginners can absorb enough Python syntax to write useful code quickly.

Python is well suited for rapid application development. It isn't unusual for coding an application in Python to take one-fifth the time it would in C or Java and to take as little as one-fifth the number of lines of the equivalent C program. This depends on the particular application, of course; for a numerical algorithm performing mostly integer arithmetic in `for` loops, there would be much less of a productivity gain. For the average application, the productivity gain can be significant.

1.2.2   *Python is expressive*

Python is a very expressive language. *Expressive* in this context means that a single line of Python code can do more than a single line of code in most other languages. The advantages of a more expressive language are obvious: The fewer lines of code you have to write, the faster you can complete the project. The fewer lines of code there are, the easier the program will be to maintain and debug.

To get an idea of how Python's expressiveness can simplify code, consider swapping the values of two variables, var1 and var2. In a language like Java, this requires three lines of code and an extra variable:

```
int temp = var1;
var1 = var2;
var2 = temp;
```

The variable temp is needed to save the value of var1 when var2 is put into it, and then that saved value is put into var2. The process isn't terribly complex, but reading those three lines and understanding that a swap has taken place takes a certain amount of overhead, even for experienced coders.

By contrast, Python lets you make the same swap in one line and in a way that makes it obvious that a swap of values has occurred:

```
var2, var1 = var1, var2
```

Of course, this is a very simple example, but you find the same advantages throughout the language.

1.2.3 *Python is readable*

Another advantage of Python is that it's easy to read. You might think that a programming language needs to be read only by a computer, but humans have to read your code as well: whoever debugs your code (quite possibly you), whoever maintains your code (could be you again), and whoever might want to modify your code in the future. In all of those situations, the easier the code is to read and understand, the better it is.

The easier code is to understand, the easier it is to debug, maintain, and modify. Python's main advantage in this department is its use of indentation. Unlike most languages, Python *insists* that blocks of code be indented. Although this strikes some people as odd, it has the benefit that your code is always formatted in a very easy-to-read style.

Following are two short programs, one written in Perl and one in Python. Both take two equal-size lists of numbers and return the pairwise sum of those lists. I think the Python code is more readable than the Perl code; it's visually cleaner and contains fewer inscrutable symbols:

```
# Perl version.
sub pairwise_sum {
    my($arg1, $arg2) = @_;
    my @result;
    for(0 .. $#$arg1) {
        push(@result, $arg1->[$_] + $arg2->[$_]);
    }
    return(\@result);
}

# Python version.
def pairwise_sum(list1, list2):
    result = []
```

```
for i in range(len(list1)):
    result.append(list1[i] + list2[i])
return result
```

Both pieces of code do the same thing, but the Python code wins in terms of readability. (There are other ways to do this in Perl, of course, some of which are much more concise—but in my opinion harder to read—than the one shown.)

1.2.4   *Python is complete—"batteries included"*

Another advantage of Python is its "batteries included" philosophy when it comes to libraries. The idea is that when you install Python, you should have everything you need to do real work without the need to install additional libraries. This is why the Python standard library comes with modules for handling email, web pages, databases, operating-system calls, GUI development, and more.

For example, with Python, you can write a web server to share the files in a directory with just two lines of code:

```
import http.server
http.server.test(HandlerClass=http.server.SimpleHTTPRequestHandler)
```

There's no need to install libraries to handle network connections and HTTP; it's already in Python, right out of the box.

1.2.5   *Python is cross-platform*

Python is also an excellent cross-platform language. Python runs on many platforms: Windows, Mac, Linux, UNIX, and so on. Because it's interpreted, the same code can run on any platform that has a Python interpreter, and almost all current platforms have one. There are even versions of Python that run on Java (Jython) and .NET (IronPython), giving you even more possible platforms that run Python

1.2.6   *Python is free*

Python is also free. Python was originally, and continues to be, developed under the open source model, and it's freely available. You can download and install practically any version of Python and use it to develop software for commercial or personal applications, and you don't need to pay a dime.

Although attitudes are changing, some people are still leery of free software because of concerns about a lack of support, fearing that they lack the clout of paying customers. But Python is used by many established companies as a key part of their business; Google, Rackspace, Industrial Light & Magic, and Honeywell are just a few examples. These companies and many others know Python for what it is: a very stable, reliable, and well-supported product with an active and knowledgeable user community. You'll get an answer to even the most difficult Python question more quickly on the Python internet newsgroup than you will on most tech-support phone lines, and the Python answer will be free and correct.

Python and open source software

Not only is Python free of cost, but also, its source code is freely available, and you're free to modify, improve, and extend it if you want. Because the source code is freely available, you have the ability to go in yourself and change it (or to hire someone to go in and do so for you). You rarely have this option at any reasonable cost with proprietary software.

If this is your first foray into the world of open source software, you should understand that you're not only free to use and modify Python, but also able (and encouraged) to contribute to it and improve it. Depending on your circumstances, interests, and skills, those contributions might be financial, as in a donation to the Python Software Foundation (PSF), or they may involve participating in one of the special interest groups (SIGs), testing and giving feedback on releases of the Python core or one of the auxiliary modules, or contributing some of what you or your company develops back to the community. The level of contribution (if any) is, of course, up to you; but if you're able to give back, definitely consider doing so. Something of significant value is being created here, and you have an opportunity to add to it.

Python has a lot going for it: expressiveness, readability, rich included libraries, and cross-platform capabilities. Also, it's open source. What's the catch?

1.3 *What Python doesn't do as well*

Although Python has many advantages, no language can do everything, so Python isn't the perfect solution for all your needs. To decide whether Python is the right language for your situation, you also need to consider the areas where Python doesn't do as well.

1.3.1 *Python isn't the fastest language*

A possible drawback with Python is its speed of execution. It isn't a fully compiled language. Instead, it's first compiled to an internal bytecode form, which is then executed by a Python interpreter. There are some tasks, such as string parsing using regular expressions, for which Python has efficient implementations and is as fast as, or faster than, any C program you're likely to write. Nevertheless, most of the time, using Python results in slower programs than in a language like C. But you should keep this in perspective. Modern computers have so much computing power that for the vast majority of applications, the speed of the program isn't as important as the speed of development, and Python programs can typically be written much more quickly. In addition, it's easy to extend Python with modules written in C or C++, which can be used to run the CPU-intensive portions of a program.

1.3.2 *Python doesn't have the most libraries*

Although Python comes with an excellent collection of libraries, and many more are available, Python doesn't hold the lead in this department. Languages like C, Java, and

Perl have even larger collections of libraries available, in some cases offering a solution where Python has none or a choice of several options where Python might have only one. These situations tend to be fairly specialized, however, and Python is easy to extend, either in Python itself or through existing libraries in C and other languages. For almost all common computing problems, Python's library support is excellent.

1.3.3 *Python doesn't check variable types at compile time*

Unlike in some languages, Python's variables don't work like containers; instead, they're more like labels that reference various objects: integers, strings, class instances, whatever. That means that although those objects themselves have types, the variables referring to them aren't bound to that particular type. It's possible (if not necessarily desirable) to use the variable x to refer to a string in one line and an integer in another:

```
>>> x = "2"
>>> x
'2'                           x is string "2"
>>> x = int(x)
>>> x
2                             x is now integer 2
```

The fact that Python associates types with objects and not with variables means that the interpreter doesn't help you catch variable type mismatches. If you intend a variable count to hold an integer, Python won't complain if you assign the string "two" to it. Traditional coders count this as a disadvantage, because you lose an additional free check on your code. But errors like this usually aren't hard to find and fix, and Python's testing features makes avoiding type errors manageable. Most Python programmers feel that the flexibility of dynamic typing more than outweighs the cost.

1.3.4 *Python doesn't have much mobile support*

In the past decade the numbers and types of mobile devices have exploded, and smartphones, tablets, phablets, Chromebooks, and more are everywhere, running on a variety of operating systems. Python isn't a strong player in this space. While options exist, running Python on mobile devices isn't always easy, and using Python to write and distribute commercial apps is problematic.

1.3.5 *Python doesn't use multiple processors well*

Multiple-core processors are everywhere now, producing significant increases in performance in many situations. However, the standard implementation of Python isn't designed to use multiple cores, due to a feature called the global interpreter lock (GIL). For more information, look for videos of GIL-related talks and posts by David Beazley, Larry Hastings, and others, or visit the GIL page on the Python wiki at https://wiki.python.org/moin/GlobalInterpreterLock. While there are ways to run concurrent processes by using Python, if you need concurrency out of the box, Python may not be for you.

1.4 *Why learn Python 3?*

Python has been around for a number of years and has evolved over that time. The first edition of this book was based on Python 1.5.2, and Python 2.x has been the dominant version for several years. This book is based on Python 3.6 but has also been tested on the alpha version of Python 3.7.

Python 3, originally whimsically dubbed Python 3000, is notable because it's the first version of Python in the history of the language to break backward compatibility. What this means is that code written for earlier versions of Python probably won't run on Python 3 without some changes. In earlier versions of Python, for example, the `print` statement didn't require parentheses around its arguments:

```
print "hello"
```

In Python 3, `print` is a function and needs the parentheses:

```
print("hello")
```

You may be thinking, "Why change details like this if it's going to break old code?" Because this kind of change is a big step for any language, the core developers of Python thought about this issue carefully. Although the changes in Python 3 break compatibility with older code, those changes are fairly small and for the better; they make the language more consistent, more readable, and less ambiguous. Python 3 isn't a dramatic rewrite of the language; it's a well-thought-out evolution. The core developers also took care to provide a strategy and tools to safely and efficiently migrate old code to Python 3, which will be discussed in a later chapter, and the Six and Future libraries are also available to make the transition easier.

Why learn Python 3? Because it's the best Python so far. Also, as projects switch to take advantage of its improvements, it will be the dominant Python version for years to come. The porting of libraries to Python 3 has been steady since its introduction, and by now many of the most popular libraries support Python 3. In fact, according to the Python Readiness page (http://py3readiness.org), 319 of the 360 most popular libraries have already been ported to Python 3. If you need a library that hasn't been converted yet, or if you're working on an established code base in Python 2, by all means stick with Python 2.x. But if you're starting to learn Python or starting a project, go with Python 3; it's not only better, but also the future.

Summary

- Python is a modern, high-level language with dynamic typing and simple, consistent syntax and semantics.
- Python is multiplatform, highly modular, and suited for both rapid development and large-scale programming.

- It's reasonably fast and can be easily extended with C or C++ modules for higher speeds.
- Python has built-in advanced features such as persistent object storage, advanced hash tables, expandable class syntax, and universal comparison functions.
- Python includes a wide range of libraries such as numeric processing, image manipulation, user interfaces, and web scripting.
- It's supported by a dynamic Python community.

Getting started 2

This chapter covers

- Installing Python
- Using IDLE and the basic interactive mode
- Writing a simple program
- Using IDLE's Python shell window

This chapter guides you through downloading, installing, and starting up Python and IDLE, an integrated development environment for Python. At this writing, Python 3.6 is the most current version, and 3.7 is under development. After years of refinement, Python 3 is the first version of the language that isn't fully backward-compatible with earlier versions, so be sure to get a version of Python 3. It should be several years before another such dramatic change occurs, and any future enhancements will be developed with concern to avoid affecting an already-significant existing code base. Therefore, the material presented after this chapter isn't likely to become dated any time soon.

2.1 *Installing Python*

Installing Python is a simple matter, regardless of which platform you're using. The first step is to obtain a recent distribution for your machine; the most recent one can always be found at www.python.org. This book is based on Python 3.6. If you have Python 3.5 or even 3.7, that's fine. In fact, you should have little trouble using most of this book with any version of Python 3.

> **Having more than one version of Python**
>
> You may already have an earlier version of Python installed on your machine. Many Linux distributions and macOS come with Python 2.x as part of the operating system. Because Python 3 isn't completely compatible with Python 2, it's reasonable to wonder whether installing both versions on the same computer will cause a conflict.
>
> There's no need to worry; you can have multiple versions of Python on the same computer. In the case of UNIX-based systems like OS X and Linux, Python 3 installs alongside the older version and doesn't replace it. When your system looks for "python," it still finds the one it expects, and when you want to access Python 3, you can run `python3` or `idle`. In Windows, the different versions are installed in separate locations and have separate menu entries.

Some basic platform-specific descriptions for the Python installation are given next. The specifics can vary quite a bit depending on your platform, so be sure to read the instructions on the download pages and for the various versions. You're probably familiar with installing software on your particular machine, so I'll keep these descriptions short:

- *Microsoft Windows*—Python can be installed in most versions of Windows by using the Python installer program, currently called python-3.6.1.exe. Download it, execute it, and follow the installer's prompts. You may need to be logged in as administrator to run the install. If you're on a network and don't have the administrator password, ask your system administrator to do the installation for you.

- *Macintosh*—You need to get a version of Python 3 that matches your OS X version and your processor. After you determine the correct version, download the disk image file, double-click to mount it, and run the installer inside. The OS X installer sets up everything automatically, and Python 3 will be in a subfolder inside the Applications folder, labeled with the version number. macOS ships with various versions of Python as part of the system, but you don't need to worry about that; Python 3 will be installed *in addition to* the system version. If you have brew installed, you can also use it to install Python by using the command `brew install python3`. You can find more information about using Python on OS X by following the links on the Python home page.

- *Linux/UNIX*—Most Linux distributions come with Python installed. But the versions of Python vary, and the version of Python installed may not be version 3;

for this book, you need to be sure you have the Python 3 packages installed. It's also possible that IDLE isn't installed by default and that you'll need to install that package separately. Although it's also possible to build Python 3 from the source code available on the www.python.org website, additional libraries are needed, and the process isn't for novices. If a precompiled version of Python exists for your distribution of Linux, I recommend using that. Use the software management system for your distribution to locate and install the correct packages for Python 3 and IDLE. Versions are also available for running Python under many other operating systems. See www.python.org for a current list of supported platforms and specifics on installation.

Anaconda: an alternative Python distribution

In addition to the distribution of Python that you can get directly from Python.org, a distribution called Anaconda is gaining popularity, particularly among scientific and data science users. Anaconda is an open data science platform with Python at its core. When you install Anaconda, you get not only Python, but also the R language and a generous collection of preinstalled data science packages, and you can add many more by using the included conda package manager. You can also install miniconda, which includes only Python and conda, and then add the packages you need.

You can get Anaconda or miniconda from www.anaconda.com/download/. Download the Python 3 version of the installer that matches your operating system, and run it according to the instructions. When that's done, you'll have a full version of Python on your machine.

Particularly if your primary interest is in data science, you may find Anaconda to be a quicker and easier way to get up and running with Python.

2.2 Basic interactive mode and IDLE

You have two built-in options for obtaining interactive access to the Python interpreter: the original basic (command-line) mode and IDLE. IDLE is available on many platforms, including Windows, Mac, and Linux, but it may not be available on others. You may need to do more work and install additional software packages to get IDLE running, but doing so will be worthwhile because IDLE offers a somewhat smoother experience than the basic interactive mode. On the other hand, even if you normally use IDLE, at times you'll likely want to fire up the basic mode. You should be familiar enough to start and use either one.

2.2.1 The basic interactive mode

The basic interactive mode is a rather primitive environment, but the interactive examples in this book are generally small. Later in this book, you learn how to easily bring code you've placed in a file into your session (by using the module mechanism). Here's how to start a basic session on Windows, macOS, and UNIX:

- *Starting a basic session on Windows*—For version 3.x of Python, you navigate to the Python 3.6 (32-bit) entry on the Python 3.6 submenu of the Programs folder on the Start menu, and click it. Alternatively, you can directly find the Python.exe executable (for example, in C:\Users\myuser\AppData\Local\Programs\Python \Python35-32) and double-click it. Doing so brings up the window shown in figure 2.1.
- *Starting a basic session on macOS*—Open a terminal window and type `python3`. If you get a "Command not found" error, run the `Update Shell Profile` command script located in the Python3 subfolder in the Applications folder.
- *Starting a basic session on UNIX*—Type `python3` at a command prompt. A version message similar to the one shown in figure 2.1 followed by the Python prompt `>>>` appears in the current window.

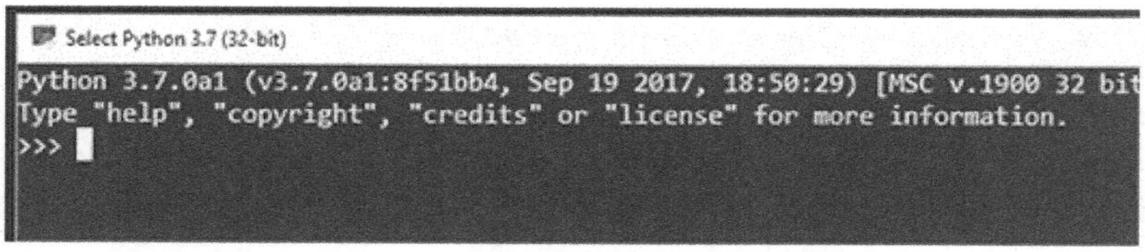

```
Select Python 3.7 (32-bit)
Python 3.7.0a1 (v3.7.0a1:8f51bb4, Sep 19 2017, 18:50:29) [MSC v.1900 32 bit
Type "help", "copyright", "credits" or "license" for more information.
>>> 
```

Figure 2.1   Basic interactive mode on Windows 10

Exiting the interactive shell
To exit from a basic session, press Ctrl-Z (if you're on Windows) or Ctrl-D (if you're on Linux or UNIX), or type `exit()` at a command prompt.

Most platforms have a command-line-editing and command-history mechanism. You can use the up and down arrows, as well as the Home, End, Page Up, and Page Down keys, to scroll through past entries and repeat them by pressing the Enter key. This is all you need to work your way through this book as you're learning Python. Another option is to use the excellent Python mode available for Emacs, which, among other things, provides access to the interactive mode of Python through an integrated shell buffer.

2.2.2   *The IDLE integrated development environment*

IDLE is the built-in development environment for Python. Its name is based on the acronym for *integrated development environment* (though of course, it may have been influenced by the last name of a certain cast member of a particular British television

show). IDLE combines an interactive interpreter with code editing and debugging tools to give you one-stop shopping as far as creating Python code is concerned. IDLE's various tools make it an attractive place to start as you learn Python. This is how you run IDLE on Windows, macOS, and Linux:

- *Starting IDLE on Windows*—For version 3.6 of Python, you navigate to the IDLE (Python GUI) entry of the Python 3.6 submenu of the All apps folder of your Windows menu, and click it. Doing so brings up the window shown in figure 2.2.
- *Starting IDLE on macOS*—Navigate to the Python 3.x subfolder in the Applications folder, and run IDLE from there.
- *Starting IDLE on Linux or UNIX*—Type `idle3` at a command prompt. This brings up a window similar to the one shown in figure 2.2. If you installed IDLE through your distribution's package manager, there should also be a menu entry for IDLE on the Programming submenu or something similar.

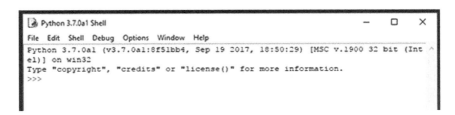

Figure 2.2   IDLE on Windows

2.2.3   *Choosing between basic interactive mode and IDLE*

Which should you use: IDLE or the basic shell window? To begin, use either IDLE or the Python shell window. Both have all you need to work through the code examples in this book until you reach chapter 10. From there, I cover writing your own modules, and IDLE will be a convenient way to create and edit files. But if you have a strong preference for another editor, you may find that a basic shell window and your favorite editor serve you just as well. If you don't have any strong editor preferences, I suggest using IDLE from the beginning.

2.3   *Using IDLE's Python shell window*

The Python shell window (figure 2.3) opens when you fire up IDLE. It provides automatic indentation and colors your code as you type it in, based on Python syntax types.

You can move around the buffer by using the mouse, the arrow keys, the Page Up and Page Down keys, and/or some of the standard Emacs key bindings. Check the Help menu for the details.

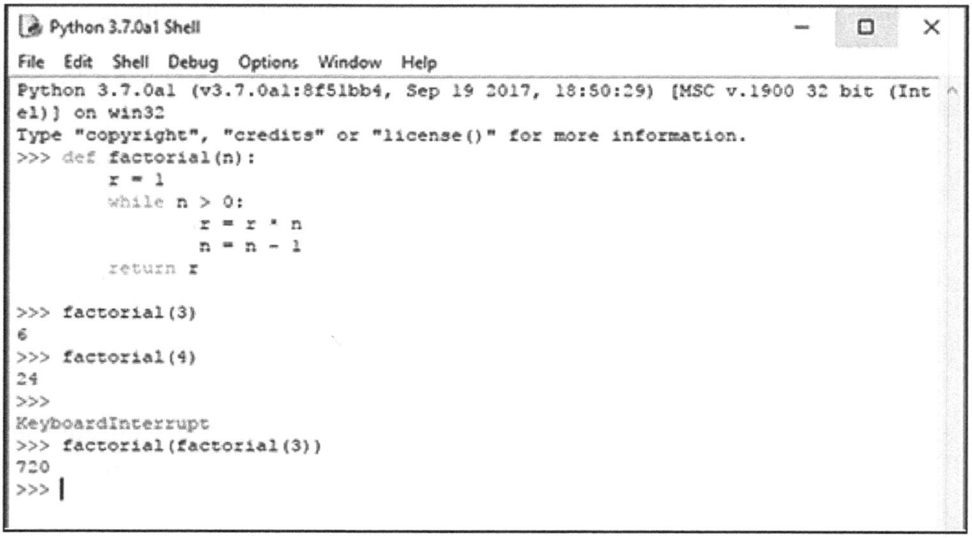

Figure 2.3 Using the Python shell in IDLE. Code is automatically colored (based on Python syntax) as it's typed in. Placing the cursor on any previous command and pressing the Enter key moves the command and the cursor to the bottom, where you can edit the command and then press Enter to send it to the interpreter. Placing the cursor at the bottom, you can toggle up and down through the history of previous commands by pressing Alt-P and Alt-N. When you have the command you want, edit it as desired and press Enter, and it will be sent to the interpreter.

Everything in your session is buffered. You can scroll or search up, place the cursor on any line, and press Enter (creating a hard return), and that line will be copied to the bottom of the screen, where you can edit it and then send it to the interpreter by pressing the Enter key again. Or, leaving the cursor at the bottom, you can toggle up and down through the previously entered commands by pressing Alt-P and Alt-N, which successively bring copies of the lines to the bottom. When you have the one you want, you can again edit it and then send it to the interpreter by pressing the Enter key. You can see a list of possible completions with Python keywords or user-defined values by pressing Tab.

If you ever find yourself in a situation where you seem to be hung and can't get a new prompt, the interpreter is likely in a state where it's waiting for you to enter something specific. Pressing Ctrl-C sends an interrupt and should get you back to a prompt. It can also be used to interrupt any running command. To exit IDLE, choose Exit from the File menu.

The Edit menu is the one you'll likely be using most to begin with. As with any of the other menus, you can tear it off by double-clicking the dotted line at its top and leaving it up beside your window.

2.4   *Hello, world*

Regardless of how you're accessing Python's interactive mode, you should see a prompt consisting of three angle braces: >>>. This prompt is the Python command prompt, and it indicates that you can type in a command to be executed or an expression to be evaluated. Start with the obligatory "Hello, World" program, which is a one-liner in Python (ending each line you type with a hard return):

```
>>> print("Hello, World")
Hello, World
```

Here, I entered the `print` function at the command prompt, and the result appeared on the screen. Executing the `print` function causes its argument to be printed to the standard output—usually, the screen. If the command had been executed while Python was running a Python program from a file, exactly the same thing would have happened: "Hello, World" would have been printed to the screen.

Congratulations! You've just written your first Python program, and I haven't even started talking about the language.

2.5   *Using the interactive prompt to explore Python*

Whether you're in IDLE or at a standard interactive prompt, a couple of handy tools can help you explore Python. The first is the `help()` function, which has two modes. You can enter `help()` at the prompt to enter the help system, where you can get help on modules, keywords, or topics. When you're in the help system, you see a `help>` prompt, and you can enter a module name, such as `math` or some other topic, to browse Python's documentation on that topic.

Usually, it's more convenient to use `help()` in a more targeted way. Entering a type or variable name as a parameter for `help()` gives you an immediate display of that type's documentation:

```
>>> x = 2
>>> help(x)
Help on int object:

class int(object)
 |  int(x=0) -> integer
 |  int(x, base=10) -> integer
 |
 |  Convert a number or string to an integer, or return 0 if no arguments
 |  are given.  If x is a number, return x.__int__().  For floating point
 |  numbers, this truncates towards zero.
 |
 |  If x is not a number or if base is given, then x must be a string,
 |  bytes, or bytearray instance representing an integer literal in the...
(continues with the documentation for an int)
```

Using `help()` in this way is handy for checking the exact syntax of a method or the behavior of an object.

The help() function is part of the pydoc library, which has several options for accessing the documentation built into Python libraries. Because every Python installation comes with complete documentation, you can have all of the official documentation at your fingertips, even if you aren't online. See appendix A for more information on accessing Python's documentation.

The other useful function is dir(), which lists the objects in a particular namespace. Used with no parameters, it lists the current globals, but it can also list objects for a module or even a type:

```
>>> dir()
['__annotations__', '__builtins__', '__doc__', '__loader__', '__name__',
    '__package__', '__spec__', 'x']
>>> dir(int)
['__abs__', '__add__', '__and__', '__bool__', '__ceil__', '__class__',
    '__delattr__', '__dir__', '__divmod__', '__doc__', '__eq__',
    '__float__', '__floor__', '__floordiv__', '__format__', '__ge__',
    '__getattribute__', '__getnewargs__', '__gt__', '__hash__', '__index__',
    '__init__', '__int__', '__invert__', '__le__', '__lshift__', '__lt__',
    '__mod__', '__mul__', '__ne__', '__neg__', '__new__', '__or__',
    '__pos__', '__pow__', '__radd__', '__rand__', '__rdivmod__',
    '__reduce__', '__reduce_ex__', '__repr__', '__rfloordiv__',
    '__rlshift__', '__rmod__', '__rmul__', '__ror__', '__round__',
    '__rpow__', '__rrshift__', '__rshift__', '__rsub__', '__rtruediv__',
    '__rxor__', '__setattr__', '__sizeof__', '__str__', '__sub__',
    '__subclasshook__', '__truediv__', '__trunc__', '__xor__', 'bit_length',
    'conjugate', 'denominator', 'from_bytes', 'imag', 'numerator', 'real',
    'to_bytes']
>>>
```

dir() is useful for finding out what methods and data are defined, for reminding yourself at a glance of all the members that belong to an object or module, and for debugging because you can see what is defined where.

Unlike dir, both globals and locals show the values associated with the objects. In the current situation, both functions return the same thing, so we have only shown the output from globals():

```
>>> globals()
{'__name__': '__main__', '__doc__': None, '__package__': None, '__loader__':
    <class '_frozen_importlib.BuiltinImporter'>, '__spec__': None,
    '__annotations__': {}, '__builtins__': <module 'builtins' (built-in)>,
    'x': 2}
```

Unlike dir, both globals and locals show the values associated with the objects. You find out more about both of these functions in chapter 10; for now, it's enough to be aware that you have several options for examining what's going on within a Python session.

Summary

- Installing Python 3 on Windows systems is as simple as downloading the latest installer from www.python.org and running it. Installation on Linux, UNIX, and Mac systems will vary.

- Refer to installation instructions on the Python website, and use your system's software package installer where possible.
- Another installation option is to install the Anaconda (or miniconda) distribution from https://www.anaconda.com/download/.
- After you've installed Python, you can use either the basic interactive shell (and later, your favorite editor) or the IDLE integrated development environment.

The Quick Python
overview

This chapter covers

- Surveying Python
- Using built-in data types
- Controlling program flow
- Creating modules
- Using object-oriented programming

The purpose of this chapter is to give you a basic feeling for the syntax, semantics, capabilities, and philosophy of the Python language. It has been designed to provide you an initial perspective or conceptual framework on which you'll be able to add details as you encounter them in the rest of the book.

On an initial read, you needn't be concerned about working through and understanding the details of the code segments. You'll be doing fine if you pick up a bit of an idea about what's being done. The subsequent chapters walk you through the specifics of these features and don't assume previous knowledge. You can always return to this chapter and work through the examples in the appropriate sections as a review after you've read the later chapters.

3.1 *Python synopsis*

Python has several built-in data types, such as integers, floats, complex numbers, strings, lists, tuples, dictionaries, and file objects. These data types can be manipulated using language operators, built-in functions, library functions, or a data type's own methods.

Programmers can also define their own classes and instantiate their own class instances.[1] These class instances can be manipulated by programmer-defined methods, as well as the language operators and built-in functions for which the programmer has defined the appropriate special method attributes.

Python provides conditional and iterative control flow through an `if-elif-else` construct along with `while` and `for` loops. It allows function definition with flexible argument-passing options. Exceptions (errors) can be raised by using the `raise` statement, and they can be caught and handled by using the `try-except-else-finally` construct.

Variables (or identifiers) don't have to be declared and can refer to any built-in data type, user-defined object, function, or module.

3.2 *Built-in data types*

Python has several built-in data types, from scalars such as numbers and Booleans to more complex structures such as lists, dictionaries, and files.

3.2.1 *Numbers*

Python's four number types are integers, floats, complex numbers, and Booleans:

- *Integers*—1, –3, 42, 355, 888888888888888, –7777777777 (integers aren't limited in size except by available memory)
- *Floats*—3.0, 31e12, –6e-4
- *Complex numbers*—3 + 2j, –4- 2j, 4.2 + 6.3j
- *Booleans*—True, False

You can manipulate them by using the arithmetic operators: + (addition), – (subtraction), * (multiplication), / (division), ** (exponentiation), and % (modulus).

The following examples use integers:

```
>>> x = 5 + 2 - 3 * 2
>>> x
1
>>> 5 / 2
2.5                          <--- 1
>>> 5 // 2
2                            <--- 2
>>> 5 % 2
```

---

[1] The Python documentation and this book use the term object to refer to instances of any Python data type, not just what many other languages would call *class instances*. This is because all Python objects are instances of one class or another.

```
1
>>> 2 ** 8
256
>>> 1000000001 ** 3
1000000003000000003000000001                          <----3
```

Division of integers with / **1** results in a float (new in Python 3.x), and division of integers with // **2** results in truncation. Note that integers are of unlimited size **3**; they grow as large as you need them to, limited only by the memory available.

These examples work with floats, which are based on the doubles in C:

```
>>> x = 4.3 ** 2.4
>>> x
33.13784737771648
>>> 3.5e30 * 2.77e45
9.695e+75
>>> 1000000001.0 ** 3
1.000000003e+27
```

These examples use complex numbers:

```
>>> (3+2j) ** (2+3j)
(0.6817665190890336-2.1207457766159625j)
>>> x = (3+2j) * (4+9j)
>>> x                          <----1
(-6+35j)
>>> x.real
-6.0
>>> x.imag
35.0
```

Complex numbers consist of both a real element and an imaginary element, suffixed with j. In the preceding code, variable x is assigned to a complex number **1**. You can obtain its "real" part by using the attribute notation x.real and obtain the "imaginary" part with x.imag.

Several built-in functions can operate on numbers. There are also the library module cmath (which contains functions for complex numbers) and the library module math (which contains functions for the other three types):

```
>>> round(3.49)                <----1
3
>>> import math
>>> math.ceil(3.49)            <----2
4
```

Built-in functions are always available and are called by using a standard function-calling syntax. In the preceding code, round is called with a float as its input argument **1**.

The functions in library modules are made available via the import statement. At **2**, the math library module is imported, and its ceil function is called using attribute notation: *module.function(arguments)*.

The following examples use Booleans:

```
>>> x = False
>>> x
False
>>> not x
True
>>> y = True * 2              ◁——❶
>>> y
2
```

Other than their representation as `True` and `False`, Booleans behave like the numbers 1 (True) and 0 (False) ❶.

3.2.2 Lists

Python has a powerful built-in list type:

```
[]
[1]
[1, 2, 3, 4, 5, 6, 7, 8, 12]
[1, "two", 3, 4.0, ["a", "b"], (5,6)]          ◁——❶
```

A list can contain a mixture of other types as its elements, including strings, tuples, lists, dictionaries, functions, file objects, and any type of number ❶.

A list can be indexed from its front or back. You can also refer to a subsegment, or *slice*, of a list by using slice notation:

```
>>> x = ["first", "second", "third", "fourth"]
>>> x[0]
'first'                        ❶
>>> x[2]
'third'
>>> x[-1]
'fourth'
>>> x[-2]                       ❷
'third'
>>> x[1:-1]
['second', 'third']
>>> x[0:3]
['first', 'second', 'third']
>>> x[-2:-1]                    ❸
['third']
>>> x[:3]
['first', 'second', 'third']
>>> x[-2:]                      ❹
['third', 'fourth']
```

Index from the front ❶ using positive indices (starting with 0 as the first element). Index from the back ❷ using negative indices (starting with -1 as the last element). Obtain a slice using `[m:n]` ❸, where m is the inclusive starting point and n is the exclusive ending point (see table 3.1). An `[:n]` slice ❹ starts at its beginning, and an `[m:]` slice goes to a list's end.

Table 3.1   List indices

x=	[	"first" ,	"second" ,	"third" ,	"fourth"	]
Positive indices		0	1	2	3	
Negative indices		-4	-3	-2	-1	

You can use this notation to add, remove, and replace elements in a list or to obtain an element or a new list that's a slice from it:

```
>>> x = [1, 2, 3, 4, 5, 6, 7, 8, 9]
>>> x[1] = "two"
>>> x[8:9] = []
>>> x
[1, 'two', 3, 4, 5, 6, 7, 8]
>>> x[5:7] = [6.0, 6.5, 7.0]                    <--1
>>> x
[1, 'two', 3, 4, 5, 6.0, 6.5, 7.0, 8]
>>> x[5:]
[6.0, 6.5, 7.0, 8]
```

The size of the list increases or decreases if the new slice is bigger or smaller than the slice it's replacing ❶.

Some built-in functions (len, max, and min), some operators (in, +, and *), the del statement, and the list methods (append, count, extend, index, insert, pop, remove, reverse, and sort) operate on lists:

```
>>> x = [1, 2, 3, 4, 5, 6, 7, 8, 9]
>>> len(x)
9
>>> [-1, 0] + x                                 <--1
[-1, 0, 1, 2, 3, 4, 5, 6, 7, 8, 9]
>>> x.reverse()                                 <--2
>>> x
[9, 8, 7, 6, 5, 4, 3, 2, 1]
```

The operators + and * each create a new list, leaving the original unchanged ❶. A list's methods are called by using attribute notation on the list itself: x.*method* (*arguments*) ❷.

Some of these operations repeat functionality that can be performed with slice notation, but they improve code readability.

3.2.3   *Tuples*

Tuples are similar to lists but are *immutable*—that is, they can't be modified after they've been created. The operators (in, +, and *) and built-in functions (len, max, and min) operate on them the same way as they do on lists because none of them modifies the original. Index and slice notation work the same way for obtaining elements or slices but can't be used to add, remove, or replace elements. Also, there are only two tuple methods: count and index. An important purpose of tuples is for use as keys for dictionaries. They're also more efficient to use when you don't need modifiability.

```
()
(1,)                           <----- ❶
(1, 2, 3, 4, 5, 6, 7, 8, 12)
(1, "two", 3L, 4.0, ["a", "b"], (5, 6))       <----- ❷
```

A one-element tuple ❶ needs a comma. A tuple, like a list, can contain a mixture of other types as its elements, including strings, tuples, lists, dictionaries, functions, file objects, and any type of number ❷.

A list can be converted to a tuple by using the built-in function `tuple`:

```
>>> x = [1, 2, 3, 4]
>>> tuple(x)
(1, 2, 3, 4)
```

Conversely, a tuple can be converted to a list by using the built-in function `list`:

```
>>> x = (1, 2, 3, 4)
>>> list(x)
[1, 2, 3, 4]
```

3.2.4 Strings

String processing is one of Python's strengths. There are many options for delimiting strings:

```
"A string in double quotes can contain 'single quote' characters."
'A string in single quotes can contain "double quote" characters.'
'''\tA string which starts with a tab; ends with a newline character.\n'''
"""This is a triple double quoted string, the only kind that can
    contain real newlines."""
```

Strings can be delimited by single (' '), double (" "), triple single (''' '''), or triple double (""" """) quotations and can contain tab (\t) and newline (\n) characters.

Strings are also immutable. The operators and functions that work with them return new strings derived from the original. The operators (in, +, and *) and built-in functions (len, max, and min) operate on strings as they do on lists and tuples. Index and slice notation works the same way for obtaining elements or slices but can't be used to add, remove, or replace elements.

Strings have several methods to work with their contents, and the `re` library module also contains functions for working with strings:

```
>>> x = "live and    let \t    \tlive"
>>> x.split()
['live', 'and', 'let', 'live']
>>> x.replace("    let \t    \tlive", "enjoy life")
'live and enjoy life'
>>> import re                              <----- ❶
>>> regexpr = re.compile(r"[\t ]+")
>>> regexpr.sub(" ", x)
'live and let live'
```

The `re` module ❶ provides regular-expression functionality. It provides more sophisticated pattern extraction and replacement capabilities than the `string` module.

The `print` function outputs strings. Other Python data types can be easily converted to strings and formatted:

```
>>> e = 2.718
>>> x = [1, "two", 3, 4.0, ["a", "b"], (5, 6)]
>>> print("The constant e is:", e, "and the list x is:", x)          ◁——❶
The constant e is: 2.718 and the list x is: [1, 'two', 3, 4.0,
['a', 'b'], (5, 6)]
>>> print("the value of %s is: %.2f" % ("e", e))          ◁——❷
the value of e is: 2.72
```

Objects are automatically converted to string representations for printing ❶. The `%` operator ❷ provides formatting capability similar to that of C's `sprintf`.

3.2.5 *Dictionaries*

Python's built-in dictionary data type provides associative array functionality implemented by using hash tables. The built-in `len` function returns the number of key-value pairs in a dictionary. The `del` statement can be used to delete a key-value pair. As is the case for lists, several dictionary methods (`clear`, `copy`, `get`, `items`, `keys`, `update`, and `values`) are available.

```
>>> x = {1: "one", 2: "two"}                    Sets the value of a new
>>> x["first"] = "one"                          key, "first", to "one"
>>> x[("Delorme", "Ryan", 1995)] = (1, 2, 3)    ◁
>>> list(x.keys())                                      ❶
['first', 2, 1, ('Delorme', 'Ryan', 1995)]
>>> x[1]
'one'
>>> x.get(1, "not available")
'one'
>>> x.get(4, "not available")          ◁——❷
'not available'
```

Keys must be of an immutable type ❶, including numbers, strings, and tuples. Values can be any kind of object, including mutable types such as lists and dictionaries. If you try to access the value of a key that isn't in the dictionary, a `KeyError` exception is raised. To avoid this error, the dictionary method `get` ❷ optionally returns a user-definable value when a key isn't in a dictionary.

3.2.6 *Sets*

A *set* in Python is an unordered collection of objects, used in situations where membership and uniqueness in the set are the main things you need to know about that object. Sets behave as collections of dictionary keys without any associated values:

```
>>> x = set([1, 2, 3, 1, 3, 5])          ◁——❶
>>> x
{1, 2, 3, 5}          ◁——❷
```

```
>>> 1 in x
True
>>> 4 in x
False
>>>
```

You can create a set by using `set` on a sequence, like a list ❶. When a sequence is made into a set, duplicates are removed ❷. The `in` keyword ❸ is used to check for membership of an object in a set.

3.2.7 *File objects*

A file is accessed through a Python file object:

```
>>> f = open("myfile", "w")
>>> f.write("First line with necessary newline character\n")
44
>>> f.write("Second line to write to the file\n")
33
>>> f.close()
>>> f = open("myfile", "r")
>>> line1 = f.readline()
>>> line2 = f.readline()
>>> f.close()
>>> print(line1, line2)
First line with necessary newline character
Second line to write to the file
>>> import os
>>> print(os.getcwd())
c:\My Documents\test
>>> os.chdir(os.path.join("c:\\", "My Documents", "images"))
>>> filename = os.path.join("c:\\", "My Documents",
"test", "myfile")
>>> print(filename)
c:\My Documents\test\myfile
>>> f = open(filename, "r")
>>> print(f.readline())
First line with necessary newline character
>>> f.close()
```

The `open` statement ❶ creates a file object. Here, the file myfile in the current working directory is being opened in write (`"w"`) mode. After writing two lines to it and closing it ❷, you open the same file again, this time in read (`"r"`) mode. The `os` module ❸ provides several functions for moving around the filesystem and working with the pathnames of files and directories. Here, you move to another directory ❹. But by referring to the file by an absolute pathname ❺, you're still able to access it.

Several other input/output capabilities are available. You can use the built-in `input` function to prompt and obtain a string from the user. The `sys` library module allows access to `stdin`, `stdout`, and `stderr`. The `struct` library module provides support for reading and writing files that were generated by, or are to be used by, C programs. The Pickle library module delivers data persistence through the ability to easily read and write the Python data types to and from files.

3.3   *Control flow structures*

Python has a full range of structures to control code execution and program flow, including common branching and looping structures.

3.3.1   *Boolean values and expressions*

Python has several ways of expressing Boolean values; the Boolean constant False, 0, the Python nil value None, and empty values (for example, the empty list [] or empty string "") are all taken as False. The Boolean constant True and everything else is considered True.

You can create comparison expressions by using the comparison operators (<, <=, ==, >, >=, !=, is, is not, in, not in) and the logical operators (and, not, or), which all return True or False.

3.3.2   *The if-elif-else statement*

The block of code after the first True condition (of an if or an elif) is executed. If none of the conditions is True, the block of code after the else is executed:

```
x = 5
if x < 5:
    y = -1
    z = 5
elif x > 5:
    y = 1
    z = 11
else:
    y = 0
    z = 10
print(x, y, z)
```

❶

❷

The elif and else clauses are optional ❶, and there can be any number of elif clauses. Python uses indentation to delimit blocks ❷. No explicit delimiters, such as brackets or braces, are necessary. Each block consists of one or more statements separated by newlines. All these statements must be at the same level of indentation. The output in the example would be 5 0 10.

3.3.3   *The while loop*

The while loop is executed as long as the condition (which here is x > y) is True:

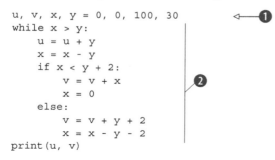

```
u, v, x, y = 0, 0, 100, 30          ◄——❶
while x > y:
    u = u + y
    x = x - y
    if x < y + 2:
        v = v + x
        x = 0
    else:
        v = v + y + 2
        x = x - y - 2
print(u, v)
```

❷

This is a shorthand notation. Here, u and v are assigned a value of 0, x is set to 100, and y obtains a value of 30 ❶. This is the loop block ❷. It's possible for a loop to contain break (which ends the loop) and continue statements (which abort the current iteration of the loop). The output would be 60 40.

3.3.4 *The for loop*

The for loop is simple but powerful because it's possible to iterate over any iterable type, such as a list or tuple. Unlike in many languages, Python's for loop iterates over each of the items in a sequence (for example, a list or tuple), making it more of a foreach loop. The following loop finds the first occurrence of an integer that's divisible by 7:

```
item_list = [3, "string1", 23, 14.0, "string2", 49, 64, 70]
for x in item_list:                                              ←── ❶
    if not isinstance(x, int):
        continue                        ←── ❷
    if not x % 7:
        print("found an integer divisible by seven: %d" % x)
        break                                       ←── ❸
```

x is sequentially assigned each value in the list ❶. If x isn't an integer, the rest of this iteration is aborted by the continue statement ❷. Flow control continues with x set to the next item from the list. After the first appropriate integer is found, the loop is ended by the break statement ❸. The output would be

```
found an integer divisible by seven: 49
```

3.3.5 *Function definition*

Python provides flexible mechanisms for passing arguments to functions:

```
>>> def funct1(x, y, z):                    ←── ❶
...     value = x + 2*y + z**2
...     if value > 0:
...         return x + 2*y + z**2              ←── ❷
...     else:
...         return 0
...
>>> u, v = 3, 4
>>> funct1(u, v, 2)
15
>>> funct1(u, z=v, y=2)          ←── ❸
23
>>> def funct2(x, y=1, z=1):              ←── ❹
...     return x + 2 * y + z ** 2
...
>>> funct2(3, z=4)
21
>>> def funct3(x, y=1, z=1, *tup):             ←── ❺
...     print((x, y, z) + tup)
...
>>> funct3(2)
```

```
(2, 1, 1)
>>> funct3(1, 2, 3, 4, 5, 6, 7, 8, 9)
(1, 2, 3, 4, 5, 6, 7, 8, 9)
>>> def funct4(x, y=1, z=1, **kwargs):          ←——6
...     print(x, y, z, kwargs)
>>> funct4(1, 2, m=5, n=9, z=3)
1 2 3 {'n': 9, 'm': 5}
```

Functions are defined by using the def statement ❶. The return statement ❷ is what a function uses to return a value. This value can be of any type. If no return statement is encountered, Python's None value is returned. Function arguments can be entered either by position or by name (keyword). Here, z and y are entered by name ❸. Function parameters can be defined with defaults that are used if a function call leaves them out ❹. A special parameter can be defined that collects all extra positional arguments in a function call into a tuple ❺. Likewise, a special parameter can be defined that collects all extra keyword arguments in a function call into a dictionary ❻.

3.3.6 Exceptions

Exceptions (errors) can be caught and handled by using the try-except-else-finally compound statement. This statement can also catch and handle exceptions you define and raise yourself. Any exception that isn't caught causes the program to exit. This listing shows basic exception handling.

Listing 3.1   File exception.py

```
class EmptyFileError(Exception):                    ←——❶
    pass
filenames = ["myfile1", "nonExistent", "emptyFile", "myfile2"]
for file in filenames:
    try:                              ←——❷
        f = open(file, 'r')
        line = f.readline()                     ←——❸
        if line == "":
            f.close()
            raise EmptyFileError("%s: is empty" % file)      ←——❹
    except IOError as error:
        print("%s: could not be opened: %s" % (file, error.strerror)
    except EmptyFileError as error:
        print(error)
    else:                              ←——❺
        print("%s: %s" % (file, f.readline()))
    finally:
        print("Done processing", file)              ←——❻
```

Here, you define your own exception type inheriting from the base Exception type ❶. If an IOError or EmptyFileError occurs during the execution of the statements in the try block, the associated except block is executed ❷. This is where an IOError might be raised ❸. Here, you raise the EmptyFileError ❹. The else clause is optional ❺; it's executed if no exception occurs in the try block. (Note that in this example, `continue` statements in the `except` blocks could have been used instead.) The `finally` clause is optional ❻; it's executed at the end of the block whether an exception was raised or not.

3.3.7 Context handling using the with keyword

A more streamlined way of encapsulating the `try-except-finally` pattern is to use the `with` keyword and a context manager. Python defines context managers for things like file access, and it's possible for the developer to define custom context managers. One benefit of context managers is that they may (and usually do) have default clean-up actions defined, which always execute whether or not an exception occurs.

This listing shows opening and reading a file by using `with` and a context manager.

Listing 3.2 File with.py

```
filename = "myfile.txt"
with open(filename, "r") as f:
    for line in f:
        print(f)
```

Here, `with` establishes a context manager which wraps the `open` function and the block that follows. In this case, the context manager's predefined clean-up action closes the file, even if an exception occurs, so as long as the expression in the first line executes without raising an exception, the file is always closed. That code is equivalent to this code:

```
filename = "myfile.txt"
try:
    f = open(filename, "r")
    for line in f:
        print(f)
except Exception as e:
    raise e
finally:
    f.close()
```

3.4   Module creation

It's easy to create your own modules, which can be imported and used in the same way as Python's built-in library modules. The example in this listing is a simple module with one function that prompts the user to enter a filename and determines the number of times that words occur in this file.

Listing 3.3 File wo.py

```
"""wo module. Contains function: words_occur()"""          ←—❶
# interface functions                                      ←—❷
def words_occur():
    """words_occur() - count the occurrences of words in a file."""
    # Prompt user for the name of the file to use.
```

```
    file_name = input("Enter the name of the file: ")
    # Open the file, read it and store its words in a list.
    f = open(file_name, 'r')
    word_list = f.read().split()                          ←──❸
    f.close()
    # Count the number of occurrences of each word in the file.
    occurs_dict = {}
    for word in word_list:
        # increment the occurrences count for this word
        occurs_dict[word] = occurs_dict.get(word, 0) + 1
    # Print out the results.
    print("File %s has %d words (%d are unique)" \          ←──❹
      % (file_name, len(word_list), len(occurs_dict)))
    print(occurs_dict)
if __name__ == '__main__':                                 ←──❺
    words_occur()
```

Documentation strings, or *docstrings*, are standard ways of documenting modules, functions, methods, and classes ❶. Comments are anything beginning with a # character ❷. read returns a string containing all the characters in a file ❸, and split returns a list of the words of a string "split out" based on whitespace. You can use a \ to break a long statement across multiple lines ❹. This if statement allows the program to be run as a script by typing python wo.py at a command line ❺.

If you place a file in one of the directories on the module search path, which can be found in sys.path, it can be imported like any of the built-in library modules by using the import statement:

```
>>> import wo
>>> wo.words_occur()          ←──❶
```

This function is called ❶ by using the same attribute syntax used for library module functions.

Note that if you change the file wo.py on disk, import won't bring your changes into the same interactive session. You use the reload function from the imp library in this situation:

```
>>> import imp
>>> imp.reload(wo)
<module 'wo'>
```

For larger projects, there is a generalization of the module concept called *packages*, which allows you to easily group modules in a directory or directory subtree and then import and hierarchically refer to them by using a *package.subpackage.module* syntax. This entails little more than creating a possibly empty initialization file for each package or subpackage.

3.5   *Object-oriented programming*

Python provides full support for OOP. Listing 3.4 is an example that might be the start of a simple shapes module for a drawing program. It's intended mainly to serve as a reference if you're already familiar with OOP. The callout notes relate Python's syntax and semantics to the standard features found in other languages.

Listing 3.4   File sh.py

```
"""sh module. Contains classes Shape, Square and Circle"""
class Shape:                                                    ← 1
    """Shape class: has method move"""
    def __init__(self, x, y):                                  ← 2
        self.x = x
        self.y = y                                              3
    def move(self, deltaX, deltaY):                            ← 4
        self.x = self.x + deltaX
        self.y = self.y + deltaY
class Square(Shape):
    """Square Class:inherits from Shape"""
    def __init__(self, side=1, x=0, y=0):
        Shape.__init__(self, x, y)
        self.side = side
class Circle(Shape):                                           ← 5
    """Circle Class: inherits from Shape and has method area"""
    pi = 3.14159                                               ← 6
    def __init__(self, r=1, x=0, y=0):
        Shape.__init__(self, x, y)                             ← 7
        self.radius = r
    def area(self):
        """Circle area method: returns the area of the circle."""
        return self.radius * self.radius * self.pi
    def __str__(self):                                         ← 8
        return "Circle of radius %s at coordinates (%d, %d)"\
                % (self.radius, self.x, self.y)
```

Classes are defined by using the class keyword **1**. The instance initializer method (constructor) for a class is always called __init__ **2**. Instance variables x and y are created and initialized here **3**. Methods, like functions, are defined by using the def keyword **4**. The first argument of any method is by convention called self. When the method is invoked, self is set to the instance that invoked the method. Class Circle inherits from class Shape **5** and is similar to, but not exactly like, a standard class variable **6**. A class must, in its initializer, explicitly call the initializer of its base class **7**. The __str__ method is used by the print function **8**. Other special method attributes permit operator overloading or are employed by built-in methods such as the length (len) function.

Importing this file makes these classes available:

```
>>> import sh
>>> c1 = sh.Circle()                          ← 1
>>> c2 = sh.Circle(5, 15, 20)
>>> print(c1)
Circle of radius 1 at coordinates (0, 0)
>>> print(c2)                                 ← 2
Circle of radius 5 at coordinates (15, 20)
```

```
>>> c2.area()
78.539749999999998
>>> c2.move(5,6)                              <--- ❸
>>> print(c2)
Circle of radius 5 at coordinates (20, 26)
```

The initializer is implicitly called, and a circle instance is created ❶. The `print` function implicitly uses the special `__str__` method ❷. Here, you see that the `move` method of `Circle`'s parent class `Shape` is available ❸. A method is called by using attribute syntax on the object instance: `object.method()`. The first (`self`) parameter is set implicitly.

Summary

- This chapter is a rapid and very high-level overview of Python; the following chapters provide more detail. This chapter ends the book's overview of Python.

- You may find it valuable to return to this chapter and work through the appropriate examples as a review after you read about the features covered in subsequent chapters.

- If this chapter was mostly a review for you, or if you'd like to learn more about only a few features, feel free to jump around, using the index or table of contents.

- You should have a solid understanding of the Python features in this chapter before skipping ahead to part 4.

Part 2

The essentials

In the chapters that follow, I show you the essentials of Python. I start from the absolute basics of what makes a Python program and move through Python's built-in data types and control structures, as well as defining functions and using modules.

The last chapter of this part moves on to show you how to write standalone Python programs, manipulate files, handle errors, and use classes.

The absolute basics

This chapter describes the absolute basics in Python: how to use assignments and expressions, how to type a number or a string, how to indicate comments in code, and so forth. It starts with a discussion of how Python block structures its code, which differs from every other major language.

4.1 Indentation and block structuring

Python differs from most other programming languages because it uses whitespace and indentation to determine block structure (that is, to determine what constitutes the body of a loop, the `else` clause of a conditional, and so on). Most languages use braces of some sort to do this. Here is C code that calculates the factorial of 9, leaving the result in the variable `r`:

```
/* This is C code  */
int n, r;
n = 9;
r = 1;
while (n > 0) {
    r *= n;
    n--;
}
```

The braces delimit the body of the `while` loop, the code that is executed with each repetition of the loop. The code is usually indented more or less as shown, to make clear what's going on, but it could also be written like this:

```
/* And this is C code with arbitrary indentation */
    int n, r;
        n = 9;
        r = 1;
    while (n > 0) {
r *=  n;
n--;
}
```

The code still would execute correctly, even though it's rather difficult to read.

Here's the Python equivalent:

```
# This is Python code. (Yea!)
n = 9
r = 1
while n > 0:
    r = r * n
    n = n - 1
```

← **Python also supports C-style r *= n**

← **Python also supports n -= 1**

Python doesn't use braces to indicate code structure; instead, the indentation itself is used. The last two lines of the previous code are the body of the `while` loop because they come immediately after the `while` statement and are indented one level further than the `while` statement. If those lines weren't indented, they wouldn't be part of the body of the `while`.

Using indentation to structure code rather than braces may take some getting used to, but there are significant benefits:

- It's impossible to have missing or extra braces. You never need to hunt through your code for the brace near the bottom that matches the one a few lines from the top.
- The visual structure of the code reflects its real structure, which makes it easy to grasp the skeleton of code just by looking at it.

- Python coding styles are mostly uniform. In other words, you're unlikely to go crazy from dealing with someone's idea of aesthetically pleasing code. Everyone's code will look pretty much like yours.

You probably use consistent indentation in your code already, so this won't be a big step for you. If you're using IDLE, it automatically indents lines. You just need to backspace out of levels of indentation when desired. Most programming editors and IDEs—Emacs, VIM, and Eclipse, to name a few—provide this functionality as well. One thing that may trip you up once or twice until you get used to it is the fact that the Python interpreter returns an error message if you have a space (or spaces) preceding the commands you enter at a prompt.

4.2 Differentiating comments

For the most part, anything following a # symbol in a Python file is a comment and is disregarded by the language. The obvious exception is a # in a string, which is just a character of that string:

```
# Assign 5 to x
x = 5
x = 3                      # Now x is 3
x = "# This is not a comment"
```

You'll put comments in Python code frequently.

4.3 Variables and assignments

The most commonly used command in Python is assignment, which looks pretty close to what you might've used in other languages. Python code to create a variable called x and assign the value 5 to that variable is

```
x = 5
```

In Python, unlike in many other computer languages, neither a variable type declaration nor an end-of-line delimiter is necessary. The line is ended by the end of the line. Variables are created automatically when they're first assigned.

> **Variables in Python: buckets or labels?**
>
> The name *variable* is somewhat misleading in Python; *name* or *label* would be more accurate. However, it seems that pretty much everyone calls variables *variables* at some time or another. Whatever you call them, you should know how they really work in Python.
>
> A common, but inaccurate, explanation is that a variable is a container that stores a value, somewhat like a bucket. This would be reasonable for many programming languages (C, for example).

(continued)

However, in Python variables aren't buckets. Instead, they're labels or tags that refer to objects in the Python interpreter's namespace. Any number of labels (or variables) can refer to the same object, and when that object changes, the value referred to by *all* of those variables also changes.

To see what this means, look at the following simple code:

```
>>> a = [1, 2, 3]
>>> b = a
>>> c = b
>>> b[1] = 5
>>> print(a, b, c)
[1, 5, 3] [1, 5, 3] [1, 5, 3]
```

If you're thinking of variables as containers, this result makes no sense. How could changing the contents of one container simultaneously change the other two? However, if variables are just labels referring to objects, it makes sense that changing the object that all three labels refer to would be reflected everywhere.

If the variables are referring to constants or immutable values, this distinction isn't quite as clear:

```
>>> a = 1
>>> b = a
>>> c = b
>>> b = 5
>>> print(a, b, c)
1 5 1
```

Because the objects they refer to can't change, the behavior of the variables in this case is consistent with either explanation. In fact, in this case, after the third line a, b, and c all refer to the same unchangeable integer object with the value 1. The next line, b = 5, makes b refer to the integer object 5 but doesn't change the references of a or c.

Python variables can be set to any object, whereas in C and many other languages, variables can store only the type of value they're declared as. The following is perfectly legal Python code:

```
>>> x = "Hello"
>>> print(x)
Hello
>>> x = 5
>>> print(x)
5
```

x starts out referring to the string object "Hello" and then refers to the integer object 5. Of course, this feature can be abused, because arbitrarily assigning the same variable name to refer successively to different data types can make code confusing to understand.

A new assignment overrides any previous assignments. The `del` statement deletes the variable. Trying to print the variable's contents after deleting it results in an error, as though the variable had never been created in the first place:

```
>>> x = 5
>>> print(x)
5
>>> del x
>>> print(x)
Traceback (most recent call last):
 File "<stdin>", line 1, in <module>
NameError: name 'x' is not defined
>>>
```

Here, you have your first look at a *traceback*, which is printed when an error, called an *exception*, has been detected. The last line tells you what exception was detected, which in this case is a `NameError` exception on x. After its deletion, x is no longer a valid variable name. In this example, the trace returns only `line 1, in <module>` because only the single line has been sent in the interactive mode. In general, the full dynamic call structure of the existing function at the time of the error's occurrence is returned. If you're using IDLE, you obtain the same information with some small differences. The code may look something like this:

```
Traceback (most recent call last):
  File "<pyshell#3>", line 1, in <module>
    print(x)
NameError: name 'x' is not defined
```

Chapter 14 describes this mechanism in more detail. A full list of the possible exceptions and what causes them is in the Python standard library documentation. Use the index to find any specific exception (such as `NameError`) you receive.

Variable names are case-sensitive and can include any alphanumeric character as well as underscores but must start with a letter or underscore. See section 4.10 for more guidance on the Pythonic style for creating variable names.

4.4 Expressions

Python supports arithmetic and similar expressions; these expressions will be familiar to most readers. The following code calculates the average of 3 and 5, leaving the result in the variable z:

```
x = 3
y = 5
z = (x + y) / 2
```

Note that arithmetic operators involving only integers do *not* always return an integer. Even though all the values are integers, division (starting with Python 3) returns a floating-point number, so the fractional part isn't truncated. If you want traditional integer division returning a truncated integer, you can use `//` instead.

Standard rules of arithmetic precedence apply. If you'd left out the parentheses in the last line, the code would've been calculated as `x + (y / 2)`.

Expressions don't have to involve just numerical values; strings, Boolean values, and many other types of objects can be used in expressions in various ways. I discuss these objects in more detail as they're used.

> **TRY THIS: VARIABLES AND EXPRESSIONS**   In the Python shell, create some variables. What happens when you try to put spaces, dashes, or other nonalphanumeric characters in the variable name? Play around with a few complex expressions, such as `x = 2 + 4 * 5 - 6 / 3`. Use parentheses to group the numbers in different ways and see how the result changes compared with the original ungrouped expression.

4.5   *Strings*

You've already seen that Python, like most other programming languages, indicates strings through the use of double quotes. This line leaves the string `"Hello, World"` in the variable `x`:

```
x = "Hello, World"
```

Backslashes can be used to escape characters, to give them special meanings. `\n` means the newline character, `\t` means the tab character, `\\` means a single normal backslash character, and `\"` is a plain double-quote character. It doesn't end the string:

```
x = "\tThis string starts with a \"tab\"."
x = "This string contains a single backslash(\\)."
```

You can use single quotes instead of double quotes. The following two lines do the same thing:

```
x = "Hello, World"
x = 'Hello, World'
```

The only difference is that you don't need to backslash `"` characters in single-quoted strings or `'` characters in double-quoted strings:

```
x = "Don't need a backslash"
x = 'Can\'t get by without a backslash'
x = "Backslash your \" character!"
x = 'You can leave the " alone'
```

You can't split a normal string across lines. This code won't work:

```
# This Python code will cause an ERROR -- you can't split the string
across two lines.
x = "This is a misguided attempt to
put a newline into a string without using backslash-n"
```

But Python offers triple-quoted strings, which let you do this and include single and double quotes without backslashes:

```
x = """Starting and ending a string with triple " characters
permits embedded newlines, and the use of " and ' without
backslashes"""
```

Now x is the entire sentence between the """ delimiters. (You can use triple single quotes—'''—instead of triple double quotes to do the same thing.)

Python offers enough string-related functionality that chapter 6 is devoted to the topic.

4.6 *Numbers*

Because you're probably familiar with standard numeric operations from other languages, this book doesn't contain a separate chapter describing Python's numeric abilities. This section describes the unique features of Python numbers, and the Python documentation lists the available functions.

Python offers four kinds of numbers: *integers, floats, complex numbers,* and *Booleans.* An integer constant is written as an integer—0, –11, +33, 123456—and has unlimited range, restricted only by the resources of your machine. A float can be written with a decimal point or in scientific notation: 3.14, –2E-8, 2.718281828. The precision of these values is governed by the underlying machine but is typically equal to double (64-bit) types in C. Complex numbers are probably of limited interest and are discussed separately later in the section. Booleans are either True or False and behave identically to 1 and 0 except for their string representations.

Arithmetic is much like it is in C. Operations involving two integers produce an integer, except for division (/), which results in a float. If the // division symbol is used, the result is an integer, with truncation. Operations involving a float always produce a float. Here are a few examples:

```
>>> 5 + 2 - 3 * 2
1
>>> 5 / 2          # floating-point result with normal division
2.5
>>> 5 / 2.0        # also a floating-point result
2.5
>>> 5 // 2         # integer result with truncation when divided using '//'
2
>>> 30000000000    # This would be too large to be an int in many languages
30000000000
>>> 30000000000 * 3
90000000000
>>> 30000000000 * 3.0
90000000000.0
>>> 2.0e-8         # Scientific notation gives back a float
2e-08
>>> 3000000 * 3000000
```

```
9000000000000
>>> int(200.2)
200
>>> int(2e2)
200
>>> float(200)
200.0
```

These are explicit conversions between types ❶. int truncates float values.

Numbers in Python have two advantages over C or Java: Integers can be arbitrarily large, and the division of two integers results in a float.

4.6.1   *Built-in numeric functions*

Python provides the following number-related functions as part of its core:

```
abs, divmod, float, hex, int, max, min, oct,
pow, round
```

See the documentation for details.

4.6.2   *Advanced numeric functions*

More advanced numeric functions such as the trig and hyperbolic trig functions, as well as a few useful constants, aren't built into Python but are provided in a standard module called math. I explain modules in detail later. For now, it's sufficient to know that you must make the math functions in this section available by starting your Python program or interactive session with the statement

```
from math import *
```

The math module provides the following functions and constants:

```
acos, asin, atan, atan2, ceil, cos, cosh, e, exp, fabs, floor, fmod,
frexp, hypot, ldexp, log, log10, mod, pi, pow, sin, sinh, sqrt, tan,
tanh
```

See the documentation for details.

4.6.3   *Numeric computation*

The core Python installation isn't well suited to intensive numeric computation because of speed constraints. But the powerful Python extension NumPy provides highly efficient implementations of many advanced numeric operations. The emphasis is on array operations, including multidimensional matrices and more advanced functions such as the Fast Fourier Transform. You should be able to find NumPy (or links to it) at www.scipy.org.

4.6.4   *Complex numbers*

Complex numbers are created automatically whenever an expression of the form nj is encountered, with n having the same form as a Python integer or float. j is, of course, standard notation for the imaginary number equal to the square root of −1, for example:

```
>>> (3+2j)
(3+2j)
```

Note that Python expresses the resulting complex number in parentheses as a way of indicating that what's printed to the screen represents the value of a single object:

```
>>> 3 + 2j - (4+4j)
(-1-2j)
>>> (1+2j) * (3+4j)
(-5+10j)
>>> 1j * 1j
(-1+0j)
```

Calculating j * j gives the expected answer of −1, but the result remains a Python complex-number object. Complex numbers are never converted automatically to equivalent real or integer objects. But you can easily access their real and imaginary parts with real and imag:

```
>>> z = (3+5j)
>>> z.real
3.0
>>> z.imag
5.0
```

Note that real and imaginary parts of a complex number are always returned as floating-point numbers.

4.6.5 *Advanced complex-number functions*

The functions in the math module don't apply to complex numbers; the rationale is that most users want the square root of −1 to generate an error, not an answer! Instead, similar functions, which can operate on complex numbers, are provided in the cmath module:

acos, acosh, asin, asinh, atan, atanh, cos, cosh, e, exp, log, log10, pi, sin, sinh, sqrt, tan, tanh.

To make clear in the code that these functions are special-purpose complex-number functions and to avoid name conflicts with the more normal equivalents, it's best to import the cmath module by saying

```
import cmath
```

and then to explicitly refer to the cmath package when using the function:

```
>>> import cmath
>>> cmath.sqrt(-1)
1j
```

> **Minimizing from <module> import ***
>
> This is a good example of why it's best to minimize the use of the `from <module>` `import *` form of the `import` statement. If you used it to import first the `math` module and then the `cmath` module, the commonly named functions in `cmath` would override those of `math`. It's also more work for someone reading your code to figure out the source of the specific functions you use. Some modules are explicitly designed to use this form of import.
>
> See chapter 10 for more details on how to use modules and module names.

The important thing to keep in mind is that by importing the `cmath` module, you can do almost anything you can do with other numbers.

> **TRY THIS: MANIPULATING STRINGS AND NUMBERS**   In the Python shell, create some string and number variables (integers, floats, *and* complex numbers). Experiment a bit with what happens when you do operations with them, including across types. Can you multiply a string by an integer, for example, or can you multiply it by a float or complex number? Also load the `math` module and try a few of the functions; then load the `cmath` module and do the same. What happens if you try to use one of those functions on an integer or float after loading the `cmath` module? How might you get the `math` module functions back?

4.7   *The None value*

In addition to standard types such as strings and numbers, Python has a special basic data type that defines a single special data object called `None`. As the name suggests, `None` is used to represent an empty value. It appears in various guises throughout Python. For example, a procedure in Python is just a function that doesn't explicitly return a value, which means that by default, it returns `None`.

None is often useful in day-to-day Python programming as a placeholder to indicate a point in a data structure where meaningful data will eventually be found, even though that data hasn't yet been calculated. You can easily test for the presence of `None` because there's only one instance of `None` in the entire Python system (all references to `None` point to the same object), and `None` is equivalent only to itself.

4.8   *Getting input from the user*

You can also use the `input()` function to get input from the user. Use the prompt string you want to display to the user as `input`'s parameter:

```
>>> name = input("Name? ")
Name? Jane
>>> print(name)
Jane
>>> age = int(input("Age? "))        ◁──┐ Converts input
Age? 28                                  └ from string to int
```

```
>>> print(age)
28
>>>
```

This is a fairly simple way to get user input. The one catch is that the input comes in as a string, so if you want to use it as a number, you have to use the `int()` or `float()` function to convert it.

> **TRY THIS: GETTING INPUT** Experiment with the `input()` function to get string and integer input. Using code similar to the previous code, what is the effect of not using `int()` around the call to `input()` for integer input? Can you modify that code to accept a float—say, 28.5? What happens if you deliberately enter the wrong type of value? Examples include a float in which an integer is expected and a string in which a number is expected—and vice versa.

4.9 Built-in operators

Python provides various built-in operators, from the standard (+, *, and so on) to the more esoteric, such as operators for performing bit shifting, bitwise logical functions, and so forth. Most of these operators are no more unique to Python than to any other language; hence, I won't explain them in the main text. You can find a complete list of the Python built-in operators in the documentation.

4.10 Basic Python style

Python has relatively few limitations on coding style with the obvious exception of the requirement to use indentation to organize code into blocks. Even in that case, the amount of indentation and type of indentation (tabs versus spaces) isn't mandated. However, there are preferred stylistic conventions for Python, which are contained in Python Enhancement Proposal (PEP) 8, which is summarized in appendix A and available online at www.python.org/dev/peps/pep-0008/. A selection of Pythonic conventions is provided in table 4.1, but to fully absorb Pythonic style, periodically reread PEP 8.

Table 4.1 Pythonic coding conventions

Situation	Suggestion	Example
Module/package names	Short, all lowercase, underscores only if needed	`imp, sys`
Function names	All lowercase, underscores_for_readablitiy	`foo(), my_func()`
Variable names	All lowercase, underscores_for_readablitiy	`my_var`
Class names	CapitalizeEachWord	`MyClass`
Constant names	ALL_CAPS_WITH_UNDERSCORES	`PI, TAX_RATE`

Table 4.1 Pythonic coding conventions *(continued)*

Situation	Suggestion	Example
Indentation	Four spaces per level, no tabs	
Comparisons	Don't compare explicitly to True or False	`if my_var:` `if not my_var:`

I strongly urge you to follow the conventions of PEP 8. They're wisely chosen and time-tested, and they'll make your code easier for you and other Python programmers to understand.

> **QUICK CHECK: PYTHONIC STYLE**   Which of the following variable and function names do you think are not good Pythonic style? Why?
>
> `bar()`, `varName`, `VERYLONGVARNAME`, `foobar`, `longvarname`, `foo_bar()`, `really_very_long_var_name`

Summary

- The basic syntax summarized above is enough to start writing Python code.
- Python syntax is predictable and consistent.
- Because the syntax offers few surprises, many programmers can get started writing code surprisingly quickly.

Lists, tuples, and sets

5

This chapter covers

- Manipulating lists and list indices
- Modifying lists
- Sorting
- Using common list operations
- Handling nested lists and deep copies
- Using tuples
- Creating and using sets

In this chapter, I discuss the two major Python sequence types: lists and tuples. At first, lists may remind you of arrays in many other languages, but don't be fooled: lists are a good deal more flexible and powerful than plain arrays.

Tuples are like lists that can't be modified; you can think of them as a restricted type of list or as a basic record type. I discuss the need for such a restricted data type later in the chapter. This chapter also discusses a newer Python collection type: sets. Sets are useful when an object's membership in the collection, as opposed to its position, is important

Most of the chapter is devoted to lists, because if you understand lists, you pretty much understand tuples. The last part of the chapter discusses the differences between lists and tuples in both functional and design terms.

5.1   *Lists are like arrays*

A list in Python is much the same thing as an array in Java or C or any other language; it's an ordered collection of objects. You create a list by enclosing a comma-separated list of elements in square brackets, like so:

```
# This assigns a three-element list to x
x = [1, 2, 3]
```

Note that you don't have to worry about declaring the list or fixing its size ahead of time. This line creates the list as well as assigns it, and a list automatically grows or shrinks as needed.

Arrays in Python

A typed `array` module available in Python provides arrays based on C data types. Information on its use can be found in the *Python Library Reference*. I suggest that you look into it only if you really need the performance improvement. If a situation calls for numerical computations, you should consider using `NumPy`, mentioned in chapter 4 and available at www.scipy.org.

Unlike lists in many other languages, Python lists can contain different types of elements; a list element can be any Python object. Here's a list that contains a variety of elements:

```
# First element is a number, second is a string, third is another list.
x = [2, "two", [1, 2, 3]]
```

Probably the most basic built-in list function is the `len` function, which returns the number of elements in a list:

```
>>> x = [2, "two", [1, 2, 3]]
>>> len(x)
3
```

Note that the `len` function doesn't count the items in the inner, nested list.

QUICK CHECK: LEN()   What would `len()` return for each of the following: `[0]`; `[]`; `[[1, 3, [4, 5], 6], 7]`?

5.2   *List indices*

Understanding how list indices work will make Python much more useful to you. Please read the whole section!

Elements can be extracted from a Python list by using a notation like C's array indexing. Like C and many other languages, Python starts counting from 0; asking for element 0 returns the first element of the list, asking for element 1 returns the second element, and so forth. Here are a few examples:

```
>>> x = ["first", "second", "third", "fourth"]
>>> x[0]
'first'
>>> x[2]
'third'
```

But Python indexing is more flexible than C indexing. If indices are negative numbers, they indicate positions counting from the end of the list, with –1 being the last position in the list, –2 being the second-to-last position, and so forth. Continuing with the same list x, you can do the following:

```
>>> a = x[-1]
>>> a
'fourth'
>>> x[-2]
'third'
```

For operations involving a single list index, it's generally satisfactory to think of the index as pointing at a particular element in the list. For more advanced operations, it's more correct to think of list indices as indicating positions *between* elements. In the list ["first", "second", "third", "fourth"], you can think of the indices as pointing like this:

x =[		"first",		"second",		"third",		"fourth"		]
Positive indices	0		1		2		3			
Negative indices	–4		–3		–2		–1			

This is irrelevant when you're extracting a single element, but Python can extract or assign to an entire sublist at once—an operation known as *slicing*. Instead of entering list[index] to extract the item just after index, enter list[index1:index2] to extract all items including index1 and up to (but not including) index2 into a new list. Here are some examples:

```
>>> x = ["first", "second", "third", "fourth"]
>>> x[1:-1]
['second', 'third']
>>> x[0:3]
['first', 'second', 'third']
>>> x[-2:-1]
['third']
```

It may seem reasonable that if the second index indicates a position in the list *before* the first index, this code would return the elements between those indices in reverse order, but this isn't what happens. Instead, this code returns an empty list:

```
>>> x[-1:2]
[]
```

When slicing a list, it's also possible to leave out index1 or index2. Leaving out index1 means "Go from the beginning of the list," and leaving out index2 means "Go to the end of the list":

```
>>> x[:3]
['first', 'second', 'third']
>>> x[2:]
['third', 'fourth']
```

Omitting both indices makes a new list that goes from the beginning to the end of the original list—that is, copies the list. This technique is useful when you want to make a copy that you can modify without affecting the original list:

```
>>> y = x[:]
>>> y[0] = '1 st'
>>> y
['1 st', 'second', 'third', 'fourth']
>>> x
['first', 'second', 'third', 'fourth']
```

> **TRY THIS: LIST SLICES AND INDEXES**   Using what you know about the len() function and list slices, how would you combine the two to get the second half of a list when you don't know what size it is? Experiment in the Python shell to confirm that your solution works.

5.3   *Modifying lists*

You can use list index notation to modify a list as well as to extract an element from it. Put the index on the left side of the assignment operator:

```
>>> x = [1, 2, 3, 4]
>>> x[1] = "two"
>>> x
[1, 'two', 3, 4]
```

Slice notation can be used here too. Saying something like lista[index1:index2] = listb causes all elements of lista between index1 and index2 to be replaced by the elements in listb. listb can have more or fewer elements than are removed from lista, in which case the length of lista is altered. You can use slice assignment to do several things, as shown here:

```
>>> x = [1, 2, 3, 4]
>>> x[len(x):] = [5, 6, 7]          ◁─┐ Appends list
>>> x                                  │ to end of list
[1, 2, 3, 4, 5, 6, 7]
```

```
>>> x[:0] = [-1, 0]
>>> x
[-1, 0, 1, 2, 3, 4, 5, 6, 7]
>>> x[1:-1] = []
>>> x
[-1, 7]
```

◁─┐ **Appends list**
  │ **to front of list**

◁─┐ **Removes elements**
  │ **from list**

Appending a single element to a list is such a common operation that there's a special append method for it:

```
>>> x = [1, 2, 3]
>>> x.append("four")
>>> x
[1, 2, 3, 'four']
```

One problem can occur if you try to append one list to another. The list gets appended as a single element of the main list:

```
>>> x = [1, 2, 3, 4]
>>> y = [5, 6, 7]
>>> x.append(y)
>>> x
[1, 2, 3, 4, [5, 6, 7]]
```

The extend method is like the append method except that it allows you to add one list to another:

```
>>> x = [1, 2, 3, 4]
>>> y = [5, 6, 7]
>>> x.extend(y)
>>> x
[1, 2, 3, 4, 5, 6, 7]
```

There's also a special insert method to insert new list elements between two existing elements or at the front of the list. insert is used as a method of lists and takes two additional arguments. The first additional argument is the index position in the list where the new element should be inserted, and the second is the new element itself:

```
>>> x = [1, 2, 3]
>>> x.insert(2, "hello")
>>> print(x)
[1, 2, 'hello', 3]
>>> x.insert(0, "start")
>>> print(x)
['start', 1, 2, 'hello', 3]
```

insert understands list indices as discussed in section 5.2, but for most uses, it's easiest to think of list.insert(n, elem) as meaning insert elem just before the *n*th element of list. insert is just a convenience method. Anything that can be done with insert can also be done with slice assignment. That is, list.insert(n, elem) is the same thing as list[n:n] = [elem] when n is nonnegative. Using `insert` makes for somewhat more readable code, and `insert` even handles negative indices:

```
>>> x = [1, 2, 3]
>>> x.insert(-1, "hello")
>>> print(x)
[1, 2, 'hello', 3]
```

The `del` statement is the preferred method of deleting list items or slices. It doesn't do anything that can't be done with slice assignment, but it's usually easier to remember and easier to read:

```
>>> x = ['a', 2, 'c', 7, 9, 11]
>>> del x[1]
>>> x
['a', 'c', 7, 9, 11]
>>> del x[:2]
>>> x
[7, 9, 11]
```

In general, `del list[n]` does the same thing as `list[n:n+1] = []`, whereas `del list[m:n]` does the same thing as `list[m:n] = []`.

The `remove` method isn't the converse of `insert`. Whereas `insert` inserts an element at a specified location, `remove` looks for the first instance of a given value in a list and removes that value from the list:

```
>>> x = [1, 2, 3, 4, 3, 5]
>>> x.remove(3)
>>> x
[1, 2, 4, 3, 5]
>>> x.remove(3)
>>> x
[1, 2, 4, 5]
>>> x.remove(3)
Traceback (innermost last):
 File "<stdin>", line 1, in ?
ValueError: list.remove(x): x not in list
```

If `remove` can't find anything to remove, it raises an error. You can catch this error by using the exception-handling abilities of Python, or you can avoid the problem by using `in` to check for the presence of something in a list before attempting to remove it.

The `reverse` method is a more specialized list modification method. It efficiently reverses a list in place:

```
>>> x = [1, 3, 5, 6, 7]
>>> x.reverse()
>>> x
[7, 6, 5, 3, 1]
```

> **TRY THIS: MODIFYING LISTS** Suppose that you have a list 10 items long. How might you move the last three items from the end of the list to the beginning, keeping them in the same order?

5.4   *Sorting lists*

Lists can be sorted by using the built-in Python `sort` method:

```
>>> x = [3, 8, 4, 0, 2, 1]
>>> x.sort()
>>> x
[0, 1, 2, 3, 4, 8]
```

This method does an in-place sort—that is, changes the list being sorted. To sort a list without changing the original list, you have two options. You can use the `sorted()` built-in function, discussed in section 5.4.2, or you can make a copy of the list and sort the copy:

```
>>> x = [2, 4, 1, 3]
>>> y = x[:]
>>> y.sort()
>>> y
[1, 2, 3, 4]
>>> x
[2, 4, 1, 3]
```

Sorting works with strings, too:

```
>>> x = ["Life", "Is", "Enchanting"]
>>> x.sort()
>>> x
['Enchanting', 'Is', 'Life']
```

The `sort` method can sort just about anything because Python can compare just about anything. But there's one caveat in sorting: The default key method used by `sort` requires all items in the list to be of comparable types. That means that using the `sort` method on a list containing both numbers and strings raises an exception:

```
>>> x = [1, 2, 'hello', 3]
>>> x.sort()
Traceback (most recent call last):
  File "<stdin>", line 1, in <module>
TypeError: '<' not supported between instances of 'str' and 'int'
```

Conversely, you can sort a list of lists:

```
>>> x = [[3, 5], [2, 9], [2, 3], [4, 1], [3, 2]]
>>> x.sort()
>>> x
[[2, 3], [2, 9], [3, 2], [3, 5], [4, 1]]
```

According to the built-in Python rules for comparing complex objects, the sublists are sorted first by ascending first element and then by ascending second element.

   `sort` is even more flexible; it has an optional `reverse` parameter that causes the sort to be in reverse order when `reverse=True`, and it's possible to use your own key function to determine how elements of a list are sorted.

5.4.1   *Custom sorting*

To use custom sorting, you need to be able to define functions—something I haven't talked about yet. In this section, I also discuss the fact that `len(string)` returns the number of characters in a string. String operations are discussed more fully in chapter 6.

By default, `sort` uses built-in Python comparison functions to determine ordering, which is satisfactory for most purposes. At times, though, you want to sort a list in a way that doesn't correspond to this default ordering. Suppose that you want to sort a list of words by the number of characters in each word, as opposed to the lexicographic sort that Python normally carries out.

To do this, write a function that returns the value, or key, that you want to sort on, and use it with the `sort` method. That function in the context of `sort` is a function that takes one argument and returns the key or value that the `sort` function is to use.

For number-of-characters ordering, a suitable key function could be

```
def compare_num_of_chars(string1):
    return len(string1)
```

This key function is trivial. It passes the length of each string back to the `sort` method, rather than the strings themselves.

After you define the key function, using it is a matter of passing it to the `sort` method by using the `key` keyword. Because functions are Python objects, they can be passed around like any other Python objects. Here's a small program that illustrates the difference between a default sort and your custom sort:

```
>>> def compare_num_of_chars(string1):
...     return len(string1)
>>> word_list = ['Python', 'is', 'better', 'than', 'C']
>>> word_list.sort()
>>> print(word_list)
['C', 'Python', 'better', 'is', 'than']
>>> word_list = ['Python', 'is', 'better', 'than', 'C']
>>> word_list.sort(key=compare_num_of_chars)
>>> print(word_list)
['C', 'is', 'than', 'Python', 'better']
```

The first list is in lexicographical order (with uppercase coming before lowercase), and the second list is ordered by ascending number of characters.

Custom sorting is very useful, but if performance is critical, it may be slower than the default. Usually, this effect is minimal, but if the key function is particularly complex, the effect may be more than desired, especially for sorts involving hundreds of thousands or millions of elements.

One particular place to avoid custom sorts is where you want to sort a list in descending, rather than ascending, order. In this case, use the `sort` method's `reverse` parameter set to `True`. If for some reason you don't want to do that, it's still better to sort the list normally and then use the `reverse` method to invert the order of the resulting list. These two operations together—the standard sort and the reverse—will still be much faster than a custom sort.

5.4.2 The sorted() function

Lists have a built-in method to sort themselves, but other iterables in Python, such as the keys of a dictionary, don't have a `sort` method. Python also has the built-in function `sorted()`, which returns a sorted list from any iterable. `sorted()` uses the same `key` and `reverse` parameters as the sort method:

```
>>> x = (4, 3, 1, 2)
>>> y = sorted(x)
>>> y
[1, 2, 3, 4]
>>> z = sorted(x, reverse=True)
>>> z
[4, 3, 2, 1]
```

> **TRY THIS: SORTING LISTS** Suppose that you have a list in which each element is in turn a list: `[[1, 2, 3], [2, 1, 3], [4, 0, 1]]`. If you wanted to sort this list by the second element in each list so that the result would be `[[4, 0, 1], [2, 1, 3], [1, 2, 3]]`, what function would you write to pass as the key value to the `sort()` method?

5.5 Other common list operations

Several other list methods are frequently useful, but they don't fall into any specific category.

5.5.1 List membership with the in operator

It's easy to test whether a value is in a list by using the `in` operator, which returns a Boolean value. You can also use the converse, the `not in` operator:

```
>>> 3 in [1, 3, 4, 5]
True
>>> 3 not in [1, 3, 4, 5]
False
>>> 3 in ["one", "two", "three"]
False
>>> 3 not in ["one", "two", "three"]
True
```

5.5.2 List concatenation with the + operator

To create a list by concatenating two existing lists, use the + (list concatenation) operator, which leaves the argument lists unchanged:

```
>>> z = [1, 2, 3] + [4, 5]
>>> z
[1, 2, 3, 4, 5]
```

5.5.3   *List initialization with the * operator*

Use the * operator to produce a list of a given size, which is initialized to a given value. This operation is a common one for working with large lists whose size is known ahead of time. Although you can use append to add elements and automatically expand the list as needed, you obtain greater efficiency by using * to correctly size the list at the start of the program. A list that doesn't change in size doesn't incur any memory real-location overhead:

```
>>> z = [None] * 4
>>> z
[None, None, None, None]
```

When used with lists in this manner, * (which in this context is called the *list multiplication operator*) replicates the given list the indicated number of times and joins all the copies to form a new list. This is the standard Python method for defining a list of a given size ahead of time. A list containing a single instance of None is commonly used in list multiplication, but the list can be anything:

```
>>> z = [3, 1] * 2
>>> z
[3, 1, 3, 1]
```

5.5.4   *List minimum or maximum with min and max*

You can use min and max to find the smallest and largest elements in a list. You'll probably use min and max mostly with numerical lists, but you can use them with lists containing any type of element. Trying to find the maximum or minimum object in a set of objects of different types causes an error if comparing those types doesn't make sense:

```
>>> min([3, 7, 0, -2, 11])
-2
>>> max([4, "Hello", [1, 2]])
Traceback (most recent call last):
  File "<pyshell#58>", line 1, in <module>
    max([4, "Hello",[1, 2]])
TypeError: '>' not supported between instances of 'str' and 'int'
```

5.5.5   *List search with index*

If you want to find where in a list a value can be found (rather than wanting to know only whether the value is in the list), use the index method. This method searches through a list looking for a list element equivalent to a given value and returns the position of that list element:

```
>>> x = [1, 3, "five", 7, -2]
>>> x.index(7)
3
>>> x.index(5)
Traceback (innermost last):
 File "<stdin>", line 1, in ?
ValueError: 5 is not in list
```

Attempting to find the position of an element that doesn't exist in the list raises an error, as shown here. This error can be handled in the same manner as the analogous error that can occur with the `remove` method (that is, by testing the list with `in` before using `index`).

5.5.6 List matches with count

`count` also searches through a list, looking for a given value, but it returns the number of times that the value is found in the list rather than positional information:

```
>>> x = [1, 2, 2, 3, 5, 2, 5]
>>> x.count(2)
3
>>> x.count(5)
2
>>> x.count(4)
0
```

5.5.7 Summary of list operations

You can see that lists are very powerful data structures, with possibilities that go far beyond those of plain old arrays. List operations are so important in Python programming that it's worth laying them out for easy reference, as shown in table 5.1.

Table 5.1 List operations

List operation	Explanation	Example
[]	Creates an empty list	x = []
len	Returns the length of a list	len(x)
append	Adds a single element to the end of a list	x.append('y')
extend	Adds another list to the end of the list	x.extend(['a', 'b'])
insert	Inserts a new element at a given position in the list	x.insert(0, 'y')
del	Removes a list element or slice	del(x[0])
remove	Searches for and removes a given value from a list	x.remove('y')
reverse	Reverses a list in place	x.reverse()
sort	Sorts a list in place	x.sort()
+	Adds two lists together	x1 + x2
*	Replicates a list	x = ['y'] * 3
min	Returns the smallest element in a list	min(x)
max	Returns the largest element in a list	max(x)
index	Returns the position of a value in a list	x.index['y']
count	Counts the number of times a value occurs in a list	x.count('y')

Table 5.1 List operations *(continued)*

List operation	Explanation	Example
sum	Sums the items (if they can be summed)	sum(x)
in	Returns whether an item is in a list	'y' in x

Being familiar with these list operations will make your life as a Python coder much easier.

> **QUICK CHECK: LIST OPERATIONS**   What would be the result of len([[1,2]] * 3)?
>
> What are two differences between using the in operator and a list's index() method?
>
> Which of the following will raise an exception?: min(["a", "b", "c"]); max([1, 2, "three"]); [1, 2, 3].count("one")

> **TRY THIS: LIST OPERATIONS**   If you have a list x, write the code to safely remove an item if—and only if—that value is in the list.
>
> Modify that code to remove the element only if the item occurs in the list more than once.

5.6   *Nested lists and deep copies*

This section covers another advanced topic that you may want to skip if you're just learning the language.

Lists can be nested. One application of nesting is to represent two-dimensional matrices. The members of these matrices can be referred to by using two-dimensional indices. Indices for these matrices work as follows:

```
>>> m = [[0, 1, 2], [10, 11, 12], [20, 21, 22]]
>>> m[0]
[0, 1, 2]
>>> m[0][1]
1
>>> m[2]
[20, 21, 22]
>>> m[2][2]
22
```

This mechanism scales to higher dimensions in the manner you'd expect.

Most of the time, this is all you need to concern yourself with. But you may run into an issue with nested lists; specifically the way that variables refer to objects and how some objects (such as lists) can be modified (are mutable). An example is the best way to illustrate:

```
>>> nested = [0]
>>> original = [nested, 1]
>>> original
[[0], 1]
```

Figure 5.1 shows what this example looks like.

Now the value in the nested list can be changed by using either the nested or the original variables:

```
>>> nested[0] = 'zero'
>>> original
[['zero'], 1]
>>> original[0][0] = 0
>>> nested
[0]
>>> original
[[0], 1]
```

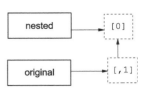

Figure 5.1   A list with its first item referring to a nested list

But if `nested` is set to another list, the connection between them is broken:

```
>>> nested = [2]
>>> original
[[0], 1]
```

Figure 5.2 illustrates this condition.

You've seen that you can obtain a copy of a list by taking a full slice (that is, `x[:]`). You can also obtain a copy of a list by using the + or * operator (for example, `x + []` or `x * 1`). These techniques are slightly less efficient than the slice method. All three create what is called a *shallow* copy of the list, which is probably what you want most of the time. But if your list has other lists nested in it, you may want to make a *deep* copy. You can do this with the deepcopy function of the copy module:

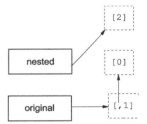

Figure 5.2   The first item of the original list is still a nested list, but the nested variable refers to a different list.

```
>>> original = [[0], 1]
>>> shallow = original[:]
>>> import copy
>>> deep = copy.deepcopy(original)
```

See figure 5.3 for an illustration.

The lists pointed at by the original or shallow variables are connected. Changing the value in the nested list through either one of them affects the other:

```
>>> shallow[1] = 2
>>> shallow
[[0], 2]
>>> original
[[0], 1]
>>> shallow[0][0] = 'zero'
>>> original
[['zero'], 1]
```

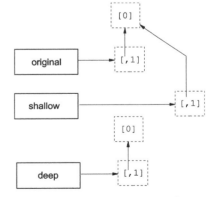

Figure 5.3   A shallow copy doesn't copy nested lists.

The deep copy is independent of the original, and no change to it has any effect on the original list:

```
>>> deep[0][0] = 5
>>> deep
[[5], 1]
>>> original
[['zero'], 1]
```

This behavior is the same for any other nested objects in a list that are modifiable (such as dictionaries).

Now that you've seen what lists can do, it's time to look at tuples.

> **TRY THIS: LIST COPIES** Suppose that you have the following list: x = [[1, 2, 3], [4, 5, 6], [7, 8, 9]] What code could you use to get a copy y of that list in which you could change the elements *without* the side effect of changing the contents of x?

5.7   *Tuples*

Tuples are data structures that are very similar to lists, but they can't be modified; they can only be created. Tuples are so much like lists that you may wonder why Python bothers to include them. The reason is that tuples have important roles that can't be efficiently filled by lists, such as keys for dictionaries.

5.7.1   *Tuple basics*

Creating a tuple is similar to creating a list: assign a sequence of values to a variable. A list is a sequence that's enclosed by [and]; a tuple is a sequence that's enclosed by (and):

```
>>> x = ('a', 'b', 'c')
```

This line creates a three-element tuple.

After a tuple is created, using it is so much like using a list that it's easy to forget that tuples and lists are different data types:

```
>>> x[2]
'c'
>>> x[1:]
('b', 'c')
>>> len(x)
3
>>> max(x)
'c'
>>> min(x)
'a'
>>> 5 in x
False
>>> 5 not in x
True
```

The main difference between tuples and lists is that tuples are immutable. An attempt to modify a tuple results in a confusing error message, which is Python's way of saying that it doesn't know how to set an item in a tuple:

```
>>> x[2] = 'd'
Traceback (most recent call last):
  File "<stdin>", line 1, in <module>
TypeError: 'tuple' object does not support item assignment
```

You can create tuples from existing ones by using the + and * operators:

```
>>> x + x
('a', 'b', 'c', 'a', 'b', 'c')
>>> 2 * x
('a', 'b', 'c', 'a', 'b', 'c')
```

A copy of a tuple can be made in any of the same ways as for lists:

```
>>> x[:]
('a', 'b', 'c')
>>> x * 1
('a', 'b', 'c')
>>> x + ()
('a', 'b', 'c')
```

If you didn't read section 5.6, you can skip the rest of this paragraph. Tuples themselves can't be modified. But if they contain any mutable objects (for example, lists or dictionaries), these objects may be changed if they're still assigned to their own variables. Tuples that contain mutable objects aren't allowed as keys for dictionaries.

5.7.2 *One-element tuples need a comma*

A small syntactical point is associated with using tuples. Because the square brackets used to enclose a list aren't used elsewhere in Python, it's clear that [] means an empty list and that [1] means a list with one element. The same thing isn't true of the parentheses used to enclose tuples. Parentheses can also be used to group items in expressions to force a certain evaluation order. If you say (x + y) in a Python program, do you mean that x and y should be added and then put into a one-element tuple, or do you mean that the parentheses should be used to force x and y to be added before any expressions to either side come into play?

This situation is a problem only for tuples with one element, because tuples with more than one element always include commas to separate the elements, and the commas tell Python that the parentheses indicate a tuple, not a grouping. In the case of one-element tuples, Python requires that the element in the tuple be followed by a comma, to disambiguate the situation. In the case of zero-element (empty) tuples, there's no problem. An empty set of parentheses must be a tuple because it's meaningless otherwise:

```
>>> x = 3
>>> y = 4
>>> (x + y)    # This line adds x and y.
```

```
7
>>> (x + y,)   # Including a comma indicates that the parentheses denote a
    tuple.
(7,)
>>> ()         # To create an empty tuple, use an empty pair of parentheses.
()
```

5.7.3 *Packing and unpacking tuples*

As a convenience, Python permits tuples to appear on the left side of an assignment operator, in which case variables in the tuple receive the corresponding values from the tuple on the right side of the assignment operator. Here's a simple example:

```
>>> (one, two, three, four) =  (1, 2, 3, 4)
>>> one
1
>>> two
2
```

This example can be written even more simply, because Python recognizes tuples in an assignment context even without the enclosing parentheses. The values on the right side are packed into a tuple and then unpacked into the variables on the left side:

```
one, two, three, four = 1, 2, 3, 4
```

One line of code has replaced the following four lines of code:

```
one = 1
two = 2
three = 3
four = 4
```

This technique is a convenient way to swap values between variables. Instead of saying

```
temp = var1
var1 = var2
var2 = temp
```

simply say

```
var1, var2 = var2, var1
```

To make things even more convenient, Python 3 has an extended unpacking feature, allowing an element marked with * to absorb any number of elements not matching the other elements. Again, some examples make this feature clearer:

```
>>> x = (1, 2, 3, 4)
>>> a, b, *c = x
>>> a, b, c
(1, 2, [3, 4])
>>> a, *b, c = x
>>> a, b, c
(1, [2, 3], 4)
```

```
>>> *a, b, c = x
>>> a, b, c
([1, 2], 3, 4)
>>> a, b, c, d, *e = x
>>> a, b, c, d, e
(1, 2, 3, 4, [])
```

Note that the starred element receives all the surplus items as a list and that if there are no surplus elements, the starred element receives an empty list.

Packing and unpacking can also be performed by using list delimiters:

```
>>> [a, b] = [1, 2]
>>> [c, d] = 3, 4
>>> [e, f] = (5, 6)
>>> (g, h) = 7, 8
>>> i, j = [9, 10]
>>> k, l = (11, 12)
>>> a
1
>>> [b, c, d]
[2, 3, 4]
>>> (e, f, g)
(5, 6, 7)
>>> h, i, j, k, l
(8, 9, 10, 11, 12)
```

5.7.4 *Converting between lists and tuples*

Tuples can be easily converted to lists with the `list` function, which takes any sequence as an argument and produces a new list with the same elements as the original sequence. Similarly, lists can be converted to tuples with the `tuple` function, which does the same thing but produces a new tuple instead of a new list:

```
>>> list((1, 2, 3, 4))
[1, 2, 3, 4]
>>> tuple([1, 2, 3, 4])
(1, 2, 3, 4)
```

As an interesting side note, `list` is a convenient way to break a string into characters:

```
>>> list("Hello")
['H', 'e', 'l', 'l', 'o']
```

This technique works because `list` (and `tuple`) apply to any Python sequence, and a string is just a sequence of characters. (Strings are discussed fully in chapter 6.)

QUICK CHECK: TUPLES Explain why the following operations aren't legal for the tuple x = (1, 2, 3, 4):

```
x.append(1)
   x[1] = "hello"
   del x[2]
```

If you had a tuple x = (3, 1, 4, 2), how might you end up with x sorted?

5.8   Sets

A *set* in Python is an unordered collection of objects used when membership and uniqueness in the set are main things you need to know about that object. Like dictionary keys (discussed in chapter 7), the items in a set must be immutable and hashable. This means that ints, floats, strings, and tuples can be members of a set, but lists, dictionaries, and sets themselves can't.

5.8.1   Set operations

In addition to the operations that apply to collections in general, such as in, len, and iteration in for loops, sets have several set-specific operations:

```
>>> x = set([1, 2, 3, 1, 3, 5])                    ← ❶
>>> x
{1, 2, 3, 5}                                        ← ❷
>>> x.add(6)                    ← ❸
>>> x
{1, 2, 3, 5, 6}
>>> x.remove(5)                                    ← ❹
>>> x
{1, 2, 3, 6}
>>> 1 in x                      ← ❺
True
>>> 4 in x                      ← ❺
False
>>> y = set([1, 7, 8, 9])
>>> x | y                       ← ❻
{1, 2, 3, 6, 7, 8, 9}
>>> x & y                                          ← ❼
{1}
>>> x ^ y                       ← ❽
{2, 3, 6, 7, 8, 9}
>>>
```

You can create a set by using set on a sequence, such as a list ❶. When a sequence is made into a set, duplicates are removed ❷. After creating a set by using the set function, you can use add ❸ and remove ❹ to change the elements in the set. The in keyword is used to check for membership of an object in a set ❺. You can also use | ❻ to get the union, or combination, of two sets, & to get their intersection ❼, and ^ ❽ to find their symmetric difference—that is, elements that are in one set or the other but not both.

These examples aren't a complete listing of set operations but are enough to give you a good idea of how sets work. For more information, refer to the official Python documentation.

5.8.2   Frozensets

Because sets aren't immutable and hashable, they can't belong to other sets. To remedy that situation, Python has another set type, frozenset, which is just like a set but can't be changed after creation. Because frozensets are immutable and hashable, they can be members of other sets:

```
>>> x = set([1, 2, 3, 1, 3, 5])
>>> z = frozenset(x)
>>> z
frozenset({1, 2, 3, 5})
>>> z.add(6)
Traceback (most recent call last):
  File "<pyshell#79>", line 1, in <module>
    z.add(6)
AttributeError: 'frozenset' object has no attribute 'add'
>>> x.add(z)
>>> x
{1, 2, 3, 5, frozenset({1, 2, 3, 5})}
```

QUICK CHECK: SETS If you were to construct a set from the following list, how many elements would the set have?: [1, 2, 5, 1, 0, 2, 3, 1, 1, (1, 2, 3)]

LAB 5: EXAMINING A LIST In this lab, the task is to read a set of temperature data (the monthly high temperatures at Heathrow Airport for 1948 through 2016) from a file and then find some basic information: the highest and lowest temperatures, the mean (average) temperature, and the median temperature (the temperature in the middle if all the temperatures are sorted).

The temperature data is in the file lab_05.txt in the source code directory for this chapter. Because I haven't yet discussed reading files, here's the code to read the files into a list:

```
temperatures = []
with open('lab_05.txt') as infile:
    for row in infile:
        temperatures.append(int(row.strip()))
```

You should find the highest and lowest temperature, the average, and the median. You'll probably want to use the `min()`, `max()`, `sum()`, `len()`, and `sort()` functions/methods.

BONUS Determine how many unique temperatures are in the list.

Summary

- Lists and tuples are structures that embody the idea of a sequence of elements, as are strings.
- Lists are like arrays in other languages, but with automatic resizing, slice notation, and many convenience functions.
- Tuples are like lists but can't be modified, so they use less memory and can be dictionary keys (see chapter 7).
- Sets are iterable collections, but they're unordered and can't have duplicate elements.

6
Strings

This chapter covers
- Understanding strings as sequences of characters
- Using basic string operations
- Inserting special characters and escape sequences
- Converting from objects to strings
- Formatting strings
- Using the byte type

Handling text—from user input to filenames to chunks of text to be processed—is a common chore in programming. Python comes with powerful tools to handle and format text. This chapter discusses the standard string and string-related operations in Python.

6.1 Strings as sequences of characters

For the purposes of extracting characters and substrings, strings can be considered to be sequences of characters, which means that you can use index or slice notation:

68

```
>>> x = "Hello"
>>> x[0]
'H'
>>> x[-1]
'o'
>>> x[1:]
'ello'
```

One use for slice notation with strings is to chop the newline off the end of a string (usually, a line that's just been read from a file):

```
>>> x = "Goodbye\n"
>>> x = x[:-1]
>>> x
'Goodbye'
```

This code is just an example. You should know that Python strings have other, better methods to strip unwanted characters, but this example illustrates the usefulness of slicing.

You can also determine how many characters are in the string by using the `len` function, just like finding out the number of elements in a list:

```
>>> len("Goodbye")
7
```

But strings aren't lists of characters. The most noticeable difference between strings and lists is that unlike lists, *strings can't be modified.* Attempting to say something like `string.append('c')` or `string[0] = 'H'` results in an error. You'll notice in the previous example that I stripped off the newline from the string by creating a string that was a slice of the previous one, not by modifying the previous string directly. This is a basic Python restriction, imposed for efficiency reasons.

6.2 *Basic string operations*

The simplest (and probably most common) way to combine Python strings is to use the string concatenation operator +:

```
>>> x = "Hello " + "World"
>>> x
'Hello World'
```

Python also has an analogous string multiplication operator that I've found to be useful sometimes, but not often:

```
>>> 8 * "x"
'xxxxxxxx'
```

6.3   *Special characters and escape sequences*

You've already seen a few of the character sequences that Python regards as special when used within strings: \n represents the newline character, and \t represents the tab character. Sequences of characters that start with a backslash and that are used to represent other characters are called *escape sequences*. Escape sequences are generally used to represent *special characters*—that is, characters (such as tab and newline) that don't have a standard one-character printable representation. This section covers escape sequences, special characters, and related topics in more detail.

6.3.1   *Basic escape sequences*

Python provides a brief list of two-character escape sequences to use in strings (see table 6.1). The same sequences also apply to bytes objects, which will be introduced at the end of this chapter.

Table 6.1   Escape sequences for string and bytes literals

Escape sequence	Character represented
\'	Single-quote character
\"	Double-quote character
\\	Backslash character
\a	Bell character
\b	Backspace character
\f	Formfeed character
\n	Newline character
\r	Carriage-return character (not the same as \n)
\t	Tab character
\v	Vertical tab character

The ASCII character set, which is the character set used by Python and the standard character set on almost all computers, defines quite a few more special characters. These characters are accessed by the numeric escape sequences, described in the next section.

6.3.2   *Numeric (octal and hexadecimal) and Unicode escape sequences*

You can include any ASCII character in a string by using an octal (base 8) or hexadecimal (base 16) escape sequence corresponding to that character. An octal escape sequence is a backslash followed by three digits defining an octal number; the ASCII character corresponding to this octal number is substituted for the octal escape sequence. A hexadecimal escape sequence is with \x rather than just \ and can consist of any number of hexadecimal digits. The escape sequence is terminated when a character is found that's not a hexadecimal digit. For example, in the ASCII character table, the character *m* happens to have decimal value 109. This value is octal value 155 and hexadecimal value 6D, so

```
>>> 'm'
'm'
>>> '\155'
'm'
>>> '\x6D'
'm'
```

All three expressions evaluate to a string containing the single character *m.* But these forms can also be used to represent characters that have no printable representation. The newline character \n, for example, has octal value 012 and hexadecimal value 0A:

```
>>> '\n'
'\n'
>>> '\012'
'\n'
>>> '\x0A'
'\n'
```

Because all strings in Python 3 are Unicode strings, they can also contain almost every character from every language available. Although a discussion of the Unicode system is far beyond the scope of this book, the following examples illustrate that you can also escape any Unicode character, either by number (as shown earlier) or by Unicode name:

```
>>> unicode_a ='\N{LATIN SMALL LETTER A}'
>>> unicode_a                                            ❶      ◁─┐ Escapes by
'a'                                                       ◁────────┘ Unicode name
>>> unicode_a_with_acute = '\N{LATIN SMALL LETTER A WITH ACUTE}'
>>> unicode_a_with_acute
'á'
>>> "\u00E1"              ◁─┐ Escapes by number,
'á'                         │ using \u
>>>
```

The Unicode character set includes the common ASCII characters ❶.

6.3.3 *Printing vs. evaluating strings with special characters*

I talked earlier about the difference between evaluating a Python expression interactively and printing the result of the same expression by using the `print` function. Although the same string is involved, the two operations can produce screen outputs that look different. A string that's evaluated at the top level of an interactive Python session is shown with all of its special characters as octal escape sequences, which makes clear what's in the string. Meanwhile, the `print` function passes the string directly to the terminal program, which may interpret special characters in special ways. Here's what happens with a string consisting of an a followed by a newline, a tab, and a b:

```
>>> 'a\n\tb'
'a\n\tb'
>>> print('a\n\tb')
a
    b
```

In the first case, the newline and tab are shown explicitly in the string; in the second, they're used as newline and tab characters.

A normal `print` function also adds a newline to the end of the string. Sometimes (that is, when you have lines from files that already end with newlines), you may not want this behavior. Giving the `print` function an `end` parameter of `""` causes the `print` function to not append the newline:

```
>>> print("abc\n")
abc

>>> print("abc\n", end="")
abc
>>>
```

6.4   *String methods*

Most of the Python string methods are built into the standard Python string class, so all string objects have them automatically. The standard `string` module also contains some useful constants. Modules are discussed in detail in chapter 10.

For the purposes of this section, you need only remember that most string methods are attached to the string object they operate on by a dot (`.`), as in `x.upper()`. That is, they're prepended with the string object followed by a dot. Because strings are immutable, the string methods are used only to obtain their return value and don't modify the string object they're attached to in any way.

I begin with those string operations that are the most useful and most commonly used; then I discuss some less commonly used but still useful operations. At the end of this section, I discuss a few miscellaneous points related to strings. Not all the string methods are documented here. See the documentation for a complete list of string methods.

6.4.1   *The split and join string methods*

Anyone who works with strings is almost certain to find the `split` and `join` methods invaluable. They're the inverse of one another: `split` returns a list of substrings in the string, and `join` takes a list of strings and puts them together to form a single string with the original string between each element. Typically, `split` uses whitespace as the delimiter to the strings it's splitting, but you can change that behavior via an optional argument.

String concatenation using + is useful but not efficient for joining large numbers of strings into a single string, because each time + is applied, a new string object is created. The previous "Hello World" example produces two string objects, one of which is immediately discarded. A better option is to use the `join` function:

```
>>> " ".join(["join", "puts", "spaces", "between", "elements"])
'join puts spaces between elements'
```

By changing the string used to `join`, you can put anything you want between the joined strings:

```
>>> "::".join(["Separated", "with", "colons"])
'Separated::with::colons'
```

You can even use an empty string, `""`, to join elements in a list:

```
>>> "".join(["Separated", "by", "nothing"])
'Separatedbynothing'
```

The most common use of `split` is probably as a simple parsing mechanism for string-delimited records stored in text files. By default, `split` splits on any whitespace, not just a single space character, but you can also tell it to split on a particular sequence by passing it an optional argument:

```
>>> x = "You\t\t can have tabs\t\n \t and newlines \n\n " \
            "mixed in"
>>> x.split()
['You', 'can', 'have', 'tabs', 'and', 'newlines', 'mixed', 'in']
>>> x = "Mississippi"
>>> x.split("ss")
['Mi', 'i', 'ippi']
```

Sometimes, it's useful to permit the last field in a joined string to contain arbitrary text, perhaps including substrings that may match what `split` splits on when reading in that data. You can do this by specifying how many splits `split` should perform when it's generating its result, via an optional second argument. If you specify n splits, `split` goes along the input string until it has performed n splits (generating a list with $n+1$ substrings as elements) or until it runs out of string. Here are some examples:

```
>>> x = 'a b c d'
>>> x.split(' ', 1)
['a', 'b c d']
>>> x.split(' ', 2)
['a', 'b', 'c d']
>>> x.split(' ', 9)
['a', 'b', 'c', 'd']
```

When using `split` with its optional second argument, you must supply a first argument. To get it to split on runs of whitespace while using the second argument, use `None` as the first argument.

I use `split` and `join` extensively, usually when working with text files generated by other programs. If you want to create more standard output files from your programs, good choices are the `csv` and `json` modules in the Python standard library.

QUICK CHECK: SPLIT AND JOIN How could you use `split` and `join` to change all the whitespace in string x to dashes, such as changing `"this is a test"` to `"this-is-a-test"`?

6.4.2 *Converting strings to numbers*

You can use the functions `int` and `float` to convert strings to integer or floating-point numbers, respectively. If they're passed a string that can't be interpreted as a number of the given type, these functions raise a `ValueError` exception. Exceptions are explained in chapter 14.

In addition, you may pass `int` an optional second argument, specifying the numeric base to use when interpreting the input string:

```
>>> float('123.456')
123.456
>>> float('xxyy')
Traceback (innermost last):
 File "<stdin>", line 1, in ?
ValueError: could not convert string to float: 'xxyy'
>>> int('3333')
3333
>>> int('123.456')                          Can't have decimal
Traceback (innermost last):                 point in integer.
 File "<stdin>", line 1, in ?
ValueError: invalid literal for int() with base 10: '123.456'
>>> int('10000', 8)                         Interprets 10000
4096                                         as octal number
>>> int('101', 2)
5
>>> int('ff', 16)
255                                          Can't interpret 123456
>>> int('123456', 6)                        as base 6 number.
Traceback (innermost last):
 File "<stdin>", line 1, in ?
ValueError: invalid literal for int() with base 6: '123456'
```

Did you catch the reason for that last error? I requested that the string be interpreted as a base 6 number, but the digit 6 can never appear in a base 6 number. Sneaky!

QUICK CHECK: STRINGS TO NUMBERS Which of the following will not be converted to numbers, and why?

```
int('a1')
int('12G', 16)
float("12345678901234567890")
int("12*2")
```

6.4.3 *Getting rid of extra whitespace*

A trio of surprisingly useful simple methods are the `strip`, `lstrip`, and `rstrip` functions. `strip` returns a new string that's the same as the original string, except that any whitespace at the *beginning or end* of the string has been removed. `lstrip` and `rstrip` work similarly, except that they remove whitespace only at the left or right end of the original string, respectively:

```
>>> x = "   Hello,     World\t\t "
>>> x.strip()
'Hello,     World'
>>> x.lstrip()
'Hello,     World\t\t '
>>> x.rstrip()
'   Hello,     World'
```

In this example, tab characters are considered to be whitespace. The exact meaning may differ across operating systems, but you can always find out what Python considers to be whitespace by accessing the `string.whitespace` constant. On my Windows system, Python returns the following:

```
>>> import string
>>> string.whitespace
' \t\n\r\x0b\x0c'
>>> " \t\n\r\v\f"
' \t\n\r\x0b\x0c'
```

The characters given in backslashed hex (\xnn) format represent the vertical tab and formfeed characters. The space character is in there as itself. It may be tempting to change the value of this variable, to attempt to affect how `strip` and so forth work, but don't do it. Such an action isn't guaranteed to give you the results you're looking for.

But you can change which characters `strip`, `rstrip`, and `lstrip` remove by passing a string containing the characters to be removed as an extra parameter:

```
>>> x = "www.python.org"
>>> x.strip("w")               ⟵┐ Strips off all ws
'.python.org'
>>> x.strip("gor")                        ⟵┐ Strips off all gs,
'www.python.'                              ❶ os, and rs
>>> x.strip(".gorw")       ⟵┐ Strips off all dots,
'python'                    │ gs, os, rs and ws
```

Note that `strip` removes any and all of the characters in the extra parameter string, no matter in which order they occur ❶.

The most common use for these functions is as a quick way to clean up strings that have just been read in. This technique is particularly helpful when you're reading lines from files (discussed in chapter 13), because Python always reads in an entire line, including the trailing newline, if one exists. When you get around to processing the line read in, you typically don't want the trailing newline. `rstrip` is a convenient way to get rid of it.

QUICK CHECK: STRIP If the string x equals `"(name,  date),\n"`, which of the following would return a string containing `"name, date"`?

```
x.rstrip("),")
x.strip("),\n")
x.strip("\n)(,")
```

6.4.4 *String searching*

The string objects provide several methods to perform simple string searches. Before I describe them, though, I'll talk about another module in Python: `re`. (This module is discussed in-depth in chapter 16.)

> **Another method for searching strings: the re module**
>
> The `re` module also does string searching but in a far more flexible manner, using *regular expressions*. Rather than search for a single specified substring, a `re` search can look for a string pattern. You could look for substrings that consist entirely of digits, for example.
>
> Why am I mentioning this when `re` is discussed fully later? In my experience, many uses of basic string searches are inappropriate. You'd benefit from a more powerful searching mechanism but aren't aware that one exists, so you don't even look for something better. Perhaps you have an urgent project involving strings and don't have time to read this entire book. If basic string searching does the job for you, that's great. But be aware that you have a more powerful alternative.

The four basic string-searching methods are similar: `find`, `rfind`, `index`, and `rindex`. A related method, `count`, counts how many times a substring can be found in another string. I describe `find` in detail and then examine how the other methods differ from it.

`find` takes one required argument: the substring being searched for. `find` returns the position of the first character of the first instance of `substring` in the `string` object, or `-1` if `substring` doesn't occur in the string:

```
>>> x = "Mississippi"
>>> x.find("ss")
2
>>> x.find("zz")
-1
```

`find` can also take one or two additional, optional arguments. The first of these arguments, if present, is an integer `start`; it causes `find` to ignore all characters before position `start` in `string` when searching for `substring`. The second optional argument, if present, is an integer `end`; it causes `find` to ignore characters at or after position `end` in `string`:

```
>>> x = "Mississippi"
>>> x.find("ss", 3)
5
>>> x.find("ss", 0, 3)
-1
```

`rfind` is almost the same as `find`, except that it starts its search at the end of `string` and so returns the position of the first character of the last occurrence of `substring` in `string`:

```
>>> x = "Mississippi"
>>> x.rfind("ss")
5
```

rfind can also take one or two optional arguments, with the same meanings as those for find.

index and rindex are identical to find and rfind, respectively, except for one difference: If index or rindex fails to find an occurrence of substring in string, it doesn't return –1 but raises a ValueError exception. Exactly what this means will be clear after you read chapter 14.

count is used identically to any of the previous four functions, but returns the number of non-overlapping times the given substring occurs in the given string:

```
>>> x = "Mississippi"
>>> x.count("ss")
2
```

You can use two other string methods to search strings: startswith and endswith. These methods return a True or False result, depending on whether the string they're used on starts or ends with one of the strings given as parameters:

```
>>> x = "Mississippi"
>>> x.startswith("Miss")
True
>>> x.startswith("Mist")
False
>>> x.endswith("pi")
True
>>> x.endswith("p")
False
```

Both startswith and endswith can look for more than one string at a time. If the parameter is a tuple of strings, both methods check for all the strings in the tuple and return True if any one of them is found:

```
>>> x.endswith(("i", "u"))
True
```

startswith and endswith are useful for simple searches where you're sure that what you're checking for is at the beginning or end of a line.

> **QUICK CHECK: STRING SEARCHING** If you wanted to check whether a line ends with the string "rejected", what string method would you use? Would there be any other ways to get the same result?

6.4.5 Modifying strings

Strings are immutable, but string objects have several methods that can operate on that string and return a new string that's a modified version of the original string. This provides much the same effect as direct modification for most purposes. You can find a more complete description of these methods in the documentation.

You can use the replace method to replace occurrences of substring (its first argument) in the string with newstring (its second argument). This method also takes an optional third argument (see the documentation for details):

```
>>> x = "Mississippi"
>>> x.replace("ss", "+++")
'Mi+++i+++ippi'
```

Like the string search functions, the re module is a much more powerful method of substring replacement.

The functions string.maketrans and string.translate may be used together to translate characters in strings into different characters. Although rarely used, these functions can simplify your life when they're needed.

Suppose that you're working on a program that translates string expressions from one computer language into another. The first language uses ~ to mean logical not, whereas the second language uses !; the first language uses ^ to mean logical and, the second language uses &; the first language uses (and), whereas the second language uses [and]. In a given string expression, you need to change all instances of ~ to !, all instances of ^ to &, all instances of (to [, and all instances of) to]. You could do this by using multiple invocations of replace, but an easier and more efficient way is

```
>>> x = "~x ^ (y % z)"
>>> table = x.maketrans("~^()", "!&[]")
>>> x.translate(table)
'!x & [y % z]'
```

The second line uses maketrans to make up a translation table from its two string arguments. The two arguments must each contain the same number of characters, and a table is made such that looking up the *n*th character of the first argument in that table gives back the *n*th character of the second argument.

Next, the table produced by maketrans is passed to translate. Then translate goes over each of the characters in its string object and checks to see whether they can be found in the table given as the second argument. If a character can be found in the translation table, translate replaces that character with the corresponding character looked up in the table to produce the translated string.

You can give translate an optional argument to specify characters that should be removed from the string. See the documentation for details.

Other functions in the string module perform more specialized tasks. string.lower converts all alphabetic characters in a string to lowercase, and upper does the opposite. capitalize capitalizes the first character of a string, and title capitalizes all words in a string. swapcase converts lowercase characters to uppercase and uppercase to lowercase in the same string. expandtabs gets rid of tab characters in a string by replacing each tab with a specified number of spaces. ljust, rjust, and center pad a string with spaces to justify it in a certain field width. zfill left-pads a numeric string with zeros. Refer to the documentation for details on these methods.

6.4.6 *Modifying strings with list manipulations*

Because strings are immutable objects, you have no way to manipulate them directly in the same way that you can manipulate lists. Although the operations that produce new strings (leaving the original strings unchanged) are useful for many things, sometimes you want to be able to manipulate a string as though it were a list of characters. In that case, turn the string into a list of characters, do whatever you want, and then turn the resulting list back into a string:

```
>>> text = "Hello, World"
>>> wordList = list(text)
>>> wordList[6:] = []          ←——  Removes everything
>>> wordList.reverse()               after comma
>>> text = "".join(wordList)
>>> print(text)                ←——  Joins with no
,olleH                               space between
```

You can also turn a string into a tuple of characters by using the built-in `tuple` function. To turn the list back into a string, use `"".join()`.

You shouldn't go overboard with this method because it causes the creation and destruction of new `string` objects, which is relatively expensive. Processing hundreds or thousands of strings in this manner probably won't have much of an impact on your program; processing millions of strings probably will.

QUICK CHECK: MODIFYING STRINGS What would be a quick way to change all punctuation in a string to spaces?

6.4.7 *Useful methods and constants*

`string` objects also have several useful methods to report various characteristics of the string, such as whether it consists of digits or alphabetic characters, or is all uppercase or lowercase:

```
>>> x = "123"
>>> x.isdigit()
True
>>> x.isalpha()
False
>>> x = "M"
>>> x.islower()
False
>>> x.isupper()
True
```

For a list of all the possible string methods, refer to the string section of the official Python documentation.

Finally, the `string` module defines some useful constants. You've already seen `string.whitespace`, which is a string made up of the characters Python thinks of as whitespace on your system. `string.digits` is the string `'0123456789'`. `string.hexdigits` includes all the characters in `string.digits`, as well as 'abcdefABCDEF', the extra characters used in hexadecimal numbers. string .octdigits contains '01234567'—only those digits used in octal numbers. string.lowercase contains all lowercase alphabetic characters; string .uppercase contains all uppercase alphabetic characters; string.letters contains all the characters in string.lowercase and string.uppercase. You might be tempted to try assigning to these constants to change the behavior of the language. Python would let you get away with this action, but it probably would be a bad idea.

Remember that strings are sequences of characters, so you can use the convenient Python in operator to test for a character's membership in any of these strings, although usually the existing string methods are simpler and easier. The most common string operations are shown in table 6.2.

Table 6.2   Common string operations

String operation	Explanation	Example
+	Adds two strings together	x = "hello " + "world"
*	Replicates a string	x = " " * 20
upper	Converts a string to uppercase	x.upper()
lower	Converts a string to lowercase	x.lower()
title	Capitalizes the first letter of each word in a string	x.title()
find, index	Searches for the target in a string	x.find(y) x.index(y)
rfind, rindex	Searches for the target in a string, from the end of the string	x.rfind(y) x.rindex(y)
startswith, endswith	Checks the beginning or end of a string for a match	x.startswith(y) x.endswith(y)
replace	Replaces the target with a new string	x.replace(y, z)
strip, rstrip, lstrip	Removes whitespace or other characters from the ends of a string	x.strip()
encode	Converts a Unicode string to a bytes object	x.encode("utf_8")

Note that these methods don't change the string itself; they return either a location in the string or a new string.

TRY THIS: STRING OPERATIONS   Suppose that you have a list of strings in which some (but not necessarily all) of the strings begin and end with the double quote character:

```
x = ['"abc"', 'def', '"ghi"', '"klm"', 'nop']
```

What code would you use on each element to remove just the double quotes?

What code could you use to find the position of the last p in Mississippi? When you've found that position, what code would you use to remove just that letter?

6.5   *Converting from objects to strings*

In Python, almost anything can be converted to some sort of a string representation by using the built-in repr function. Lists are the only complex Python data types you're familiar with so far, so here, I turn some lists into their representations:

```
>>> repr([1, 2, 3])
'[1, 2, 3]'
>>> x = [1]
>>> x.append(2)
>>> x.append([3, 4])
>>> 'the list x is ' + repr(x)
'the list x is [1, 2, [3, 4]]'
```

The example uses repr to convert the list x to a string representation, which is then concatenated with the other string to form the final string. Without the use of repr, this code wouldn't work. In an expression like "string" + [1, 2] + 3, are you trying to add strings, add lists, or just add numbers? Python doesn't know what you want in such a circumstance, so it does the safe thing (raises an error) rather than make any assumptions. In the previous example, all the elements had to be converted to string representations before the string concatenation would work.

Lists are the only complex Python objects that I've described to this point, but repr can be used to obtain some sort of string representation for almost any Python object. To see this, try repr around a built-in complex object, which is an actual Python function:

```
>>> repr(len)
'<built-in function len>'
```

Python hasn't produced a string containing the code that implements the len function, but it has at least returned a string—<built-in function len>—that describes what that function is. If you keep the repr function in mind and try it on each Python data type (dictionaries, tuples, classes, and the like) in the book, you'll see that no matter what type of Python object you have, you can get a string that describes something about that object.

This is great for debugging programs. If you're in doubt about what's held in a variable at a certain point in your program, use repr and print out the contents of that variable.

I've covered how Python can convert any object to a string that describes that object. The truth is, Python can do this in either of two ways. The repr function always returns what might be loosely called the *formal string representation* of a Python object. More specifically, repr returns a string representation of a Python object from which the original object can be rebuilt. For large, complex objects, this may not be the sort of thing you want to see in debugging output or status reports.

Python also provides the built-in `str` function. In contrast to `repr`, `str` is intended to produce *printable* string representations, and it can be applied to any Python object. `str` returns what might be called the *informal string representation* of the object. A string returned by `str` need not define an object fully and is intended to be read by humans, not by Python code.

You won't notice any difference between `repr` and `str` when you start using them, because until you begin using the object-oriented features of Python, there's no difference. `str` applied to any built-in Python object always calls `repr` to calculate its result. Only when you start defining your own classes does the difference between `str` and `repr` become important, as discussed in chapter 15.

So why talk about this now? I want you to be aware that there's more going on behind the scenes with `repr` than just being able to easily write `print` functions for debugging. As a matter of good style, you may want to get into the habit of using `str` rather than `repr` when creating strings for displaying information.

6.6   *Using the format method*

You can format strings in Python 3 in two ways. The newer way is to use the string class's `format` method. The `format` method combines a format string containing replacement fields marked with { } with replacement values taken from the parameters given to the `format` command. If you need to include a literal { or } in the string, you double it to {{ or }}. The `format` command is a powerful string-formatting mini-language that offers almost endless possibilities for manipulating string formatting. Conversely, it's fairly simple to use for the most common use cases, so I look at a few basic patterns in this section. Then, if you need to use the more advanced options, you can refer to the string-formatting section of the standard library documentation.

6.6.1   *The format method and positional parameters*

A simple way to use the string `format` method is with numbered replacement fields that correspond to the parameters passed to the `format` function:

```
>>> "{0} is the {1} of {2}".format("Ambrosia", "food", "the gods")   ◁────①
'Ambrosia is the food of the gods'
>>> "{{Ambrosia}} is the {0} of {1}".format("food", "the gods")   ◁────②
'{Ambrosia} is the food of the gods'
```

Note that the `format` method is applied to the format string, which can also be a string variable ①. Doubling the { } characters escapes them so that they don't mark a replacement field ②.

This example has three replacement fields, {0}, {1}, and {2}, which are in turn filled by the first, second, and third parameters. No matter where in the format string you place {0}, it's always be replaced by the first parameter, and so on.

You can also use the named parameters.

6.6.2 *The format method and named parameters*

The `format` method also recognizes named parameters and replacement fields:

```
>>> "{food} is the food of {user}".format(food="Ambrosia",
...        user="the gods")
'Ambrosia is the food of the gods'
```

In this case, the replacement parameter is chosen by matching the name of the replacement field with the name of the parameter given to the `format` command.

You can also use both positional and named parameters, and you can even access attributes and elements within those parameters:

```
>>> "{0} is the food of {user[1]}".format("Ambrosia",
...        user=["men", "the gods", "others"])
'Ambrosia is the food of the gods'
```

In this case, the first parameter is positional, and the second, `user[1]`, refers to the second element of the named parameter `user`.

6.6.3 *Format specifiers*

Format specifiers let you specify the result of the formatting with even more power and control than the formatting sequences of the older style of string formatting. The format specifier lets you control the fill character, alignment, sign, width, precision, and type of the data when it's substituted for the replacement field. As noted earlier, the syntax of format specifiers is a mini-language in its own right and too complex to cover completely here, but the following examples give you an idea of its usefulness:

```
>>> "{0:10} is the food of gods".format("Ambrosia")          <--(1)
'Ambrosia   is the food of gods'
>>> "{0:{1}} is the food of gods".format("Ambrosia", 10)     <--(2)
'Ambrosia   is the food of gods'
>>> "{food:{width}} is the food of gods".format(food="Ambrosia", width=10)
'Ambrosia   is the food of gods'
>>> "{0:>10} is the food of gods".format("Ambrosia")         <--(3)
'  Ambrosia is the food of gods'
>>> "{0:&>10} is the food of gods".format("Ambrosia")        <--(4)
'&&Ambrosia is the food of gods'
```

`:10` is a format specifier that makes the field 10 spaces wide and pads with spaces (1). `:{1}` takes the width from the second parameter (2). `:>10` forces right-justification of the field and pads with spaces (3). `:&>10` forces right-justification and pads with `&` instead of spaces (4).

QUICK CHECK: THE FORMAT() METHOD What will be in x when the following snippets of code are executed?:

```
x = "{1:{0}}".format(3, 4)
x = "{0:$>5}".format(3)
x = "{a:{b}}".format(a=1, b=5)
x = "{a:{b}}:{0:$>5}".format(3, 4, a=1, b=5, c=10)
```

6.7   *Formatting strings with %*

This section covers formatting strings with the *string modulus* (%) operator. This operator is used to combine Python values into formatted strings for printing or other use. C users will notice a strange similarity to the `printf` family of functions. The use of % for string formatting is the old style of string formatting, and I cover it here because it was the standard in earlier versions of Python, and you're likely to see it in code that's been ported from earlier versions of Python or was written by coders who are familiar with those versions. This style of formatting shouldn't be used in new code, however, because it's slated to be deprecated and then removed from the language in the future.

Here's an example:

```
>>> "%s is the %s of %s" % ("Ambrosia", "food", "the gods")
'Ambrosia is the food of the gods'
```

The string modulus operator (the bold % that occurs in the middle, not the three instances of %s that come before it in the example) takes two parts: the left side, which is a string, and the right side, which is a tuple. The string modulus operator scans the left string for special *formatting sequences* and produces a new string by substituting the values on the right side for those formatting sequences, in order. In this example, the only formatting sequences on the left side are the three instances of %s, which stands for "Stick a string in here."

Passing in different values on the right side produces different strings:

```
>>> "%s is the %s of %s" % ("Nectar", "drink", "gods")
'Nectar is the drink of gods'
>>> "%s is the %s of the %s" % ("Brussels Sprouts", "food",
...        "foolish")
'Brussels Sprouts is the food of the foolish'
```

The members of the tuple on the right have `str` applied to them automatically by %s, so they don't have to already be strings:

```
>>> x = [1, 2, "three"]
>>> "The %s contains: %s" % ("list", x)
"The list contains: [1, 2, 'three']"
```

6.7.1   *Using formatting sequences*

All formatting sequences are substrings contained in the string on the left side of the central %. Each formatting sequence begins with a percent sign and is followed by one or more characters that specify what is to be substituted for the formatting sequence and how the substitution is to be accomplished. The %s formatting sequence used previously is the simplest formatting sequence; it indicates that the corresponding string from the tuple on the right side of the central % should be substituted in place of the %s.

Other formatting sequences can be more complex. The following sequence specifies the field width (total number of characters) of a printed number to be six, specifies the number of characters after the decimal point to be two, and left-justifies the
number in its field. I've put this formatting sequence in angle brackets so you can see
where extra spaces are inserted into the formatted string:

```
>>> "Pi is <%-6.2f>" % 3.14159 # use of the formatting sequence: %-6.2f
'Pi is <3.14  >'
```

All the options for characters that are allowable in formatting sequences are given in
the documentation. There are quite a few options, but none is particularly difficult to
use. Remember that you can always try a formatting sequence interactively in Python
to see whether it does what you expect it to do.

6.7.2 *Named parameters and formatting sequences*

Finally, one additional feature available with the % operator can be useful in certain
circumstances. Unfortunately, to describe it, I have to employ a Python feature that I
haven't yet discussed in detail: *dictionaries*, commonly called *hash tables* or *associative
arrays* in other languages. You can skip ahead to chapter 7 to learn about dictionaries;
skip this section for now and come back to it later; or read straight through, trusting
the examples to make things clear.

Formatting sequences can specify what should be substituted for them by name
rather than by position. When you do this, each formatting sequence has a name in
parentheses immediately following the initial % of the formatting sequence, like so:

```
"%(pi).2f"            ⟵── Note name in parentheses.
```

In addition, the argument to the right of the % operator is no longer given as a single
value or tuple of values to be printed, but as a dictionary of values to be printed, with
each named formatting sequence having a correspondingly named key in the dictionary. Using the previous formatting sequence with the string modulus operator, you
might produce code like this:

```
>>> num_dict = {'e': 2.718, 'pi': 3.14159}
>>> print("%(pi).2f - %(pi).4f - %(e).2f" % num_dict)
3.14 - 3.1416 - 2.72
```

This code is particularly useful when you're using format strings that perform a large
number of substitutions, because you no longer have to keep track of the positional
correspondences of the right-side tuple of elements with the formatting sequences in
the format string. The order in which elements are defined in the dict argument is
irrelevant, and the template string may use values from dict more than once (as it
does with the 'pi' entry).

Controlling output with the print function

Python's built-in `print` function also has some options that can make handling simple string output easier. When used with one parameter, `print` prints the value and a newline character, so that a series of calls to `print` prints each value on a separate line:

```
>>> print("a")
a
>>> print("b")
b
```

But `print` can do more. You can also give the `print` function several arguments, and those arguments are printed on the same line, separated by spaces and ending with a newline:

```
>>> print("a", "b", "c")
a b c
```

If that's not quite what you need, you can give the `print` function additional parameters to control what separates each item and what ends the line:

```
>>> print("a", "b", "c", sep="|")
a|b|c
>>> print("a", "b", "c", end="\n\n")
a b c

>>>
```

Finally, the `print` function can be used to print to files as well as console output.

```
>>> print("a", "b", "c", file=open("testfile.txt", "w"))
```

Using the `print` function's options gives you enough control for simple text output, but more complex situations are best served by using the `format` method.

> **QUICK CHECK: FORMATTING STRINGS WITH %**   What would be in the variable x after the following snippets of code have executed?
>
> ```
> x = "%.2f" % 1.1111
> x = "%(a).2f" % {'a':1.1111}
> x = "%(a).08f" % {'a':1.1111}
> ```

6.8   *String interpolation*

Starting in Python 3.6, there's a way to create string constants containing arbitrary values, which is called *string interpolation*. String interpolation is a way to include the values of Python expressions inside literal strings. These f-strings, as they're commonly called because they are prefixed with f, use a syntax similar to that of the format method, but with a little less overhead. The following examples should give you a basic idea of how f-strings work:

```
>>> value = 42
>>> message = f"The answer is {value}"
```

```
>>> print(message)
The answer is 42
```

Just as with the format method, format specifiers may be added:

```
>>> pi = 3.1415
>>> print(f"pi is {pi:{10}.{2}}")
pi is        3.1
```

Because string interpolation is a new feature, it's not yet clear how it will be used. For the complete documentation on f-strings and format specifiers, refer to PEP-498 in the online Python documentation.

6.9 *Bytes*

A `bytes` object is similar to a `string` object but with an important difference: A `string` is an immutable sequence of Unicode characters, whereas a `bytes` object is a sequence of integers with values from 0 to 256. Bytes can be necessary when you're dealing with binary data, such as reading from a binary data file.

The key thing to remember is that `bytes` objects may look like strings, but they can't be used exactly like strings or combined with strings:

```
>>> unicode_a_with_acute = '\N{LATIN SMALL LETTER A WITH ACUTE}'
>>> unicode_a_with_acute
'á'
>>> xb = unicode_a_with_acute.encode()        ←———      ❶
>>> xb
b'\xc3\xa1'                        ←——❷
>>> xb += 'A'                                  ←———
Traceback (most recent call last):                     ❸
  File "<pyshell#35>", line 1, in <module>
    xb += 'A'
TypeError: can't concat str to bytes           ❹
>>> xb.decode()                                ←———
'á'
```

The first thing you can see is that to convert from a regular (Unicode) string to `bytes`, you need to call the string's `encode` method ❶. After it's encoded to a `bytes` object, the character is 2 bytes and no longer prints the same way that the string did ❷. Further, if you attempt to add a `bytes` object and a string object together, you get a type error because the two types are incompatible ❸. Finally, to convert a `bytes` object back to a string, you need to call that object's `decode` method ❹.

Most of the time, you shouldn't need to think about Unicode or bytes at all. But when you need to deal with international character sets (an increasingly common issue), you must understand the difference between regular strings and `bytes`.

QUICK CHECK: BYTES For which of the following kinds of data would you want to use a string? For which could you use bytes?

❶ Data file storing binary data
❷ Text in a language with accented characters

❸ Text with only uppercase and lowercase roman characters

❹ A series of integers no larger than 255

LAB 6: PREPROCESSING TEXT   In processing raw text, it's quite often necessary to clean and normalize the text before doing anything else. If you want to find the frequency of words in text, for example, you can make the job easier if, before you start counting, you make sure that everything is lowercase (or uppercase, if you prefer) and that all punctuation has been removed. You can also make things easier by breaking the text into a series of words. In this lab, the task is to read the first part of the first chapter of *Moby Dick* (found in the book's source code), make sure that everything is one case, remove all punctuation, and write the words one per line to a second file. Because I haven't yet covered reading and writing files, here's the code for those operations:

```
with open("moby_01.txt") as infile, open("moby_01_clean.txt", "w") as outfile:
    for line in infile:
        # make all one case
        # remove punctuation
        # split into words
        # write all words for line
        outfile.write(cleaned_words)
```

Summary

- Python strings have powerful text-processing features, including searching and replacing, trimming characters, and changing case.
- Strings are immutable; they can't be changed in place.
- Operations that appear to change strings actually return a copy with the changes.
- The `re` (regular expression) module has even more powerful string capabilities, which are discussed in chapter 16.

Dictionaries 7

This chapter discusses dictionaries, Python's name for associative arrays or maps, which it implements by using hash tables. Dictionaries are amazingly useful, even in simple programs.

Because dictionaries are less familiar to many programmers than other basic data structures such as lists and strings, some of the examples illustrating dictionary use are slightly more complex than the corresponding examples for other built-in data structures. It may be necessary to read parts of chapter 8 to fully understand some of the examples in this chapter.

7.1   *What is a dictionary?*

If you've never used associative arrays or hash tables in other languages, a good way to start understanding the use of dictionaries is to compare them with lists:

- Values in lists are accessed by means of integers called *indices*, which indicate where in the list a given value is found.
- Dictionaries access values by means of integers, strings, or other Python objects called *keys*, which indicate where in the dictionary a given value is found. In other words, both lists and dictionaries provide indexed access to arbitrary values, but the set of items that can be used as dictionary indices is much larger than, and contains, the set of items that can be used as list indices. Also, the mechanism that dictionaries use to provide indexed access is quite different from that used by lists.
- Both lists and dictionaries can store objects of any type.
- Values stored in a list are implicitly *ordered* by their positions in the list, because the indices that access these values are consecutive integers. You may or may not care about this ordering, but you can use it if desired. Values stored in a dictionary are *not* implicitly ordered relative to one another because dictionary keys aren't just numbers. Note that if you're using a dictionary but also care about the order of the items (the order in which they were added, that is), you can use an *ordered dictionary*, which is a dictionary subclass that can be imported from the `collections` module. You can also define an order on the items in a dictionary by using another data structure (often a list) to store such an ordering explicitly; this won't change the fact that basic dictionaries have no implicit (built-in) ordering.

In spite of the differences between them, the use of dictionaries and lists often appears to be the same. As a start, an empty dictionary is created much like an empty list, but with curly braces instead of square brackets:

```
>>> x = []
>>> y = {}
```

Here, the first line creates a new, empty list and assigns it to x. The second line creates a new, empty dictionary and assigns it to y.

After you create a dictionary, you may store values in it as though it were a list:

```
>>> y[0] = 'Hello'
>>> y[1] = 'Goodbye'
```

Even in these assignments, there's already a significant operational difference between the dictionary and list usage. Trying to do the same thing with a list would result in an error, because in Python, it's illegal to assign to a position in a list that doesn't exist. For example, if you try to assign to the *0*th element of the list x, you receive an error:

```
>>> x[0] = 'Hello'
Traceback (innermost last):
  File "<stdin>", line 1, in ?
IndexError: list assignment index out of range
```

This isn't a problem with dictionaries; new positions in dictionaries are created as necessary.

Having stored some values in the dictionary, now you can access and use them:

```
>>> print(y[0])
Hello
>>> y[1] + ", Friend."
'Goodbye, Friend.'
```

All in all, this makes a dictionary look pretty much like a list. Now for the big difference. Store (and use) some values under keys that aren't integers:

```
>>> y["two"] = 2
>>> y["pi"] = 3.14
>>> y["two"] * y["pi"]
6.28
```

This is definitely something that can't be done with lists! Whereas list indices must be integers, dictionary keys are much less restricted; they may be numbers, strings, or one of a wide range of other Python objects. This makes dictionaries a natural for jobs that lists can't do. For example, it makes more sense to implement a telephone-directory application with dictionaries than with lists because the phone number for a person can be stored indexed by that person's last name.

A dictionary is a way of mapping from one set of arbitrary objects to an associated but equally arbitrary set of objects. Actual dictionaries, thesauri, or translation books are good analogies in the real world. To see how natural this correspondence is, here's the start of an English-to-French color translator:

```
>>> english_to_french = {}                              Creates empty
                                                         dictionary
>>> english_to_french['red'] = 'rouge'
>>> english_to_french['blue'] = 'bleu'                   Stores three
>>> english_to_french['green'] = 'vert'                  words in it
>>> print("red is", english_to_french['red'])   C
red is rouge                                             Obtains value
                                                         for 'red'
```

> **TRY THIS: CREATE A DICTIONARY** Write the code to ask the user for three names and three ages. After the names and ages are entered, ask the user for one of the names, and print the correct age.

7.2 *Other dictionary operations*

Besides basic element assignment and access, dictionaries support several operations. You can define a dictionary explicitly as a series of key-value pairs separated by commas:

```
>>> english_to_french = {'red': 'rouge', 'blue': 'bleu', 'green': 'vert'}
```

`len` returns the number of entries in a dictionary:

```
>>> len(english_to_french)
3
```

You can obtain all the keys in the dictionary with the `keys` method. This method is often used to iterate over the contents of a dictionary using Python's `for` loop, described in chapter 8:

```
>>> list(english_to_french.keys())
['green', 'blue', 'red']
```

In Python 3.5 and earlier, the order of the keys in a list returned by `keys` has no meaning; the keys aren't necessarily sorted, and they don't necessarily occur in the order in which they were created. Your Python code may print out the keys in a different order than my Python code did. If you need keys sorted, you can store them in a list variable and then sort that list. However, starting with Python 3.6, dictionaries preserve the order that the keys were created and return them in that order.

It's also possible to obtain all the values stored in a dictionary by using `values`:

```
>>> list(english_to_french.values())
 ['vert', 'bleu', 'rouge']
```

This method isn't used nearly as often as `keys`.

You can use the `items` method to return all keys and their associated values as a sequence of tuples:

```
>>> list(english_to_french.items())
[('green', 'vert'), ('blue', 'bleu'), ('red', 'rouge')]
```

Like `keys`, this method is often used in conjunction with a `for` loop to iterate over the contents of a dictionary.

The `del` statement can be used to remove an entry (key-value pair) from a dictionary:

```
>>> list(english_to_french.items())
[('green', 'vert'), ('blue', 'bleu'), ('red', 'rouge')]
>>> del english_to_french['green']
>>> list(english_to_french.items())
 [('blue', 'bleu'), ('red', 'rouge')]
```

Dictionary view objects

The `keys`, `values`, and `items` methods return not lists, but *views* that behave like sequences but are dynamically updated whenever the dictionary changes. That's why you need to use the `list` function to make them appear as a list in these examples. Otherwise, they behave like sequences, allowing code to iterate over them in a `for` loop, using `in` to check membership in them, and so on.

The view returned by `keys` (and in some cases the view returned by `items`) also behaves like a set, with union, difference, and intersection operations.

Attempting to access a key that isn't in a dictionary is an error in Python. To handle this error, you can test the dictionary for the presence of a key with the `in` keyword, which returns `True` if a dictionary has a value stored under the given key and `False` otherwise:

```
>>> 'red' in english_to_french
True
>>> 'orange' in english_to_french
False
```

Alternatively, you can use the `get` function. This function returns the value associated with a key if the dictionary contains that key, but returns its second argument if the dictionary doesn't contain the key:

```
>>> print(english_to_french.get('blue', 'No translation'))
bleu
>>> print(english_to_french.get('chartreuse', 'No translation'))
No translation
```

The second argument is optional. If that argument isn't included, `get` returns `None` if the dictionary doesn't contain the key.

Similarly, if you want to safely get a key's value *and* make sure that it's set to a default in the dictionary, you can use the `setdefault` method:

```
>>> print(english_to_french.setdefault('chartreuse', 'No translation'))
No translation
```

The difference between `get` and `setdefault` is that after the `setdefault` call, there's a key in the dictionary `'chartreuse'` with the value `'No translation'`.

You can obtain a copy of a dictionary by using the `copy` method:

```
>>> x = {0: 'zero', 1: 'one'}
>>> y = x.copy()
>>> y
{0: 'zero', 1: 'one'}
```

This method makes a shallow copy of the dictionary, which is likely to be all you need in most situations. For dictionaries that contain any modifiable objects as values (for example, lists or other dictionaries), you may want to make a deep copy by using the `copy.deepcopy` function. See chapter 5 for an introduction to the concept of shallow and deep copies.

The `update` method updates a first dictionary with all the key-value pairs of a second dictionary. For keys that are common to both dictionaries, the values from the second dictionary override those of the first:

```
>>> z = {1: 'One', 2: 'Two'}
>>> x = {0: 'zero', 1: 'one'}
>>> x.update(z)
>>> x
{0: 'zero', 1: 'One', 2: 'Two'}
```

Dictionary methods give you a full set of tools to manipulate and use dictionaries. For quick reference, table 7.1 lists some of the main dictionary functions.

Table 7.1   Dictionary operations

Dictionary operation	Explanation	Example
`{}`	Creates an empty dictionary	`x = {}`
`len`	Returns the number of entries in a dictionary	`len(x)`
`keys`	Returns a view of all keys in a dictionary	`x.keys()`
`values`	Returns a view of all values in a dictionary	`x.values()`
`items`	Returns a view of all items in a dictionary	`x.items()`
`del`	Removes an entry from a dictionary	`del(x[key])`
`in`	Tests whether a key exists in a dictionary	`'y' in x`
`get`	Returns the value of a key or a configurable default	`x.get('y', None)`
`setdefault`	Returns the value if the key is in the dictionary; otherwise, sets the value for the key to the default and returns the value	`x.setdefault('y', None)`
`copy`	Makes a shallow copy of a dictionary	`y = x.copy()`
`update`	Combines the entries of two dictionaries	`x.update(z)`

This table isn't a complete list of all dictionary operations. For a complete list, refer to the Python standard library documentation.

> **QUICK CHECK: DICTIONARY OPERATIONS**   Assume that you have a dictionary `x = {'a':1, 'b':2, 'c':3, 'd':4}` and a dictionary `y = {'a':6, 'e':5, 'f':6}`. What would be the contents of `x` after the following snippets of code have executed?:
>
> ```
> del x['d']
> z = x.setdefault('g', 7)
> x.update(y)
> ```

7.3   *Word counting*

Assume that you have a file that contains a list of words, one word per line. You want to know how many times each word occurs in the file. You can use dictionaries to perform this task easily:

```
>>> sample_string = "To be or not to be"
>>> occurrences = {}
>>> for word in sample_string.split():
...     occurrences[word] = occurrences.get(word, 0) + 1        ◁──┐
...                                                              ❶
```

```
>>> for word in occurrences:
...     print("The word", word, "occurs", occurrences[word], \
...             "times in the string")
...
The word To occurs 1 times in the string
The word be occurs 2 times in the string
The word or occurs 1 times in the string
The word not occurs 1 times in the string
The word to occurs 1 times in the string
```

Increment the occurrences count for each word ❶. This is a good example of the power of dictionaries. The code is simple, but because dictionary operations are highly optimized in Python, it's also quite fast. This pattern is so handy, in fact, that it's been standardized as the Counter class in the collections module of the standard library.

7.4   *What can be used as a key?*

The previous examples use strings as keys, but Python permits more than just strings to be used in this manner. Any Python object that is immutable and hashable can be used as a key to a dictionary.

In Python, as discussed earlier, any object that can be modified is called *mutable*. Lists are mutable because list elements can be added, changed, or removed. Dictionaries are also mutable for the same reason. Numbers are immutable. If a variable x is referring to the number 3, and you assign 4 to x, you've made x refer to a different number (4), but you haven't changed the number 3 itself; 3 still has to be 3. Strings are also immutable. list[n] returns the *n*th element of list, string[n] returns the *n*th character of string, and list[n] = value changes the *n*th element of list, but string[n] = character is illegal in Python and causes an error, because strings in Python are immutable.

Unfortunately, the requirement that keys be immutable and hashable means that lists can't be used as dictionary keys, but in many instances, it would be convenient to have a listlike key. For example, it's convenient to store information about a person under a key consisting of the person's first and last names, which you could easily do if you could use a two-element list as a key.

Python solves this difficulty by providing tuples, which are basically immutable lists; they're created and used similarly to lists, except that once created, they can't be modified. There's one further restriction: Keys must also be hashable, which takes things a step further than just immutable. To be hashable, a value must have a hash value (provided by a __hash__ method) that never changes throughout the life of the value. That means that tuples containing mutable values are *not* hashable, although the tuples themselves are technically immutable. Only tuples that don't contain any mutable objects nested within them are hashable and valid to use as keys for dictionaries. Table 7.2 illustrates which of Python's built-in types are immutable, hashable, and eligible to be dictionary keys.

Table 7.2 Python values eligible to be used as dictionary keys

Python type	Immutable?	Hashable?	Dictionary key?
int	Yes	Yes	Yes
float	Yes	Yes	Yes
boolean	Yes	Yes	Yes
complex	Yes	Yes	Yes
str	Yes	Yes	Yes
bytes	Yes	Yes	Yes
bytearray	No	No	No
list	No	No	No
tuple	Yes	Sometimes	Sometimes
set	No	No	No
frozenset	Yes	Yes	Yes
dictionary	No	No	No

The next sections give examples illustrating how tuples and dictionaries can work together.

> **QUICK CHECK: WHAT CAN BE A KEY?**   Decide which of the following expressions can be a dictionary key: 1; 'bob'; ('tom', [1, 2, 3]); ["file-name"]; "filename"; ("filename", "extension")

7.5   *Sparse matrices*

In mathematical terms, a *matrix* is a two-dimensional grid of numbers, usually written in textbooks as a grid with square brackets on each side, as shown here.

$$\begin{bmatrix} 3 & 0 & -2 & 11 \\ 0 & 9 & 0 & 0 \\ 0 & 7 & 0 & 0 \\ 0 & 0 & 0 & -5 \end{bmatrix}$$

A fairly standard way to represent such a matrix is by means of a list of lists. In Python, a matrix is presented like this:

```
matrix = [[3, 0, -2, 11], [0, 9, 0, 0], [0, 7, 0, 0], [0, 0, 0, -5]]
```

Elements in the matrix can be accessed by row and column number:

```
element = matrix[rownum][colnum]
```

But in some applications, such as weather forecasting, it's common for matrices to be very large—thousands of elements to a side, meaning millions of elements in total. It's also common for such matrices to contain many zero elements. In some applications, all but a small percentage of the matrix elements may be set to zero. To conserve memory, it's common for such matrices to be stored in a form in which only the non-zero elements are actually stored. Such representations are called *sparse matrices*.

It's simple to implement sparse matrices by using dictionaries with tuple indices. For example, the previous sparse matrix can be represented as follows:

```
matrix = {(0, 0): 3, (0, 2): -2, (0, 3): 11,
          (1, 1): 9, (2, 1): 7, (3, 3): -5}
```

Now you can access an individual matrix element at a given row and column number by this bit of code:

```
if (rownum, colnum) in matrix:
    element = matrix[(rownum, colnum)]
else:
    element = 0
```

A slightly less clear (but more efficient) way of doing this is to use the dictionary get method, which you can tell to return 0 if it can't find a key in the dictionary and otherwise return the value associated with that key, preventing one of the dictionary lookups:

```
element = matrix.get((rownum, colnum), 0)
```

If you're considering doing extensive work with matrices, you may want to look into NumPy, the numeric computation package.

7.6   Dictionaries as caches

This section shows how dictionaries can be used as *caches*, data structures that store results to avoid recalculating those results over and over. Suppose that you need a function called sole, which takes three integers as arguments and returns a result. The function might look something like this:

```
def sole(m, n, t):
    # . . . do some time-consuming calculations . . .
    return(result)
```

But if this function is very time-consuming, and if it's called tens of thousands of times, the program might run too slowly.

Now suppose that sole is called with about 200 different combinations of arguments during any program run. That is, you might call sole(12, 20, 6) 50 or more times during the execution of your program and similarly for many other combinations of arguments. By eliminating the recalculation of sole on identical arguments, you'd save a huge amount of time. You could use a dictionary with tuples as keys, like so:

```
sole_cache = {}
def sole(m, n, t):
    if (m, n, t) in sole_cache:
        return sole_cache[(m, n, t)]
    else:
        # . . . do some time-consuming calculations . . .
        sole_cache[(m, n, t)] = result
        return result
```

The rewritten `sole` function uses a global variable to store previous results. The global variable is a dictionary, and the keys of the dictionary are tuples corresponding to argument combinations that have been given to `sole` in the past. Then any time `sole` passes an argument combination for which a result has already been calculated, it returns that stored result rather than recalculating it.

> **TRY THIS: USING DICTIONARIES**   Suppose that you're writing a program that works like a spreadsheet. How might you use a dictionary to store the contents of a sheet? Write some sample code to both store a value and retrieve a value in a particular cell. What might be some drawbacks to this approach?

7.7   *Efficiency of dictionaries*

If you come from a traditional compiled-language background, you may hesitate to use dictionaries, worrying that they're less efficient than lists (arrays). The truth is that the Python dictionary implementation is quite fast. Many of the internal language features rely on dictionaries, and a lot of work has gone into making them efficient. Because all of Python's data structures are heavily optimized, you shouldn't spend much time worrying about which is faster or more efficient. If the problem can be solved more easily and cleanly by using a dictionary than by using a list, do it that way, and consider alternatives only if it's clear that dictionaries are causing an unacceptable slowdown.

> **LAB 7: WORD COUNTING**   In the previous lab, you took the text of the first chapter of *Moby Dick*, normalized the case, removed punctuation, and wrote the separated words to a file. In this lab, you read that file, use a dictionary to count the number of times each word occurs, and then report the most common and least common words.

Summary

- Dictionaries are powerful data structures, used for many purposes even within Python itself.
- Dictionary keys must be immutable, but any immutable object can be a dictionary key.
- Using keys means accessing collections of data more directly and with less code than many other solutions.

Control flow

8

This chapter covers

- Repeating code with a `while` loop
- Making decisions: the `if-elif-else` statement
- Iterating over a list with a `for` loop
- Using list and dictionary comprehensions
- Delimiting statements and blocks with indentation
- Evaluating Boolean values and expressions

Python provides a complete set of control-flow elements, with loops and conditionals. This chapter examines each element in detail.

8.1 The while loop

You've come across the basic `while` loop several times already. The full `while` loop looks like this:

```
while condition:
    body
else:
    post-code
```

condition is a Boolean expression—that is, one that evaluates to a True or False value. As long as it's True, the body is executed repeatedly. When the condition evaluates to False, the while loop executes the post-code section and then terminates. If the condition starts out by being False, the body won't be executed at all—just the post-code section. The body and post-code are each sequences of one or more Python statements that are separated by newlines and are at the same level of indentation. The Python interpreter uses this level to delimit them. No other delimiters, such as braces or brackets, are necessary.

Note that the else part of the while loop is optional and not often used. That's because as long as there's no break in the body, this loop

```
while condition:
    body
else:
    post-code
```

and this loop

```
while condition:
    body
post-code
```

do the same things—and the second is simpler to understand. I probably wouldn't mention the else clause except that if you don't know about it, you may find it confusing if you run across this syntax in another person's code. Also, it's useful in some situations.

The two special statements break and continue can be used in the body of a while loop. If break is executed, it immediately terminates the while loop, and not even the post-code (if there is an else clause) is executed. If continue is executed, it causes the remainder of the body to be skipped over; the condition is evaluated again, and the loop proceeds as normal.

8.2   *The if-elif-else statement*

The most general form of the if-then-else construct in Python is

```
if condition1:
    body1
elif condition2:
    body2
elif condition3:
    body3
.
.
.
elif condition(n-1):
    body(n-1)


else:
    body(n)
```

It says: If condition1 is True, execute body1; otherwise, if condition2 is True, execute body2; otherwise . . . and so on until it either finds a condition that evaluates to True or hits the else clause, in which case it executes body(n). As with the while loop, the body sections are again sequences of one or more Python statements that are separated by newlines and are at the same level of indentation.

You don't need all that luggage for every conditional, of course. You can leave out the elif parts, the else part, or both. If a conditional can't find any body to execute (no conditions evaluate to True, and there's no else part), it does nothing.

The body after the if statement is required. But you can use the pass statement here (as you can anywhere in Python where a statement is required). The pass statement serves as a placeholder where a statement is needed, but it performs no action:

```
if x < 5:
    pass
else:
    x = 5
```

There's no case (or switch) statement in Python.

Where's the case statement in Python?

As just mentioned, there's no case statement in Python. In most cases where a case or switch statement would be used in other languages, Python gets by just fine with a ladder of if... elif... elif... else. In the few cases where that gets cumbersome, a dictionary of functions usually works, as in this example:

```
def do_a_stuff():
    #process a
def do_b_stuff():
    #process b
def do_c_stiff():
    #process c

func_dict = {'a' : do_a_stuff,
             'b' : do_b_stuff,
             'c' : do_c_stuff }

x = 'a'                          run function
func_dict[x]()                  from dictionary
```

In fact, there have been proposals (see PEP 275 and PEP 3103) to add a case statement to Python, but overall consensus has been that it's not needed or worth the trouble.

8.3 The for loop

A for loop in Python is different from for loops in some other languages. The traditional pattern is to increment and test a variable on each iteration, which is what C for loops usually do. In Python, a for loop iterates over the values returned by any iterable object—that is, any object that can yield a sequence of values. For example, a for loop can iterate over every element in a list, a tuple, or a string. But an iterable object can also be a special function called range or a special type of function called a *generator* or a generator expression, which can be quite powerful. The general form is

```
for item in sequence:
    body
else:
    post-code
```

body is executed once for each element of sequence. item is set to be the first element of sequence, and body is executed; then item is set to be the second element of sequence, and body is executed, and so on for each remaining element of the sequence.

The else part is optional. Like the else part of a while loop, it's rarely used. break and continue do the same thing in a for loop as in a while loop.

This small loop prints out the reciprocal of each number in x:

```
x = [1.0, 2.0, 3.0]
for n in x:
    print(1 / n)
```

8.3.1   *The range function*

Sometimes, you need to loop with explicit indices (such as the positions at which values occur in a list). You can use the range command together with the len command on the list to generate a sequence of indices for use by the for loop. This code prints out all the positions in a list where it finds negative numbers:

```
x = [1, 3, -7, 4, 9, -5, 4]
for i in range(len(x)):
    if x[i] < 0:
        print("Found a negative number at index ", i)
```

Given a number n, range(n) returns a sequence 0, 1, 2, ..., $n - 2$, $n - 1$. So passing it the length of a list (found using len) produces a sequence of the indices for that list's elements. The range function doesn't build a Python list of integers; it just appears to. Instead, it creates a range object that produces integers on demand. This is useful when you're using explicit loops to iterate over really large lists. Instead of building a list with 10 million elements in it, for example, which would take up quite a bit of memory, you can use range(10000000), which takes up only a small amount of memory and generates a sequence of integers from 0 up to (but *not* including) 10000000 as needed by the for loop.

8.3.2   *Controlling range with starting and stepping values*

You can use two variants on the range function to gain more control over the sequence it produces. If you use range with two numeric arguments, the first argument is the starting number for the resulting sequence, and the second number is the number the resulting sequence goes up to (but doesn't include). Here are a few examples:

```
>>> list(range(3, 7))          ◁——❶
[3, 4, 5, 6]
>>> list(range(2, 10))         ◁——❶
[2, 3, 4, 5, 6, 7, 8, 9]
>>> list(range(5, 3))
[]
```

`list()` is used only to force the items `range` would generate to appear as a list. It's not normally used in actual code ❶.

This still doesn't allow you to count backward, which is why the value of `list(range(5, 3))` is an empty list. To count backward, or to count by any amount other than 1, you need to use the optional third argument to `range`, which gives a step value by which counting proceeds:

```
>>> list(range(0, 10, 2))
[0, 2, 4, 6, 8]
>>> list(range(5, 0, -1))
[5, 4, 3, 2, 1]
```

Sequences returned by `range` always include the starting value given as an argument to `range` and never include the ending value given as an argument.

8.3.3 Using break and continue in for loops

The two special statements `break` and `continue` can also be used in the body of a `for` loop. If `break` is executed, it immediately terminates the `for` loop, and not even the `post-code` (if there is an `else` clause) is executed. If `continue` is executed in a `for` loop, it causes the remainder of the `body` to be skipped over, and the loop proceeds as normal with the next item.

8.3.4 The for loop and tuple unpacking

You can use tuple unpacking to make some `for` loops cleaner. The following code takes a list of two-element tuples and calculates the value of the sum of the products of the two numbers in each tuple (a moderately common mathematical operation in some fields):

```
somelist = [(1, 2), (3, 7), (9, 5)]
result = 0
for t in somelist:
    result = result + (t[0] * t[1])
```

Here's the same thing, but cleaner:

```
somelist = [(1, 2), (3, 7), (9, 5)]
result = 0

for x, y in somelist:
    result = result + (x * y)
```

This code uses a tuple `x`, `y` immediately after the `for` keyword instead of the usual single variable. On each iteration of the `for` loop, x contains element 0 of the current tuple from `list`, and y contains element 1 of the current tuple from `list`. Using a tuple in this manner is a convenience of Python, and doing this indicates to Python that each element of the list is expected to be a tuple of appropriate size to unpack into the variable names mentioned in the tuple after the `for`.

8.3.5   *The enumerate function*

You can combine tuple unpacking with the `enumerate` function to loop over both the items and their index. This is similar to using `range` but has the advantage that the code is clearer and easier to understand. Like the previous example, the following code prints out all the positions in a list where it finds negative numbers:

```
x = [1, 3, -7, 4, 9, -5, 4]
for i, n in enumerate(x):          ←—❶
    if n < 0:                          ←—❷
        print("Found a negative number at index ", i)   ←—❸
```

The `enumerate` function returns tuples of (index, item) ❶. You can access the item without the index ❷. The index is also available ❸.

8.3.6   *The zip function*

Sometimes, it's useful to combine two or more iterables before looping over them. The `zip` function takes the corresponding elements from one or more iterables and combines them into tuples until it reaches the end of the shortest iterable:

```
>>> x = [1, 2, 3, 4]
>>> y = ['a', 'b', 'c']          ←┐ y is 3 elements;
>>> z = zip(x, y)                 │ x is 4 elements.
>>> list(z)                                      ┌ z has only
[(1, 'a'), (2, 'b'), (3, 'c')]          ←─┘ 3 elements.
```

> **TRY THIS: LOOPING AND IF STATEMENTS** Suppose that you have a list `x = [1, 3, 5, 0, -1, 3, -2]`, and you need to remove all negative numbers from that list. Write the code to do this.
>
> How would you count the total number of negative numbers in a list `y = [[1, -1, 0], [2, 5, -9], [-2, -3, 0]]`?
>
> What code would you use to print `very low` if the value of x is below -5, `low` if it's from -5 up to 0, `neutral` if it's equal to 0, `high` if it's greater than 0 up to 5, and `very high` if it's greater than 5?

8.4   *List and dictionary comprehensions*

The pattern of using a `for` loop to iterate through a list, modify or select individual elements, and create a new list or dictionary is very common. Such loops often look a lot like the following:

```
>>> x = [1, 2, 3, 4]
>>> x_squared = []
```

```
>>> for item in x:
...     x_squared.append(item * item)
...
>>> x_squared
[1, 4, 9, 16]
```

This sort of situation is so common that Python has a special shortcut for such operations, called a *comprehension*. You can think of a list or dictionary comprehension as a one-line for loop that creates a new list or dictionary from a sequence. The pattern of a list comprehension is as follows:

```
new_list = [expression1 for variable in old_list if expression2]
```

and a dictionary comprehension looks like this:

```
new_dict = {expression1:expression2 for variable in list if expression3}
```

In both cases, the heart of the expression is similar to the beginning of a for loop—for variable in list—with some expression using that variable to create a new key or value and an optional conditional expression using the value of the variable to select whether it's included in the new list or dictionary. The following code does exactly the same thing as the previous code but is a list comprehension:

```
>>> x = [1, 2, 3, 4]
>>> x_squared = [item * item for item in x]
>>> x_squared
[1, 4, 9, 16]
```

You can even use if statements to select items from the list:

```
>>> x = [1, 2, 3, 4]
>>> x_squared = [item * item for item in x if item > 2]

>>> x_squared
[9, 16]
```

Dictionary comprehensions are similar, but you need to supply both a key and a value. If you want to do something similar to the previous example but have the number be the key and the number's square be the value in a dictionary, you can use a dictionary comprehension, like so:

```
>>> x = [1, 2, 3, 4]
>>> x_squared_dict = {item: item * item for item in x}
>>> x_squared_dict
{1: 1, 2: 4, 3: 9, 4: 16}
```

List and dictionary comprehensions are very flexible and powerful, and when you get used to them, they make list-processing operations much simpler. I recommend that you experiment with them and try them any time you find yourself writing a for loop to process a list of items.

8.4.1   *Generator expressions*

Generator expressions are similar to list comprehensions. A generator expression looks a lot like a list comprehension, except that in place of square brackets, it uses parentheses. The following example is the generator-expression version of the list comprehension already discussed:

```
>>> x = [1, 2, 3, 4]
>>> x_squared = (item * item for item in x)
>>> x_squared
<generator object <genexpr> at 0x102176708>
>>> for square in x_squared:
...     print(square,)
...
1 4 9 16
```

Other than the change from square brackets, notice that this expression doesn't return a list. Instead, it returns a generator object that could be used as the iterator in a for loop, as shown, which is very similar to what the range() function does. The advantage of using a generator expression is that the entire list isn't generated in memory, so arbitrarily large sequences can be generated with little memory overhead.

> **TRY THIS: COMPREHENSIONS**   What list comprehension would you use to process the list x so that all negative values are removed?
>
> Create a generator that returns only odd numbers from 1 to 100. (Hint: A number is odd if there is a remainder if divided by 2; use % 2 to get the remainder of division by 2.)
>
> Write the code to create a dictionary of the numbers and their cubes from 11 through 15.

8.5   *Statements, blocks, and indentation*

Because the control flow constructs you've encountered in this chapter are the first to make use of blocks and indentation, this is a good time to revisit the subject.

Python uses the indentation of the statements to determine the delimitation of the different blocks (or bodies) of the control-flow constructs. A block consists of one or more statements, which are usually separated by newlines. Examples of Python statements are the assignment statement, function calls, the print function, the placeholder pass statement, and the del statement. The control-flow constructs (if-elif-else, while, and for loops) are compound statements:

```
compound statement clause:
    block
compound statement clause:
    block
```

A compound statement contains one or more clauses that are each followed by indented blocks. Compound statements can appear in blocks just like any other statements. When they do, they create nested blocks.

You may also encounter a couple of special cases. Multiple statements may be placed on the same line if they're separated by semicolons. A block containing a single line may be placed on the same line after the semicolon of a clause of a compound statement:

```
>>> x = 1; y = 0; z = 0
>>> if x > 0: y = 1; z = 10
... else: y = -1
...
>>> print(x, y, z)
1 1 10
```

Improperly indented code results in an exception being raised. You may encounter two forms of this exception. The first is

```
>>>
>>>    x = 1
File "<stdin>", line 1
    x = 1
    ^
    IndentationError: unexpected indent
>>>
```

This code indented a line that shouldn't have been indented. In the basic mode, the carat (^) indicates the spot where the problem occurred. In the IDLE Python shell (see figure 8.1), the invalid indent is highlighted. The same message would occur if the code didn't indent where necessary (that is, the first line after a compound statement clause).

Figure 8.1 Indentation error

One situation where this can occur can be confusing. If you're using an editor that displays tabs in four-space increments (or Windows interactive mode, which indents the first tab only four spaces from the prompt) and indent one line with four spaces and then the next line with a tab, the two lines may appear to be at the same level of indentation. But you receive this exception because Python maps the tab to eight spaces. The best way to avoid this problem is to use only spaces in Python code. If you must use tabs for indentation, or if you're dealing with code that uses tabs, be sure never to mix them with spaces.

On the subject of the basic interactive mode and the IDLE Python shell, you've likely noticed that you need an extra line after the outermost level of indentation:

```
>>> x = 1
>>> if x == 1:
...     y = 2
...     if v > 0:
...         z = 2
...         v = 0
...
>>> x = 2
```

No line is necessary after the line z = 2, but one is needed after the line v = 0. This line is unnecessary if you're placing your code in a module in a file.

The second form of exception occurs if you indent a statement in a block less than the legal amount:

```
>>> x = 1
>>> if x == 1:
        y = 2
      z = 2
File "<stdin>", line 3
    z = 2
    ^
IndentationError: unindent does not match any outer indentation level
```

In this example, the line containing z = 2 isn't lined up properly below the line containing y = 2. This form is rare, but I mention it again because in a similar situation, it may be confusing.

Python allows you to indent any amount and won't complain regardless of how much you vary indentation as long as you're consistent within a single block. Please don't take improper advantage of this flexibility. The recommended standard is to use four spaces for each level of indentation.

Before leaving indentation, I'll cover breaking up statements across multiple lines, which of course is necessary more often as the level of indentation increases. You can explicitly break up a line by using the backslash character. You can also implicitly break any statement between tokens when within a set of (), {}, or [] delimiters (that is, when typing a set of values in a list, a tuple, or a dictionary; a set of arguments in a function call; or any expression within a set of brackets). You can indent the continuation line of a statement to any level you desire:

```
>>> print('string1', 'string2', 'string3' \
...     , 'string4', 'string5')
string1 string2 string3 string4 string5
>>> x = 100 + 200 + 300 \
...     + 400 + 500
>>> x
1500
>>> v = [100, 300, 500, 700, 900,
...     1100, 1300]
```

```
>>> v
[100, 300, 500, 700, 900, 1100, 1300]
>>> max(1000, 300, 500,
...         800, 1200)
1200
>>> x = (100 + 200 + 300
...          + 400 + 500)
>>> x
1500
```

You can break a string with a \ as well. But any indentation tabs or spaces become part of the string, and the line *must* end with the \. To avoid this situation, remember that any string literals separated by whitespace are automatically concatenated by the Python interpreter:

```
>>> "strings separated by whitespace "     \
...    """are automatically"""  ' concatenated'
'strings separated by whitespace are automatically concatenated'
>>> x = 1
>>> if x > 0:
...         string1 = "this string broken by a backslash will end up \
...                 with the indentation tabs in it"
...
>>> string1
'this string broken by a backslash will end up \t\t\twith
    the indentation tabs in it'
>>> if x > 0:
...         string1 = "this can be easily avoided by splitting the " \
...             "string in this way"
...
>>> string1
'this can be easily avoided by splitting the string in this way'
```

8.6   Boolean values and expressions

The previous examples of control flow use conditional tests in a fairly obvious manner but never really explain what constitutes true or false in Python or what expressions can be used where a conditional test is needed. This section describes these aspects of Python.

Python has a Boolean object type that can be set to either `True` or `False`. Any expression with a Boolean operation returns `True` or `False`.

8.6.1   Most Python objects can be used as Booleans

In addition, Python is similar to C with respect to Boolean values, in that C uses the integer 0 to mean false and any other integer to mean true. Python generalizes this idea: 0 or empty values are `False`, and any other values are `True`. In practical terms, this means the following:

- The numbers 0, 0.0, and 0+0j are all `False`; any other number is `True`.
- The empty string `""` is `False`; any other string is `True`.
- The empty list `[]` is `False`; any other list is `True`.

- The empty dictionary { } is `False`; any other dictionary is `True`.
- The empty set `set()` is `False`; any other set is `True`.
- The special Python value `None` is always `False`.

We haven't looked at some Python data structures yet, but generally, the same rule applies. If the data structure is empty or 0, it's taken to mean false in a Boolean context; otherwise, it's taken to mean true. Some objects, such as file objects and code objects, don't have a sensible definition of a 0 or empty element, and these objects shouldn't be used in a Boolean context.

8.6.2   *Comparison and Boolean operators*

You can compare objects by using normal operators: `<`, `<=`, `>`, `>=`, and so forth. `==` is the equality test operator, and `!=` is the "not equal to" test. There are also `in` and `not in` operators to test membership in sequences (lists, tuples, strings, and dictionaries), as well as `is` and `is not` operators to test whether two objects are the same.

Expressions that return a Boolean value may be combined into more complex expressions using the `and`, `or`, and `not` operators. This code snippet checks to see whether a variable is within a certain range:

```
if 0 < x and x < 10:
    ...
```

Python offers a nice shorthand for this particular type of compound statement. You can write it as you would in a math paper:

```
if 0 < x < 10:
    ...
```

Various rules of precedence apply; when in doubt, you can use parentheses to make sure that Python interprets an expression the way you want it to. Using parentheses is probably a good idea for complex expressions, regardless of whether it's necessary, because it makes clear to future maintainers of the code exactly what's happening. See the Python documentation for more details on precedence.

The rest of this section provides more advanced information. If you're reading this book as you're learning the language, you may want to skip that material for now.

The `and` and `or` operators return objects. The `and` operator returns either the first false object (that an expression evaluates to) or the last object. Similarly, the `or` operator returns either the first true object or the last object. This may seem a little confusing, but it works correctly; if an expression with `and` has even one false element, that element makes the entire expression evaluate as `False`, and that `False` value is returned. If all of the elements are `True`, the expression is `True`, and the last value, which must also be `True`, is returned. The converse is true for `or`; only one `True` element makes the statement logically `True`, and the first `True` value found is returned. If no `True` values are found, the last (`False`) value is returned. In other words, as with many other languages, evaluation stops as soon as a true expression is found for the or operator or as soon as a false expression is found for the and operator:

```
>>> [2] and [3, 4]
[3, 4]
>>> [] and 5
[]
>>> [2] or [3, 4]
[2]
>>> [] or 5
5
>>>
```

The == and != operators test to see whether their operands contains the same values. == and != are used in most situations, as opposed to is and is not operators, which test to see whether their operands are the same object:

```
>>> x = [0]
>>> y = [x, 1]                    ⌐ They reference the
>>> x is y[0]          ◁────────┘   same object.
True
>>> x = [0]            ◁────┐
>>> x is y[0]              │ x has been assigned
False                      └ to a different object.
>>> x == y[0]
True
```

Revisit section 5.6, "Nested lists and deep copies," if this example isn't clear to you.

> **QUICK CHECK: BOOLEANS AND TRUTHINESS** Decide whether the following statements are true or false: 1, 0, -1, [0], 1 and 0, 1 > 0 or [].

8.7 *Writing a simple program to analyze a text file*

To give you a better sense of how a Python program works, this section looks at a small sample that roughly replicates the UNIX wc utility and reports the number of lines, words, and characters in a file. The sample in this listing is deliberately written to be clear to programmers who are new to Python and to be as simple as possible.

> **Listing 8.1   word_count.py**

```
#!/usr/bin/env python3

""" Reads a file and returns the number of lines, words,
    and characters - similar to the UNIX wc utility
"""
                                        ⌐ Opens file
infile = open('word_count.tst')    ◁────┘
                                            ⌐ Reads file;
lines = infile.read().split("\n")    ◁──────┘ splits into lines

line_count = len(lines)          ◁──┐ Gets number of
                                    │ lines with len()
```

```
word_count = 0                          Initializes other counts
char_count = 0

                                                            Iterates
for line in lines:                                          through lines

    words = line.split()                        Splits into words
    word_count += len(words)
                                        Returns number
    char_count += len(line)             of characters

print("File has {0} lines, {1} words, {2} characters".format      Prints
                    (line_count, word_count, char_count))         answers
```

To test, you can run this sample against a sample file containing the first paragraph of this chapter's summary, like this.

Listing 8.2   word_count.tst

```
Python provides a complete set of control flow elements,
including while and for loops, and conditionals.
Python uses the level of indentation to group blocks
of code with control elements.
```

Upon running word_count.py, you get the following output:

```
naomi@mac:~/quickpythonbook/code $ python3.1 word_count.py
File has 4 lines, 30 words, 189 characters
```

This code can give you an idea of a Python program. There isn't much code, and most of the work gets done in three lines of code in the `for` loop. In fact, this program could be made even shorter and more idiomatic. Most Pythonistas see this conciseness as one of Python's great strengths.

> **LAB 8: REFACTOR WORD_COUNT**   Rewrite the word-count program from section 8.7 to make it shorter. You may want to look at the string and list operations already discussed, as well as think about different ways to organize the code. You may also want to make the program smarter so that only alphabetic strings (not symbols or punctuation) count as words.

Summary

- Python uses indentation to group blocks of code.
- Python has loops using `while` and `for`, and conditionals using `if-elif-else`.
- Python has the Boolean values `True` and `False`, which can be referenced by variables.
- Python also considers any 0 or empty value to be `False` and any nonzero or nonempty value to be `True`.

Functions

9

This chapter assumes that you're familiar with function definitions in at least one other computer language and with the concepts that correspond to function definitions, arguments, parameters, and so forth.

9.1 Basic function definitions

The basic syntax for a Python function definition is

```
def name(parameter1, parameter2, . . .):
    body
```

113

As it does with control structures, Python uses indentation to delimit the body of the function definition. The following simple example puts the factorial code from a previous section into a function body, so you can call a `fact` function to obtain the factorial of a number:

```
>>> def fact(n):
...     """Return the factorial of the given number."""     ◁——①
...     r = 1
...     while n > 0:
...         r = r * n
...         n = n - 1                    ②
...     return r                    ◁
...
```

The second line ① is an optional *documentation string*, or *docstring*. You can obtain its value by printing `fact.__doc__`. The intention of docstrings is to describe the external behavior of a function and the parameters it takes, whereas comments should document internal information about how the code works. Docstrings are strings that immediately follow the first line of a function definition and are usually triple quoted to allow for multiline descriptions. Browsing tools are available that extract the first line of document strings. It's standard practice for multiline documentation strings to give a synopsis of the function in the first line, follow this synopsis with a blank second line, and end with the rest of the information. This line indicates that the value after the return is sent back to the code calling the function ②.

Procedure or function?

In some languages, a function that doesn't return a value is called a *procedure*. Although you can (and will) write functions that don't have a `return` statement, they aren't really procedures. All Python procedures are functions; if no explicit `return` is executed in the procedure body, the special Python value `None` is returned, and if `return arg` is executed, the value `arg` is immediately returned. Nothing else in the function body is executed after a `return` has been executed. Because Python doesn't have true procedures, I'll refer to both types as *functions*.

Although all Python functions return values, it's up to you whether a function's return value is used:

```
>>> fact(4)              ◁——①
24
>>> x = fact(4)          ◁         ②
>>> x                    ③
24
>>>
```

The return value isn't associated with a variable ①. The `fact` function's value is printed in the interpreter only ②. The return value is associated with the variable x ③.

9.2 *Function parameter options*

Most functions need parameters, and each language has its own specifications for how function parameters are defined. Python is flexible and provides three options for defining function parameters. These options are outlined in this section.

9.2.1 *Positional parameters*

The simplest way to pass parameters to a function in Python is by position. In the first line of the function, you specify variable names for each parameter; when the function is called, the parameters used in the calling code are matched to the function's parameter variables based on their order. The following function computes x to the power of y:

```
>>> def power(x, y):
...     r = 1
...     while y > 0:
...         r = r * x
...         y = y - 1
...     return r
...
>>> power(3, 3)
27
```

This method requires that the number of parameters used by the calling code exactly matches the number of parameters in the function definition; otherwise, a `Type-Error` exception is raised:

```
>>> power(3)
Traceback (most recent call last):
  File "<stdin>", line 1, in <module>
TypeError: power() missing 1 required positional argument: 'y'
>>>
```

Default values

Function parameters can have default values, which you declare by assigning a default value in the first line of the function definition, like so:

```
def fun(arg1, arg2=default2, arg3=default3, . . .)
```

Any number of parameters can be given default values. Parameters with default values must be defined as the last ones in the parameter list because Python, like most languages, pairs arguments with parameters on a positional basis. There must be enough arguments to a function that the last parameter in that function's parameter list without a default value gets an argument. See section 9.2.2, "Passing arguments by parameter name," for a more flexible mechanism.

The following function also computes x to the power of y. But if y isn't given in a call to the function, the default value of 2 is used, and the function is just the square function:

```
>>> def power(x, y=2):
...     r = 1
...     while y > 0:
...         r = r * x
...         y = y - 1
...     return r
...
```

You can see the effect of the default argument in the following interactive session:

```
>>> power(3, 3)
27
>>> power(3)
9
```

9.2.2 *Passing arguments by parameter name*

You can also pass arguments into a function by using the name of the corresponding function parameter rather than its position. Continuing with the previous interactive example, you can type

```
>>> power(2, 3)
8
>>> power(3, 2)
9
>>> power(y=2, x=3)
9
```

Because the arguments to power in the final invocation are named, their order is irrelevant; the arguments are associated with the parameters of the same name in the definition of power, and you get back 3^2. This type of argument passing is called *keyword passing*.

Keyword passing, in combination with the default argument capability of Python functions, can be highly useful when you're defining functions with large numbers of possible arguments, most of which have common defaults. Consider a function that's intended to produce a list with information about files in the current directory and that uses Boolean arguments to indicate whether that list should include information such as file size, last modified date, and so forth, for each file. You can define such a function along these lines

```
def list_file_info(size=False, create_date=False, mod_date=False, ...):
    ...get file names...
    if size:
        # code to get file sizes goes here
    if create_date:
        # code to get create dates goes here
    # do any other stuff desired

    return fileinfostructure
```

and then call it from other code using keyword argument passing to indicate that you want only certain information (in this example, the file size and modification date but *not* the creation date):

```
fileinfo = list_file_info(size=True, mod_date=True)
```

This type of argument handling is particularly suited for functions with very complex behavior, and one place where such functions occur is in a graphical user interface (GUI). If you ever use the Tkinter package to build GUIs in Python, you'll find that the use of optional, keyword-named arguments like this is invaluable.

9.2.3 *Variable numbers of arguments*

Python functions can also be defined to handle variable numbers of arguments, which you can do in two ways. One way handles the relatively familiar case in which you want to collect an unknown number of arguments at the end of the argument list into a list. The other method can collect an arbitrary number of keyword-passed arguments, which have no correspondingly named parameter in the function parameter list, into a dictionary. These two mechanisms are discussed next.

DEALING WITH AN INDEFINITE NUMBER OF POSITIONAL ARGUMENTS

Prefixing the final parameter name of the function with a * causes all excess non-keyword arguments in a call of a function (that is, those positional arguments not assigned to another parameter) to be collected together and assigned as a tuple to the given parameter. Here's a simple way to implement a function to find the maximum in a list of numbers.

First, implement the function:

```
>>> def maximum(*numbers):
...     if len(numbers) == 0:
...         return None
...     else:
...         maxnum = numbers[0]
...         for n in numbers[1:]:
...             if n > maxnum:
...                 maxnum = n
...         return maxnum
...
```

Now test the behavior of the function:

```
>>> maximum(3, 2, 8)
8
>>> maximum(1, 5, 9, -2, 2)
9
```

DEALING WITH AN INDEFINITE NUMBER OF ARGUMENTS PASSED BY KEYWORD

An arbitrary number of keyword arguments can also be handled. If the final parameter in the parameter list is prefixed with **, it collects all excess *keyword-passed* arguments into a dictionary. The key for each entry in the dictionary is the keyword (parameter name) for the excess argument. The value of that entry is the argument itself. An argument passed by keyword is excess in this context if the keyword by which it was passed doesn't match one of the parameter names in the function definition.

For example:

```
>>> def example_fun(x, y, **other):
...     print("x: {0}, y: {1}, keys in 'other': {2}".format(x,
...         y, list(other.keys())))
...     other_total = 0
...     for k in other.keys():
...         other_total = other_total + other[k]
...     print("The total of values in 'other' is {0}".format(other_total))
```

Trying out this function in an interactive session reveals that it can handle arguments passed in under the keywords `foo` and `bar`, even though `foo` and `bar` aren't parameter names in the function definition:

```
>>> example_fun(2, y="1", foo=3, bar=4)
x: 2, y: 1, keys in 'other': ['foo', 'bar']
The total of values in 'other' is 7
```

9.2.4 *Mixing argument-passing techniques*

It's possible to use all of the argument-passing features of Python functions at the same time, although it can be confusing if not done with care. The general rule for using mixed argument-passing is that positional arguments come first, then named arguments, followed by the indefinite positional argument with a single *, and last of all the indefinite keyword argument with **. See the documentation for full details.

> **QUICK CHECK: FUNCTIONS AND PARAMETERS** How would you write a function that could take any number of unnamed arguments and print their values out in reverse order?
>
> What do you need to do to create a procedure or void function—that is, a function with no return value?
>
> What happens if you capture the return value of a function with a variable?

9.3 *Mutable objects as arguments*

Arguments are passed in by object reference. The parameter becomes a new reference to the object. For immutable objects (such as tuples, strings, and numbers), what is done with a parameter has no effect outside the function. But if you pass in a mutable object (such as a list, dictionary, or class instance), any change made to the object changes what the argument is referencing outside the function. Reassigning the parameter doesn't affect the argument, as shown in figures 9.1 and 9.2:

```
>>> def f(n, list1, list2):
...     list1.append(3)
...     list2 = [4, 5, 6]
...     n = n + 1
...
>>> x = 5
>>> y = [1, 2]
```

```
>>> z = [4, 5]
>>> f(x, y, z)
>>> x, y, z
(5, [1, 2, 3], [4, 5])
```

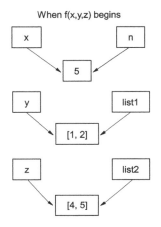

When f(x,y,z) begins

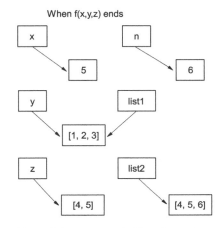

When f(x,y,z) ends

Figure 9.1 **At the beginning of function f(), both the initial variables and the function parameters refer to the same objects.**

Figure 9.2 **At the end of function f(), y (list1 inside the function) has been changed internally, whereas n and list2 refer to different objects.**

Figures 9.1 and 9.2 illustrate what happens when function f is called. The variable x isn't changed because it's immutable. Instead, the function parameter n is set to refer to the new value of 6. Likewise, variable z is unchanged because inside function f, its corresponding parameter list2 was set to refer to a new object, [4, 5, 6]. Only y sees a change because the actual list it points to was changed.

> **QUICK CHECK: MUTABLE FUNCTION PARAMETERS** What would be the result of changing a list or dictionary that was passed into a function as a parameter value? Which operations would be likely to create changes that would be visible outside the function? What steps might you take to minimize that risk?

9.4   *Local, nonlocal, and global variables*

Here, you return to the definition of fact from the beginning of this chapter:

```
def fact(n):
    """Return the factorial of the given number."""
    r = 1
    while n > 0:
        r = r * n
        n = n - 1
    return r
```

Both the variables r and n are *local* to any particular call of the factorial function; changes to them made when the function is executing have no effect on any variables outside the function. Any variables in the parameter list of a function, and any variables created within a function by an assignment (like r = 1 in fact), are local to the function.

You can explicitly make a variable global by declaring it so before the variable is used, using the global statement. Global variables can be accessed and changed by the function. They exist outside the function and can also be accessed and changed by other functions that declare them global or by code that's not within a function. Here's an example that shows the difference between local and global variables:

```
>>> def fun():
...     global a
...     a = 1
...     b = 2
...
```

This example defines a function that treats a as a global variable and b as a local variable, and attempts to modify both a and b.

Now test this function:

```
>>> a = "one"
>>> b = "two"

>>> fun()
>>> a
1
>>> b
'two'
```

The assignment to a within fun is an assignment to the global variable a also existing outside fun. Because a is designated global in fun, the assignment modifies that global variable to hold the value 1 instead of the value "one". The same isn't true for b; the local variable called b inside fun starts out referring to the same value as the variable b outside fun, but the assignment causes b to point to a new value that's local to the function fun.

Similar to the global statement is the nonlocal statement, which causes an identifier to refer to a previously bound variable in the closest enclosing scope. I discuss scopes and namespaces in more detail in chapter 10, but the point is that global is used for a top-level variable, whereas nonlocal can refer to any variable in an enclosing scope, as the example in listing 9.1 illustrates.

Listing 9.1 File nonlocal.py

```
g_var = 0                                              g_var in inner_test
nl_var = 0                                              binds top-level g_var.
print("top level-> g_var: {0} nl_var: {1}".format(g_var, nl_var))
def test():
    nl_var = 2                              ← nl_var in
    print("in test-> g_var: {0} nl_var: {1}".format(g_var, nl_var))    inner_test
    def inner_test():                          binds to
                                              nl_var in test.
```

nl_var in inner_test binds to nl_var in test.

```
        global g_var
        nonlocal nl_var                 g_var in inner_test
        g_var = 1                       binds top-level g_var.
        nl_var = 4
        print("in inner_test-> g_var: {0} nl_var: {1}".format(g_var,
                                                              nl_var))

    inner_test()
    print("in test-> g_var: {0} nl_var: {1}".format(g_var, nl_var))

test()
print("top level-> g_var: {0} nl_var: {1}".format(g_var, nl_var))
```

When run, this code prints the following:

```
top level-> g_var: 0 nl_var: 0
in test-> g_var: 0 nl_var: 2
in inner_test-> g_var: 1 nl_var: 4
in test-> g_var: 1 nl_var: 4
top level-> g_var: 1 nl_var: 0
```

Note that the value of the top-level nl_var hasn't been affected, which would happen if inner_test contained the line global nl_var.

The bottom line is that if you want to assign to a variable existing outside a function, you must explicitly declare that variable to be nonlocal or global. But if you're accessing a variable that exists outside the function, you don't need to declare it nonlocal or global. If Python can't find a variable name in the local function scope, it attempts to look up the name in the global scope. Hence, accesses to global variables are automatically sent through to the correct global variable. Personally, I don't recommend using this shortcut. It's much clearer to a reader if all global variables are explicitly declared as global. Further, you probably want to limit the use of global variables within functions to rare occasions.

> **TRY THIS: GLOBAL VS. LOCAL VARIABLES**   Assuming that x = 5, what will be the value of x after funct_1() below executes? After funct_2() executes?
>
> ```
> def funct_1():
>     x = 3
> def funct_2():
>     global x
>     x = 2
> ```

9.5   *Assigning functions to variables*

Functions can be assigned, like other Python objects, to variables, as shown in this example:

```
>>> def f_to_kelvin(degrees_f):         Defines the f_to_kelvin
...     return 273.15 + (degrees_f - 32) * 5 / 9    kelvin function
...
>>> def c_to_kelvin(degrees_c):         Defines the c_to_kelvin
...     return 273.15 + degrees_c       function
```

```
...
>>> abs_temperature = f_to_kelvin
>>> abs_temperature(32)
273.15
>>> abs_temperature = c_to_kelvin
>>> abs_temperature(0)
273.15
```

⟵ **Assigns function to variable**

⟵ **Assigns function to variable**

You can place functions in lists, tuples, or dictionaries:

```
>>> t = {'FtoK': f_to_kelvin, 'CtoK': c_to_kelvin}
>>> t['FtoK'](32)
273.15
>>> t['CtoK'](0)
273.15
```

⟵ ❶

⟵ **Accesses the f_to_kelvin function as value in dictionary**

⟵ **Accesses the c_to_kelvin function as value in dictionary**

A variable that refers to a function can be used in exactly the same way as the function ❶. This last example shows how you can use a dictionary to call different functions by the value of the strings used as keys. This pattern is common in situations in which different functions need to be selected based on a string value, and in many cases, it takes the place of the switch structure found in languages such as C and Java.

9.6   *lambda expressions*

Short functions like those you just saw can also be defined by using lambda expressions of the form

```
lambda parameter1, parameter2, . . .: expression
```

lambda expressions are anonymous little functions that you can quickly define inline. Often, a small function needs to be passed to another function, like the key function used by a list's sort method. In such cases, a large function is usually unnecessary, and it would be awkward to have to define the function in a separate place from where it's used. The dictionary in the previous subsection can be defined all in one place with

```
>>> t2 = {'FtoK': lambda deg_f: 273.15 + (deg_f - 32) * 5 / 9,
...       'CtoK': lambda deg_c: 273.15 + deg_c}
>>> t2['FtoK'](32)
273.15
```

⟵ ❶

This example defines lambda expressions as values of the dictionary ❶. Note that lambda expressions don't have a return statement because the value of the expression is automatically returned.

9.7   *Generator functions*

A *generator* function is a special kind of function that you can use to define your own iterators. When you define a generator function, you return each iteration's value using the yield keyword. The generator will stop returning values when there are no more iterations, or it encounters either an empty return statement or the end of the function. Local variables in a generator function are saved from one call to the next, unlike in normal functions:

```
>>> def four():
...     x = 0
...     while x < 4:
...         print("in generator, x =", x)
...         yield x
...         x += 1
...
>>> for i in four():
...     print(i)
...
in generator, x = 0
0
in generator, x = 1
1
in generator, x = 2
2
in generator, x = 3
3
```

Sets initial value of x to 0

Returns current value of x

Increments value of x

Note that this generator function has a `while` loop that limits the number of times the generator executes. Depending on how it's used, a generator that doesn't have some condition to halt it could cause an endless loop when called.

yield vs. yield from

Starting with Python 3.3, the new key word for generators, `yield from`, joins `yield`. Basically, `yield from` makes it possible to string generators together. `yield from` behaves the same way as `yield`, except that it delegates the generator machinery to a subgenerator. So in a simple case, you could do this:

```
>>> def subgen(x):
...     for i in range(x):
...         yield i
...
>>> def gen(y):
...     yield from subgen(y)
...
>>> for q in gen(6):
...     print(q)
...
0
1
2
3
4
5
```

This example allows the `yield` expression to be moved out of the main generator, making refactoring easier.

You can also use generator functions with `in` to see whether a value is in the series that the generator produces:

```
>>> 2 in four()
in generator, x = 0
in generator, x = 1
in generator, x = 2
True
>>> 5 in four()
in generator, x = 0
in generator, x = 1
in generator, x = 2
in generator, x = 3
False
```

> **QUICK CHECK: GENERATOR FUNCTIONS**   What would you need to modify in the previous code for the function `four()` to make it work for any number? What would you need to add to allow the starting point to also be set?

9.8   *Decorators*

Because functions are first-class objects in Python, they can be assigned to variables, as you've seen. Functions can also be passed as arguments to other functions and passed back as return values from other functions.

It's possible, for example, to write a Python function that takes another function as its parameter, wraps it in another function that does something related, and then returns the new function. This new combination can be used instead of the original function:

```
>>> def decorate(func):
...     print("in decorate function, decorating", func.__name__)
...     def wrapper_func(*args):
...         print("Executing", func.__name__)
...         return func(*args)
...     return wrapper_func
...
>>> def myfunction(parameter):
...     print(parameter)
...
>>> myfunction = decorate(myfunction)
in decorate function, decorating myfunction
>>> myfunction("hello")
Executing myfunction
hello
```

A decorator is syntactic sugar for this process and lets you wrap one function inside another with a one-line addition. It still gives you exactly the same effect as the previous code, but the resulting code is much cleaner and easier to read.

Very simply, using a decorator involves two parts: defining the function that will be wrapping or "decorating" other functions and then using an @ followed by the decorator immediately before the wrapped function is defined. The decorator function should take a function as a parameter and return a function, as follows:

```
>>> def decorate(func):
...     print("in decorate function, decorating", func.__name__)     ◁——❶
...     def wrapper_func(*args):
...         print("Executing", func.__name__)
...         return func(*args)
...     return wrapper_func                    ◁——❷
...
>>> @decorate                                  ◁——❸
... def myfunction(parameter):
...     print(parameter)
...
in decorate function, decorating myfunction    ◁——❹
>>> myfunction("hello")
Executing myfunction
hello
```

The `decorate` function prints the name of the function it's wrapping when the function is defined ❶. When it's finished, the decorator returns the wrapped function ❷. `myfunction` is decorated using `@decorate` ❸. The wrapped function is called after the decorator function has completed ❹.

Using a decorator to wrap one function in another can be handy for several purposes. In web frameworks such as Django, decorators are used to make sure that a user is logged in before executing a function; and in graphics libraries, decorators can be used to register a function with the graphics framework.

> **TRY THIS: DECORATORS** How would you modify the code for the decorator function to remove unneeded messages and enclose the return value of the wrapped function in `"<html>"` and `"</html>"`, so that `myfunction("hello")` would return `"<html>hello<html>"`?

> **LAB 9: USEFUL FUNCTIONS** Looking back at the labs in chapters 6 and 7, refactor that code into functions for cleaning and processing the data. The goal should be that most of the logic is moved into functions. Use your own judgment as to the types of functions and parameters, but keep in mind that functions should do just one thing, and they shouldn't have any side effects that carry over outside the function.

Summary

- External variables can easily be accessed within a function by using the `global` statement.
- Arguments may be passed by position or by parameter name.
- Default values may be provided for function parameters.
- Functions can collect arguments into tuples, giving you the ability to define functions that take an indefinite number of arguments.

- Functions can collect arguments into dictionaries, giving you the ability to define functions that take an indefinite number of arguments passed by parameter name.
- Functions are first-class objects in Python, which means that they can be assigned to variables, accessed by way of variables, and decorated.

Modules and scoping rules

10

Modules are used to organize larger Python projects. The Python standard library is split into modules to make it more manageable. You don't need to organize your own code into modules, but if you're writing any programs that are more than a few pages long or any code that you want to reuse, you should probably do so.

10.1 What is a module?

A *module* is a file containing code. It defines a group of Python functions or other objects, and the name of the module is derived from the name of the file.

Modules most often contain Python source code, but they can also be compiled C or C++ object files. Compiled modules and Python source modules are used the same way.

As well as grouping related Python objects, modules help avert name-clash problems. You might write a module for your program called mymodule, which defines a function called reverse. In the same program, you might also want to use somebody else's module called othermodule, which also defines a function called reverse but does something different from your reverse function. In a language without modules, it would be impossible to use two different functions named reverse. In Python, the process is trivial; you refer to the functions in your main program as mymodule.reverse and othermodule.reverse.

Using the module names keeps the two reverse functions straight because Python uses namespaces. A *namespace* is essentially a dictionary of the identifiers available to a block, function, class, module, and so on. I discuss namespaces a bit more at the end of this chapter, but be aware that each module has its own namespace, which helps prevent naming conflicts.

Modules are also used to make Python itself more manageable. Most standard Python functions aren't built into the core of the language but are provided via specific modules, which you can load as needed.

10.2 *A first module*

The best way to learn about modules is probably to make one, so you get started in this section.

Create a text file called mymath.py, and in that text file, enter the Python code in listing 10.1. (If you're using IDLE, choose File > New Window and start typing, as shown in figure 10.1.)

> **Listing 10.1   File mymath.py**

```
"""mymath - our example math module"""
pi = 3.14159
def area(r):
    """area(r): return the area of a circle with radius r."""
    global pi
    return(pi * r * r)
```

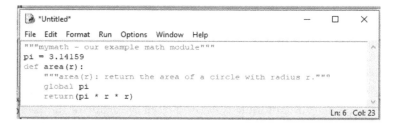

Figure 10.1   An IDLE edit window provides the same editing functionality as the shell window, including automatic indentation and colorization.

Save this code for now in the directory where your Python executable is. This code merely assigns `pi` a value and defines a function. The .py filename suffix is strongly suggested for all Python code files; it identifies that file to the Python interpreter as consisting of Python source code. As with functions, you have the option of putting in a document string as the first line of your module.

Now start up the Python shell and type the following:

```
>>> pi
Traceback (innermost last):
  File "<stdin>", line 1, in ?
NameError: name 'pi' is not defined
>>> area(2)
Traceback (innermost last):
  File "<stdin>", line 1, in ?
NameError: name 'area' is not defined
```

In other words, Python doesn't have the constant `pi` or the function `area` built in.

Now type

```
>>> import mymath
>>> pi
Traceback (innermost last):
  File "<stdin>", line 1, in ?
NameError: name 'pi' is not defined
>>> mymath.pi
3.14159
>>> mymath.area(2)
12.56636
>>> mymath.__doc__
'mymath - our example math module'
>>> mymath.area.__doc__
'area(r): return the area of a circle with radius r.'
```

You've brought in the definitions for `pi` and `area` from the mymath.py file, using the `import` statement (which automatically adds the .py suffix when it searches for the file defining the module named `mymath`). But the new definitions aren't directly accessible; typing `pi` by itself gave an error, and typing `area(2)` by itself would give an error. Instead, you access `pi` and `area` by *prepending* them with the name of the module that contains them, which guarantees name safety. Another module out there may also define `pi` (maybe the author of that module thinks that pi is 3.14 or 3.14159265), but that module is of no concern. Even if that other module is imported, its version of `pi` will be accessed by `othermodulename.pi`, which is different from `mymath.pi`. This form of access is often referred to as *qualification* (that is, the variable `pi` is being qualified by the module `mymath`). You may also refer to `pi` as an *attribute* of `mymath`.

Definitions within a module can access other definitions within that module without prepending the module name. The `mymath.area` function accesses the `mymath.pi` constant as just `pi`.

If you want to, you can also specifically ask for names from a module to be imported in such a manner that you don't have to prepend them with the module name. Type

```
>>> from mymath import pi
>>> pi
3.14159
>>> area(2)
Traceback (innermost last):
  File "<stdin>", line 1, in ?
NameError: name 'area' is not defined
```

The name `pi` is now directly accessible because you specifically requested it by using `from mymath import pi`. The function `area` still needs to be called as `mymath.area`, though, because it wasn't explicitly imported.

You may want to use the basic interactive mode or IDLE's Python shell to incrementally test a module as you're creating it. But if you change your module on disk, retyping the `import` command won't cause it to load again. You need to use the `reload` function from the `importlib` module for this purpose. The `importlib` module provides an interface to the mechanisms behind importing modules:

```
>>> import mymath, importlib
>>> importlib.reload(mymath)
<module 'mymath' from '/home/doc/quickpythonbook/code/mymath.py'>
```

When a module is reloaded (or imported for the first time), all of its code is parsed. A syntax exception is raised if an error is found. On the other hand, if everything is okay, a .pyc file (for example, mymath.pyc) containing Python byte code is created.

Reloading a module doesn't put you back into exactly the same situation as when you start a new session and import it for the first time. But the differences won't normally cause you any problems. If you're interested, you can look up `reload` in the section on the `importlib` module in the *Python Language Reference,* found at https://docs.python.org/3/reference/import.html in this page's importlib section, to find the details.

Modules don't need to be used only from the interactive Python shell, of course. You can also import them into scripts (or other modules, for that matter); enter suitable `import` statements at the beginning of your program file. Internally to Python, the interactive session and a script are considered to be modules as well.

To summarize:

- A module is a file defining Python objects.
- If the name of the module file is modulename.py, the Python name of the module is `modulename`.
- You can bring a module named `modulename` into use with the `import modulename` statement. After this statement is executed, objects defined in the module can be accessed as `modulename.objectname`.

- Specific names from a module can be brought directly into your program by using the `from modulename import objectname` statement. This statement makes `objectname` accessible to your program without your needing to prepend it with `modulename`, and it's useful for bringing in names that are often used.

10.3 The import statement

The `import` statement takes three different forms. The most basic is

```
import modulename
```

which searches for a Python module of the given name, parses its contents, and makes it available. The importing code can use the contents of the module, but any references by that code to names within the module must still be prepended with the module name. If the named module isn't found, an error is generated. I discuss exactly where Python looks for modules in section 10.4.

The second form permits specific names from a module to be explicitly imported into the code:

```
from modulename import name1, name2, name3, . . .
```

Each of `name1`, `name2`, and so forth from within `modulename` is made available to the importing code; code after the `import` statement can use any of `name1`, `name2`, `name3`, and so on without your prepending the module name.

Finally, there's a general form of the `from . . . import . . .` statement:

```
from modulename import *
```

The `*` stands for all the exported names in `modulename`. `from modulename import *` imports all public names from `modulename`—that is, those that don't begin with an underscore—and makes them available to the importing code without the necessity of prepending the module name. But if a list of names called `__all__` exists in the module (or the package's `__init__.py`), the names are the ones imported, whether or not they begin with an underscore.

You should take care when using this particular form of importing. If two modules both define a name, and you import both modules using this form of importing, you'll end up with a name clash, and the name from the second module will replace the name from the first. This technique also makes it more difficult for readers of your code to determine where the names you're using originate. When you use either of the two previous forms of the import statement, you give your reader explicit information about where they're from.

But some modules (such as `tkinter`) name their functions to make it obvious where they originate and to make it unlikely that name clashes will occur. It's also common to use the general import to save keystrokes when using an interactive shell.

10.4   *The module search path*

Exactly where Python looks for modules is defined in a variable called `path`, which you can access through a module called `sys`. Enter the following:

```
>>> import sys
>>> sys.path
_list of directories in the search path_
```

The value shown in place of `_list of directories in the search path_` depends on the configuration of your system. Regardless of the details, the string indicates a list of directories that Python searches (in order) when attempting to execute an `import` statement. The first module found that satisfies the `import` request is used. If there's no satisfactory module in the module search path, an `ImportError` exception is raised.

If you're using IDLE, you can graphically look at the search path and the modules on it by using the Path Browser window, which you can start from the File menu of the Python shell window.

The `sys.path` variable is initialized from the value of the environment (operating system) variable `PYTHONPATH`, if it exists, or from a default value that's dependent on your installation. In addition, whenever you run a Python script, the `sys.path` variable for that script has the directory containing the script inserted as its first element, which provides a convenient way of determining where the executing Python program is located. In an interactive session such as the previous one, the first element of `sys.path` is set to the empty string, which Python takes as meaning that it should first look for modules in the current directory.

10.4.1   *Where to place your own modules*

In the example that starts this chapter, the `mymath` module is accessible to Python because (1) when you execute Python interactively, the first element of `sys.path` is `""`, telling Python to look for modules in the current directory; and (2) you executed Python in the directory that contained the mymath.py file. In a production environment, neither of these conditions typically is true. You won't be running Python interactively, and Python code files won't be located in your current directory. To ensure that your programs can use the modules you coded, you need to:

- Place your modules in one of the directories that Python normally searches for modules.
- Place all the modules used by a Python program in the same directory as the program.
- Create a directory (or directories) to hold your modules, and modify the `sys.path` variable so that it includes this new directory (or directories).

Of these three options, the first is apparently the easiest and is also an option that you should *never* choose unless your version of Python includes local code directories in its default module search path. Such directories are specifically intended for site-specific code (that is, code specific to your machine) and aren't in danger of being overwritten by a new Python install because they're not part of the Python installation. If your `sys.path` refers to such directories, you can put your modules there.

The second option is a good choice for modules that are associated with a particular program. Just keep them with the program.

The third option is the right choice for site-specific modules that will be used in more than one program at that site. You can modify `sys.path` in various ways. You can assign to it in your code, which is easy, but doing so hardcodes directory locations into your program code. You can set the `PYTHONPATH` environment variable, which is relatively easy, but it may not apply to all users at your site; or you can add it to the default search path by using a .pth file.

Examples of how to set `PYTHONPATH` are in the Python documentation in the Python Setup and Usage section (under Command line and environment). The directory or directories you set it to are prepended to the `sys.path` variable. If you use `PYTHONPATH`, be careful that you don't define a module with the same name as one of the existing library modules that you're using. If you do that your module will be found before the library module. In some cases, this may be what you want, but probably not often.

You can avoid this issue by using a .pth file. In this case, the directory or directories you added will be appended to `sys.path`. The last of these mechanisms is best illustrated by an example. On Windows, you can place a .pth file in the directory pointed to by `sys.prefix`. Assume your `sys.prefix` is `c:\program files \python`, and place the file in this listing in that directory.

> **Listing 10.2 File myModules.pth**

```
mymodules
c:\Users\naomi\My Documents\python\modules
```

The next time a Python interpreter is started, `sys.path` will have `c:\program files \python\mymodules` and `c:\Users\naomi\My Documents\python\modules` added to it, if they exist. Now you can place your modules in these directories. Note that the mymodules directory still runs the danger of being overwritten with a new installation. The modules directory is safer. You also may have to move or create a mymodules.pth file when you upgrade Python. See the description of the `site` module in the *Python Library Reference* if you want more details on using .pth files.

10.5 *Private names in modules*

I mentioned earlier in the chapter that you can enter `from module import *` to import *almost* all names from a module. The exception is that identifiers in the module beginning with an underscore can't be imported with `from module import *`. People can write modules that are intended for importation with `from module import *` but still keep certain function or variables from being imported. By starting all internal names (that is, names that shouldn't be accessed outside the module) with an underscore, you can ensure that from module import * brings in only those names that the user will want to access.

To see this technique in action, assume that you have a file called modtest.py containing this code.

Listing 10.3   File modtest.py

```
"""modtest: our test module"""
def f(x):
    return x
def _g(x):
    return x
a = 4
_b = 2
```

Now start up an interactive session and enter the following:

```
>>> from modtest import *
>>> f(3)
3
>>> _g(3)
Traceback (innermost last):
  File "<stdin>", line 1, in ?
NameError: name '_g' is not defined
>>> a
4
>>> _b
Traceback (innermost last):
  File "<stdin>", line 1, in ?
NameError: name '_b' is not defined
```

As you can see, the names f and a are imported, but the names _g and _b remain hidden outside modtest. Note that this behavior occurs only with from ... import *. You can do the following to access _g or _b:

```
>>> import modtest
>>> modtest._b
2
>>> from modtest import _g
>>> _g(5)
5
```

The convention of leading underscores to indicate private names is used throughout Python, not just in modules.

10.6   *Library and third-party modules*

At the beginning of this chapter, I mentioned that the standard Python distribution is split into modules to make it more manageable. After you've installed Python, all the functionality in these library modules is available to you. All that's needed is to import the appropriate modules, functions, classes, and so forth explicitly, before you use them.

Many of the most common and useful standard modules are discussed throughout this book. But the standard Python distribution includes far more than what this book describes. At the very least, you should browse the table of contents of the *Python Library Reference*.

In IDLE, you can easily browse to and look at those modules written in Python by using the Path Browser window. You can also search for example code that uses modules with the Find in Files dialog box, which you can open from the Edit menu of the Python shell window. You can search your own modules as well in this way.

Available third-party modules and links to them are identified in the Python Package Index (pyPI), which I discuss in chapter 19. You need to download these modules and install them in a directory in your module search path to make them available for import into your programs.

> **QUICK CHECK: MODULES** Suppose that you have a module called `new_math` that contains a function called `new_divide`. What are the ways that you might import and then use that function? What are the pros and cons of each method?
>
> Suppose that the `new_math` module contains a function call `_helper_math()`. How will the underscore character affect the way that `_helper_math()` is imported?

10.7 Python scoping rules and namespaces

Python's scoping rules and namespaces will become more interesting as your experience as a Python programmer grows. If you're new to Python, you probably don't need to do anything more than quickly read through the text to get the basic ideas. For more details, look up *namespaces* in the *Python Language Reference*.

The core concept here is that of a namespace. A *namespace* in Python is a mapping from identifiers to objects—that is, how Python keeps track of what variables and identifiers are active and what they point to. So a statement like `x = 1` adds `x` to a namespace (assuming that it isn't already there) and associates it with the value `1`. When a block of code is executed in Python, it has three namespaces: *local*, *global*, and *built-in* (see figure 10.2).

When an identifier is encountered during execution, Python first looks in the *local*

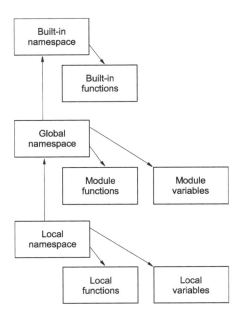

Figure 10.2 The order in which namespaces are checked to locate identifiers

namespace for it. If the identifier isn't found, the *global namespace* is looked in next. If the identifier still hasn't been found, the *built-in namespace* is checked. If it doesn't exist there, this situation is considered to be an error, and a `NameError` exception occurs.

For a module, a command executed in an interactive session, or a script running from a file, the global and local namespaces are the same. Creating any variable or function or importing anything from another module results in a new entry, or *binding*, being made in this namespace.

But when a function call is made, a local namespace is created, and a binding is entered in it for each parameter of the call. Then a new binding is entered into this local namespace whenever a variable is created within the function. The global namespace of a function is the global namespace of the containing block of the function (that of the module, script file, or interactive session). It's independent of the dynamic context from which it's called.

In all of these situations, the built-in namespace is that of the __builtins__ module. This module contains, among other things, all the built-in functions you've encountered (such as `len`, `min`, `max`, `int`, `float`, `list`, `tuple`, `range`, `str`, and `repr`) and the other built-in classes in Python, such as the exceptions (like `NameError`).

One thing that sometimes trips up new Python programmers is the fact that you can override items in the built-in module. If, for example, you create a list in your program and put it in a variable called `list`, you can't subsequently use the built-in `list` function. The entry for your list is found first. There's no differentiation between names for functions and modules and other objects. The most recent occurrence of a binding for a given identifier is used.

Enough talk—it's time to explore some examples. The examples use two built-in functions: `locals` and `globals`. These functions return dictionaries containing the bindings in the local and global namespaces, respectively.

Start a new interactive session:

```
>>> locals()
{'__builtins__': <module 'builtins' (built-in)>, '__name__': '__main__',
 '__doc__': None, '__package__': None}
>>> globals()
{'__builtins__': <module 'builtins' (built-in)>, '__name__': '__main__',
 '__doc__': None, '__package__': None}>>>
```

The local and global namespaces for this new interactive session are the same. They have three initial key-value pairs that are for internal use: (1) an empty documentation string __doc__, (2) the main module name __name__ (which for interactive sessions and scripts run from files is always __main__), and (3) the module used for the built-in namespace __builtins__ (the module __builtins__).

Now if you continue by creating a variable and importing from modules, you see several bindings created:

```
>>> z = 2
>>> import math
>>> from cmath import cos
>>> globals()
{'cos': <built-in function cos>, '__builtins__': <module 'builtins'
 (built-in)>, '__package__': None, '__name__': '__main__', 'z': 2,
 '__doc__': None, 'math': <module 'math' from
 '/usr/local/lib/python3.0/libdynload/math.so'>}
>>> locals()
{'cos': <built-in function cos>, '__builtins__':
 <module 'builtins' (built-in)>, '__package__': None, '__name__':
 '__main__', 'z': 2, '__doc__': None, 'math': <module 'math' from
 '/usr/local/lib/python3.0/libdynload/math.so'>}
>>> math.ceil(3.4)
4
```

As expected, the local and global namespaces continue to be equivalent. Entries have been added for z as a number, math as a module, and cos from the cmath module as a function.

You can use the del statement to remove these new bindings from the namespace (including the module bindings created with the import statements):

```
>>> del z, math, cos
>>> locals()
{'__builtins__': <module 'builtins' (built-in)>, '__package__': None,
'__name__': '__main__', '__doc__': None}
>>> math.ceil(3.4)
Traceback (innermost last):
  File "<stdin>", line 1, in <module>
NameError: math is not defined
>>> import math
>>> math.ceil(3.4)
4
```

The result isn't drastic, because you're able to import the math module and use it again. Using del in this manner can be handy when you're in the interactive mode.[1]

For the trigger-happy, yes, it's also possible to use del to remove the __doc__, __main__, and __builtins__ entries. But resist doing this, because it wouldn't be good for the health of your session!

Now look at a function created in an interactive session:

```
>>> def f(x):
...     print("global: ", globals())
...     print("Entry local: ", locals())
...     y = x
...     print("Exit local: ", locals())
...
>>> z = 2
```

---

[1] Using del and then import again won't pick up changes made to a module on disk. It isn't removed from memory and then loaded from disk again. The binding is taken out of and then put back into your namespace. You still need to use importlib.reload if you want to pick up changes made to a file.

```
>>> globals()
{'f': <function f at 0xb7cbfeac>, '__builtins__': <module 'builtins'
⮑ (built-in)>, '__package__': None, '__name__': '__main__', 'z': 2,
⮑ '__doc__': None}
>>> f(z)
global:  {'f': <function f at 0xb7cbfeac>, '__builtins__': <module
⮑ 'builtins' (built-in)>, '__package__': None, '__name__': '__main__',
⮑ 'z': 2, '__doc__': None}
Entry local:  {'x': 2}
Exit local:  {'y': 2, 'x': 2}
>>>
```

If you dissect this apparent mess, you see that as expected, upon entry the parameter x is the original entry in f's local namespace, but y is added later. The global namespace is the same as that of your interactive session, which is where f was defined. Note that it contains z, which was defined after f.

In a production environment, you normally call functions that are defined in modules. Their global namespace is that of the module in which the functions are defined. Assume that you've created the file in this listing.

Listing 10.4   File scopetest.py

```python
"""scopetest: our scope test module"""
v = 6
def f(x):
    """f: scope test function"""
    print("global: ", list(globals().keys()))
    print("entry local:", locals())
    y = x
    w = v
    print("exit local:", locals().keys())
```

Note that you'll be printing only the keys (identifiers) of the dictionary returned by globals to reduce clutter in the results. You print only the keys because modules are optimized to store the whole __builtins__ dictionary as the value field for the __builtins__ key:

```
>>> import scopetest
>>> z = 2
>>> scopetest.f(z)
global:  ['__name__', '__doc__', '__package__', '__loader__', '__spec__',
    '__file__', '__cached__', '__builtins__', 'v', 'f']
entry local: {'x': 2}
exit local: dict_keys(['x', 'w', 'y'])
```

Now the global namespace is that of the scopetest module and includes the function f and integer v (but not z from your interactive session). Thus, when creating a module, you have complete control over the namespaces of its functions.

I've covered local and global namespaces. Next, I move on to the built-in namespace. This example introduces another built-in function, `dir`, which, given a module, returns a list of the names defined in it:

```
>>> dir(__builtins__)
['ArithmeticError', 'AssertionError', 'AttributeError', 'BaseException',
    'BlockingIOError', 'BrokenPipeError', 'BufferError', 'BytesWarning',
    'ChildProcessError', 'ConnectionAbortedError', 'ConnectionError',
    'ConnectionRefusedError', 'ConnectionResetError', 'DeprecationWarning',
    'EOFError', 'Ellipsis', 'EnvironmentError', 'Exception', 'False',
    'FileExistsError', 'FileNotFoundError', 'FloatingPointError',
    'FutureWarning', 'GeneratorExit', 'IOError', 'ImportError',
    'ImportWarning', 'IndentationError', 'IndexError', 'InterruptedError',
    'IsADirectoryError', 'KeyError', 'KeyboardInterrupt', 'LookupError',
    'MemoryError', 'ModuleNotFoundError', 'NameError', 'None',
    'NotADirectoryError', 'NotImplemented', 'NotImplementedError',
    'OSError', 'OverflowError', 'PendingDeprecationWarning',
    'PermissionError', 'ProcessLookupError', 'RecursionError',
    'ReferenceError', 'ResourceWarning', 'RuntimeError', 'RuntimeWarning',
    'StopAsyncIteration', 'StopIteration', 'SyntaxError', 'SyntaxWarning',
    'SystemError', 'SystemExit', 'TabError', 'TimeoutError', 'True',
    'TypeError', 'UnboundLocalError', 'UnicodeDecodeError',
    'UnicodeEncodeError', 'UnicodeError', 'UnicodeTranslateError',
    'UnicodeWarning', 'UserWarning', 'ValueError', 'Warning',
    'ZeroDivisionError', '__build_class__', '__debug__', '__doc__',
    '__import__', '__loader__', '__name__', '__package__', '__spec__',
    'abs', 'all', 'any', 'ascii', 'bin', 'bool', 'bytearray', 'bytes',
    'callable', 'chr', 'classmethod', 'compile', 'complex', 'copyright',
    'credits', 'delattr', 'dict', 'dir', 'divmod', 'enumerate', 'eval',
    'exec', 'exit', 'filter', 'float', 'format', 'frozenset', 'getattr',
    'globals', 'hasattr', 'hash', 'help', 'hex', 'id', 'input', 'int',
    'isinstance', 'issubclass', 'iter', 'len', 'license', 'list', 'locals',
    'map', 'max', 'memoryview', 'min', 'next', 'object', 'oct', 'open',
    'ord', 'pow', 'print', 'property', 'quit', 'range', 'repr', 'reversed',
    'round', 'set', 'setattr', 'slice', 'sorted', 'staticmethod', 'str',
    'sum', 'super', 'tuple', 'type', 'vars', 'zip']
```

There are a lot of entries here. Those entries ending in `Error` and `Exit` are the names of the exceptions built into Python, which I discuss in chapter 14.

The last group (from `abs` to `zip`) is built-in functions of Python. You've already seen many of these functions in this book and will see more, but I don't cover all of them here. If you're interested, you can find details on the rest in the *Python Library Reference*. You can also easily obtain the documentation string for any of them by using the `help()` function or by printing the docstring directly:

```
>>> print(max.__doc__)
max(iterable[, key=func]) -> value
max(a, b, c, ...[, key=func]) -> value

With a single iterable argument, return its largest item.
With two or more arguments, return the largest argument.
```

As I mentioned earlier, it's not unheard-of for a new Python programmer to inadvertently override a built-in function:

```
>>> list("Peyto Lake")
['P', 'e', 'y', 't', 'o', ' ', 'L', 'a', 'k', 'e']
>>> list = [1, 3, 5, 7]
>>> list("Peyto Lake")
Traceback (innermost last):
  File "<stdin>", line 1, in ?
TypeError: 'list' object is not callable
```

The Python interpreter won't look beyond the new binding for list as a list, even though you're using the built-in list function syntax.

The same thing happens, of course, if you try to use the same identifier twice in a single namespace. The previous value is overwritten, regardless of its type:

```
>>> import mymath
>>> mymath = mymath.area
>>> mymath.pi
Traceback (most recent call last):
  File "<stdin>", line 1, in <module>
AttributeError: 'function' object has no attribute 'pi'
```

When you're aware of this situation, it isn't a significant issue. Reusing identifiers, even for different types of objects, wouldn't make for the most readable code anyway. If you do inadvertently make one of these mistakes when in interactive mode, it's easy to recover. You can use del to remove your binding, to regain access to an overridden built-in, or to import your module again to regain access:

```
>>> del list
>>> list("Peyto Lake")
['P', 'e', 'y', 't', 'o', ' ', 'L', 'a', 'k', 'e']
>>> import mymath
>>> mymath.pi
3.14159
```

The locals and globals functions can be useful as simple debugging tools. The dir function doesn't give the current settings, but if you call it without parameters, it returns a sorted list of the identifiers in the local namespace. This practice helps you catch the mistyped variable error that compilers usually catch for you in languages that require declarations:

```
>>> x1 = 6
>>> x1 = x1 - 2
>>> x1
6
>>> dir()
['__annotations__', '__builtins__', '__doc__', '__loader__', '__name__',
    '__package__', '__spec__', 'x1', 'xl']
```

The debugger that's bundled with IDLE has settings that allow you to view the local and global variable settings as you step through your code; it displays the output of the `locals` and `globals` functions.

> **QUICK CHECK: NAMESPACES AND SCOPE** Consider a variable `width` that's in the module `make_window.py`. In which of the following contexts is `width` in scope?:
>
> (A) within the module itself
> (B) inside the `resize()` function in the module
> (C) within the script that imported the `make_window.py` module

> **LAB 10: CREATE A MODULE** Package the functions created at the end of chapter 9 as a standalone module. Although you can include code to run the module as the main program, the goal should be for the functions to be completely usable from another script.

Summary

- Python modules allow you to put related code and objects into a file.
- Using modules also helps prevent conflicting variable names, because imported objects are normally named in association with their module.

Python programs

11

Up until now, you've been using the Python interpreter mainly in interactive mode. For production use, you'll want to create Python programs or scripts. Several of the sections in this chapter focus on command-line programs. If you come from a Linux/UNIX background, you may be familiar with scripts that can be started from a command line and given arguments and options that can be used to pass in information and possibly redirect their input and output. If you're from a Windows or Mac background, these things may be new to you, and you may be more inclined to question their value.

It's true that command-line scripts are sometimes less convenient to use in a GUI environment, but the Mac has the option of a UNIX command-line shell, and

Windows also offers enhanced command-line options. It will be well worth your time to read the bulk of this chapter at some point. You may find occasions when these techniques are useful, or you may run across code you need to understand that uses some of them. In particular, command-line techniques are very useful when you need to process large numbers of files.

11.1 Creating a very basic program

Any group of Python statements placed sequentially in a file can be used as a program, or *script*. But it's more standard and useful to introduce additional structure. In its most basic form, this task is a simple matter of creating a controlling function in a file and calling that function.

> **Listing 11.1 File script1.py**

```
def main():                                              ◁─┐ Controlling
    print("this is our first test script file")            │ function main
main()                                          ◁── Calls main
```

In this script, `main` is the controlling—and only—function. First, it's defined, and then it's called. Although it doesn't make much difference in a small program, this structure can give you more options and control when you create larger applications, so it's a good idea to make using it a habit from the beginning.

11.1.1 Starting a script from a command line

If you're using Linux/UNIX, make sure that Python is on your path and you're in the same directory as your script. Then type the following on your command line to start the script:

```
python script1.py
```

If you're using a Macintosh running OS X, the procedure is the same as for other UNIX systems. You need to open a terminal program, which is in the Utilities folder of the Applications folder. You have several other options for running scripts on OS X, which I discuss shortly.

If you're using Windows, open Command Prompt (this can be found in different menu locations depending on the version of Windows; in Windows 10, it's in the Windows System menu) or PowerShell. Either of these opens in your home folder, and if necessary, you can use the `cd` command to change to a subdirectory. Running script1.py if it was saved on your desktop would look like this:

```
C:\Users\naomi> cd Desktop                      ◁─┐ Changes to
                                                   │ Desktop folder
C:\Users\naomi\Desktop> python script1.py                        ◁─┐
this is our first test script file     ◁──┐                         │ Runs script1.py
                                          │
C:\Users\naomi\Desktop>                   │ Output of script1.py
```

I look at other options for calling scripts later in this chapter, but stick with this option for now.

11.1.2   *Command-line arguments*

A simple mechanism is available for passing in command-line arguments.

> **Listing 11.2   File script2.py**

```
import sys
def main():
    print("this is our second test script file")
    print(sys.argv)
main()
```

If you call this with the line

```
python script2.py arg1 arg2 3
```

you get

```
this is our second test script file
['script2.py', 'arg1', 'arg2', '3']
```

You can see that the command-line arguments have been stored in `sys.argv` as a list of strings.

11.1.3   *Redirecting the input and output of a script*

You can redirect the input and/or the output for a script by using command-line options. To show this technique, I use this short script.

> **Listing 11.3   File replace.py**

```
import sys
def main():
    contents = sys.stdin.read()                              ◁──┐ Reads from stdin
    sys.stdout.write(contents.replace(sys.argv[1], sys.argv[2]))  ◁──┘ into contents
main()
```

Reads from stdin into contents

Replaces first argument with second

This script reads its standard input and writes to its standard output whatever it reads, with all occurrences of its first argument replaced with its second argument. Called as follows, the script places in `outfile` a copy of `infile` with all occurrences of `zero` replaced by `0`:

```
python replace.py zero 0 < infile > outfile
```

Note that this script works on UNIX, but on Windows, redirection of input and/or output works only if you start a script from a command-prompt window.

In general, the line

```
python script.py arg1 arg2 arg3 arg4 < infile > outfile
```

has the effect of having any `input` or `sys.stdin` operations directed out of `infile` and any `print` or `sys.stdout` operations directed into `outfile`. The effect is as though you set `sys.stdin` to `infile` with `'r'` (read) mode and `sys.stdout` to `outfile` with `'w'` (write):

```
python replace.py a A < infile >> outfile
```

This line causes the output to be appended to `outfile` rather than to overwrite it, as happened in the previous example.

You can also *pipe* in the output of one command as the input of another command:

```
python replace.py 0 zero < infile | python replace.py 1 one > outfile
```

This code results in `outfile` containing the contents of `infile`, with all occurrences of `0` changed to `zero` and all occurrences of `1` changed to `one`.

11.1.4 *The argparse module*

You can configure a script to accept command-line options as well as arguments. The `argparse` module provides support for parsing different types of arguments and can even generate usage messages.

To use the `argparse` module, you create an instance of `ArgumentParser`, populate it with arguments, and then read both the optional and positional arguments. This listing illustrates the module's use.

Listing 11.4 File opts.py

```
from argparse import ArgumentParser

def main():
    parser = ArgumentParser()
    parser.add_argument("indent", type=int, help="indent for report")
    parser.add_argument("input_file", help="read data from this file")    ◁─┐
    parser.add_argument("-f", "--file", dest="filename",                  ◁─┤  ❶
                help="write report to FILE", metavar="FILE")                 ❷
    parser.add_argument("-x", "--xray",
                help="specify xray strength factor")
    parser.add_argument("-q", "--quiet",
                action="store_false", dest="verbose", default=True,       ◁─┐
                help="don't print status messages to stdout")                ❸

    args = parser.parse_args()

    print("arguments:", args)
main()
```

This code creates an instance of `ArgumentParser` and then adds two positional arguments, `indent` and `input_file`, which are the arguments entered after all of the optional arguments have been parsed. *Positional arguments* are those without a prefix character (usually (`"-"`) and are required, and in this case, the `indent` argument must also be parsable as an `int` ❶.

The next line adds an optional filename argument with either `'-f'` or `'--file'` ❷. The final option added, the `"quiet"` option, also adds the ability to turn off the verbose option, which is `True` by default (`action="store_false"`). The fact that these options begin with the prefix character `"-"` tells the parser that they're optional.

The final argument, `"-q"`, also has a default value (`True`, in this case) that will be set if the option isn't specified. The `action="store_false"` parameter specifies that if the argument *is* specified, a value of `False` will be stored in the destination. ❸

The `argparse` module returns a Namespace object containing the arguments as attributes. You can get the values of the arguments by using dot notation. If there's no argument for an option, its value is `None`. Thus, if you call the previous script with the line

```
python opts.py -x100 -q -f outfile 2 arg2
```

    ← **Options come after script name.**

the following output results:

```
arguments: Namespace(filename='outfile', indent=2, input_file='arg2',
    verbose=False, xray='100')
```

If an invalid argument is found, or if a required argument isn't given, `parse_args` raises an error:

```
python opts.py -x100 -r
```

This line results in the following response:

```
usage: opts.py [-h] [-f FILE] [-x XRAY] [-q] indent input_file
opts.py: error: the following arguments are required: indent, input_file
```

11.1.5 *Using the fileinput module*

The `fileinput` module is sometimes useful for scripts. It provides support for processing lines of input from one or more files. It automatically reads the command-line arguments (out of `sys.argv`) and takes them as its list of input files. Then it allows you to sequentially iterate through these lines. The simple example script in this listing (which strips out any lines starting with ##) illustrates the module's basic use.

Listing 11.5   File script4.py

```python
import fileinput
def main():
    for line in fileinput.input():
        if not line.startswith('##'):
            print(line, end="")
main()
```

Now assume that you have the data files shown in the next two listings.

Listing 11.6   File sole1.tst

```
## sole1.tst: test data for the sole function
0 0 0
0 100 0
##
0 100 100
```

Listing 11.7   File sole2.tst

```
## sole2.tst: more test data for the sole function
12 15 0
##
100 100 0
```

Also assume that you make this call:

```
python script4.py sole1.tst sole2.tst
```

You obtain the following result with the comment lines stripped out and the data from the two files combined:

```
0 0 0
0 100 0
0 100 100
12 15 0
100 100 0
```

If no command-line arguments are present, the standard input is all that is read. If one of the arguments is a hyphen (-), the standard input is read at that point.

The module provides several other functions. These functions allow you at any point to determine the total number of lines that have been read (lineno), the number of lines that have been read out of the current file (filelineno), the name of the current file (filename), whether this is the first line of a file (isfirstline), and/or whether standard input is currently being read (isstdin). You can at any point skip to the next file (nextfile) or close the whole stream (close). The short script in the following listing (which combines the lines in its input files and adds file-start delimiters) illustrates how you can use these functions.

Listing 11.8   File script5.py

```
import fileinput
def main():
    for line in fileinput.input():
        if fileinput.isfirstline():
            print("<start of file {0}>".format(fileinput.filename()))
        print(line, end="")
main()
```

Using the call

```
python script5.py file1 file2
```

results in the following (where the dotted lines indicate the lines in the original files):

```
<start of file file1>
.....................
.....................
<start of file file2>
.....................
.....................
```

Finally, if you call `fileinput.input` with an argument of a single filename or a list of filenames, they're used as its input files rather than the arguments in `sys.argv`. `fileinput.input` also has an `inplace` option that leaves its output in the same file as its input while optionally leaving the original around as a backup file. See the documentation for a description of this last option.

QUICK CHECK: SCRIPTS AND ARGUMENTS   Match the following ways of interacting with the command line and the correct use case for each:

Multiple argurments and options	`sys.agrv`
No arguments or just one argument	Use `file_input` module
Processing multiple files	Redirect standard input and output
Using the script as a filter	Use `argparse` module

11.2 *Making a script directly executable on UNIX*

If you're on UNIX, you can easily make a script directly executable. Add the following line to its top, and change its mode appropriately (that is, `chmod +x replace.py`):

```
#! /usr/bin/env python
```

Note that if Python 3.x isn't your default version of Python, you may need to change the `python` in the snippet to `python3,  python3.6`, or something similar to specify that you want to use Python 3.x instead of an earlier default version.

Then if you place your script somewhere on your path (for example, in your bin directory), you can execute it regardless of the directory you're in by typing its name and the desired arguments:

```
replace.py zero 0 < infile > outfile
```

On UNIX, you'll have input and output redirection and, if you're using a modern shell, command history and completion.

If you're writing administrative scripts on UNIX, several library modules are available that you may find useful. These modules include `grp` for accessing the group database, `pwd` for accessing the password database, `resource` for accessing resource usage information, `syslog` for working with the syslog facility, and `stat` for working with information about a file or directory obtained from an `os.stat` call. You can find information on these modules in the *Python Library Reference*.

11.3 Scripts on macOS

In many ways, Python scripts on macOS behave the same way as they do on Linux/ UNIX. You can run Python scripts from a terminal window exactly the same way as on any UNIX box. But on the Mac, you can also run Python programs from the Finder, either by dragging the script file to the Python Launcher app or by configuring Python Launcher as the default application for opening your script (or, optionally, all files with a .py extension.)

You have several options for using Python on a Mac. The specifics of all the options are beyond the scope of this book, but you can get a full explanation by going to the www.python.org website and checking out the Mac section of the "Using Python" section of the documentation for your version of Python. You should also see section 11.6 of the documentation, "Distributing Python applications," for more information on how to distribute Python applications and libraries for the Mac platform.

If you're interested in writing administrative scripts for macOS, you should look at packages that bridge the gap between Apple's Open Scripting Architectures (OSA) and Python. Two such packages are `appscript` and `PyOSA`.

11.4 Script execution options in Windows

If you're on Windows, you have several options for starting a script that vary in their capability and ease of use. Unfortunately, exactly what those options might be and how they are configured can vary considerably across the various versions of Windows currently in use. This book focuses on running Windows from a command prompt or PowerShell. For information on the other options for running Python on your system, you should consult the online Python documentation for your version of Python and look for "Using Python on Windows."

11.4.1 Starting a script from a command window or PowerShell

To run a script from a command window or PowerShell window, open a command prompt or PowerShell window. When you're at the command prompt and have navigated to the folder where your scripts are located, you can use Python to run your scripts in much the same way as on UNIX/Linux/MacOS systems:

```
> python replace.py zero 0 < infile > outfile
```

> **Python doesn't run?**
> If Python doesn't run when you enter `python` at the Windows command prompt, it probably means that the location of the Python executable isn't on your command path. You either need to add the Python executable to your system's PATH environment variable manually or rerun the installer to have it do the job. To get more help on setting up Python on Windows, refer to the Python Setup and Usage section of the online Python documentation. There, you'll find a section on using Python on Windows, with instructions for installing Python.

This is the most flexible of the ways to run a script on Windows because it allows you to use input and output redirection.

11.4.2 *Other Windows options*

Other options are available to explore. If you're familiar with writing batch files, you can wrap your commands in them. A port of the GNU BASH shell comes with the Cygwin tool set, which you can read about at www.cygwin.com and which provides UNIX-like shell capability for Windows.

On Windows, you can edit the environment variables (see the previous section) to add .py as a magic extension, making your scripts automatically executable:

```
PATHEXT=.COM;.EXE;.BAT;.CMD;.VBS;.JS;.PY
```

> **TRY THIS: MAKING A SCRIPT EXECUTABLE** Experiment with executing scripts on your platform. Also try to redirect input and output into and out of your scripts.

11.5 *Programs and modules*

For small scripts that contain only a few lines of code, a single function works well. But if the script grows beyond this size, separating your controlling function from the rest of the code is a good option to take. The rest of this section illustrates this technique and some of its benefits. I start with an example using a simple controlling function. The script in the next listing returns the English-language name for a given number between 0 and 99.

Listing 11.9   File script6.py

```
#! /usr/bin/env python3
import sys
# conversion mappings
_1to9dict = {'0': '', '1': 'one', '2': 'two', '3': 'three', '4': 'four',
             '5': 'five', '6': 'six', '7': 'seven', '8': 'eight',
             '9': 'nine'}
_10to19dict = {'0': 'ten', '1': 'eleven', '2': 'twelve',
               '3': 'thirteen', '4': 'fourteen', '5': 'fifteen',
               '6': 'sixteen', '7': 'seventeen', '8': 'eighteen',
               '9': 'nineteen'}
_20to90dict = {'2': 'twenty', '3': 'thirty', '4': 'forty', '5': 'fifty',
               '6': 'sixty', '7': 'seventy', '8': 'eighty', '9': 'ninety'}
def num2words(num_string):
    if num_string == '0':
        return'zero'
    if len(num_string) > 2:
        return "Sorry can only handle 1 or 2 digit numbers"
    num_string = '0' + num_string          ◁─┐ Pads on left in case it's
    tens, ones = num_string[-2], num_string[-1]  │ a single-digit number
    if tens == '0':
        return _1to9dict[ones]
```

```
        elif tens == '1':
            return _10to19dict[ones]
        else:
            return _20to90dict[tens] + ' ' + _1to9dict[ones]
def main():
    print(num2words(sys.argv[1]))
main()
```

If you call it with

```
python script6.py 59
```

you get this result:

```
fifty nine
```

The controlling function here calls the function num2words with the appropriate argument and prints the result ❶. It's standard to have the call at the bottom, but sometimes you'll see the controlling function's definition at the top of the file. I prefer this function at the bottom, just above the call, so that I don't have to scroll back up to find it after going to the bottom to find out its name. This practice also cleanly separates the scripting plumbing from the rest of the file, which is useful when combining scripts and modules.

People combine scripts with modules when they want to make functions they've created in a script available to other modules or scripts. Also, a module may be instrumented so it can run as a script either to provide a quick interface to it for users or to provide hooks for automated module testing.

Combining a script and a module is a simple matter of putting the following conditional test around the controlling function:

```
if __name__ == '__main__':
    main()
else:
    # module-specific initialization code if any
```

If it's called as a script, it will be run with the name __main__, and the controlling function, main, will be called. If the test has been imported into an interactive session or another module, its name will be its filename.

When creating a script, I often set it as a module as well right from the start. This practice allows me to import it into a session and interactively test and debug my functions as I create them. Only the controlling function needs to be debugged externally. If the script grows, or if I find myself writing functions I might be able to use elsewhere, I can separate those functions into their own module or have other modules import this module.

The script in listing 11.10 is an extension of the previous script but modified to be used as a module. The functionality has also been expanded to allow the entry of a number from 0 to 999999999999999 rather than just from 0 to 99. The controlling

function (main) does the checking of the validity of its argument and also strips out
any commas in it, allowing more user-readable input like 1,234,567.

Listing 11.10   File n2w.py

```
#! /usr/bin/env python3
"""n2w: number to words conversion module: contains function
   num2words. Can also be run as a script
usage as a script: n2w num
            (Convert a number to its English word description)
            num: whole integer from 0 and 999,999,999,999,999 (commas are
            optional)
example: n2w 10,003,103
            for 10,003,103 say: ten million three thousand one hundred three
"""
import sys, string, argparse
_1to9dict = {'0': '', '1': 'one', '2': 'two', '3': 'three', '4': 'four',
             '5': 'five', '6': 'six', '7': 'seven', '8': 'eight',
             '9': 'nine'}
_10to19dict = {'0': 'ten', '1': 'eleven', '2': 'twelve',
               '3': 'thirteen', '4': 'fourteen', '5': 'fifteen',
               '6': 'sixteen', '7': 'seventeen', '8': 'eighteen',
               '9': 'nineteen'}
_20to90dict = {'2': 'twenty', '3': 'thirty', '4': 'forty', '5': 'fifty',
               '6': 'sixty', '7': 'seventy', '8': 'eighty', '9': 'ninety'}
_magnitude_list = [(0, ''), (3, ' thousand '), (6, ' million '),
                   (9, ' billion '), (12, ' trillion '),(15, '')]
def num2words(num_string):
    """num2words(num_string): convert number to English words"""
    if num_string == '0':
        return 'zero'
    num_string = num_string.replace(",", "")
    num_length = len(num_string)
    max_digits = _magnitude_list[-1][0]
    if num_length > max_digits:
        return "Sorry, can't handle numbers with more than  " \
               "{0} digits".format(max_digits)
    num_string = '00' + num_string
    word_string = ''
    for mag, name in _magnitude_list:
        if mag >= num_length:
            return word_string
        else:
            hundreds, tens, ones = num_string[-mag-3], \
                   num_string[-mag-2], num_string[-mag-1]
            if not (hundreds == tens == ones == '0'):
                word_string = _handle1to999(hundreds, tens, ones) + \
                                     name + word_string
def _handle1to999(hundreds, tens, ones):
    if hundreds == '0':
        return _handle1to99(tens, ones)
    else:
```

Usage message; includes example

Conversion mappings

Handles special conditions (number is zero or too large)

Removes commas from number

Pads number on left

Initiates string for number

Creates string containing number

```
            return _1to9dict[hundreds] + ' hundred ' + _handle1to99(tens, ones)
def _handle1to99(tens, ones):
    if tens == '0':
        return _1to9dict[ones]
    elif tens == '1':
        return _10to19dict[ones]
    else:
        return _20to90dict[tens] + ' ' + _1to9dict[ones]
def test():                                          ◁──┐  Function for module
    values = sys.stdin.read().split()                   │  test mode
    for val in values:
        print("{0} = {1}".format(val, num2words(val)))
def main():
    parser = argparse.ArgumentParser(usage=__doc__)
    parser.add_argument("num", nargs='*')            ◁──┐  Gathers all values for
    parser.add_argument("-t", "--test", dest="test",    │  that argument into a list
                        action='store_true', default=False,
                        help="Test mode: reads from stdin")
    args = parser.parse_args()
    if args.test:            ◁──┐ Runs in test mode
        test()                  │ if test variable is set
    else:
        try:                                            ┐  Catches KeyErrors
            result = num2words(args.num[0])             │  due to argument
        except KeyError:                         ◁──────┘  containing nondigits
            parser.error('argument contains non-digits')
        else:
            print("For {0}, say: {1}".format(args.num[0], result))
if __name__ == '__main__':
    main()                                   ◁──┐
else:                                            ❶
    print("n2w  loaded as a module")
```

If it's called as a script, the name will be __main__. If it's imported as a module, it will be named n2w ❶.

This main function illustrates the purpose of a controlling function for a command-line script, which in effect is to create a simple UI for the user. It may handle the following tasks:

- Ensure that there's the right number of command-line arguments and that they're of the right types. Inform the user, giving usage information if not. Here, the function ensures that there is a single argument, but it doesn't explicitly test to ensure that the argument contains only digits.

- Possibly handle a special mode. Here, a '--test' argument puts you in a test mode.

- Map the command-line arguments to those required by the functions, and call them in the appropriate manner. Here, commas are stripped out, and the single function num2words is called.

- Possibly catch and print a more user-friendly message for exceptions that may be expected. Here, KeyErrors are caught, which occurs if the argument contains nondigits.[1]
- Map the output if necessary to a more user-friendly form, which is done here in the print statement. If this were a script to run on Windows, you'd probably want to let the user open it with the double-click method—that is, to use the input to query for the parameter, rather than have it as a command-line option and keep the screen up to display the output by ending the script with the line

```
input("Press the Enter key to exit")
```

But you may still want to leave the test mode in as a command-line option.

The test mode in the following listing provides a regression test capability for the module and its num2words function. In this case, you use it by placing a set of numbers in a file.

Listing 11.11   File n2w.tst

```
0 1 2 3 4 5 6 7 8 9 10 11 12 13 14 15 16 17 18 19 20 21 98 99 100
101 102 900 901 999
999,999,999,999,999
1,000,000,000,000,000
```

Then type

```
python n2w.py --test < n2w.tst > n2w.txt
```

The output file can be easily checked for correctness. This example was run several times during its creation and can be rerun any time num2words or any of the functions it calls are modified. And yes, I'm aware that full exhaustive testing certainly didn't occur. I admit that well over 999 trillion valid inputs for this program haven't been checked!

Often, the provision of a test mode for a module is the only function of a script. I know of at least one company in which part of the development policy is to always create one for every Python module developed. Python's built-in data object types and methods usually make this process easy, and those who practice this technique seem to be unanimously convinced that it's well worth the effort. See chapter 21 to find out more about testing your Python code.

Another option is to create a separate file with only the portion of the main function that handles the argument and import n2w into this file. Then only the test mode would be left in the main function of n2w.py.

---

[1] A better way to do this would be to explicitly check for nondigits in the argument using the regular expression module that will be introduced later. This would ensure that we don't hide KeyErrors that occur due to other reasons.

QUICK CHECK: PROGRAMS AND MODULES What issue is the use of `if __name__ == "__main__":` meant to prevent, and how does it do that? Can you think of any other way to prevent this issue?

11.6 *Distributing Python applications*

You can distribute your Python scripts and applications in several ways. You can share the source files, of course, probably bundled in a zip or tar file. Assuming that the applications were written portably, you could also ship only the bytecode as .pyc files. Both of those options, however, usually leave a lot to be desired.

11.6.1 *Wheels packages*

The current standard way of packaging and distributing Python modules and applications is to use packages called wheels. Wheels are designed to make installing Python code more reliable and to help manage dependencies. The details of how to create wheels are beyond the scope of this chapter, but full details about the requirements and the process for creating wheels are in the Python Packaging User Guide at https://packaging.python.org.

11.6.2 *zipapp and pex*

If you have an application that's in multiple modules, you can also distribute it as an executable zip file. This format relies on two facts about Python.

First, if a zip file contains a file named `__main__.py`, Python can use that file as the entry point to the archive and execute the `__main__.py` file directly. In addition, the zip file's contents are added to `sys.path`, so they're available to be imported and executed by `__main__.py`.

Second, zip files allow arbitrary contents to be added to the beginning of the archive. If you add a shebang line pointing to a Python interpreter, such as `#!/usr/bin/env python3`, and give the file the needed permissions, the file can become a self-contained executable.

In fact, it's not that difficult to manually create an executable zipapp. Create a zip file containing a `__main__.py`, add the shebang line to the beginning, and set the permissions.

Starting with Python 3.5, the zipapp module is included in the standard library; it can create zipapps either from the command line or via the library's API.

A more powerful tool, pex, isn't in the standard library but is available from the package index via pip. pex does the same basic job but offers many more features and options, and it's available for Python 2.7, if needed. Either way, zip file apps are convenient ways to package and distribute multifile Python apps ready to run.

11.6.3 *py2exe and py2app*

Although it's not the purpose of this book to dwell on platform-specific tools, it's worth mentioning that `py2exe` creates standalone Windows programs and that `py2app` does the same on the macOS platform. By *standalone*, I mean that they're single executables that can run on machines that don't have Python installed. In many ways, standalone executables aren't ideal, because they tend to be larger and less flexible than native Python applications. But in some situations, they're the best—and sometimes the only—solution.

11.6.4   *Creating executable programs with freeze*

It's also possible to create an executable Python program that runs on machines that don't have Python installed by using the `freeze` tool. You'll find the instructions for this in the Readme file inside the freeze directory in the Tools subdirectory of the Python source directory. If you're planning to use `freeze`, you'll probably need to download the Python source distribution.

In the process of "freezing" a Python program, you create C files, which are then compiled and linked using a C compiler, which you need to have installed on your system. The frozen application will run only on the platform for which the C compiler you use provides its executables.

Several other tools try in one way or another to convert and package a Python interpreter/environment with an application in a standalone application. In general, however, this path is still difficult and complex, and you probably want to avoid it unless you have a strong need and the time and resources to make the process work.

> **LAB 11: CREATING A PROGRAM**   In chapter 8, you created a version of the UNIX `wc` utility to count the lines, words, and characters in a file. Now that you have more tools at your disposal, refactor that program to make it work more like the original. In particular, the program should have options to show only lines (`-l`), only words (`-w`), and only characters (`-c`). If none of those options is given, all three stats are displayed. But if any of these options is present, only the specified stats are shown.
>
> For an extra challenge, have a look at the `man` page for `wc` on a Linux/UNIX system, and add the `-L` to show the longest line length. Feel free to try to implement the complete behavior as listed in the man page and test it against your system's `wc` utility.

Summary

- Python scripts and modules in their most basic form are just sequences of Python statements placed in a file.
- Modules can be instrumented to run as scripts, and scripts can be set up so that they can be imported as modules.
- Scripts can be made executable on the UNIX, macOS, or Windows command lines. They can be set up to support command-line redirection of their input and output, and with the `argparse` module, it's easy to parse out complex combinations of command-line arguments.
- On macOS, you can use the Python Launcher to run Python programs, either individually or as the default application for opening Python files.

- On Windows, you can call scripts in several ways: by opening them with a double-click, using the Run window, or using a command-prompt window.
- Python scripts can be distributed as scripts, as bytecode, or in special packages called wheels.
- `py2exe`, `py2app`, and the `freeze` tool provide an executable Python program that runs on machines that don't contain a Python interpreter.
- Now that you have an idea of the ways to create scripts and applications, the next step is looking at how Python can interact with and manipulate filesystems.

Using the filesystem

Working with files involves one of two things: basic I/O (described in chapter 13, "Reading and writing files") and working with the filesystem (for example, naming, creating, moving, or referring to files), which is a bit tricky, because different operating systems have different filesystem conventions.

It would be easy enough to learn how to perform basic file I/O without learning all the features Python has provided to simplify cross-platform filesystem interaction—but I wouldn't recommend it. Instead, read at least the first part of this chapter, which gives you the tools you need to refer to files in a manner that doesn't depend on your particular operating system. Then, when you use the basic I/O operations, you can open the relevant files in this manner.

12.1 *os and os.path vs. pathlib*

The traditional way that file paths and filesystem operations have been handled in Python is by using functions included in the os and os.path modules. These functions have worked well enough but often resulted in more verbose code than necessary. Since Python 3.5, a new library, pathlib, has been added; it offers a more object-oriented and more unified way of doing the same operations. Because a lot of code out there still uses the older style, I've retained those examples and their explanations. On the other hand, pathlib has a lot going for it and is likely to become the new standard, so after each example of the old method, I include an example (and brief explanation, where necessary) of how the same thing would be done with pathlib.

12.2 *Paths and pathnames*

All operating systems refer to files and directories with strings naming a given file or directory. Strings used in this manner are usually called *pathnames* (or sometimes just *paths*), which is the word I'll use for them. The fact that pathnames are strings introduces possible complications into working with them. Python does a good job of providing functions that help avert these complications; but to use these Python functions effectively, you need to understand the underlying problems. This section discusses these details.

Pathname semantics across operating systems are very similar because the filesystem on almost all operating systems is modeled as a tree structure, with a disk being the root and folders, subfolders, and so on being branches, subbranches, and so on. This means that most operating systems refer to a specific file in fundamentally the same manner: with a pathname that specifies the path to follow from the root of the filesystem tree (the disk) to the file in question. (This characterization of the root corresponding to a hard disk is an oversimplification, but it's close enough to the truth to serve for this chapter.) This pathname consists of a series of folders to descend into to get to the desired file.

Different operating systems have different conventions regarding the precise syntax of pathnames. The character used to separate sequential file or directory names in a Linux/UNIX pathname is /, whereas the character used to separate file or directory names in a Windows pathname is \. In addition, the UNIX filesystem has a single root (which is referred to by having a / character as the first character in a pathname), whereas the Windows filesystem has a separate root for each drive, labeled A:\, B:\, C:\, and so forth (with C: usually being the main drive). Because of these differences, files have different pathname representations on different operating systems. A file called C:\data\myfile in MS Windows might be called /data/myfile on UNIX and on the Mac OS. Python provides functions and constants that allow you to perform common pathname manipulations without worrying about such syntactic details. With a little care, you can write your Python programs in such a manner that they'll run correctly no matter what the underlying filesystem happens to be.

12.2.1 *Absolute and relative paths*

These operating systems allow two types of pathnames:

- *Absolute* pathnames specify the exact location of a file in a filesystem without any ambiguity; they do this by listing the entire path to that file, starting from the root of the filesystem.
- *Relative* pathnames specify the position of a file relative to some other point in the filesystem, and that other point isn't specified in the relative pathname itself; instead, the absolute starting point for relative pathnames is provided by the context in which they're used.

As examples, here are two Windows absolute pathnames:

```
C:\Program Files\Doom
D:\backup\June
```

and here are two Linux absolute pathnames and a Mac absolute pathname:

```
/bin/Doom
/floppy/backup/June
/Applications/Utilities
```

and here are two Windows relative pathnames:

```
mydata\project1\readme.txt
games\tetris
```

and these are Linux/UNIX/Mac relative pathnames:

```
mydata/project1/readme.txt
games/tetris
Utilities/Java
```

Relative paths need context to anchor them. This context is typically provided in one of two ways.

The simpler way is to append the relative path to an existing absolute path, producing a new absolute path. You might have a relative Windows path, `Start Menu\Programs\Startup`, and an absolute path, `C:\Users\Administrator`. By appending the two, you have a new absolute path: `C:\Users\Administrator\Start Menu\Programs\Startup`, which refers to a specific location in the filesystem. By appending the same relative path to a different absolute path (say, `C:\Users\myuser`), you produce a path that refers to the Startup folder in a different user's (myuser's) Profiles directory.

The second way in which relative paths may obtain a context is via an implicit reference to the *current working directory*, which is the particular directory where a Python program considers itself to be at any point during its execution. Python commands may implicitly make use of the current working directory when they're given a relative path as an argument. If you use the `os.listdir(path)` command with a relative path argument, for example, the anchor for that relative path is the current working directory, and the result of the command is a list of the filenames in the directory whose path is formed by appending the current working directory with the relative path argument.

12.2.2 *The current working directory*

Whenever you edit a document on a computer, you have a concept of where you are in that computer's file structure because you're in the same directory (folder) as the file you're working on. Similarly, whenever Python is running, it has a concept of where in the directory structure it is at any moment. This fact is important because the program may ask for a list of files stored in the current directory. The directory that a Python program is in is called the *current working directory* for that program. This directory may be different from the directory the program resides in.

To see this in action, start Python and use the `os.getcwd` (get current working directory) command to find Python's initial current working directory:

```
>>> import os
>>> os.getcwd()
```

Note that `os.getcwd` is used as a zero-argument function call, to emphasize the fact that the value it returns isn't a constant but will change as you issue commands that alter the value of the current working directory. (That directory probably will be either the directory the Python program itself resides in or the directory you were in when you started Python. On a Linux machine, the result is /home/myuser, which is the home directory.) On Windows machines, you'll see extra backslashes inserted into the path because Windows uses \ as its path separator, and in Python strings (as discussed in section 6.3.1), \ has a special meaning unless it's itself backslashed.

Now type

```
>>> os.listdir(os.curdir)
```

The constant `os.curdir` returns whatever string your system happens to use as the same directory indicator. On both UNIX and Windows, the current directory is represented as a single dot, but to keep your programs portable, you should always use `os.curdir` instead of typing just the dot. This string is a relative path, meaning that `os.listdir` appends it to the path for the current working directory, giving the same path. This command returns a list of all the files or folders inside the current working directory. Choose some folder name, and type

```
>>> os.chdir(folder name)    ◁─┐  "Change directory"
>>> os.getcwd()                │  function
```

As you can see, Python moves into the folder specified as an argument of the `os.chdir` function. Another call to `os.listdir(os.curdir)` would return a list of files in `folder`, because `os.curdir` would then be taken relative to the new current working directory. Many Python filesystem operations use the current working directory in this manner.

12.2.3 *Accessing directories with pathlib*

To get the current directory with `pathlib`, you could do the following:

```
>>> import pathlib
>>> cur_path = pathlib.Path()
>>> cur_path.cwd()
PosixPath('/home/naomi')
```

There's no way for `pathlib` to change the current directory in the way that `os.chdir()` does (see the preceding section), but you could work with a new folder by creating a new path object, as discussed in section 12.2.5, "Manipulating pathnames with pathlib."

12.2.4 *Manipulating pathnames*

Now that you have the background to understand file and directory pathnames, it's time to look at the facilities Python provides for manipulating these pathnames. These facilities consist of several functions and constants in the `os.path` submodule, which you can use to manipulate paths without explicitly using any operating-system-specific syntax. Paths are still represented as strings, but you need never think of them or manipulate them as such.

To start, construct a few pathnames on different operating systems, using the `os.path.join` function. Note that importing `os` is sufficient to bring in the `os.path` submodule also; there's no need for an explicit `import os.path` statement.

First, start Python under Windows:

```
>>> import os
>>> print(os.path.join('bin', 'utils', 'disktools'))
bin\utils\disktools
```

The `os.path.join` function interprets its arguments as a series of directory names or filenames, which are to be joined to form a single string understandable as a relative path by the underlying operating system. In a Windows system, that means path component names should be joined with backslashes, which is what was produced.

Now try the same thing in UNIX:

```
>>> import os
>>> print(os.path.join('bin', 'utils', 'disktools'))
bin/utils/disktools
```

The result is the same path, but using the Linux/UNIX convention of forward slash separators rather than the Windows convention of backslash separators. In other words, `os.path.join` lets you form file paths from a sequence of directory or filenames without any worry about the conventions of the underlying operating system.

`os.path.join` is the fundamental way by which file paths may be built in a manner that doesn't constrain the operating systems on which your program will run.

The arguments to `os.path.join` need not be a single directory or filename; they may also be subpaths that are then joined to make a longer pathname. The following example illustrates this in the Windows environment and is also a case in which you'd find it necessary to use double backslashes in your strings. Note that you could enter the pathname with forward slashes (/) as well, because Python converts them before accessing the Windows operating system:

```
>>> import os
>>> print(os.path.join('mydir\\bin', 'utils\\disktools\\chkdisk'))
mydir\bin\utils\disktools\chkdisk
```

If you always use `os.path.join` to build up your paths, of course, you'll rarely need to worry about this situation. To write this example in a portable manner, you should enter

```
>>> path1 = os.path.join('mydir', 'bin');
>>> path2 = os.path.join('utils', 'disktools', 'chkdisk')
>>> print(os.path.join(path1, path2))
mydir\bin\utils\disktools\chkdisk
```

The `os.path.join` command also has some understanding of absolute versus relative pathnames. In Linux/UNIX, an *absolute* path always begins with a / (because a single slash denotes the topmost directory of the entire system, which contains everything else, including the various floppy and CD drives that might be available). A *relative* path in UNIX is any legal path that does *not* begin with a slash. Under any of the Windows operating systems, the situation is more complicated because the way in which Windows handles relative and absolute paths is messier. Rather than go into all of the details, I'll just say that the best way to handle this situation is to work with the following simplified rules for Windows paths:

- A pathname beginning with a drive letter followed by a colon and a backslash and then a path is an absolute path: C:\Program Files\Doom. (Note that C: by itself, without a trailing backslash, can't reliably be used to refer to the top-level directory on the C: drive. You must use C:\ to refer to the top-level directory on C:. This requirement is a result of DOS conventions, not Python design.)
- A pathname beginning with neither a drive letter nor a backslash is a relative path: `mydirectory\letters\business`.
- A pathname beginning with \\ followed by the name of a server is the path to a network resource.
- Anything else can be considered to be an invalid pathname.[1]

Regardless of the operating system used, the `os.path.join` command doesn't perform sanity checks on the names it's constructing. It's possible to construct pathnames

---

[1] Microsoft Windows allows some other constructs, but it's probably best to stick to the given definitions.

containing characters that, according to your OS, are forbidden in pathnames. If such checks are a requirement, probably the best solution is to write a small path-validity-checker function yourself.

The `os.path.split` command returns a two-element tuple splitting the base-name of a path (the single file or directory name at the end of the path) from the rest of the path. You might use this example on a Windows system:

```
>>> import os
>>> print(os.path.split(os.path.join('some', 'directory', 'path')))
('some\\directory', 'path')
```

The `os.path.basename` function returns only the basename of the path, and the `os.path.dirname` function returns the path up to but not including the last name, as in this example:

```
>>> import os
>>> os.path.basename(os.path.join('some', 'directory', 'path.jpg'))
'path.jpg'
>>> os.path.dirname(os.path.join('some', 'directory', 'path.jpg'))
'some\\directory'
```

To handle the dotted extension notation used by most filesystems to indicate file type (the Macintosh is a notable exception), Python provides `os.path.splitext`:

```
>>> os.path.splitext(os.path.join('some', 'directory', 'path.jpg'))
('some/directory/path', '.jpg')
```

The last element of the returned tuple contains the dotted extension of the indicated file (if there was a dotted extension). The first element of the returned tuple contains everything from the original argument except the dotted extension.

You can also use more specialized functions to manipulate pathnames. `os.path.commonprefix(path1, path2, ...)` finds the common prefix (if any) for a set of paths. This technique is useful if you want to find the lowest-level directory that contains every file in a set of files. `os.path.expanduser` expands username shortcuts in paths, such as for UNIX. Similarly, `os.path.expandvars` does the same for environment variables. Here's an example on a Windows 10 system:

```
>>> import os
>>> os.path.expandvars('$HOME\\temp')
'C:\\Users\\administrator\\personal\\temp'
```

12.2.5 *Manipulating pathnames with pathlib*

Just as you did in the preceding section, start by constructing a few pathnames on different operating systems, using the path object's methods.

First, start Python under Windows:

```
>>> from pathlib import Path
>>> cur_path = Path()
>>> print(cur_path.joinpath('bin', 'utils', 'disktools'))
bin\utils\disktools
```

The same result can be achieved by using the slash operator:

```
>>> cur_path / 'bin' / 'utils' / 'disktools'
WindowsPath('bin/utils/disktools')
```

Note that in the representation of the path object, forward slashes are always used, but Windows Path objects have the forward slashes converted to backslashes as required by the OS. So if you try the same thing in UNIX:

```
>>> cur_path = Path()
>>> print(cur_path.joinpath('bin', 'utils', 'disktools'))
bin/utils/disktools
```

The `parts` property returns a tuple of all the components of a path. You might use this example on a Windows system:

```
>>> a_path = WindowsPath('bin/utils/disktools')
>>> print(a_path.parts)
('bin', 'utils', 'disktools')
```

The `name` property returns only the basename of the path, the `parent` property returns the path up to but not including the last name, and the `suffix` property handles the dotted extension notation used by most filesystems to indicate file type (but the Macintosh is a notable exception). Here's an example:

```
>>> a_path = Path('some', 'directory', 'path.jpg')
>>> a_path.name
'path.jpg'
>>> print(a_path.parent)
some\directory
>>> a_path.suffix
'.jpg'
```

Several other methods associated with `Path` objects allow flexible manipulation of both pathnames and files themselves, so you should review the documentation of the `pathlib` module. It's likely that the `pathlib` module will make your life easier and your file-handling code more concise.

12.2.6 *Useful constants and functions*

You can access several useful path-related constants and functions to make your Python code more system-independent than it otherwise would be. The most basic of these constants are `os.curdir` and `os.pardir`, which respectively define the symbol used by the operating system for the directory and parent directory path indicators. In Windows as well as Linux/UNIX and macOS, these indicators are . and .. respectively, and they can be used as normal path elements. This example

```
os.path.isdir(os.path.join(path, os.pardir, os.curdir))
```

asks whether the parent of the parent of `path` is a directory. `os.curdir` is particularly useful for requesting commands on the current working directory. This example

```
os.listdir(os.curdir)
```

returns a list of filenames in the current working directory (because `os.curdir` is a relative path, and `os.listdir` always takes relative paths as being relative to the current working directory).

The `os.name` constant returns the name of the Python module imported to handle the operating system–specific details. Here's an example on my Windows XP system:

```
>>> import os
>>> os.name
'nt'
```

Note that `os.name` returns `'nt'` even though the actual version of Windows could be Windows 10. Most versions of Windows, except for Windows CE, are identified as `'nt'`.

On a Mac running OS X and on Linux/UNIX, the response is `posix`. You can use this response to perform special operations, depending on the platform you're working on:

```
import os
if os.name == 'posix':
    root_dir = "/"
elif os.name == 'nt':
    root_dir = "C:\\"
else:
    print("Don't understand this operating system!")
```

You may also see programs use `sys.platform`, which gives more exact information. On Windows 10, `sys.platform` is set to `win32`—even if the machine is running the 64-bit version of the operating system. On Linux, you may see `linux2`, whereas on Solaris, it may be set to `sunos5` depending on the version you're running.

All your environment variables and the values associated with them are available in a dictionary called `os.environ`. On most operating systems, this directory includes variables related to paths—typically, search paths for binaries and so forth. If what you're doing requires this directory, you know where to find it now.

At this point, you've received an introduction to the major aspects of working with pathnames in Python. If your immediate need is to open files for reading or writing, you can jump directly to the next chapter. Continue reading for further information about pathnames, testing what they point to, useful constants, and so forth.

> **QUICK CHECK: MANIPULATING PATHS** How would you use the `os` module's functions to take a path to a file called `test.log` and create a new file path in the same directory for a file called `test.log.old`? How would you do the same thing using the `pathlib` module?
>
> What path would you get if you created a pathlib `Path` object from `os.pardir`? Try it and find out.

12.3   *Getting information about files*

File paths are supposed to indicate actual files and directories on your hard drive. You're probably passing a path around, of course, because you want to know something about what it points to. Various Python functions are available for this purpose.

The most commonly used Python path-information functions are os.path.exists, os.path.isfile, and os.path.isdir, all of which take a single path as an argument. os.path.exists returns True if its argument is a path corresponding to something that exists in the filesystem. os.path.isfile returns True if and only if the path it's given indicates a normal data file of some sort (executables fall under this heading), and it returns False otherwise, including the possibility that the path argument doesn't indicate anything in the filesystem. os.path.isdir returns True if and only if its path argument indicates a directory; it returns False otherwise. These examples are valid on my system. You may need to use different paths on yours to investigate the behavior of these functions:

```
>>> import os
>>> os.path.exists('C:\\Users\\myuser\\My Documents')
True
>>> os.path.exists('C:\\Users\\myuser\\My Documents\\Letter.doc')
True
>>> os.path.exists('C:\\Users\\myuser\\\My Documents\\ljsljkflkjs')
False
>>> os.path.isdir('C:\\Users\\myuser\\My Documents')
True
>>> os.path.isfile('C:\\Users\\ myuser\\My Documents')
False
>>> os.path.isdir('C:\\Users\\ myuser\\My Documents
\\Letter.doc')
False
>>> os.path.isfile('C:\\Users\\ myuser\\My Documents\\Letter.doc')
True
```

Several similar functions provide more specialized queries. os.path.islink and os.path.ismount are useful in the context of Linux and other UNIX operating systems that provide file links and mount points; they return True if, respectively, a path indicates a file that's a link or a mount point. os.path.islink does *not* return True on Windows shortcuts files (files ending with .lnk), for the simple reason that such files aren't true links. However, os.path.islink returns True on Windows systems for true symbolic links created with the mklink() command. The OS doesn't assign them a special status, and programs can't transparently use them as though they were the actual file. os.path.samefile(path1, path2) returns True if and only if the two path arguments point to the same file. os.path.isabs(path) returns True if its argument is an absolute path; it returns False otherwise. os.path.getsize(path), os.path.getmtime(path), and os.path.getatime(path) return the size, last modify time, and last access time of a pathname, respectively.

12.3.1 *Getting information about files with scandir*

In addition to the os.path functions listed, you can get more complete information about the files in a directory by using os.scandir, which returns an iterator of os.DirEntry objects. os.DirEntry objects expose the file attributes of a directory entry, so using os.scandir can be faster and more efficient than combining os.listdir (discussed in the next section) with the os.path operations. If, for example, you need to know whether the entry refers to a file or directory, os.scandir's ability to access more directory information than just the name will be a plus. os.DirEntry objects have methods that correspond to the os.path functions mentioned in the previous section, including exists, is_dir, is_file, is_socket, and is_symlink.

os.scandir also supports a context manager using with, and using one is recommended to ensure resources are properly disposed of. This example code iterates over all of the entries in a directory and prints both the name of the entry and whether it's a file:

```
>>> with os.scandir(".") as my_dir:
...     for entry in my_dir:
...         print(entry.name, entry.is_file())
...
pip-selfcheck.json True
pyvenv.cfg True
include False
test.py True
lib False
lib64 False
bin False
```

12.4 *More filesystem operations*

In addition to obtaining information about files, Python lets you perform certain filesystem operations directly through a set of basic but highly useful commands in the os module.

I describe only those true cross-platform operations in this section. Many operating systems have access to more advanced filesystem functions, and you need to check the main Python library documentation for the details.

You've already seen that to obtain a list of files in a directory, you use os.listdir:

```
>>> os.chdir(os.path.join('C:', 'my documents', 'tmp'))
>>> os.listdir(os.curdir)
['book1.doc.tmp', 'a.tmp', '1.tmp', '7.tmp', '9.tmp', 'registry.bkp']
```

Note that unlike the list-directory command in many other languages or shells, Python does *not* include the os.curdir and os.pardir indicators in the list returned by os.listdir.

The glob function from the glob module (named after an old UNIX function that did pattern matching) expands Linux/UNIX shell-style wildcard characters and character sequences in a pathname, returning the files in the current working directory that match. A * matches any sequence of characters. A ? matches any single character. A character sequence ([h,H] or [0-9]) matches any single character in that sequence:

```
>>> import glob
>>> glob.glob("*")
['book1.doc.tmp', 'a.tmp', '1.tmp', '7.tmp', '9.tmp', 'registry.bkp']
>>> glob.glob("*bkp")
['registry.bkp']
>>> glob.glob("?.tmp")
['a.tmp', '1.tmp', '7.tmp', '9.tmp']
>>> glob.glob("[0-9].tmp")
['1.tmp', '7.tmp', '9.tmp']
```

To rename (move) a file or directory, use os.rename:

```
>>> os.rename('registry.bkp', 'registry.bkp.old')
>>> os.listdir(os.curdir)
['book1.doc.tmp', 'a.tmp', '1.tmp', '7.tmp', '9.tmp', 'registry.bkp.old']
```

You can use this command to move files across directories as well as within directories.

Remove or delete a data file with os.remove:

```
>>> os.remove('book1.doc.tmp')
>>> os.listdir(os.curdir)
['a.tmp', '1.tmp', '7.tmp', '9.tmp', 'registry.bkp.old']
```

Note that you can't use os.remove to delete directories. This restriction is a safety feature, to ensure that you don't accidentally delete an entire directory substructure.

Files can be created by writing to them, as discussed in chapter 11. To create a directory, use os.makedirs or os.mkdir. The difference between them is that os.mkdir doesn't create any necessary intermediate directories, but os.makedirs does:

```
>>> os.makedirs('mydir')
>>> os.listdir(os.curdir)
['mydir', 'a.tmp', '1.tmp', '7.tmp', '9.tmp', 'registry.bkp.old']
>>> os.path.isdir('mydir')
True
```

To remove a directory, use os.rmdir. This function removes only empty directories. Attempting to use it on a nonempty directory raises an exception:

```
>>> os.rmdir('mydir')
>>> os.listdir(os.curdir)
['a.tmp', '1.tmp', '7.tmp', '9.tmp', 'registry.bkp.old']
```

To remove nonempty directories, use the shutil.rmtree function. It recursively removes all files in a directory tree. See the Python standard library documentation for details on its use.

12.4.1 *More filesystem operations with pathlib*

Path objects have most of the same methods mentioned earlier. Some differences exist, however. The `iterdir` method is similar to the `os.path.listdir` function except that it returns an iterator of paths rather than a list of strings:

```
>>> new_path = cur_path.joinpath('C:', 'my documents', 'tmp'))
>>> list(new_path.iterdir())
[WindowsPath('book1.doc.tmp'), WindowsPath('a.tmp'), WindowsPath('1.tmp'),
    WindowsPath('7.tmp'), WindowsPath('9.tmp'), WindowsPath('registry.bkp')]
```

Note that in a Windows environment, the paths returned are `WindowsPath` objects, whereas on Mac OS or Linux, they're `PosixPath` objects.

`pathlib` path objects also have a `glob` method built in, which again returns not a list of strings but an iterator of path objects. Otherwise, this function behaves very much like the `glob.glob` function demonstrated above:

```
>>> list(cur_path.glob("*"))
[WindowsPath('book1.doc.tmp'), WindowsPath('a.tmp'), WindowsPath('1.tmp'),
    WindowsPath('7.tmp'), WindowsPath('9.tmp'), WindowsPath('registry.bkp')]
>>> list(cur_path.glob("*bkp"))
[WindowsPath('registry.bkp')]
>>> list(cur_path.glob("?.tmp"))
[WindowsPath('a.tmp'), WindowsPath('1.tmp'), WindowsPath('7.tmp'),
    WindowsPath('9.tmp')]
>>> list(cur_path.glob("[0-9].tmp"))
[WindowsPath('1.tmp'), WindowsPath('7.tmp'), WindowsPath('9.tmp')]
```

To rename (move) a file or directory, use the path object's `rename` method:

```
>>> old_path = Path('registry.bkp')
>>> new_path = Path('registry.bkp.old')
>>> old_path.rename(new_path)
>>> list(cur_path.iterdir())
[WindowsPath('book1.doc.tmp'), WindowsPath('a.tmp'), WindowsPath('1.tmp'),
    WindowsPath('7.tmp'), WindowsPath('9.tmp'),
    WindowsPath('registry.bkp.old')]
```

You can use this command to move files across directories as well as within directories.

Remove or delete a data file with `unlink`:

```
>>> new_path = Path('book1.doc.tmp')
>>> new_path.unlink()
>>> list(cur_path.iterdir())
[WindowsPath('a.tmp'), WindowsPath('1.tmp'), WindowsPath('7.tmp'),
    WindowsPath('9.tmp'), WindowsPath('registry.bkp.old')]
```

Note that as with `os.remove`, you can't use the `unlink` method to delete directories. This restriction is a safety feature, to ensure that you don't accidentally delete an entire directory substructure.

To create a directory by using a path object, use the path object's `mkdir` method. If you give the `mkdir` method a `parents=True` parameter, it creates any necessary intermediate directories; otherwise, it raises a `FileNotFoundError` if an intermediate directory isn't there:

```
>>> new_path = Path ('mydir')
>>> new_path.mkdir(parents=True)
>>> list(cur_path.iterdir())
[WindowsPath('mydir'), WindowsPath('a.tmp'), WindowsPath('1.tmp'),
    WindowsPath('7.tmp'), WindowsPath('9.tmp'),
    WindowsPath('registry.bkp.old')]]
>>> new_path.is_dir('mydir')
True
```

To remove a directory, use the `rmdir` method. This method removes only empty directories. Attempting to use it on a nonempty directory raises an exception:

```
>>> new_path = Path('mydir')
>>> new_path.rmdir()
>>> list(cur_path.iterdir())
[WindowsPath('a.tmp'), WindowsPath('1.tmp'), WindowsPath('7.tmp'),
    WindowsPath('9.tmp'), WindowsPath('registry.bkp.old')]
```

> **LAB 12: MORE FILE OPERATIONS** How might you calculate the total size of all files ending with .txt that aren't symlinks in a directory? If your first answer was using `os.path`, also try it with `pathlib`, and vice versa.
>
> Write some code that builds off your solution to move the same .txt files in the lab question to a new subdirectory called backup in the same directory.

12.5 *Processing all files in a directory subtree*

Finally, a highly useful function for traversing recursive directory structures is the `os.walk` function. You can use it to walk through an entire directory tree, returning three things for each directory it traverses: the root, or path, of that directory; a list of its subdirectories; and a list of its files.

`os.walk` is called with the path of the starting, or top, directory and can have three optional arguments: `os.walk(directory, topdown=True, onerror=None, followlinks= False)`. `directory` is a starting directory path; if `topdown` is `True` or not present, the files in each directory are processed *before* its subdirectories, resulting in a listing that starts at the top and goes down; whereas if `topdown` is `False`, the subdirectories of each directory are processed *first*, giving a bottom-up traversal of the tree. The `onerror` parameter can be set to a function to handle any errors that result from calls to `os.listdir`, which are ignored by default. `os.walk` by default doesn't walk down into folders that are symbolic links unless you give it the `followlinks=True` parameter.

When called, `os.walk` creates an iterator that recursively applies itself to all the directories contained in the `top` parameter. In other words, for each subdirectory `subdir` in `names`, `os.walk` recursively invokes a call to itself, of the form `os.walk(subdir, ...)`. Note that if `topdown` is `True` or not given, the list of subdirectories may be modified (using any of the list-modification operators or methods) before its items are used for the next level of recursion; you can use this to control into which—if any—subdirectories os.walk will descend.

To get a feel for os.walk, I recommend iterating over the tree and printing out the values returned for each directory. As an example of the power of os.walk, list the current working directory and all of its subdirectories along with a count of the number of entries in each of them, excluding any .git directories:

```
import os
for root, dirs, files in os.walk(os.curdir):
    print("{0} has {1} files".format(root, len(files)))     ◁──┐ Checks for directory
    if ".git" in dirs:                                      ◁──┘ named .git
        dirs.remove(".git")              ◁──┐ Removes .git (only the .git
                                            │ directory) from directory list
```

This example is complex, and if you want to use os.walk to its fullest extent, you should probably play around with it quite a bit to understand the details of what's going on.

The copytree function of the shutil module recursively makes copies of all the files in a directory and all of its subdirectories, preserving permission mode and stat (that is, access/modify times) information. shutil also has the already-mentioned rmtree function for removing a directory and all of its subdirectories, as well as several functions for making copies of individual files. See the standard library documentation for details.

Summary

- Python provides a group of functions and constants that handle filesystem references (pathnames) and filesystem operations in a manner independent of the underlying operating system.
- For more advanced and specialized filesystem operations that typically are tied to a certain operating system or systems, look at the main Python documentation for the os, pathlib, and posix modules.
- For convenience, a summary of the functions discussed in this chapter is given in table 12.1 and table 12.2.

Table 12.1 Summary of filesystem values and functions

Function	Filesystem value or operation
os.getcwd(), Path.cwd()	Gets the current directory
os.name	Provides generic platform identification
sys.platform	Provides specific platform information
os.environ	Maps the environment
os.listdir(path)	Gets files in a directory
os.scandir(path)	Gets an iterator of os.DirEntry objects for a directory

Table 12.1 Summary of filesystem values and functions *(continued)*

Function	Filesystem value or operation
`os.chdir(path)`	Changes directory
`os.path.join(elements)`, `Path.joinpath(elements)`	Combines elements into a path
`os.path.split(path)`	Splits the path into a base and tail (the last element of the path)
`Path.parts`	A tuple of the path's elements
`os.path.splitext(path)`	Splits the path into a base and a file extension
`Path.suffix`	The path's file extension
`os.path.basename(path)`	Gets the base of the path
`Path.name`	The base name of the path
`os.path.commonprefix(list_of_paths)`	Gets the common prefix for all paths on a list
`os.path.expanduser(path)`	Expands ~ or ~user to a full pathname
`os.path.expandvars(path)`	Expands environment variables
`os.path.exists(path)`	Tests to see if a path exists
`os.path.isdir(path)`, `Path.is_dir()`	Tests to see if a path is a directory
`os.path.isfile(path)`, `Path.is_file()`	Tests to see if a path is a file
`os.path.islink(path)`, `Path.is_link()`	Tests to see if a path is a symbolic link (not a Windows shortcut)
`os.path.ismount(path)`	Tests to see if a path is a mount point
`os.path.isabs(path)`, `Path.is_absolute()`	Tests to see if a path is an absolute path
`os.path.samefile(path_1, path_2)`	Tests to see if two paths refer to the same file
`os.path.getsize(path)`	Gets the size of a file
`os.path.getmtime(path)`	Gets the modification time
`os.path.getatime(path)`	Gets the access time
`os.rename(old_path, new_path)`	Renames a file
`os.mkdir(path)`	Creates a directory
`os.makedirs(path)`	Creates a directory and any needed parent directories
`os.rmdir(path)`	Removes a directory

Table 12.1 Summary of filesystem values and functions *(continued)*

Function	Filesystem value or operation
`glob.glob(pattern)`	Gets matches to a wildcard pattern
`os.walk(path)`	Gets all filenames in a directory tree

Table 12.2 Partial list of pathlib properties and functions

Method or property	Value or operation
`Path.cwd()`	Gets the current directory
`Path.joinpath(elements)` or `Path / element / element`	Combines elements into a new path
`Path.parts`	A tuple of the path's elements
`Path.suffix`	The path's file extension
`Path.name`	The base name of the path
`Path.exists()`	Tests to see if a path exists
`Path.is_dir()`	Tests to see if a path is a directory
`Path.is_file()`	Tests to see if a path is a file
`Path.is_symlink()`	Tests to see if a path is a symbolic link (not a Windows shortcut)
`Path.is_absolute()`	Tests to see if a path is an absolute path
`Path.samefile(Path2)`	Tests to see if two paths refer to the same file
`Path1.rename(Path2)`	Renames a file
`Path.mkdir([parents=True])`	Creates a directory, if `parents` is `True` also creates needed parent directories
`Path.rmdir()`	Removes a directory
`Path.glob(pattern)`	Gets matches to a wildcard pattern

Reading and writing files

13

This chapter covers

- Opening files and `file` objects
- Closing files
- Opening files in different modes
- Reading and writing text or binary data
- Redirecting screen input/output
- Using the `struct` module
- Pickling objects into files
- Shelving objects

13.1 Opening files and file objects

Probably the single most common thing you'll want to do with files is open and read them.

In Python, you open and read a file by using the built-in `open` function and various built-in reading operations. The following short Python program reads in one line from a text file named myfile:

```python
with open('myfile', 'r') as file_object:
    line = file_object.readline()
```

open doesn't read anything from the file; instead, it returns an object called a `file` object that you can use to access the opened file. A `file` object keeps track of a file and how much of the file has been read or written. All Python file I/O is done using `file` objects rather than filenames.

The first call to `readline` returns the first line in the `file` object, everything up to and including the first newline character or the entire file if there's no newline character in the file; the next call to `readline` returns the second line, if it exists, and so on.

The first argument to the `open` function is a pathname. In the previous example, you're opening what you expect to be an existing file in the current working directory. The following opens a file at an absolute location—`c:\My Documents\test \myfile`:

```
import os
file_name = os.path.join("c:", "My Documents", "test", "myfile")
file_object = open(file_name, 'r')
```

Note also that this example uses the `with` keyword, indicating that the file will be opened with a context manager, which I explain more in chapter 14. For now, it's enough to note that this style of opening files better manages potential I/O errors and is generally preferred.

13.2   *Closing files*

After all data has been read from or written to a `file` object, it should be closed. Closing a `file` object frees up system resources, allows the underlying file to be read or written to by other code, and in general makes the program more reliable. For small scripts, not closing a `file` object generally doesn't have much of an effect; `file` objects are automatically closed when the script or program terminates. For larger programs, too many open `file` objects may exhaust system resources, causing the program to abort.

You close a `file` object by using the `close` method when the `file` object is no longer needed. The earlier short program then becomes this:

```
file_object = open("myfile", 'r')
line = file_object.readline()
# . . . any further reading on the file_object . . .
file_object.close()
```

Using a context manager and the keyword `with` is also a good way to automatically close files when you're done:

```
with open("myfile", 'r') as file_object:
    line = file_object.readline()
        # . . . any further reading on the file_object . . .
```

13.3   *Opening files in write or other modes*

The second argument of the `open` command is a string denoting how the file should be opened. `'r'` means "Open the file for reading," `'w'` means "Open the file for writing" (any data already in the file will be erased), and `'a'` means "Open the file for appending" (new data will be appended to the end of any data already in the file). If you want to open the file for reading, you can leave out the second argument; `'r'` is the default. The following short program writes "Hello, World" to a file:

```
file_object = open("myfile", 'w')
file_object.write("Hello, World\n")
file_object.close()
```

Depending on the operating system, `open` may also have access to additional file modes. These modes aren't necessary for most purposes. As you write more advanced Python programs, you may want to consult the Python reference manuals for details.

open can take an optional third argument, which defines how reads or writes for that file are buffered. *Buffering* is the process of holding data in memory until enough data has been requested or written to justify the time cost of doing a disk access. Other parameters to `open` control the encoding for text files and the handling of newline characters in text files. Again, these features aren't things you typically need to worry about, but as you become more advanced in your use of Python, you may want to read up on them.

13.4 *Functions to read and write text or binary data*

I've already presented the most common text file–reading function, `readline`. This function reads and returns a single line from a `file` object, including any newline character on the end of the line. If there's nothing more to be read from the file, `readline` returns an empty string, which makes it easy to (for example) count the number of lines in a file:

```
file_object = open("myfile", 'r')
count = 0
while file_object.readline() != "":
    count = count + 1
print(count)
file_object.close()
```

For this particular problem, an even shorter way to count all the lines is to use the built-in `readlines` method, which reads *all* the lines in a file and returns them as a list of strings, one string per line (with trailing newlines still included):

```
file_object = open("myfile", 'r')
print(len(file_object.readlines()))
file_object.close()
```

If you happen to be counting all the lines in a huge file, of course, this method may cause your computer to run out of memory because it reads the entire file into memory at once. It's also possible to overflow memory with `readline` if you have the misfortune to try to read a line from a huge file that contains no newline characters, although this situation is highly unlikely. To handle such circumstances, both `readline` and `readlines` can take an optional argument affecting the amount of data they read at any one time. See the Python reference documentation for details.

Another way to iterate over all of the lines in a file is to treat the `file` object as an iterator in a `for` loop:

```
file_object = open("myfile", 'r')
count = 0
for line in file_object:
    count = count + 1
print(count)
file_object.close()
```

This method has the advantage that the lines are read into memory as needed, so even with large files, running out of memory isn't a concern. The other advantage of this method is that it's simpler and easier to read.

A possible problem with the `read` method may arise due to the fact that on Windows and Macintosh machines, text-mode translations occur if you use the `open` command in text mode—that is, without adding a `b` to the mode. In text mode, on a Macintosh any `\r` is converted to `"\n"`, whereas on Windows `"\r\n"` pairs are converted to `"\n"`. You can specify the treatment of newline characters by using the newline parameter when you open the file and specifying `newline="\n"`, `"\r"`, or `"\r\n"`, which forces only that string to be used as a newline:

```
input_file = open("myfile", newline="\n")
```

This example forces only `"\n"` to be considered to be a newline. If the file has been opened in binary mode, the newline parameter isn't needed, because all bytes are returned exactly as they are in the file.

The write methods that correspond to the `readline` and `readlines` methods are the `write` and `writelines` methods. Note that there's no `writeline` function. `write` writes a single string, which can span multiple lines if newline characters are embedded within the string, as in this example:

```
myfile.write("Hello")
```

`write` doesn't write out a newline after it writes its argument; if you want a newline in the output, you must put it there yourself. If you open a file in text mode (using `w`), any `\n` characters are mapped back to the platform-specific line endings (that is, `'\r\n'` on Windows or `'\r'` on Macintosh platforms). Again, opening the file with a specified newline prevents this situation.

`writelines` is something of a misnomer because it doesn't necessarily write lines; it takes a list of strings as an argument and writes them, one after the other, to the given `file` object without writing newlines. If the strings in the list end with newlines, they're written as lines; otherwise, they're effectively concatenated in the file. But `writelines` is a precise inverse of `readlines` in that it can be used on the list returned by `readlines` to write a file identical to the file `readlines` read from.

Assuming that myfile.txt exists and is a text file, this bit of code creates an exact copy of myfile.txt called myfile2.txt:

```
input_file = open("myfile.txt", 'r')
lines = input_file.readlines()
input_file.close()
output = open("myfile2.txt", 'w')
output.writelines(lines)
output.close()
```

13.4.1 *Using binary mode*

On some occasions, you may want to read all the data in a file into a single `bytes` object, especially if the data isn't a string, and you want to get it all into memory so you can treat it as a byte sequence. Or you may want to read data from a file as `bytes` objects of a fixed size. You may be reading data without explicit newlines, for example, where each line is assumed to be a sequence of characters of a fixed size. To do so, use the `read` method. Without any argument, this method reads all of a file from the current position and returns that data as a `bytes` object. With a single-integer argument, it reads that number of bytes (or less, if there isn't enough data in the file to satisfy the request) and returns a `bytes` object of the given size:

```
input_file = open("myfile", 'rb')
header = input_file.read(4)
data = input_file.read()
input_file.close()
```

The first line opens a file for reading in binary mode, the second line reads the first four bytes as a header string, and the third line reads the rest of the file as a single piece of data.

Keep in mind that files open in binary mode deal only in bytes, not strings. To use the data as strings, you must decode any `bytes` objects to `string` objects. This point is often important in dealing with network protocols, where data streams often behave as files but need to be interpreted as bytes, not strings.

> **QUICK CHECK:** What is the significance of adding a `"b"` to the file open mode string, as in `open("file", "wb")`?
>
> Suppose that you want to open a file named `myfile.txt` and write additional data on the end of it. What command would you use to open `myfile.txt`? What command would you use to reopen the file to read from the beginning?

13.5 *Reading and writing with pathlib*

In addition to its path-manipulation powers discussed in chapter 12, a `Path` object can be used to read and write text and binary files. This capability can be convenient because no open or close is required, and separate methods are used for text and binary operations. One limitation, however, is that you have no way to append by using `Path` methods, because writing replaces any existing content:

```
>>> from pathlib import Path
>>> p_text = Path('my_text_file')
>>> p_text.write_text('Text file contents')
18
>>> p_text.read_text()
'Text file contents'
>>> p_binary = Path('my_binary_file')
>>> p_binary.write_bytes(b'Binary file contents')
20
>>> p_binary.read_bytes()
b'Binary file contents'
```

13.6   *Screen input/output and redirection*

You can use the built-in `input` method to prompt for and read an input string:

```
>>> x = input("enter file name to use: ")
enter file name to use: myfile
>>> x
'myfile'
```

The prompt line is optional, and the newline at the end of the input line is stripped off. To read in numbers by using `input`, you need to explicitly convert the string that `input` returns to the correct number type. The following example uses `int`:

```
>>> x = int(input("enter your number: "))
enter your number: 39
>>> x
39
```

`input` writes its prompt to the *standard output* and reads from the *standard input.* Lower-level access to these and *standard error* can be obtained by using the `sys` module, which has `sys.stdin`, `sys.stdout`, and `sys.stderr` attributes. These attributes can be treated as specialized `file` objects.

For `sys.stdin`, you have the `read`, `readline`, and `readlines` methods. For `sys.stdout` and `sys.stderr`, you can use the standard `print` function as well as the `write` and `writelines` methods, which operate as they do for other `file` objects:

```
>>> import sys
>>> print("Write to the standard output.")
Write to the standard output.
>>> sys.stdout.write("Write to the standard output.\n")
Write to the standard output.
30                              ⟵┐  sys.stdout.write returns the
>>> s = sys.stdin.readline()      │  number of characters written.
An input line
>>> s
'An input line\n'
```

You can redirect standard input to read from a file. Similarly, standard output or standard error can be set to write to files and then programmatically restored to their original values by using sys.__stdin__, sys.__stdout__, and sys.__stderr__:

```
>>> import sys
>>> f = open("outfile.txt", 'w')
>>> sys.stdout = f
>>> sys.stdout.writelines(["A first line.\n", "A second line.\n"])
>>> print("A line from the print function")
>>> 3 + 4
>>> sys.stdout = sys.__stdout__
>>> f.close()
>>> 3 + 4
7
```

After this line outfile.txt
contains two lines:
A first line
A second line

outfile.txt now contains
three lines:
A first line
A second line
A line from the print function

The print function also can be redirected to any file without changing standard output:

```
>>> import sys
>>> f = open("outfile.txt", 'w')
>>> print("A first line.\n", "A second line.\n", file=f)
>>> 3 + 4
7
>>> f.close()
>>> 3 + 4
7
```

outfile.txt contains:
A first line
A second line

While the standard output is redirected, you receive prompts and tracebacks from errors but no other output. If you're using IDLE, these examples using sys.__stdout__ won't work as indicated; you have to use the interpreter's interactive mode directly.

You'd normally use this technique when you're running from a script or program. But if you're using the interactive mode on Windows, you may want to temporarily redirect standard output to capture what might otherwise scroll off the screen. The short module shown here implements a set of functions that provides this capability.

Listing 13.1   File mio.py

```
"""mio: module, (contains functions capture_output, restore_output,
    print_file, and clear_file )"""
import sys
_file_object = None
def capture_output(file="capture_file.txt"):
    """capture_output(file='capture_file.txt'): redirect the standard
    output to 'file'."""
    global _file_object
    print("output will be sent to file: {0}".format(file))
    print("restore to normal by calling 'mio.restore_output()'")
    _file_object = open(file, 'w')
    sys.stdout = _file_object
```

```
def restore_output():
    """restore_output(): restore the standard output back to the
            default (also closes the capture file)"""
    global _file_object
    sys.stdout = sys.__stdout__
    _file_object.close()
    print("standard output has been restored back to normal")

def print_file(file="capture_file.txt"):
    """print_file(file="capture_file.txt"): print the given file to the
        standard output"""
    f = open(file, 'r')
    print(f.read())
    f.close()

def clear_file(file="capture_file.txt"):
    """clear_file(file="capture_file.txt"): clears the contents of the
        given file"""
    f = open(file, 'w')
    f.close()
```

Here, `capture_output()` redirects standard output to a file that defaults to `"capture_file.txt"`. The function `restore_output()` restores standard output to the default. Assuming `capture_output` hasn't been executed, `print_file()` prints this file to the standard output, and `clear_file()` clears its current contents.

> **TRY THIS: REDIRECTING INPUT AND OUTPUT** Write some code to use the mio.py module in listing 13.1 to capture all the print output of a script to a file named myfile.txt, reset the standard output to the screen, and print that file to screen.

13.7   *Reading structured binary data with the struct module*

Generally speaking, when working with your own files, you probably don't want to read or write binary data in Python. For very simple storage needs, it's usually best to use text or bytes input and output. For more sophisticated applications, Python provides the ability to easily read or write arbitrary Python objects (*pickling*, described in section 13.8). This ability is much less error-prone than directly writing and reading your own binary data and is highly recommended.

But there's at least one situation in which you'll likely need to know how to read or write binary data: when you're dealing with files that are generated or used by other programs. This section describes how to do this by using the `struct` module. Refer to the Python reference documentation for more details.

As you've seen, Python supports explicit binary input or output by using bytes instead of strings if you open the file in binary mode. But because most binary files rely on a particular structure to help parse the values, writing your own code to read and split them into variables correctly is often more work than it's worth. Instead, you can use the standard `struct` module to permit you to treat those strings as formatted byte sequences with some specific meaning.

Assume that you want to read in a binary file called data, containing a series of records generated by a C program. Each record consists of a C short integer, a C double float, and a sequence of four characters that should be taken as a four-character string. You want to read this data into a Python list of tuples, with each tuple containing an integer, a floating-point number, and a string.

The first thing to do is define a *format string* understandable to the struct module, which tells the module how the data in one of your records is packed. The format string uses characters meaningful to struct to indicate what type of data is expected where in a record. The character 'h', for example, indicates the presence of a single C short integer, and the character 'd' indicates the presence of a single C double-precision floating-point number. Not surprisingly, 's' indicates the presence of a string. Any of these may be preceded by an integer to indicate the number of values; in this case, '4s' indicates a string consisting of four characters. For your records, the appropriate format string is therefore 'hd4s'. struct understands a wide range of numeric, character, and string formats. See the *Python Library Reference* for details.

Before you start reading records from your file, you need to know how many bytes to read at a time. Fortunately, struct includes a calcsize function, which takes your format string as an argument and returns the number of bytes used to contain data in such a format.

To read each record, you use the read method described earlier in this chapter. Then the struct.unpack function conveniently returns a tuple of values by parsing a read record according to your format string. The program to read your binary data file is remarkably simple:

```python
import struct
record_format = 'hd4s'
record_size = struct.calcsize(record_format)
result_list = []
input = open("data", 'rb')
while 1:
    record = input.read(record_size)        # Reads in a single record
    if record == '':
        input.close()                        # 1
        break
    result_list.append(struct.unpack(record_format, record))   # Unpacks record into a tuple; appends to results
```

If the record is empty, you're at the end of the file, so you quit the loop ❶. Note that there's no checking for file consistency; if the last record is an odd size, the struct.unpack function raises an error.

As you may already have guessed, struct also provides the ability to take Python values and convert them to packed byte sequences. This conversion is accomplished through the struct.pack function, which is almost, but not quite, an inverse of struct.unpack. The *almost* comes from the fact that whereas struct.unpack returns a tuple of Python values, struct.pack doesn't take a tuple of Python values; rather, it takes a format string as its first argument and then enough additional arguments to satisfy the format string. To produce a binary record of the form used in the previous example, you might do something like this:

```
>>> import struct
>>> record_format = 'hd4s'
>>> struct.pack(record_format, 7, 3.14, b'gbye')
b'\x07\x00\x00\x00\x00\x00\x00\x00\x1f\x85\xebQ\xb8\x1e\t@gbye'
```

struct gets even better; you can insert other special characters into the format string to indicate that data should be read/written in big-endian, little-endian, or machine-native-endian format (default is machine-native) and to indicate that things like a C short integer should be sized either as native to the machine (the default) or as standard C sizes. If you need these features, it's nice to know that they exist. See the *Python Library Reference* for details.

> **QUICK CHECK: STRUCT** What use cases can you think of in which the struct module would be useful for either reading or writing binary data?

13.8 *Pickling objects files*

Python can write any data structure into a file, read that data structure back out of a file, and re-create it with just a few commands. This capability is unusual but can be useful, because it can save you many pages of code that do nothing but dump the state of a program into a file (and can save a similar amount of code that does nothing but read that state back in).

Python provides this capability via the pickle module. Pickling is powerful but simple to use. Assume that the entire state of a program is held in three variables: a, b, and c. You can save this state to a file called state as follows:

```
import pickle
.
.
.
file = open("state", 'wb')
pickle.dump(a, file)
pickle.dump(b, file)
pickle.dump(c, file)
file.close()
```

It doesn't matter what was stored in a, b, and c. The content might be as simple as numbers or as complex as a list of dictionaries containing instances of user-defined classes. pickle.dump saves everything.

Now, to read that data back in on a later run of the program, just write

```
import pickle
file = open("state", 'rb')
a = pickle.load(file)
b = pickle.load(file)
c = pickle.load(file)
file.close()
```

Any data that was previously in the variables a, b, or c is restored to them by pickle.load.

The pickle module can store almost anything in this manner. It can handle lists, tuples, numbers, strings, dictionaries, and just about anything made up of these types of objects, which includes all class instances. It also handles shared objects, cyclic references, and other complex memory structures correctly, storing shared objects only once and restoring them as shared objects, not as identical copies. But code objects (what Python uses to store byte-compiled code) and system resources (like files or sockets) can't be pickled.

More often than not, you won't want to save your entire program state with pickle. Most applications can have multiple documents open at one time, for example. If you saved the entire state of the program, you would effectively save all open documents in one file. An easy and effective way of saving and restoring only data of interest is to write a save function that stores all data you want to save into a dictionary and then uses pickle to save the dictionary. Then you can use a complementary restore function to read the dictionary back in (again using pickle) and to assign the values in the dictionary to the appropriate program variables. This technique also has the advantage that there's no possibility of reading values back in an incorrect order— that is, an order different from the order in which the values were stored. Using this approach with the previous example, you get code looking something like this:

```
import pickle
.
.
.
def save_data():
    global a, b, c
    file = open("state", 'wb')
    data = {'a': a, 'b': b, 'c': c}
    pickle.dump(data, file)
    file.close()

def restore_data():
    global a, b, c
    file = open("state", 'rb')
    data = pickle.load(file)
    file.close()
    a = data['a']
    b = data['b']
    c = data['c']
    .
    .
```

This example is somewhat contrived. You probably won't be saving the state of the top-level variables of your interactive mode very often.

A real-life application is an extension of the cache example given in chapter 7. In that chapter, you called a function that performed a time-intensive calculation based on its three arguments. During the course of a program run, many of your calls to that

function ended up using the same set of arguments. You were able to obtain a significant performance improvement by caching the results in a dictionary, keyed by the
arguments that produced them. But it was also the case that many sessions of this program were being run many times over the course of days, weeks, and months. Therefore, by pickling the cache, you can avoid having to start over with every session. Here
is a pared-down version of the module you might use for this purpose.

Listing 13.2   File sole.py

```
"""sole module: contains functions sole, save, show"""
import pickle
_sole_mem_cache_d = {}
_sole_disk_file_s = "solecache"              Initialization code executes
file = open(_sole_disk_file_s, 'rb')     ◁── when module loads.
_sole_mem_cache_d = pickle.load(file)
file.close()
                                              Public functions
def sole(m, n, t):                       ◁──
    """sole(m, n, t): perform the sole calculation using the cache."""
    global _sole_mem_cache_d
    if _sole_mem_cache_d.has_key((m, n, t)):
        return _sole_mem_cache_d[(m, n, t)]
    else:
        # . . . do some time-consuming calculations . . .
        _sole_mem_cache_d[(m, n, t)] = result
        return result

def save():
    """save(): save the updated cache to disk."""
    global _sole_mem_cache_d, _sole_disk_file_s
    file = open(_sole_disk_file_s, 'wb')
    pickle.dump(_sole_mem_cache_d, file)
    file.close()

def show():
    """show(): print the cache"""
    global _sole_mem_cache_d
    print(_sole_mem_cache_d)
```

This code assumes that the cache file already exists. If you want to play around with it,
use the following to initialize the cache file:

```
>>> import pickle
>>> file = open("solecache",'wb')
>>> pickle.dump({}, file)
>>> file.close()
```

You also, of course, need to replace the comment # . . . do some time-consuming calculations with an actual calculation. Note that for production code, this
situation is one in which you'd probably use an absolute pathname for your cache file.
Also, concurrency isn't being handled here. If two people run overlapping sessions,

you end up with only the additions of the last person to save. If this situation were an issue, you could limit the overlap window significantly by using the dictionary update method in the `save` function.

13.8.1 *Reasons not to pickle*

Although it may make some sense to use a pickled object in the previous scenario, you should also be aware of the drawbacks to pickles:

- Pickling is neither particularly fast nor space-efficient as a means of serialization. Even using JSON to store serialized objects is faster and results in smaller files on disk.
- Pickling isn't secure, and loading a pickle with malicious content can result in the execution of arbitrary code on your machine. Therefore, you should avoid pickling if there's *any* chance at all that the pickle file will be accessible to anyone who might alter it.

QUICK CHECK: PICKLES Think about why a pickle would or would not be a good solution in the following use cases:

- Saving some state variables from one run to the next
- Keeping a high-score list for a game
- Storing usernames and passwords
- Storing a large dictionary of English terms

13.9 *Shelving objects*

This topic is somewhat advanced but certainly not difficult. You can think of a `shelve` object as being a dictionary that stores its data in a file on disk rather than in memory, which means that you still have the convenience of access with a key, but you don't have the limitations of the amount of available RAM.

This section is likely of most interest to people whose work involves storing or accessing pieces of data in large files, because the Python `shelve` module does exactly that: permits the reading or writing of pieces of data in large files without reading or writing the entire file. For applications that perform many accesses of large files (such as database applications), the savings in time can be spectacular. Like the `pickle` module (which it uses), the `shelve` module is simple.

In this section, you explore this module through an address book. This sort of thing usually is small enough that an entire address file can be read in when the application is started and written out when the application is done. If you're an extremely friendly sort of person and your address book is too big for this example, it would be better to use `shelve` and not worry about it.

Assume that each entry in your address book consists of a tuple of three elements, giving the first name, phone number, and address of a person. Each entry is indexed by the last name of the person the entry refers to. This setup is so simple that your application will be an interactive session with the Python shell.

First, import the `shelve` module, and open the address book. `shelve.open` creates the address book file if it doesn't exist:

```
>>> import shelve
>>> book = shelve.open("addresses")
```

Now add a couple of entries. Notice that you're treating the object returned by `shelve.open` as a dictionary (although it's a dictionary that can use only strings as keys):

```
>>> book['flintstone'] = ('fred', '555-1234', '1233 Bedrock Place')
>>> book['rubble'] = ('barney', '555-4321', '1235 Bedrock Place')
```

Finally, close the file and end the session:

```
>>> book.close()
```

So what? Well, in that same directory, start Python again, and open the same address book:

```
>>> import shelve
>>> book = shelve.open("addresses")
```

But now, instead of entering something, see whether what you put in before is still around:

```
>>> book['flintstone']
('fred', '555-1234', '1233 Bedrock Place')
```

The addresses file created by `shelve.open` in the first interactive session has acted just like a persistent dictionary. The data you entered before was stored to disk, even though you did no explicit disk writes. That's exactly what `shelve` does.

More generally, `shelve.open` returns a `shelf` object that permits basic dictionary operations, key assignment or lookup, `del`, `in`, and the `keys` method. But unlike a normal dictionary, `shelf` objects store their data on disk, not in memory. Unfortunately, `shelf` objects do have one significant restriction compared with dictionaries: They can use only strings as keys, versus the wide range of key types allowable in dictionaries.

It's important to understand the advantage `shelf` objects give you over dictionaries when dealing with large data sets. `shelve.open` makes the file accessible; it doesn't read an entire `shelf` object file into memory. File accesses are done only when needed (typically, when an element is looked up), and the file structure is maintained in such a manner that lookups are very fast. Even if your data file is really large, only a couple of disk accesses will be required to locate the desired object in the file, which can improve your program in several ways. The program may start faster, because it doesn't need to read a potentially large file into memory. Also, the program may execute faster because more memory is available to the rest of the program; thus, less code must be swapped out into virtual memory. You can operate on data sets that are otherwise too large to fit in memory.

You have a few restrictions when using the `shelve` module. As previously mentioned, `shelf` object keys can be only strings, but any Python object that can be pickled can be stored under a key in a `shelf` object. Also, `shelf` objects aren't suitable for multiuser databases because they provide no control for concurrent access. Make sure that you close a `shelf` object when you're finished; closing is sometimes required for the changes you've made (entries or deletions) to be written back to disk.

As written, the cache example in listing 13.1 is an excellent candidate to be handled with shelves. You wouldn't, for example, have to rely on the user to explicitly save their work to the disk. The only possible issue is that you wouldn't have the low-level control when you write back to the file.

QUICK CHECK: SHELVE Using a `shelf` object looks very much like using a dictionary. In what ways is using a `shelf` object different? What disadvantages would you expect in using a `shelf` object?

LAB 13: FINAL FIXES TO WC If you look at the `man` page for the `wc` utility, you see two command-line options that do very similar things. `-c` makes the utility count the bytes in the file, and `-m` makes it count characters (which in the case of some Unicode characters can be two or more bytes long). In addition, if a file is given, it should read from and process that file, but if no file is given, it should read from and process `stdin`.

Rewrite your version of the `wc` utility to implement both the distinction between bytes and characters and the ability to read from files and standard input.

Summary

- File input and output in Python uses various built-in functions to open, read, write, and close files.
- In addition to reading and writing text, the `struct` module gives you the ability to read or write packed binary data.
- The `pickle` and `shelve` modules provide simple, safe, and powerful ways of saving and accessing arbitrarily complex Python data structures.

14

Exceptions

This chapter covers

- Understanding exceptions
- Handling exceptions in Python
- Using the `with` keyword

This chapter discusses exceptions, which are language features specifically aimed at handling unusual circumstances during the execution of a program. The most common use for exceptions is to handle errors that arise during the execution of a program, but they can also be used effectively for many other purposes. Python provides a comprehensive set of exceptions, and new ones can be defined by users for their own purposes.

The concept of exceptions as an error-handling mechanism has been around for some time. C and Perl, the most commonly used systems and scripting languages, don't provide any exception capabilities, and even programmers who use languages such as C++, which does include exceptions, are often unfamiliar with them. This chapter doesn't assume familiarity with exceptions on your part but instead provides detailed explanations.

14.1 Introduction to exceptions

The following sections provide an introduction to exceptions and how they're used. If you're already familiar with exceptions, you can skip directly to "Exceptions in Python" (section 14.2).

14.1.1 General philosophy of errors and exception handling

Any program may encounter errors during its execution. For the purposes of illustrating exceptions, I look at the case of a word processor that writes files to disk and that therefore may run out of disk space before all of its data is written. There are various ways of coming to grips with this problem.

SOLUTION 1: DON'T HANDLE THE PROBLEM

The simplest way to handle this disk-space problem is to assume that there'll always be adequate disk space for whatever files you write and that you needn't worry about it. Unfortunately, this option seems to be the most commonly used. It's usually tolerable for small programs dealing with small amounts of data, but it's completely unsatisfactory for more mission-critical programs.

SOLUTION 2: ALL FUNCTIONS RETURN SUCCESS/FAILURE STATUS

The next level of sophistication in error handling is realizing that errors will occur and defining a methodology using standard language mechanisms for detecting and handling them. There are numerous ways to do this, but a typical method is to have each function or procedure return a status value that indicates whether that function or procedure call executed successfully. Normal results can be passed back in a call-by-reference parameter.

Consider how this solution might work with a hypothetical word-processing program. Assume that the program invokes a single high-level function, `save_to_file`, to save the current document to file. This function calls subfunctions to save different parts of the entire document to the file, such as `save_text_to_file` to save the actual document text, `save_prefs_to_file` to save user preferences for that document, `save_formats_to_file` to save user-defined formats for the document, and so forth. Any of these subfunctions may in turn call its own subfunctions, which save smaller pieces to the file. At the bottom are built-in system functions, which write primitive data to the file and report on the success or failure of the file-writing operations.

You could put error-handling code into every function that might get a disk-space error, but that practice makes little sense. The only thing the error handler will be able to do is put up a dialog box telling the user that there's no more disk space and asking the user to remove some files and save again. It wouldn't make sense to duplicate this code everywhere you do a disk write. Instead, put one piece of error-handling code into the main disk-writing function: `save_to_file`.

Unfortunately, for `save_to_file` to be able to determine when to call this error-handling code, every function it calls that writes to disk must itself check for disk space errors and return a status value indicating the success or failure of the disk write. In addition, the `save_to_file` function must explicitly check every call to a function that writes to disk, even though it doesn't care about which function fails. The code, using C-like syntax, looks something like this:

```
const ERROR = 1;
const OK = 0;
int save_to_file(filename) {
    int status;
    status = save_prefs_to_file(filename);
    if (status == ERROR) {
        ...handle the error...
    }
    status = save_text_to_file(filename);
    if (status == ERROR) {
        ...handle the error...
    }
    status = save_formats_to_file(filename);
    if (status == ERROR) {
        ...handle the error...
    }
    .
    .
    .
}
int save_text_to_file(filename) {
    int status;
    status = ...lower-level call to write size of text...
    if (status == ERROR) {
        return(ERROR);
    }
    status = ...lower-level call to write actual text data...
    if (status == ERROR) {
        return(ERROR);
    }
    .
    .
    .
}
```

The same applies to `save_prefs_to_file`, `save_formats_to_file`, and all other functions that either write to `filename` directly or (in any way) call functions that write to `filename`.

Under this methodology, code to detect and handle errors can become a significant portion of the entire program, because every function and procedure containing calls that might result in an error needs to contain code to check for an error. Often, programmers don't have the time or the energy to put in this type of complete error checking, and programs end up being unreliable and crash-prone.

SOLUTION 3: THE EXCEPTION MECHANISM

It's obvious that most of the error-checking code in the previous type of program is largely repetitive: The code checks for errors on each attempted file write and passes an error status message back up to the calling procedure if an error is detected. The disk-space error is handled in only one place: the top-level `save_to_file`. In other words, most of the error-handling code is plumbing code that connects the place where an error is generated with the place where it's handled. What you really want to do is get rid of this plumbing and write code that looks something like this:

```
def save_to_file(filename)
    try to execute the following block
        save_text_to_file(filename)
        save_formats_to_file(filename)
        save_prefs_to_file(filename)
        .
        .
        .

    except that, if the disk runs out of space while
        executing the above block, do this
        ...handle the error...

def save_text_to_file(filename)
    ...lower-level call to write size of text...
    ...lower-level call to write actual text data...
        .
        .
        .
```

The error-handling code is completely removed from the lower-level functions; an error (if it occurs) is generated by the built-in file writing routines and propagates directly to the `save_to_file` routine, where your error-handling code will (presumably) take care of it. Although you can't write this code in C, languages that offer exceptions permit exactly this sort of behavior—and of course, Python is one such language. Exceptions let you write clearer code and handle error conditions better.

14.1.2 *A more formal definition of exceptions*

The act of generating an exception is called *raising* or *throwing* an exception. In the previous example, all exceptions are raised by the disk-writing functions, but exceptions can also be raised by any other functions or can be explicitly raised by your own code. In the previous example, the low-level disk-writing functions (not seen in the code) would throw an exception if the disk were to run out of space.

The act of responding to an exception is called *catching* an exception, and the code that handles an exception is called *exception-handling code* or just an *exception handler*. In the example, the `except that...` line catches the disk-write exception, and the code that would be in place of the `...handle the error...` line would be an exception handler for disk-write (out of space) exceptions. There may be other exception handlers for other types of exceptions or even other exception handlers for the same type of exception but at another place in your code.

14.1.3 *Handling different types of exceptions*

Depending on exactly what event causes an exception, a program may need to take different actions. An exception raised when disk space is exhausted needs to be handled quite differently from an exception that's raised if you run out of memory, and both of these exceptions are completely different from an exception that arises when a divide-by-zero error occurs. One way to handle these different types of exceptions is to globally record an error message indicating the cause of the exception, and have all exception handlers examine this error message and take appropriate action. In practice, a different method has proved to be much more flexible.

Rather than defining a single kind of exception, Python, like most modern languages that implement exceptions, defines different types of exceptions corresponding to various problems that may occur. Depending on the underlying event, different types of exceptions may be raised. In addition, the code that catches exceptions may be told to catch only certain types. This feature is used in the pseudocode in solution 3 earlier in this chapter that said except that, if the disk runs out of space . . ., do this; this pseudocode specifies that this particular exception-handling code is interested only in disk-space exceptions. Another type of exception wouldn't be caught by that exception-handling code. That exception would be caught by an exception handler that was looking for numeric exceptions, or (if no such exception handler existed) it would cause the program to exit prematurely with an error.

14.2 *Exceptions in Python*

The remaining sections of this chapter talk specifically about the exception mechanisms built into Python. The entire Python exception mechanism is built around an object-oriented paradigm, which makes it both flexible and expandable. If you aren't familiar with object-oriented programming (OOP), you don't need to learn object-oriented techniques to use exceptions.

An exception is an object generated automatically by Python functions with a raise statement. After the object is generated, the raise statement, which raises an exception, causes execution of the Python program to proceed in a manner different from what would normally occur. Instead of proceeding with the next statement after the raise or whatever generated the exception, the current call chain is searched for a handler that can handle the generated exception. If such a handler is found, it's invoked and may access the exception object for more information. If no suitable exception handler is found, the program aborts with an error message.

Easier to ask forgiveness than permission

The way that Python thinks about handling error situations in general is different from that common in languages such as Java, for example. Those languages rely on checking for possible errors as much as possible before they occur, since handling exceptions after they occur tends to be costly in various ways. This style is described in the first section of this chapter and is sometimes described as a look before you leap (LBYL) approach.

Python, on the other hand, is more likely to rely on exceptions to deal with errors after they occur. Although this reliance may seem to be risky, if exceptions are used well, the code is less cumbersome and easier to read, and errors are dealt with only as they occur. This Pythonic approach to handling errors is often described by the phrase "easier to ask forgiveness than permission" (EAFP).

14.2.1   *Types of Python exceptions*

It's possible to generate different types of exceptions to reflect the actual cause of the error or exceptional circumstance being reported. Python 3.6 provides several exception types:

```
BaseException
    SystemExit
    KeyboardInterrupt
    GeneratorExit
    Exception
        StopIteration
        ArithmeticError
            FloatingPointError
            OverflowError
            ZeroDivisionError
        AssertionError
        AttributeError
        BufferError
        EOFError
        ImportError
            ModuleNoteFoundError
        LookupError
            IndexError
            KeyError
        MemoryError
        NameError
            UnboundLocalError
        OSError
            BlockingIOError
            ChildProcessError
            ConnectionError
                BrokenPipeError
                ConnectionAbortedError
                ConnectionRefusedError
                ConnectionResetError
            FileExistsError
            FileNotFoundError
            InterruptedError
            IsADirectoryError
            NotADirectoryError
            PermissionError
            ProcessLookupError
```

```
        TimeoutError
    ReferenceError
    RuntimeError
        NotImplementedError
        RecursionError
    SyntaxError
        IndentationError
            TabError
    SystemError
    TypeError
    ValueError
        UnicodeError
            UnicodeDecodeError
            UnicodeEncodeError
            UnicodeTranslateError
    Warning
        DeprecationWarning
        PendingDeprecationWarning
        RuntimeWarning
        SyntaxWarning
        UserWarning
        FutureWarning
        ImportWarning
        UnicodeWarning
        BytesWarningException
        ResourceWarning
```

The Python exception set is hierarchically structured, as reflected by the indentation in this list of exceptions. As you saw in a previous chapter, you can obtain an alphabetized list from the `__builtins__` module.

Each type of exception is a Python class, which inherits from its parent exception type. But if you're not into OOP yet, don't worry about that. An `IndexError`, for example, is also a `LookupError` and (by inheritance) an `Exception` and also a `BaseException`.

This hierarchy is deliberate: Most exceptions inherit from `Exception`, and it's strongly recommended that any user-defined exceptions also subclass `Exception`, not `BaseException`. The reason is that if you have code set up like this

```
try:
    # do stuff
except Exception:
    # handle exceptions
```

you could still interrupt the code in the `try` block with Ctrl-C without triggering the exception-handling code, because the `KeyboardInterrupt` exception is *not* a subclass of `Exception`.

You can find an explanation of the meaning of each type of exception in the documentation, but you'll rapidly become acquainted with the most common types as you program!

14.2.2 *Raising exceptions*

Exceptions are raised by many of the Python built-in functions:

```
>>> alist = [1, 2, 3]
>>> element = alist[7]
Traceback (innermost last):
  File "<stdin>", line 1, in ?
IndexError: list index out of range
```

Error-checking code built into Python detects that the second input line requests an element at a list index that doesn't exist and raises an `IndexError` exception. This exception propagates all the way back to the top level (the interactive Python interpreter), which handles it by printing out a message stating that the exception has occurred.

Exceptions may also be raised explicitly in your own code through the use of the `raise` statement. The most basic form of this statement is

```
raise exception(args)
```

The `exception(args)` part of the code creates an exception. The arguments to the new exception are typically values that aid you in determining what happened—something that I discuss next. After the exception has been created, `raise` throws it upward along the stack of Python functions that were invoked in getting to the line containing the `raise` statement. The new exception is thrown up to the nearest (on the stack) exception catcher looking for that type of exception. If no catcher is found on the way to the top level of the program, the program terminates with an error or (in an interactive session) causes an error message to be printed to the console.

Try the following:

```
>>> raise IndexError("Just kidding")
Traceback (innermost last):
  File "<stdin>", line 1, in ?
IndexError: Just kidding
```

The use of `raise` here generates what at first glance looks similar to all the Python list-index error messages you've seen so far. Closer inspection reveals this isn't the case. The actual error reported isn't as serious as those other ones.

The use of a string argument when creating exceptions is common. Most of the built-in Python exceptions, if given a first argument, assume that the argument is a message to be shown to you as an explanation of what happened. This isn't always the case, though, because each exception type is its own class, and the arguments expected when a new exception of that class is created are determined entirely by the class definition. Also, programmer-defined exceptions, created by you or by other programmers, are often used for reasons other than error handling; as such, they may not take a text message.

14.2.3 *Catching and handling exceptions*

The important thing about exceptions isn't that they cause a program to halt with an error message. Achieving that function in a program is never much of a problem. What's special about exceptions is that they don't have to cause the program to halt. By defining appropriate exception handlers, you can ensure that commonly encountered exceptional circumstances don't cause the program to fail; perhaps they display an error message to the user or do something else, perhaps even fix the problem, but they don't crash the program.

The basic Python syntax for exception catching and handling is as follows, using the try, except, and sometimes else keywords:

```
try:
    body
except exception_type1 as var1:
    exception_code1
except exception_type2 as var2:
    exception_code2
      .
      .
      .
except:
    default_exception_code
else:
    else_body
finally:
    finally_body
```

A try statement is executed by first executing the code in the body part of the statement. If this execution is successful (that is, no exceptions are thrown to be caught by the try statement), the else_body is executed, and the try statement is finished. Because there is a finally statement, finally_body is executed. If an exception is thrown to the try, the except clauses are searched sequentially for one whose associated exception type matches that which was thrown. If a matching except clause is found, the thrown exception is assigned to the variable named after the associated exception type, and the exception code body associated with the matching exception is executed. If the line except exception_type as var: matches some thrown exception exc, the variable var is created, and exc is assigned as the value of var before the exception-handling code of the except statement is executed. You don't need to put in var; you can say something like except exception_type:, which still catches exceptions of the given type but doesn't assign them to any variable.

If no matching except clause is found, the thrown exception can't be handled by that try statement, and the exception is thrown farther up the call chain in hope that some enclosing try will be able to handle it.

The last except clause of a try statement can optionally refer to no exception types at all, in which case it handles all types of exceptions. This technique can be convenient for some debugging and extremely rapid prototyping but generally isn't a good idea: all errors are hidden by the except clause, which can lead to some confusing behavior on the part of your program.

The `else` clause of a `try` statement is optional and rarely used. This clause is executed if and only if the `body` of the `try` statement executes without throwing any errors.

The `finally` clause of a `try` statement is also optional and executes after the `try`, `except`, and `else` sections have executed. If an exception is raised in the `try` block and isn't handled by any of the `except` blocks, that exception is raised again after the `finally` block executes. Because the `finally` block always executes, it gives you a chance to include code to clean up after any exception handling by closing files, resetting variables, and so on.

> **TRY THIS: CATCHING EXCEPTIONS** Write code that gets two numbers from the user and divides the first number by the second. Check for and catch the exception that occurs if the second number is zero (`ZeroDivisionError`).

14.2.4 *Defining new exceptions*

You can easily define your own exception. The following two lines do this for you:

```
class MyError(Exception):
    pass
```

This code creates a class that inherits everything from the base `Exception` class. But you don't have to worry about that if you don't want to.

You can raise, catch, and handle this exception like any other exception. If you give it a single argument (and you don't catch and handle it), it's printed at the end of the traceback:

```
>>> raise MyError("Some information about what went wrong")
Traceback (most recent call last):
  File "<stdin>", line 1, in <module>
__main__.MyError: Some information about what went wrong
```

This argument, of course, is available to a handler you write as well:

```
try:
    raise MyError("Some information about what went wrong")
except MyError as error:
    print("Situation:", error)
```

The result is

```
Situation: Some information about what went wrong
```

If you raise your exception with multiple arguments, these arguments are delivered to your handler as a tuple, which you can access through the `args` variable of the error:

```
try:
    raise MyError("Some information", "my_filename", 3)
except MyError as error:
    print("Situation: {0} with file {1}\n error code: {2}".format(
        error.args[0],
 error.args[1], error.args[2]))
```

The result is

```
Situation: Some information with file my_filename
error code: 3
```

Because an exception type is a regular class in Python and happens to inherit from the root Exception class, it's a simple matter to create your own subhierarchy of exception types for use by your own code. You don't have to worry about this process on a first read of this book. You can always come back to it after you've read chapter 15. Exactly how you create your own exceptions depends on your particular needs. If you're writing a small program that may generate only a few unique errors or exceptions, subclass the main Exception class as you've done here. If you're writing a large, multifile code library with a special goal in mind—say, weather forecasting—you may decide to define a unique class called WeatherLibraryException and then define all the unique exceptions of the library as subclasses of WeatherLibrary-Exception.

> **QUICK CHECK: EXCEPTIONS AS CLASSES**   If MyError inherits from Exception, what is the difference between except Exception as e and except MyError as e?

14.2.5   *Debugging programs with the assert statement*

The assert statement is a specialized form of the raise statement:

```
assert expression, argument
```

The AssertionError exception with the optional argument is raised if the expression evaluates to False and the system variable __debug__ is True. The __debug__ variable defaults to True and is turned off by starting the Python interpreter with the -O or -OO option or by setting the system variable PYTHONOPTIMIZE to True. The optional argument can be used to include an explanation of the assertion.

The code generator creates no code for assertion statements if __debug__ is False. You can use assert statements to instrument your code with debug statements during development and leave them in the code for possible future use with no runtime cost during regular use:

```
>>> x = (1, 2, 3)
>>> assert len(x) > 5, "len(x) not > 5"
Traceback (most recent call last):
  File "<stdin>", line 1, in <module>
AssertionError: len(x) not > 5
```

> **TRY THIS: THE ASSERT STATEMENT**   Write a simple program that gets a number from the user and then uses the assert statement to raise an exception if the number is zero. Test to make sure that the assert statement fires; then turn it off, using one of the methods mentioned in this section.

14.2.6 *The exception inheritance hierarchy*

In this section, I expand on an earlier notion that Python exceptions are hierarchically structured and on what that structure means in terms of how except clauses catch exceptions.

The following code

```
try:
    body
except LookupError as error:
    exception code
except IndexError as error:
    exception code
```

catches two types of exceptions: IndexError and LookupError. It just so happens that IndexError is a subclass of LookupError. If body throws an IndexError, that error is first examined by the except LookupError as error: line, and because an IndexError is a LookupError by inheritance, the first except succeeds. The second except clause is never used because it's subsumed by the first except clause.

Conversely, flipping the order of the two except clauses could potentially be useful; then the first clause would handle IndexError exceptions, and the second clause would handle any LookupError exceptions that aren't IndexError errors.

14.2.7 *Example: a disk-writing program in Python*

In this section, I revisit the example of a word-processing program that needs to check for disk out-of-space conditions as it writes a document to disk:

```
def save_to_file(filename) :
    try:
        save_text_to_file(filename)
        save_formats_to_file(filename)
        save_prefs_to_file(filename)
        .
        .
        .

    except IOError:
        ...handle the error...
def save_text_to_file(filename):
    ...lower-level call to write size of text...
    ...lower-level call to write actual text data...
    .
    .
    .
```

Notice how unobtrusive the error-handling code is; it's wrapped around the main sequence of disk-writing calls in the save_to_file function. None of the subsidiary disk-writing functions needs any error-handling code. It would be easy to develop the program first and add error-handling code later. That's often what programmers do, although this practice isn't the optimal ordering of events.

As another note of interest, this code doesn't respond specifically to disk-full errors; rather, it responds to IOError exceptions, which Python's built-in functions raise automatically whenever they can't complete an I/O request, for whatever reason. That's probably satisfactory for your needs, but if you need to identify disk-full conditions, you can do a couple of things. The except body can check to see how much room is available on disk. If the disk is out of space, clearly, the problem is a disk-full problem and should be handled in this except body; otherwise, the code in the except body can throw the IOError farther up the call chain to be handled by some other except. If that solution isn't sufficient, you can do something more extreme, such as going into the C source for the Python disk-writing functions and raising your own DiskFull exceptions as necessary. I don't recommend the latter option, but it's nice to know that this possibility exists if you need to use it.

14.2.8   *Example: exceptions in normal evaluation*

Exceptions are most often used in error handling but can also be remarkably useful in certain situations involving what you'd think of as normal evaluation. Consider the problems in implementing something that works like a spreadsheet. Like most spreadsheets, it would have to permit arithmetic operations involving cells, and it would also permit cells to contain values other than numbers. In such an application, blank cells used in a numerical calculation might be considered to contain the value 0, and cells containing any other nonnumeric string might be considered invalid and represented as the Python value None. Any calculation involving an invalid value should return an invalid value.

The first step is to write a function that evaluates a string from a cell of the spreadsheet and returns an appropriate value:

```
def cell_value(string):
    try:
        return float(string)
    except ValueError:
        if string == "":
            return 0
        else:
            return None
```

Python's exception-handling ability makes this function a simple one to write. The code tries to convert the string from the cell to a number and return it in a try block using the float built-in function. float raises the ValueError exception if it can't convert its string argument to a number, so the code catches that exception and returns either 0 or None, depending on whether the argument string is empty or nonempty.

The next step is handling the fact that some of the arithmetic might have to deal with a value of None. In a language without exceptions, the normal way to do this is to define a custom set of arithmetic functions, which check their arguments for None, and then use those functions rather than the built-in arithmetic functions to perform all of the spreadsheet arithmetic. This process is time-consuming and error-prone, however, and it leads to slow execution because you're effectively building an interpreter in your spreadsheet. This project takes a different approach. All the spreadsheet formulas can actually be Python functions that take as arguments the x and y coordinates of the cell being evaluated and the spreadsheet itself, and calculate the result for the given cell by using standard Python arithmetic operators, using `cell_value` to extract the necessary values from the spreadsheet. You can define a function called `safe_apply` that applies one of these formulas to the appropriate arguments in a `try` block and returns either the formula's result or `None`, depending on whether the formula evaluated successfully:

```
def safe_apply(function, x, y, spreadsheet):
    try:
        return function(x, y, spreadsheet)
    except TypeError:
        return None
```

These two changes are enough to integrate the idea of an empty (`None`) value into the semantics of the spreadsheet. Trying to develop this ability without the use of exceptions is a highly educational exercise.

14.2.9 *Where to use exceptions*

Exceptions are natural choices for handling almost any error condition. It's an unfortunate fact that error handling is often added when the rest of the program is largely complete, but exceptions are particularly good at intelligibly managing this sort of after-the-fact error-handling code (or, more optimistically, when you're adding more error handling after the fact).

Exceptions are also highly useful in circumstances where a large amount of processing may need to be discarded after it becomes obvious that a computational branch in your program has become untenable. The spreadsheet example is one such case; others are branch-and-bound algorithms and parsing algorithms.

> **QUICK CHECK: EXCEPTIONS** Do Python exceptions force a program to halt?
>
> Suppose that you want accessing a dictionary x to always return None if a key doesn't exist in the dictionary (that is, if a KeyError exception is raised). What code would you use?

> **TRY THIS: EXCEPTIONS** What code would you use to create a custom Value-TooLarge exception and raise that exception if the variable x is over 1000?

14.3 *Context managers using the with keyword*

Some situations, such as reading files, follow a predictable pattern with a set beginning and end. In the case of reading from a file, quite often the file needs to be open only one time: while data is being read. Then the file can be closed. In terms of exceptions, you can code this kind of file access like this:

```
try:
    infile = open(filename)
    data = infile.read()
finally:
    infile.close()
```

Python 3 offers a more generic way of handling situations like this: context managers. *Context managers* wrap a block and manage requirements on *entry* and *departure* from the block and are marked by the `with` keyword. File objects are context managers, and you can use that capability to read files:

```
with open(filename) as infile:
    data = infile.read()
```

These two lines of code are equivalent to the five previous lines. In both cases, you know that the file will be closed immediately after the last read, whether or not the operation was successful. In the second case, closure of the file is also assured because it's part of the file object's context management, so you don't need to write the code. In other words, by using `with` combined with a context management (in this case a file object), you don't need to worry about the routine cleanup.

As you might expect, it's also possible to create your own context managers if you need them. You can learn a bit more about how to create context managers and the various ways they can be manipulated by checking out the documentation for the `contextlib` module of the standard library.

Context managers are great for things like locking and unlocking resources, closing files, committing database transactions, and so on. Since their introduction, context managers have become standard best practice for such use cases.

QUICK CHECK: CONTEXT MANAGERS   Assume that you're using a context manager in a script that reads and/or writes several files. Which of the following approaches do you think would be best?

- Put the entire script in a block managed by a `with` statement.
- Use one `with` statement for all file reads and another for all file writes.
- Use a `with` statement each time you read a file or write a file (for each line, for example).
- Use a `with` statement for each file that you read or write.

LAB 14: CUSTOM EXCEPTIONS   Think about the module you wrote in chapter 9 to count word frequencies. What errors might reasonably occur in those functions? Refactor those functions to handle those exception conditions appropriately.

Summary

- Python's exception-handling mechanism and exception classes provide a rich system to handle runtime errors in your code.
- By using `try`, `except`, `else`, and `finally` blocks, and by selecting and even creating the types of exceptions caught, you can have very fine-grained control over how exceptions are handled and ignored.
- Python's philosophy is that errors shouldn't pass silently unless they're explicitly silenced.
- Python exception types are organized in a hierarchy because exceptions, like all objects in Python, are based on classes.

Part 3

Advanced language features

The previous chapters have been a survey of the basic features of Python: the features that most programmers will use most of the time. What follows is a look at some more advanced features, which you may not use every day (depending on your needs) but which are vital when you need them.

Classes and object-oriented programming

This chapter covers

- Defining classes
- Using instance variables and `@property`
- Defining methods
- Defining class variables and methods
- Inheriting from other classes
- Making variables and methods private
- Inheriting from multiple classes

In this chapter, I discuss Python classes, which can be used to hold both data and code. Although most programmers are probably familiar with classes or objects in other languages, I make no particular assumptions about knowledge of a specific language or paradigm. In addition, this chapter is a description only of the constructs available in Python; it's not an exposition on object-oriented programming (OOP) itself.

15.1   Defining classes

A *class* in Python is effectively a data type. All the data types built into Python are classes, and Python gives you powerful tools to manipulate every aspect of a class's behavior. You define a class with the `class` statement:

```
class MyClass:
    body
```

`body` is a list of Python statements—typically, variable assignments and function definitions. No assignments or function definitions are required. The body can be just a single `pass` statement.

By convention, class identifiers are in CapCase—that is, the first letter of each component word is capitalized, to make the identifiers stand out. After you define the class, you can create a new object of the class type (an instance of the class) by calling the class name as a function:

```
instance = MyClass()
```

15.1.1   Using a class instance as a structure or record

Class instances can be used as structures or records. Unlike C structures or Java classes, the data fields of an instance don't need to be declared ahead of time; they can be created on the fly. The following short example defines a class called `Circle`, creates a `Circle` instance, assigns a value to the `radius` field of the circle, and then uses that field to calculate the circumference of the circle:

```
>>> class Circle:
...     pass
...
>>> my_circle = Circle()
>>> my_circle.radius = 5
>>> print(2 * 3.14 * my_circle.radius)
31.4
```

As in Java and many other languages, the fields of an instance/structure are accessed and assigned to by using dot notation.

You can initialize fields of an instance automatically by including an `__init__` initialization method in the class body. This function is run every time an instance of the class is created, with that new instance as its first argument, `self`. The `__init__` method is similar to a constructor in Java, but it doesn't really *construct* anything; it *initializes* fields of the class. Also unlike those in Java and C++, Python classes may only have one `__init__` method. This example creates circles with a radius of 1 by default:

```
class Circle:
    def __init__(self):          ①
        self.radius = 1
my_circle = Circle()             ②                    ③
print(2 * 3.14 * my_circle.radius)
```

```
6.28
my_circle.radius = 5
print(2 * 3.14 * my_circle.radius)
31.400000000000002
```

By convention, `self` is always the name of the first argument of `__init__`. `self` is set to the newly created circle instance when `__init__` is run ❶. Next, the code uses the class definition. You first create a `Circle` instance object ❷. The next line makes use of the fact that the radius field is already initialized ❸. You can also overwrite the radius field ❹; as a result, the last line prints a different result from the previous `print` statement ❺.

Python also has something more like a constructor: the `__new__` method, which is what is called on object creation and returns an uninitialized object. Unless you're subclassing an immutable type, like `str` or `int`, or using a metaclass to modify the object creation process, it's rare to override the existing `__new__` method.

You can do a great deal more by using true OOP, and if you're not familiar with it, I urge you to read up on it. Python's OOP constructs are the subject of the remainder of this chapter.

15.2 Instance variables

Instance variables are the most basic feature of OOP. Take a look at the `Circle` class again:

```
class Circle:
    def __init__(self):
        self.radius = 1
```

`radius` is an *instance variable* of `Circle` instances. That is, each instance of the `Circle` class has its own copy of `radius`, and the value stored in that copy may be different from the values stored in the `radius` variable in other instances. In Python, you can create instance variables as necessary by assigning to a field of a class instance:

```
instance.variable = value
```

If the variable doesn't already exist, it's created automatically, which is how `__init__` creates the `radius` variable.

All uses of instance variables, both assignment and access, require *explicit mention* of the containing instance—that is, `instance.variable`. A reference to `variable` by itself is a reference not to an instance variable, but to a local variable in the executing method. This is different from C++ and Java, where instance variables are referred to in the same manner as local method function variables. I rather like Python's requirement for explicit mention of the containing instance because it clearly distinguishes instance variables from local function variables.

> **TRY THIS: INSTANCE VARIABLES** What code would you use to create a `Rectangle` class?

15.3 *Methods*

A *method* is a function associated with a particular class. You've already seen the special __init__ method, which is called on a new instance when that instance is created. In the following example, you define another method, area, for the Circle class; this method can be used to calculate and return the area for any Circle instance. Like most user-defined methods, area is called with a *method invocation syntax* that resembles instance variable access:

```
>>> class Circle:
...     def __init__(self):
...         self.radius = 1
...     def area(self):
...         return self.radius * self.radius * 3.14159
...
>>> c = Circle()
>>> c.radius = 3
>>> print(c.area())
28.27431
```

Method invocation syntax consists of an instance, followed by a period, followed by the method to be invoked on the instance. When a method is called in this way, it's a *bound* method invocation. However, a method *can* also be invoked as an *unbound* method by accessing it through its containing class. This practice is less convenient and is almost never done, because when a method is invoked in this manner, its first argument must be an instance of the class in which that method is defined and is less clear:

```
>>> print(Circle.area(c))
28.27431
```

Like __init__, the area method is defined as a function within the body of the class definition. The first argument of any method is the instance it was invoked by or on, named self by convention. In many languages the instance, often called this, is implicit and is never explicitly passed, but Python's design philosophy prefers to make things explicit.

Methods can be invoked with arguments if the method definitions accept those arguments. This version of Circle adds an argument to the __init__ method so that you can create circles of a given radius without needing to set the radius after a circle is created:

```
class Circle:
    def __init__(self, radius):
        self.radius = radius
    def area(self):
        return self.radius * self.radius * 3.14159
```

Note the two uses of radius here. self.radius is the instance variable called radius. radius by itself is the local function parameter called radius. The two aren't the same! In practice, you'd probably call the local function parameter something like r or rad to avoid any possibility of confusion.

Using this definition of Circle, you can create circles of any radius with one call on the Circle class. The following creates a Circle of radius 5:

```
c = Circle(5)
```

All the standard Python function features—default argument values, extra arguments, keyword arguments, and so forth—can be used with methods. You could have defined the first line of __init__ to be

```
def __init__(self, radius=1):
```

Then calls to circle would work with or without an extra argument; Circle() would return a circle of radius 1, and Circle(3) would return a circle of radius 3.

There's nothing magical about method invocation in Python, which can be considered to be shorthand for normal function invocation. Given a method invocation instance.method(arg1, arg2, . . .), Python transforms it into a normal function call by using the following rules:

1 Look for the method name in the instance namespace. If a method has been changed or added for this instance, it's invoked in preference over methods in the class or superclass. This lookup is the same sort of lookup discussed in section 15.4.1 later in this chapter.
2 If the method isn't found in the instance namespace, look up the class type class of instance, and look for the method there. In the previous examples, class is Circle—the type of the instance c.
3 If the method still isn't found, look for the method in the superclasses.
4 When the method has been found, make a direct call to it as a normal Python function, using the instance as the first argument of the function and shifting all the other arguments in the method invocation one space over to the right. So instance.method(arg1, arg2, . . .) becomes class.method (instance, arg1, arg2, . . .).

> **TRY THIS: INSTANCE VARIABLES AND METHODS** Update the code for a Rectangle class so that you can set the dimensions when an instance is created, just as for the Circle class above. Also, add an area() method.

15.4 *Class variables*

A *class variable* is a variable associated with a class, not an instance of a class, and is accessible by *all* instances of the class. A class variable might be used to keep track of some class-level information, such as how many instances of the class have been created at any point. Python provides class variables, although using them requires slightly more effort than in most other languages. Also, you need to watch out for an interaction between class and instance variables.

A class variable is created by an assignment in the *class* body, not in the __init__ function. After it has been created, it can be seen by all instances of the class. You can use a class variable to make a value for `pi` accessible to all instances of the `Circle` class:

```
class Circle:
    pi = 3.14159
    def __init__(self, radius):
        self.radius = radius
    def area(self):
        return self.radius * self.radius * Circle.pi
```

With the definition entered, you can type

```
>>> Circle.pi
3.14159
>>> Circle.pi = 4
>>> Circle.pi
4
>>> Circle.pi = 3.14159
>>> Circle.pi
3.14159
```

This example is exactly how you'd expect a class variable to act; it's associated with and contained in the class that defines it. Notice in this example that you're accessing `Circle.pi` before any circle instances have been created. Obviously, `Circle.pi` exists independently of any specific instances of the `Circle` class.

You can also access a class variable from a method of a class, through the class name. You do so in the definition of `Circle.area`, where the `area` function makes specific reference to `Circle.pi`. In operation, this has the desired effect; the correct value for `pi` is obtained from the class and used in the calculation:

```
>>> c = Circle(3)
>>> c.area()
28.27431
```

You may object to hardcoding the name of a class inside that class's methods. You can avoid doing so through use of the special __class__ attribute, available to all Python class instances. This attribute returns the class of which the instance is a member, for example:

```
>>> Circle
<class '__main__.Circle'>
>>> c.__class__
<class '__main__.Circle'>
```

The class named `Circle` is represented internally by an abstract data structure, and that data structure is exactly what is obtained from the __class__ attribute of c, an instance of the `Circle` class. This example lets you obtain the value of `Circle.pi` from c without ever explicitly referring to the `Circle` class name:

```
>>> c.__class__.pi
3.14159
```

You could use this code internally in the `area` method to get rid of the explicit reference to the `Circle` class; replace `Circle.pi` with `self.__class__.pi`.

15.4.1 *An oddity with class variables*

There's a bit of an oddity with class variables that can trip you up if you aren't aware of it. When Python is looking up an instance variable, if it can't find an instance variable of that name, it tries to find and return the value in a class variable of the same name. Only if it can't find an appropriate class variable will Python signal an error. Class variables make it efficient to implement default values for instance variables; just create a class variable with the same name and appropriate default value, and avoid the time and memory overhead of initializing that instance variable every time a class instance is created. But this also makes it easy to inadvertently refer to an instance variable rather than a class variable without signaling an error. In this section, I look at how class variables operate in conjunction with the previous example.

First, you can refer to the variable `c.pi`, even though `c` doesn't have an associated instance variable named `pi`. Python first tries to look for such an instance variable; when it can't find an instance variable, Python looks for and finds a class variable `pi` in `Circle`:

```
>>> c = Circle(3)
>>> c.pi
3.14159
```

This result may or may not be what you want. This technique is convenient but can be prone to error, so be careful.

Now, what happens if you attempt to use `c.pi` as a true class variable by changing it from one instance with the intention that all instances should see the change? Again, you use the earlier definition for `Circle`:

```
>>> c1 = Circle(1)
>>> c2 = Circle(2)
>>> c1.pi = 3.14
>>> c1.pi
3.14
>>> c2.pi
3.14159
>>> Circle.pi
3.14159
```

This example doesn't work as it would for a true class variable; `c1` now has its own copy of `pi`, distinct from the `Circle.pi` accessed by `c2`. This happens because the assignment to `c1.pi` *creates* an instance variable in `c1`; it doesn't affect the class variable `Circle.pi` in any way. Subsequent lookups of `c1.pi` return the value in that instance variable, whereas subsequent lookups of `c2.pi` look for an instance variable pi in c2, fail to find it, and resort to returning the value of the class variable `Circle.pi`. If you want to change the value of a class variable, access it through the class name, not through the instance variable `self`.

15.5   *Static methods and class methods*

Python classes can also have methods that correspond explicitly to static methods in a language such as Java. In addition, Python has *class* methods, which are a bit more advanced.

15.5.1   *Static methods*

Just as in Java, you can invoke static methods even though no instance of that class has been created, although you *can* call them by using a class instance. To create a static method, use the `@staticmethod` decorator, as shown here.

Listing 15.1   File circle.py

```
"""circle module: contains the Circle class."""
class Circle:
    """Circle class"""
    all_circles = []
    pi = 3.14159
    def __init__(self, r=1):
        """Create a Circle with the given radius"""
        self.radius = r
        self.__class__.all_circles.append(self)
    def area(self):
        """determine the area of the Circle"""
        return self.__class__.pi * self.radius * self.radius

    @staticmethod
    def total_area():
        """Static method to total the areas of all Circles """
        total = 0
        for c in Circle.all_circles:
            total = total + c.area()
        return total
```

> **Class variable containing list of all circles that have been created**

> **When an instance is initialized, it adds itself to the all_circles list.**

Now interactively type the following:

```
>>> import circle
>>> c1 = circle.Circle(1)
>>> c2 = circle.Circle(2)
>>> circle.Circle.total_area()
15.70795
>>> c2.radius = 3
>>> circle.Circle.total_area()
31.415899999999997
```

Also notice that documentation strings are used. In a real module, you'd probably put in more informative strings, indicating in the class docstring what methods are available and including usage information in the method docstrings:

```
>>> circle.__doc__
'circle module: contains the Circle class.'
>>> circle.Circle.__doc__
'Circle class'
>>> circle.Circle.area.__doc__
'determine the area of the Circle'
```

15.5.2 *Class methods*

Class methods are similar to static methods in that they can be invoked before an object of the class has been instantiated or by using an instance of the class. But class methods are implicitly passed the class they belong to as their first parameter, so you can code them more simply, as here.

Listing 15.2   File circle_cm.py

```
"""circle_cm module: contains the Circle class."""
class Circle:
    """Circle class"""
    all_circles = []                        ◄──┐  Variable containing list of all
    pi = 3.14159                               │  circles that have been created
    def __init__(self, r=1):
        """Create a Circle with the given radius"""
        self.radius = r
        self.__class__.all_circles.append(self)
    def area(self):
        """determine the area of the Circle"""
        return self.__class__.pi * self.radius * self.radius

    @classmethod                    ◄──❶
    def total_area(cls):            ◄──❷
        total = 0
        for c in cls.all_circles:   ◄──┐
            total = total + c.area()   ❸
        return total
>>> import circle_cm
>>> c1 = circle_cm.Circle(1)
>>> c2 = circle_cm.Circle(2)
>>> circle_cm.Circle.total_area()
15.70795
>>> c2.radius = 3
>>> circle_cm.Circle.total_area()
31.415899999999997
```

The @classmethod decorator is used before the method def ❶. The class parameter is traditionally cls ❷. You can use cls instead of self.__class__ ❸.

By using a class method instead of a static method, you don't have to hardcode the class name into total_area. As a result, any subclasses of Circle can still call total_area and refer to their own members, not those in Circle.

> **TRY THIS: CLASS METHODS** Write a class method similar to total_area() that returns the total circumference of all circles.

15.6 *Inheritance*

Inheritance in Python is easier and more flexible than inheritance in compiled languages such as Java and C++ because the dynamic nature of Python doesn't force as many restrictions on the language.

To see how inheritance is used in Python, start with the `Circle` class discussed earlier in this chapter, and generalize. You might want to define an additional class for squares:

```
class Square:
    def __init__(self, side=1):
        self.side = side
```
Length of any
side of square

Now, if you want to use these classes in a drawing program, they must define some sense of where on the drawing surface each instance is. You can do so by defining an x coordinate and a y coordinate in each instance:

```
class Square:
    def __init__(self, side=1, x=0, y=0):
        self.side = side
        self.x = x
        self.y = y
class Circle:
    def __init__(self, radius=1, x=0, y=0):
        self.radius = radius
        self.x = x
        self.y = y
```

This approach works but results in a good deal of repetitive code as you expand the number of shape classes, because you presumably want each shape to have this concept of position. No doubt you know where I'm going here; this situation is a standard one for using inheritance in an object-oriented language. Instead of defining the x and y variables in each shape class, you can abstract them out into a general `Shape` class and have each class defining a specific shape inherit from that general class. In Python, that technique looks like this:

```
class Shape:
    def __init__(self, x, y):
        self.x = x
        self.y = y
class Square(Shape):
    def __init__(self, side=1, x=0, y=0):
        super().__init__(x, y)
        self.side = side
class Circle(Shape):
    def __init__(self, r=1, x=0, y=0):
        super().__init__(x, y)
        self.radius = r
```
Says Square inherits
from Shape

Must call __init__ method
of Shape

Says Circle inherits
from Shape

Must call __init__ method
of Shape

There are (generally) two requirements in using an inherited class in Python, both of which you can see in the bolded code in the `Circle` and `Square` classes. The first requirement is defining the inheritance hierarchy, which you do by giving the classes inherited from, in parentheses, immediately after the name of the class being defined with the `class` keyword. In the previous code, `Circle` and `Square` both inherit from `Shape`. The second and more subtle element is the necessity to explicitly call the `__init__` method of inherited classes. Python doesn't automatically do this for you, but you can use the `super` function to have Python figure out which inherited class to use. This task is accomplished in the example code by the `super().__init__(x,y)` lines. This code calls the `Shape` initialization function with the instance being initialized and the appropriate arguments. Otherwise, in the example, instances of `Circle` and `Square` wouldn't have their x and y instance variables set.

Instead of using `super`, you could call `Shape`'s `__init__` by explicitly naming the inherited class using `Shape.__init__(self, x, y)`, which would also call the `Shape` initialization function with the instance being initialized. This technique wouldn't be as flexible in the long run because it hardcodes the inherited class's name, which could be a problem later if the design and the inheritance hierarchy change. On the other hand, the use of `super` can be tricky in more complex cases. Because the two methods don't exactly mix well, clearly document whichever approach you use in your code.

Inheritance also comes into effect when you attempt to use a method that isn't defined in the base classes but is defined in the superclass. To see this effect, define another method in the `Shape` class called `move`, which moves a shape by a given displacement. This method modifies the x and y coordinates of the shape by an amount determined by arguments to the method. The definition for `Shape` now becomes

```
class Shape:
    def __init__(self, x, y):
        self.x = x
        self.y = y
    def move(self, delta_x, delta_y):
        self.x = self.x + delta_x
        self.y = self.y + delta_y
```

If you enter this definition for `Shape` and the previous definitions for `Circle` and `Square`, you can engage in the following interactive session:

```
>>> c = Circle(1)
>>> c.move(3, 4)
>>> c.x
3
>>> c.y
4
```

If you try this code in an interactive session, be sure to reenter the `Circle` class after the redefinition of the `Shape` class.

The `Circle` class in the example didn't define a `move` method immediately within itself, but because it inherits from a class that implements `move`, all instances of `Circle` can make use of `move`. In more traditional OOP terms, you could say that all

Python methods are virtual—that is, if a method doesn't exist in the current class, the list of superclasses is searched for the method, and the first one found is used.

> **TRY THIS: INHERITANCE** Rewrite the code for a `Rectangle` class to inherit from `Shape`. Because squares and rectangles are related, would it make sense to inherit one from the other? If so, which would be the base class, and which would inherit?
>
> How would you write the code to add an `area()` method for the `Square` class? Should the `area` method be moved into the base `Shape` class and inherited by circle, square, and rectangle? If so, what issues would result?

15.7 *Inheritance with class and instance variables*

Inheritance allows an instance to inherit attributes of the class. Instance variables are associated with object instances, and only one instance variable of a given name exists for a given instance.

Consider the following example. Using these class definitions,

```
class P:
    z = "Hello"
    def set_p(self):
        self.x = "Class P"
    def print_p(self):
        print(self.x)
class C(P):
    def set_c(self):
        self.x = "Class C"
    def print_c(self):
        print(self.x)
```

execute the following code:

```
>>> c = C()
>>> c.set_p()
>>> c.print_p()
Class P
>>> c.print_c()
Class P
>>> c.set_c()
>>> c.print_c()
Class C
>>> c.print_p()
Class C
```

The object c in this example is an instance of class C. C inherits from P but c doesn't inherit from some invisible instance of class P. It inherits methods and class variables directly from P. Because there is only one instance (c), any reference to the instance variable x in a method invocation on c must refer to c.x. This is true regardless of which class defines the method being invoked on c. As you can see, when they're invoked on c, both set_p and print_p, defined in class P, and refer to the same variable, which is referred to by set_c and print_c when they're invoked on c.

In general, this behavior is what is desired for instance variables, because it makes sense that references to instance variables of the same name should refer to the same variable. Occasionally, somewhat different behavior is desired, which you can achieve by using private variables (see section 15.9).

Class variables are inherited, but you should take care to avoid name clashes and be aware of a generalization of the behavior you saw in the subsection on class variables. In the example, a class variable z is defined for the superclass P and can be accessed in three ways: through the instance c, through the derived class C, or directly through the superclass P:

```
>>> c.z; C.z; P.z
'Hello'
'Hello'
'Hello'
```

But if you try setting the class variable z through the class C, a new class variable is created for the class C. This result has no effect on P's class variable itself (as accessed through P). But future accesses through the class C or its instance c will see this new variable rather than the original:

```
>>> C.z = "Bonjour"
>>> c.z; C.z; P.z
'Bonjour'
'Bonjour'
'Hello'
```

Similarly, if you try setting z through the instance c, a new instance variable is created, and you end up with three different variables:

```
>>> c.z = "Ciao"
>>> c.z; C.z; P.z
'Ciao'
'Bonjour'
'Hello'
```

15.8 Recap: Basics of Python classes

The points I've discussed so far are the basics of using classes and objects in Python. Before I go any farther, I'll bring the basics together in a single example. In this section, you create a couple of classes with the features discussed earlier, and then you see how those features behave.

First, create a base class:

```
class Shape:
    def __init__(self, x, y):
        self.x = x
        self.y = y
    def move(self, delta_x, delta_y):
        self.x = self.x + delta_x
        self.y = self.y + delta_y
```

__init__ method takes instance (self) and two parameters

Instance variables accessed through self.

move method takes instance (self) and two parameters

Instance variable set inside move method

Next, create a subclass that inherits from the base class `Shape`:

Circle class inherits from Shape class

Circle's __init__ takes instance (self) and 3 parameters, all with defaults

pi and all_circles are class variables for Circle.

total_area is a class method and takes the class itself (cls) as parameter.

Circle's __init__ uses super() to call Shape's __init__

In the __init__ method the instance adds itself to all_circles list

Uses the cls parameter to access static method circle_area

circle_area is a static method that doesn't get self or cls as parameters.

Accesses class variable pi; could also use __class__.pi

```python
class Circle(Shape):
    pi = 3.14159
    all_circles = []
    def __init__(self, r=1, x=0, y=0):
        super().__init__(x, y)
        self.radius = r
        all_circles.append(self)
    @classmethod
    def total_area(cls):
        area = 0
        for circle in cls.all_circles:
            area += cls.circle_area(circle.radius)
        return area
    @staticmethod
    def circle_area(radius):
        return Circle.pi * radius * radius
```

Now you can create some instances of the `Circle` class and put them through their paces. Because `Circle`'s `__init__` method has default parameters, you can create a `Circle` without giving any parameters:

```
>>> c1 = Circle()
>>> c1.radius, c1.x, c1.y
(1, 0, 0)
```

If you do give parameters, they are used to set the instance's values:

```
>>> c2 = Circle(2, 1, 1)
>>> c2.radius, c2.x, c2.y
(2, 1, 1)
```

If you call the `move()` method, Python doesn't find a `move()` in the `Circle` class, so it moves up the inheritance hierarchy and uses `Shape`'s `move()` method:

```
>>> c2.move(2, 2)
>>> c2.radius, c2.x, c2.y
(2, 3, 3)
```

Also, because part of what the `__init__` method does is add each instance to a list that is a class variable, you get the `Circle` instances:

```
>>> Circle.all_circles
[<__main__.Circle object at 0x7fa88835e9e8>, <__main__.Circle object at
    0x7fa88835eb00>]
>>> [c1, c2]
[<__main__.Circle object at 0x7fa88835e9e8>, <__main__.Circle object at
    0x7fa88835eb00>]
```

You can also call the `Circle` class's `total_area()` class method, either through the class itself or through an instance:

```
>>> Circle.total_area()
15.70795
>>> c2.total_area()
15.70795
```

Finally, you can call the static method `circle_area()`, again either via the class itself or an instance. As a static method, `circle_area` doesn't get passed the instance or the class, and it behaves more like an independent function that's inside the class's namespace. In fact, quite often, static methods are used to bundle utility functions with a class:

```
>>> Circle.circle_area(c1.radius)
3.14159
>>> c1.circle_area(c1.radius)
3.14159
```

These examples show the basic behavior of classes in Python. Now that you've got the basics of classes down, you can move on to more advanced topics.

15.9 *Private variables and private methods*

A *private variable* or *private method* is one that can't be seen outside the methods of the class in which it's defined. Private variables and methods are useful for two reasons: They enhance security and reliability by selectively denying access to important or delicate parts of an object's implementation, and they prevent name clashes that can arise from the use of inheritance. A class may define a private variable and inherit from a class that defines a private variable of the same name, but this doesn't cause a problem, because the fact that the variables are private ensures that separate copies of them are kept. Private variables make it easier to read code, because they explicitly indicate what's used only internally in a class. Anything else is the class's interface.

Most languages that define private variables do so through the use of the keyword "private" or something similar. The convention in Python is simpler, and it also makes it easier to immediately see what is private and what isn't. Any method or instance variable whose name begins—but doesn't end—with a *double underscore (__)* is private; anything else isn't private.

As an example, consider the following class definition:

```
class Mine:
    def __init__(self):
        self.x = 2
        self.__y = 3          Defines __y as private by using
    def print_y(self):        leading double underscores
        print(self.__y)
```

Using this definition, create an instance of the class:

```
>>> m = Mine()
```

x isn't a private variable, so it's directly accessible:

```
>>> print(m.x)
2
```

__y is a private variable. Trying to access it directly raises an error:

```
>>> print(m.__y)
Traceback (innermost last):
  File "<stdin>", line 1, in ?
AttributeError: 'Mine' object has no attribute '__y'
```

The print_y method isn't private, and because it's in the Mine class, it can access __y and print it:

```
>>> m.print_y()
3
```

Finally, you should note that the mechanism used to provide privacy *mangles* the name of private variables and private methods when the code is compiled to bytecode. What specifically happens is that _classname is prepended to the variable name:

```
>>> dir(m)
['_Mine__y', 'x', ...]
```

The purpose is to prevent any accidental accesses. If someone wanted to, he could deliberately simulate the mangling and access the value. But performing the mangling in this easily readable form makes debugging easy.

> **TRY THIS: PRIVATE INSTANCE VARIABLES**   Modify the Rectangle class's code to make the dimension variables private. What restriction will this modification impose on using the class?

15.10 *Using @property for more flexible instance variables*

Python allows you as the programmer to access instance variables directly, without the extra machinery of the getter and setter methods often used in Java and other object-oriented languages. This lack of getters and setters makes writing Python classes cleaner and easier, but in some situations, using getter and setter methods can be handy. Suppose that you want a value before you put it into an instance variable or where it would be handy to figure out an attribute's value on the fly. In both cases, getter and setter methods would do the job, but at the cost of losing Python's easy instance-variable access.

The answer is to use a property. A *property* combines the ability to pass access to an instance variable through methods like getters and setters and the straightforward access to instance variables through dot notation.

To create a property, you use the property decorator with a method that has the property's name:

```
class Temperature:
    def __init__(self):
        self._temp_fahr = 0
    @property
    def temp(self):
        return (self._temp_fahr - 32) * 5 / 9
```

Without a setter, such a property is read-only. To change the property, you need to add a setter:

```
    @temp.setter
    def temp(self, new_temp):
        self._temp_fahr = new_temp * 9 / 5 + 32
```

Now you can use standard dot notation to both get and set the property `temp`. Notice that the name of the method remains the same, but the decorator changes to the property name (`temp`, in this case), plus `.setter` indicates that a setter for the `temp` property is being defined:

```
>>> t = Temperature()
>>> t._temp_fahr
0
>>> t.temp
-17.77777777777778

>>> t.temp = 34          ◄────┐
>>> t._temp_fahr            ❶
93.2

>>> t.temp      ◄────┐
34.0              ❷
```

The `0` in `_temp_fahr` is converted to centigrade before it's returned ❶. The `34` is converted back to Fahrenheit by the setter ❷.

One big advantage of Python's ability to add properties is that you can do initial development with plain-old instance variables and then seamlessly change to properties whenever and wherever you need to without changing any client code. The access is still the same, using dot notation.

> **TRY THIS: PROPERTIES** Update the dimensions of the `Rectangle` class to be properties with getters and setters that don't allow negative sizes.

15.11 *Scoping rules and namespaces for class instances*

Now you have all the pieces to put together a picture of the scoping rules and namespaces for a class instance.

When you're in a method of a class, you have direct access to the *local namespace* (parameters and variables declared in the method), the *global namespace* (functions and variables declared at the module level), and the *built-in namespace* (built-in functions and built-in exceptions). These three namespaces are searched in the following order: local, global, and built-in (see figure 15.1).

You also have access through the `self` variable to the *instance's namespace* (instance variables, private instance variables, and superclass instance variables), its *class's namespace* (methods, class variables, private methods, and private class variables), and its *superclass's namespace* (superclass methods and superclass class variables). These three namespaces are searched in the order instance, class, and then superclass (see figure 15.2).

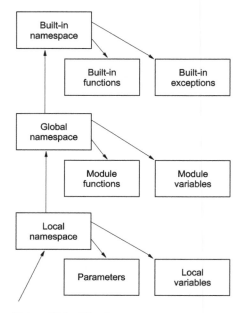

Figure 15.1   Direct namespaces

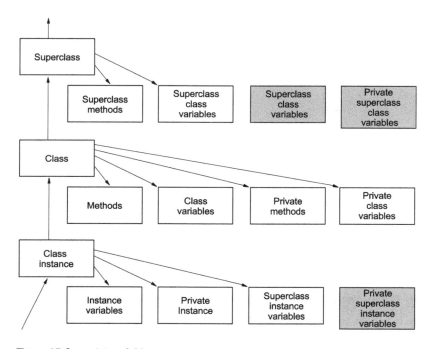

Figure 15.2 `self` **variable namespaces**

Private superclass instance variables, private superclass methods, and private superclass class variables can't be accessed by using `self`. A class is able to hide these names from its children.

The module in listing 15.3 puts these two examples together to concretely demonstrate what can be accessed from within a method.

Listing 15.3   File cs.py

```
"""cs module: class scope demonstration module."""
mv ="module variable: mv"
def mf():
    return "module function (can be used like a class method in " \
            "other languages): mf()"
class SC:
    scv = "superclass class variable: self.scv"
    __pscv = "private superclass class variable: no access"
    def __init__(self):
        self.siv = "superclass instance variable: self.siv " \
                    "(but use SC.siv for assignment)"
        self.__psiv = "private superclass instance variable: " \
                        "no access"
    def sm(self):
        return "superclass method: self.sm()"
    def __spm(self):
        return "superclass private method: no access"
class C(SC):
    cv = "class variable: self.cv (but use C.cv for assignment)"
    __pcv = "class private variable: self.__pcv (but use C.__pcv " \
            "for assignment)"
    def __init__(self):
        SC.__init__(self)
        self.__piv = "private instance variable: self.__piv"
    def m2(self):
        return "method: self.m2()"
    def __pm(self):
        return "private method: self.__pm()"
    def m(self, p="parameter: p"):
        lv = "local variable: lv"
        self.iv = "instance variable: self.xi"
        print("Access local, global and built-in " \
                "namespaces directly")
        print("local namespace:", list(locals().keys()))    ⟵⎯┤ Parameter
        print(p)
                                                              ⟵⎯┤ Local variable
        print(lv)
        print("global namespace:", list(globals().keys()))

        print(mv)            ⟵⎯┐ Module variable
                                                              ⟵⎯┤ Module function
        print(mf())
        print("Access instance, class, and superclass namespaces " \


                "through 'self'")
        print("Instance namespace:",dir(self))
```

```
print(self.iv)                          ← Instance variable

print(self.__piv)                       ← Private instance variable

print(self.siv)                         ← Superclass instance
print("Class namespace:",dir(C))          variable
print(self.cv)                          ← Class variable

print(self.m2())                        ← Method

print(self.__pcv)                       ← Private class variable

print(self.__pm())                      ← Private method
print("Superclass namespace:",dir(SC))
print(self.sm())                        ← Superclass method
                                          Superclass class variable
print(self.scv)                         ← through instance
```

This output is considerable, so we'll look at it in pieces.

In the first part, class C's method m's local namespace contains the parameters self (which is the instance variable) and p along with the local variable lv (all of which can be accessed directly):

```
>>> import cs
>>> c = cs.C()
>>> c.m()
Access local, global and built-in namespaces directly
local namespace: ['lv', 'p', 'self']
parameter: p
local variable: lv
```

Next, method m's global namespace contains the module variable mv and the module function mf (which, as described in a previous section, you can use to provide a class method functionality). There are also the classes defined in the module (the class C and the superclass SC). All these classes can be directly accessed:

```
global namespace: ['C', 'mf', '__builtins__', '__file__', '__package__',
    'mv', 'SC', '__name__', '__doc__']
module variable: mv
module function (can be used like a class method in other languages): mf()
```

Instance C's namespace contains instance variable iv and the superclass's instance variable siv (which, as described in a previous section, is no different from the regular instance variable). It also has the mangled name of private instance variable __piv (which you can access through self) and the mangled name of the superclass's private instance variable __psiv (which you can't access):

```
Access instance, class, and superclass namespaces through 'self'
Instance namespace: ['_C__pcv', '_C__piv', '_C__pm', '_SC__pscv',
    '_SC__psiv', '_SC__spm', '__class__', '__delattr__', '__dict__',
    '__doc__', '__eq__', '__format__', '__ge__', '__getattribute__',
    '__gt__', '__hash__', '__init__', '__le__', '__lt__', '__module__',
```

```
           '__ne__', '__new__', '__reduce__', '__reduce_ex__', '__repr__',
           '__setattr__', '__sizeof__', '__str__', '__subclasshook__',
           '__weakref__', 'cv', 'iv', 'm', 'm2', 'scv', 'siv', 'sm']
instance variable: self.xi
private instance variable: self.__piv
superclass instance variable: self.siv (but use SC.siv for assignment)
```

Class C's namespace contains the class variable cv and the mangled name of the private class variable __pcv. Both can be accessed through self, but to assign to them, you need to use class C. Class C also has the class's two methods m and m2, along with the mangled name of the private method __pm (which can be accessed through self):

```
Class namespace: ['_C__pcv', '_C__pm', '_SC__pscv', '_SC__spm', '__class__',
           '__delattr__', '__dict__', '__doc__', '__eq__', '__format__', '__ge__',
           '__getattribute__', '__gt__', '__hash__', '__init__', '__le__',
           '__lt__', '__module__', '__ne__', '__new__', '__reduce__',
           '__reduce_ex__', '__repr__', '__setattr__', '__sizeof__', '__str__',
           '__subclasshook__', '__weakref__', 'cv', 'm', 'm2', 'scv', 'sm']
class variable: self.cv (but use C.cv for assignment)
method: self.m2()
class private variable: self.__pcv (but use C.__pcv for assignment)
private method: self.__pm()
```

Finally, superclass SC's namespace contains superclass class variable scv (which can be accessed through self, but to assign to it, you need to use the superclass SC) and superclass method sm. It also contains the mangled names of private superclass method __spm and private superclass class variable __pscv, neither of which can be accessed through self:

```
Superclass namespace: ['_SC__pscv', '_SC__spm', '__class__', '__delattr__',
           '__dict__', '__doc__', '__eq__', '__format__', '__ge__',
           '__getattribute__', '__gt__', '__hash__', '__init__', '__le__',
           '__lt__', '__module__', '__ne__', '__new__', '__reduce__',
           '__reduce_ex__', '__repr__', '__setattr__', '__sizeof__', '__str__',
           '__subclasshook__', '__weakref__', 'scv', 'sm']
superclass method: self.sm()
superclass class variable: self.scv
```

This example is a rather full one to decipher at first. You can use it as a reference or a base for your own exploration. As with most other concepts in Python, you can build a solid understanding of what's going on by playing around with a few simplified examples.

15.12 *Destructors and memory management*

You've already seen class initializers (the __init__ methods). A destructor can be defined for a class as well. But unlike in C++, creating and calling a destructor isn't necessary to ensure that the memory used by your instance is freed. Python provides automatic memory management through a reference-counting mechanism. That is, it keeps track of the number of references to your instance; when this number reaches zero, the memory used by your instance is reclaimed, and any Python objects refer-enced by your instance have their reference counts decremented by one. *You almost never need to define a destructor.*

You may occasionally encounter a situation in which you need to deallocate an external resource explicitly when an object is removed. In such a situation, the best practice is to use a context manager, as discussed in chapter 14. As mentioned there, you can use the `contextlib` module from the standard library to create a custom context manager for your situation.

15.13 *Multiple inheritance*

Compiled languages place severe restrictions on the use of *multiple inheritance*—the ability of objects to inherit data and behavior from more than one parent class. The rules for using multiple inheritance in C++, for example, are so complex that many people avoid using it. In Java, multiple inheritance is disallowed, although Java does have the interface mechanism.

Python places no such restrictions on multiple inheritance. A class can inherit from any number of parent classes in the same way that it can inherit from a single parent class. In the simplest case, none of the involved classes, including those inherited indi-rectly through a parent class, contains instance variables or methods of the same name. In such a case, the inheriting class behaves like a synthesis of its own definitions and all of its ancestors' definitions. Suppose that class A inherits from classes B, C, and D; class B inherits from classes E and F; and class D inherits from class G (see figure 15.3). Also suppose that none of these classes shares method names. In this case, an instance of class A can be used as though it were an instance of any of the classes B–G, as well as A; an instance of class B can be used as though it were an instance of class E or F as well as class B; and an instance of class D can be used as though it were an instance of class G as well as class D. In terms of code, the class definitions look like this:

```
class E:
    . . .
class F:
    . . .
class G:
    . . .
class D(G):
    . . .
class C:
    . . .
class B(E, F):
    . . .
class A(B, C, D):
    . . .
```

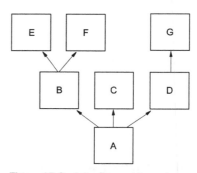

Figure 15.3   Inheritance hierarchy

The situation is more complex when some of the classes share method names, because Python must decide which of the identical names is the correct one. Suppose that you want to resolve a method invocation a.f() on an instance a of class A, where f isn't defined in A but is defined in all of F, C, and G. Which of the various methods will be invoked?

The answer lies in the order in which Python searches base classes when looking for a method not defined in the original class on which the method was invoked. In the simplest cases, Python looks through the base classes of the original class in left-to-right order, but it always looks through all of the ancestor classes of a base class before looking in the next base class. In attempting to execute a.f(), the search goes something like this:

1. Python first looks in the class of the invoking object, class A.
2. Because A doesn't define a method f, Python starts looking in the base classes of A. The first base class of A is B, so Python starts looking in B.
3. Because B doesn't define a method f, Python continues its search of B by looking in the base classes of B. It starts by looking in the first base class of B, class E.
4. E doesn't define a method f and also has no base classes, so there's no more searching to be done in E. Python goes back to class B and looks in the next base class of B, class F.

Class F does contain a method f, and because it was the first method found with the given name, it's the method used. The methods called f in classes C and G are ignored.

Using internal logic like this isn't likely to lead to the most readable or maintainable of programs, of course. And with more complex hierarchies, other factors come into play to make sure that no class is searched twice and to support cooperative calls to super.

But this hierarchy is probably more complex than you'd expect to see in practice. If you stick to the more standard uses of multiple inheritance, as in the creation of mixin or addin classes, you can easily keep things readable and avoid name clashes.

Some people have a strong conviction that multiple inheritance is a bad thing. It can certainly be misused, and nothing in Python forces you to use it. One of the biggest dangers seems to be creating inheritance hierarchies that are too deep, and multiple inheritance can sometimes be used to help keep this problem from happening. That issue is beyond the scope of this book. The example I use here only illustrates how multiple inheritance works in Python and doesn't attempt to explain the use cases for it (such as in mixin or addin classes).

LAB 15: HTML CLASSES In this lab, you create classes to represent an HTML document. To keep things simple, assume that each element can contain only text and one subelement. So the <html> element contains only a <body> element, and the <body> element contains (optional) text and a <p> element that contains only text.

The key feature to implement is the __str__() method, which in turn calls its subelement's __str__() method, so that the entire document is returned when the str() function is called on an <html> element. You can assume that any text comes before the subelement.

Here's example output from using the classes:

```
para = p(text="this is some body text")
doc_body = body(text="This is the body", subelement=para)
doc = html(subelement=doc_body)
print(doc)

<html>
<body>
This is the body
<p>
this is some body text
</p>
</body>
</html>
```

Summary

- Defining a class in effect creates a new data type.
- __init__ is used to initialize data when a new instance of a class is created, but it isn't a constructor.
- The self parameter refers to the current instance of the class and is passed as the first parameter to methods of a class.
- Static methods can be called without creating an instance of the class, so they don't receive a self parameter.
- Class methods are passed a cls parameter, which is a reference to the class, instead of self.
- All Python methods are virtual. That is, if a method isn't overridden in the sub-class or private to the superclass, it's accessible by all subclasses.
- Class variables are inherited from superclasses unless they begin with two underscores (__), in which case they're private and can't be seen by subclasses. Methods can be made private in the same way.
- Properties let you have attributes with defined getter and setter methods, but they still behave like plain instance attributes.
- Python allows multiple inheritance, which is often used with mixin classes.

Regular expressions

This chapter covers

- Understanding regular expressions
- Creating regular expressions with special characters
- Using raw strings in regular expressions
- Extracting matched text from strings
- Substituting text with regular expressions

Some might wonder why I'm discussing regular expressions in this book at all. Regular expressions are implemented by a single Python module and are advanced enough that they don't even come as part of the standard library in languages like C or Java. But if you're using Python, you're probably doing text parsing; if you're doing that, regular expressions are too useful to be ignored. If you've used Perl, Tcl, or Linux/UNIX, you may be familiar with regular expressions; if not, this chapter goes into them in some detail.

16.1   *What is a regular expression?*

A *regular expression* (regex) is a way of recognizing and often extracting data from certain patterns of text. A regex that recognizes a piece of text or a string is said to *match* that text or string. A regex is defined by a string in which certain characters (the so-called *metacharacters*) can have a special meaning, which enables a single regex to match many different specific strings.

It's easier to understand this through example than through explanation. Here's a program with a regular expression that counts how many lines in a text file contain the word *hello*. A line that contains *hello* more than once is counted only once:

```
import re
regexp = re.compile("hello")
count = 0
file = open("textfile", 'r')
for line in file.readlines():
    if regexp.search(line):
        count = count + 1
file.close()
print(count)
```

The program starts by importing the Python regular expression module, called re. Then it takes the text string "hello" as a *textual regular expression* and compiles it into a *compiled regular expression*, using the re.compile function. This compilation isn't strictly necessary, but compiled regular expressions can significantly increase a program's speed, so they're almost always used in programs that process large amounts of text.

What can the regex compiled from "hello" be used for? You can use it to recognize other instances of the word "hello" within another string; in other words, you can use it to determine whether another string contains "hello" as a substring. This task is accomplished by the search method, which returns None if the regular expression isn't found in the string argument; Python interprets None as false in a Boolean context. If the regular expression is found in the string, Python returns a special object that you can use to determine various things about the match (such as where in the string it occurred). I discuss this topic later.

16.2   *Regular expressions with special characters*

The previous example has a small flaw: It counts how many lines contain "hello" but ignores lines that contain "Hello" because it doesn't take capitalization into account.

One way to solve this problem would be to use two regular expressions—one for "hello" and one for "Hello"—and test each against every line. A better way is to use the more advanced features of regular expressions. For the second line in the program, substitute

```
regexp = re.compile("hello|Hello")
```

This regular expression uses the vertical-bar special character |. A *special character* is a character in a regex that isn't interpreted as itself; it has some special meaning. | means *or*, so the regular expression matches "hello" *or* "Hello".

Another way of solving this problem is to use

```
regexp = re.compile("(h|H)ello")
```

In addition to using |, this regular expression uses the *parentheses* special characters to group things, which in this case means that the | chooses between a small or capital *H*. The resulting regex matches either an *h* or an *H*, followed by *ello*.

Another way to perform the match is

```
regexp = re.compile("[hH]ello")
```

The special characters [and] take a string of characters between them and match any single character in that string. There's a special shorthand to denote ranges of characters in [and]; [a-z] match a single character between *a* and *z*, [0-9A-Z] match any digit or any uppercase character, and so forth. Sometimes, you may want to include a real hyphen in the [], in which case you should put it as the first character to avoid defining a range; [-012] match a hyphen, a *0*, a *1*, or a *2*, and nothing else.

Quite a few special characters are available in Python regular expressions, and describing all of the subtleties of using them in regular expressions is beyond the scope of this book. A complete list of the special characters available in Python regular expressions, as well as descriptions of what they mean, is in the online documentation of the regular expression re module in the standard library. For the remainder of this chapter, I describe the special characters I use as they appear.

> **QUICK CHECK: SPECIAL CHARACTERS IN REGULAR EXPRESSIONS** What regular expression would you use to match strings that represent the numbers -5 through 5?
>
> What regular expression would you use to match a hexadecimal digit? Assume that allowed hexadecimal digits are 1, 2, 3, 4, 5, 6, 7, 8, 9, 0, A, a, B, b, C, c, D, d, E, e, F, and f.

16.3 *Regular expressions and raw strings*

The functions that compile regular expressions, or search for matches to regular expressions, understand that certain character sequences in strings have special meanings in the context of regular expressions. regex functions understand that \n represents a newline character, for example. But if you use normal Python strings as regular expressions, the regex functions typically never see such special sequences, because many of these sequences also possess a special meaning in normal strings. \n, for example, also means newline in the context of a normal Python string, and Python automatically replaces the string sequence \n with a newline character before the regex function ever sees that sequence. The regex function, as a result, compiles strings with embedded newline characters—not with embedded \n sequences.

In the case of \n, this situation makes no difference because regex functions interpret a newline character as exactly that and do the expected thing: attempt to match the character with another newline character in the text being searched.

Now look at another special sequence, \\, which represents a *single* backslash to regular expressions. Assume that you want to search text for an occurrence of the string "\ten". Because you know that you have to represent a backslash as a double backslash, you might try

```
regexp = re.compile("\\ten")
```

This example compiles without complaining, but it's wrong. The problem is that \\ also means a single backslash in Python strings. Before re.compile is invoked, Python interprets the string you typed as meaning \ten, which is what is passed to re.compile. In the context of regular expressions, \t means *tab*, so your compiled regular expression searches for a tab character followed by the two characters *en*.

To fix this problem while using regular Python strings, you need four backslashes. Python interprets the first two backslashes as a special sequence representing a single backslash, and likewise for the second pair of backslashes, resulting in two *actual* backslashes in the Python string. Then that string is passed in to re.compile, which interprets the two actual backslashes as a regex special sequence representing a single backslash. Your code looks like this:

```
regexp = re.compile("\\\\ten")
```

That seems confusing, and it's why Python has a way of defining strings that doesn't apply the normal Python rules to special characters. Strings defined this way are called *raw strings*.

16.3.1 *Raw strings to the rescue*

A raw string looks similar to a normal string except that it has a leading *r* character immediately preceding the initial quotation mark of the string. Here are some raw strings:

```
r"Hello"
r"""\tTo be\n\tor not to be"""
r'Goodbye'
r'''12345'''
```

As you can see, you can use raw strings with either the single or double quotation marks and with the regular or triple-quoting convention. You can also use a leading *R* instead of *r* if you want to. No matter how you do it, raw-string notation can be taken as an instruction to Python saying "Don't process special sequences in this string." In the previous examples, all the raw strings are equivalent to their normal string counterparts except the second example, in which the \t and \n sequences aren't interpreted as tabs or newlines but are left as two-string character sequences begin-ning with a backslash.

Raw strings aren't different types of strings. They represent a different way of *defin-ing* strings. It's easy to see what's happening by running a few examples interactively:

```
>>> r"Hello" == "Hello"
True
>>> r"\the" == "\\the"
True
>>> r"\the" == "\the"
False
>>> print(r"\the")
\the
>>> print("\the")
    he
```

Using raw strings with regular expressions means that you don't need to worry about any funny interactions between string special sequences and regex special sequences. You use the regex special sequences. Then the previous regex example becomes

```
regexp = re.compile(r"\\ten")
```

which works as expected. The compiled regex looks for a single backslash followed by the letters *ten*.

You should get into the habit of using raw strings whenever defining regular expressions, and you'll do so for the remainder of this chapter.

16.4　*Extracting matched text from strings*

One of the most common uses of regular expressions is to perform simple pattern-based parsing on text. This task is something you should know how to do, and it's also a good way to learn more regex special characters.

Assume that you have a list of people and phone numbers in a text file. Each line of the file looks like this:

```
surname, firstname middlename: phonenumber
```

You have a surname followed by a comma and space, followed by a first name, fol-lowed by a space, followed by a middle name, followed by colon and a space, followed by a phone number.

But to make things complicated, a middle name may not exist, and a phone num-ber may not have an area code. (It might be 800-123-4567 or 123-4567.) You *could* write code to explicitly parse data out from such a line, but that job would be tedious and error-prone. Regular expressions provide a simpler answer.

Start by coming up with a regex that matches lines of the given form. The next few paragraphs throw quite a few special characters at you. Don't worry if you don't get them all on the first read; as long as you understand the gist of things, that's all right.

For simplicity's sake, assume that first names, surnames, and middle names consist of letters and possibly hyphens. You can use the [] special characters discussed in the previous section to define a pattern that defines only name characters:

`[-a-zA-z]`

This pattern matches a single hyphen, a single lowercase letter, or a single uppercase letter.

To match a full name (such as McDonald), you need to repeat this pattern. The + metacharacter repeats whatever comes before it one or more times as necessary to match the string being processed. So the pattern

`[-a-zA-Z]+`

matches a single name, such as Kenneth or McDonald or Perkin-Elmer. It also matches some strings that aren't names, such as — or -a-b-c-, but that's all right for purposes of this example.

Now, what about the phone number? The special sequence \d matches any digit, and a hyphen outside [] is a normal hyphen. A good pattern to match the phone number is

`\d\d\d-\d\d\d-\d\d\d\d`

That's three digits followed by a hyphen, followed by three digits, followed by a hyphen, followed by four digits. This pattern matches only phone numbers with an area code, and your list may contain numbers that don't have one. The best solution is to enclose the area-code part of the pattern in (); group it; and follow that group with a ? special character, which says that the thing coming immediately before the ? is optional:

`(\d\d\d-)?\d\d\d-\d\d\d\d`

This pattern matches a phone number that may or may not contain an area code. You can use the same sort of trick to account for the fact that some of the people in your list have middle names (or initials) included and others don't. (To do so, make the middle name optional by using grouping and the ? special character.)

You can also use {} to indicate the number of times that a pattern should repeat, so for the phone-number examples above, you could use:

`(\d{3}-)?\d{3}-\d{4}`

This pattern also means an optional group of three digits plus a hyphen, three digits followed by a hyphen, and then four digits.

Commas, colons, and spaces don't have any special meanings in regular expressions; they mean themselves.

Putting everything together, you come up with a pattern that looks like this:

`[-a-zA-Z]+, [-a-zA-Z]+( [-a-zA-Z]+)?: (\d{3}-)?\d{3}-\d{4}`

A real pattern probably would be a bit more complex, because you wouldn't assume that there's exactly one space after the comma, exactly one space after the first and middle names, and exactly one space after the colon. But that's easy to add later.

The problem is that, whereas the above pattern lets you check to see whether a line has the anticipated format, you can't extract any data yet. All you can do is write a program like this:

```
import re
regexp = re.compile(r"[-a-zA-Z]+,"          Last name
                                              and comma
                    r" [-a-zA-Z]+"                         First name
                    r"( [-a-zA-Z]+)?"                              Optional
                    r": (\d{3}-)?\d{3}-\d{4}"                      middle name
                    )
file = open("textfile", 'r')                  Colon and
for line in file.readlines():                 phone number
    if regexp.search(line):
        print("Yeah, I found a line with a name and number. So what?")
file.close()
```

Notice that you've split your regex pattern, using the fact that Python implicitly concatenates any set of strings separated by whitespace. As your pattern grows, this technique can be a great aid in keeping the pattern maintainable and understandable. It also solves the problem with the line length possibly increasing beyond the right edge of the screen.

Fortunately, you can use regular expressions to extract data from patterns, as well as to see whether the patterns exist. The first step is to group each subpattern corresponding to a piece of data you want to extract by using the () special characters. Then give each subpattern a unique name with the special sequence ?P<name>, like this:

```
(?P<last>[-a-zA-Z]+), (?P<first>[-a-zA-Z]+)( (?P<middle>([-a-zA-Z]+)))?:
(?P<phone>(\d{3}-)?\d{3}-\d{4}
```

(Please note that you should enter these lines as a single line, with no line breaks. Due to space constraints, the code can't be represented here in that manner.)

There's an obvious point of confusion here: The question marks in ?P<...> and the question-mark special characters indicating that the middle name and area code are optional have nothing to do with one another. It's an unfortunate semi-coincidence that they happen to be the same character.

Now that you've named the elements of the pattern, you can extract the matches for those elements by using the group method. You can do so because when the search function returns a successful match, it doesn't return just a truth value; it also returns a data structure that records what was matched. You can write a simple program to extract names and phone numbers from your list and print them out again, as follows:

```
import re
regexp = re.compile(r"(?P<last>[-a-zA-Z]+),"          Last name
                                                        and comma
First      r" (?P<first>[-a-zA-Z]+)"                              Optional
name       r"( (?P<middle>([-a-zA-Z]+)))?"                        middle name
```

```
             r": (?P<phone>(\(\d{3}-)?\d{3}-\d{4})"          ◄──┐ Colon and
             )                                                   │ phone number
file = open("textfile", 'r')
for line in file.readlines():
    result = regexp.search(line)
    if result == None:
        print("Oops, I don't think this is a record")
    else:
        lastname = result.group('last')
        firstname = result.group('first')
        middlename = result.group('middle')
        if middlename == None:
            middlename = ""
        phonenumber = result.group('phone')
    print('Name:', firstname, middlename, lastname,' Number:', phonenumber)
file.close()
```

There are some points of interest here:

- You can find out whether a match succeeded by checking the value returned by search. If the value is None, the match failed; otherwise, the match succeeded, and you can extract information from the object returned by search.
- group is used to extract whatever data matched your named subpatterns. You pass in the name of the subpattern you're interested in.
- Because the middle subpattern is optional, you can't count on it to have a value, even if the match as a whole is successful. If the match succeeds, but the match for the middle name doesn't, using group to access the data associated with the middle subpattern returns the value None.
- Part of the phone number is optional, but part isn't. If the match succeeds, the phone subpattern must have some associated text, so you don't have to worry about it having a value of None.

TRY THIS: EXTRACTING MATCHED TEXT Making international calls usually requires a + and the country code. Assuming that the country code is two digits, how would you modify the code above to extract the + and the country code as part of the number? (Again, not all numbers have a country code.) How would you make the code handle country codes of one to three digits?

16.5   *Substituting text with regular expressions*

In addition to extracting strings from text, you can use Python's regex module to find strings in text and substitute other strings in place of those that were found. You accomplish this task by using the regular substitution method sub. The following example replaces instances of "the the" (presumably, a typo) with single instances of "the":

```
>>> import re
>>> string = "If the the problem is textual, use the the re module"
>>> pattern = r"the the"
>>> regexp = re.compile(pattern)
```

```
>>> regexp.sub("the", string)
'If the problem is textual, use the re module'
```

The sub method uses the invoking regex (regexp, in this case) to scan its second argument (string, in the example) and produces a new string by replacing all matching substrings with the value of the first argument ("the", in this example).

But what if you want to replace the matched substrings with new ones that reflect the value of those that matched? This is where the elegance of Python comes into play. The first argument to sub—the replacement substring, "the" in the example—doesn't have to be a string at all. Instead, it can be a function. If it's a function, Python calls it with the current match object; then it lets that function compute and return a replacement string.

To see this function in action, build an example that takes a string containing integer values (no decimal point or decimal part) and returns a string with the same numerical values but as floating numbers (with a trailing decimal point and zero):

```
>>> import re
>>> int_string = "1 2 3 4 5"
>>> def int_match_to_float(match_obj):
...     return(match_obj.group('num') + ".0")
...
>>> pattern = r"(?P<num>[0-9]+)"
>>> regexp = re.compile(pattern)
>>> regexp.sub(int_match_to_float, int_string)
'1.0 2.0 3.0 4.0 5.0'
```

In this case, the pattern looks for a number consisting of one or more digits (the [0-9]+ part). But it's also given a name (the ?P<num>... part) so that the replacement string function can extract any matched substring by referring to that name. Then the sub method scans down the argument string "1 2 3 4 5", looking for anything that matches [0-9]+. When sub finds a substring that matches, it makes a match object defining exactly which substring matched the pattern, and it calls the int_match_to_float function with that match object as the sole argument. int_match_to_float uses group to extract the matching substring from the match object (by referring to the group name num) and produces a new string by concatenating the matched substring with a ".0". sub returns the new string and incorporates it as a substring into the overall result. Finally, sub starts scanning again right after the place where it found the last matching substring, and it keeps going like that until it can't find any more matching substrings.

> **TRY THIS: REPLACING TEXT** In the checkpoint in section 16.4, you extended a phone-number regular expression to also recognize a country code. How would you use a function to make any numbers that didn't have a country code now have +1 (the country code for the United States and Canada)?

> **LAB 16: PHONE-NUMBER NORMALIZER** In the United States and Canada, phone numbers consist of ten digits, usually separated into a three-digit area code, a

three-digit exchange code, and a four-digit station code. As mentioned in section 16.4, they may or may not be preceded by +1, the country code. In practice, however, you have many ways to format a phone number, such as (NNN) NNN-NNNN, NNN-NNN-NNNN, NNN NNN-NNNN, NNN.NNN.NNNN, and NNN NNN NNNN, to name a few. Also, the country code may not be present, may not have a +, and usually (not always) is separated from the number by a space or dash. Whew!

In this lab, your task is to create a phone-number normalizer that takes any of the formats and returns a normalized phone number 1-NNN-NNN-NNNN.

The following are all possible phone numbers:

+1 223-456-7890	1-223-456-7890	+1 223 456-7890
(223) 456-7890	1 223 456 7890	223.456.7890

Bonus: The first digit of the area code and the exchange code can only be 2-9, and the second digit of an area code can't be 9. Use this information to validate the input and return a `ValueError` exception of `invalid phone number` if the number is invalid.

Summary

- For a complete list and explanation of the regex special characters, refer to the Python documentation.
- In addition to the `search` and `sub` methods, many other methods can be used to split strings, extract more information from `match` objects, look for the positions of substrings in the main argument string, and precisely control the iteration of a regex search over an argument string.
- Besides the `\d` special sequence, which can be used to indicate a digit character, many other special sequences are listed in the documentation.
- There are also regex flags, which you can use to control some of the more esoteric aspects of how extremely sophisticated matches are carried out.

Data types as objects

This chapter covers

- Treating types as objects
- Using types
- Creating user-defined classes
- Understanding duck typing
- Using special method attributes
- Subclassing built-in types

By now, you've learned the basic Python types as well as how to create your own data types using classes. For many languages, that would be pretty much it as far as data types are concerned. But Python is dynamically typed, meaning that types are determined at runtime, not at compile time. This fact is one of the reasons Python is so easy to use. It also makes it possible, and sometimes necessary, to compute with the types of objects (not just the objects themselves).

17.1   *Types are objects, too*

Fire up a Python session, and try out the following:

```
>>> type(5)
<class 'int'>
>>> type(['hello', 'goodbye'])
<class 'list'>
```

This example is the first time you've seen the built-in type function in Python. It can be applied to any Python object and returns the type of that object. In this example, the function tells you that 5 is an int (integer) and that ['hello', 'goodbye'] is a list—things that you probably already knew.

Of greater interest is the fact that Python returns objects in response to the calls to type; <class 'int'> and <class 'list'> are the screen representations of the returned objects. What sort of object is returned by a call of type(5)? You have an easy way of finding out. Just use type on that result:

```
>>> type_result = type(5)
>>> type(type_result)
<class 'type'>
```

The object returned by type is an object whose type happens to be <class 'type'>; you can call it a *type object*. A type object is another kind of Python object whose only outstanding feature is the confusion that its name sometime causes. Saying a type object is of type <class 'type'> has about the same degree of clarity as the old Abbott and Costello "Who's on First?" comedy routine.

17.2   *Using types*

Now that you know that data types can be represented as Python type objects, what can you do with them? You can compare them, because any two Python objects can be compared:

```
>>> type("Hello") == type("Goodbye")
True
>>> type("Hello") == type(5)
False
```

The types of "Hello" and "Goodbye" are the same (they're both strings), but the types of "Hello" and 5 are different. Among other things, you can use this technique to provide type checking in your function and method definitions.

17.3   *Types and user-defined classes*

The most common reason to be interested in the types of objects, particularly instances of user-defined classes, is to find out whether a particular object is an instance of a class. After determining that an object is of a particular type, the code can treat it appropriately. An example makes things much clearer. To start, define a couple of empty classes so as to set up a simple inheritance hierarchy:

```
>>> class A:
...     pass
...
>>> class B(A):
...     pass
...
```

Now create an instance of class B:

```
>>> b = B()
```

As expected, applying the `type` function to b tells you that b is an instance of the class B that's defined in your current __main__ namespace:

```
>>> type(b)
<class '__main__.B'>
```

You can also obtain exactly the same information by accessing the instance's special __class__ attribute:

```
>>> b.__class__
<class '__main__.B'>
```

You'll be working with that class quite a bit to extract further information, so store it somewhere:

```
>>> b_class = b.__class__
```

Now, to emphasize that everything in Python is an object, prove that the class you obtained from b is the class you defined under the name B:

```
>>> b_class == B
True
```

In this example, you didn't need to store the class of b—you already had it—but I want to make clear that a class is just another Python object and can be stored or passed around like any Python object.

Given the class of b, you can find the name of that class by using its __name__ attribute:

```
>>> b_class.__name__
'B'
```

And you can find out what classes a class inherits from by accessing its __bases__ attribute, which contains a tuple of all of its base classes:

```
>>> b_class.__bases__
(<class '__main__.A'>,)
```

Used together, __class__, __bases__, and __name__ allow a full analysis of the class inheritance structure associated with any instance.

But two built-in functions provide a more user-friendly way of obtaining most of the information you usually need: `isinstance` and `issubclass`. The `isinstance` function is what you should use to determine whether, for example, a class passed into a function or method is of the expected type:

```
>>> class C:
...     pass
...
>>> class D:
...     pass
...
>>> class E(D):
...     pass
...
>>> x = 12
>>> c = C()
>>> d = D()
>>> e = E()
>>> isinstance(x, E)
False
>>> isinstance(c, E)
False
>>> isinstance(e, E)
True
>>> isinstance(e, D)
True
>>> isinstance(d, E)
False
>>> y = 12
>>> isinstance(y, type(5))
True
```

1 **2** **3** **4**

The `issubclass` function is only for class types.

```
>>> issubclass(C, D)
False
>>> issubclass(E, D)
True
>>> issubclass(D, D)
True
>>> issubclass(e.__class__, D)
True
```

5

For class instances, check against the class **1**. e is an instance of class D because E inherits from D **2**. But d isn't an instance of class E **3**. For other types, you can use an example **4**. A class is considered to be a subclass of itself **5**.

> **QUICK CHECK: TYPES**   Suppose that you want to make sure that object x is a list before you try appending to it. What code would you use? What would be the difference between using `type()` and `isinstance()`? Would this be the look before you leap (LBYL) or easier to ask forgiveness than permission (EAFP) of programming? What other options might you have besides checking the type explicitly?

17.4 Duck typing

Using `type`, `isinstance`, and `issubclass` makes it fairly easy to make code correctly determine an object's or class's inheritance hierarchy. Although this process is easy, Python also has a feature that makes using objects even easier: duck typing. *Duck typing* (as in "If it walks like a duck and quacks like a duck, it probably *is* a duck") refers to Python's way of determining whether an object is the required type for an operation, focusing on an object's interface rather than its type. If an operation needs an iterator, for example, the object used doesn't need to be a subclass of any particular iterator or of any iterator at all. All that matters is that the object used as an iterator is able to yield a series of objects in the expected way.

By contrast, in a language like Java, stricter rules of inheritance are enforced. In short, duck typing means that in Python, you don't need to (and probably shouldn't) worry about type-checking function or method arguments and the like. Instead, you should rely on readable and documented code combined with thorough testing to make sure that an object "quacks like a duck" as needed.

Duck typing can increase the flexibility of well-written code and, combined with the more advanced object-oriented features, gives you the ability to create classes and objects to cover almost any situation.

17.5 What is a special method attribute?

A *special method attribute* is an attribute of a Python class with a special meaning to Python. It's defined as a method but isn't intended to be used directly as such. Special methods aren't usually directly invoked; instead, they're called automatically by Python in response to a demand made on an object of that class.

Perhaps the simplest example is the `__str__` special method attribute. If it's defined in a class, any time an instance of that class is used where Python requires a user-readable string representation of that instance, the `__str__` method attribute is invoked, and the value it returns is used as the required string. To see this attribute in action, define a class representing red, green, and blue (RGB) colors as a triplet of numbers, one each for red, green, and blue intensities. As well as defining the standard `__init__` method to initialize instances of the class, define a `__str__` method to return strings representing instances in a reasonably human-friendly format. Your definition should look something like this.

Listing 17.1 File color_module.py

```python
class Color:
    def __init__(self, red, green, blue):
        self._red = red
        self._green = green
        self._blue = blue
    def __str__(self):
        return "Color: R={0:d}, G={1:d}, B={2:d}".format (self._red,
                                    self._green, self._blue)
```

If you put this definition into a file called color_module.py, you can load it and use it in the normal manner:

```
>>> from color_module import Color
>>> c = Color(15, 35, 3)
```

You can see the presence of the __str__ special method attribute if you use `print` to print out c:

```
>>> print(c)
Color: R=15, G=35, B=3
```

Even though your __str__ special method attribute hasn't been explicitly invoked by any of your code, it has nonetheless been used by Python, which knows that the __str__ attribute (if present) defines a method to convert objects into user-readable strings. This characteristic is the defining one of special method attributes; it allows you to define functionality that hooks into Python in special ways. Among other things, special method attributes can be used to define classes whose objects behave in a fashion that's syntactically and semantically equivalent to lists or dictionaries. You could, for example, use this ability to define objects that are used in exactly the same manner as Python lists but that use balanced trees rather than arrays to store data. To a programmer, such objects would appear to be lists, but with faster inserts, slower iterations, and certain other performance differences that presumably would be advantageous in the problem at hand.

The rest of this chapter covers longer examples using special method attributes. The chapter doesn't discuss all of Python's available special method attributes, but it does expose you to the concept in enough detail that you can easily use the other special attribute methods, all of which are defined in the standard library documentation for built-in types.

17.6 *Making an object behave like a list*

This sample problem involves a large text file containing records of people; each record consists of a single line containing the person's name, age, and place of residence, with a double semicolon (::) between the fields. A few lines from such a file might look like this:

```
.
.
.
John Smith::37::Springfield, Massachusetts
Ellen Nelle::25::Springfield, Connecticut
Dale McGladdery::29::Springfield, Hawaii
.
.
.
```

Suppose that you need to collect information about the distribution of ages of people in the file. There are many ways the lines in this file could be processed. Here's one way:

```
fileobject = open(filename, 'r')
lines = fileobject.readlines()
fileobject.close()
for line in lines:
    . . . do whatever . . .
```

That technique would work in theory, but it reads the entire file into memory at once. If the file were too large to be held in memory (and these files potentially are that large), the program wouldn't work.

Another way to attack the problem is this:

```
fileobject = open(filename, 'r')
for line in fileobject:
    . . . do whatever . . .
fileobject.close()
```

This code would get around the problem of having too little memory by reading in only one line at a time. It would work fine, but suppose that you wanted to make opening the file even simpler and that you wanted to get only the first two fields (name and age) of the lines in the file. You'd need something that could, at least for the purposes of a `for` loop, treat a text file as a list of lines but without reading the entire text file in at once.

17.7 The __getitem__ special method attribute

A solution is to use the `__getitem__` special method attribute, which you can define in any user-defined class, to enable instances of that class to respond to list access syntax and semantics. If `AClass` is a Python class that defines `__getitem__`, and `obj` is an instance of that class, things like `x = obj[n]` and `for x in obj:` are meaningful; `obj` may be used in much the same way as a list.

Here's the resulting code (explanations follow):

```
class LineReader:
    def __init__(self, filename):
        self.fileobject = open(filename, 'r')         ◁── Opens file
                                                           for reading
    def __getitem__(self, index):
        line = self.fileobject.readline()             ◁── Tries to read line
        if line == "":                                ◁── If no more data ...
            self.fileobject.close()                        ◁── ... closes fileobject ...
            raise IndexError                          ◁── ... and raises
                                                           IndexError
        else:
            return line.split("::")[:2]               ◁── Otherwise, splits line,
                                                           returns first two fields

for name, age in LineReader("filename"):
    . . . do whatever . . .
```

At first glance, this example may look worse than the previous solution because there's more code, and it's difficult to understand. But most of that code is in a class, which can be put into its own module, such as the `myutils` module. Then the program becomes

```
import myutils
for name, age in myutils.LineReader("filename"):
    . . . do whatever . . .
```

The `LineReader` class handles all the details of opening the file, reading in lines one at a time, and closing the file. At the cost of somewhat more initial development time, it provides a tool that makes working with one-record-per-line large text files easier and less error-prone. Note that Python already has several powerful ways to read files, but this example has the advantage that it's fairly easy to understand. When you get the idea, you can apply the same principle in many situations.

17.7.1 *How it works*

`LineReader` is a class, and the `__init__` method opens the named file for reading and stores the opened `fileobject` for later access. To understand the use of the `__getitem__` method, you need to know the following three points:

- Any object that defines `__getitem__` as an instance method can return elements as though it were a list: all accesses of the form `object[i]` are transformed by Python into a method invocation of the form `object.__getitem__(i)`, which is handled as a normal method invocation. It's ultimately executed as `__getitem__(object, i)`, using the version of `__getitem__` defined in the class. The first argument of each call of `__getitem__` is the object from which data is being extracted, and the second argument is the index of that data.
- Because `for` loops access each piece of data in a list, one at a time, a loop of the form `for arg in sequence:` works by calling `__getitem__` over and over again, with sequentially increasing indexes. The `for` loop first sets `arg` to `sequence.__getitem__(0)`, then to `sequence.__getitem__(1)`, and so on.
- A `for` loop catches `IndexError` exceptions and handles them by exiting the loop. This process is how `for` loops are terminated when used with normal lists or sequences.

The `LineReader` class is intended for use only with and inside a `for` loop, and the `for` loop always generates calls with a uniformly increasing index: `__getitem__(self, 0)`, `__getitem__(self, 1)`, `__getitem__(self, 2)`, and so on. The previous code takes advantage of this knowledge and returns lines one after the other, ignoring the `index` argument.

   With this knowledge, understanding how a `LineReader` object emulates a sequence in a `for` loop is easy. Each iteration of the loop causes the special Python attribute method `__getitem__` to be invoked on the object; as a result, the object reads in the next line from its stored `fileobject` and examines that line. If the line is nonempty, it's returned. An empty line means that the end of the file has been reached; the object closes the `fileobject` and raises the `IndexError` exception. `IndexError` is caught by the enclosing `for` loop, which then terminates.

Remember that this example is here for illustrative purposes only. Usually, iterating over the lines of a file by using the `for line in fileobject:` type of loop is sufficient, but this example does show how easy it is in Python to create objects that behave like lists or other types.

> **QUICK CHECK: __GETITEM__**   The example use of __getitem__ is very limited and won't work correctly in many situations. What are some cases in which the implementation above will fail or work incorrectly?

17.7.2   *Implementing full list functionality*

In the previous example, an object of the `LineReader` class behaves like a list object only to the extent that it correctly responds to sequential accesses of the lines in the file it's reading from. You may wonder how this functionality can be expanded to make `LineReader` (or other) objects behave more like a list.

First, the __getitem__ method should handle its index argument in some way. Because the whole point of the `LineReader` class is to avoid reading a large file into memory, it wouldn't make sense to have the entire file in memory and return the appropriate line. Probably the smartest thing to do would be to check that each index in a __getitem__ call is one greater than the index from the previous __getitem__ call (or is 0, for the first call of __getitem__ on a `LineReader` instance) and to raise an error if this isn't the case. This practice would ensure that `LineReader` instances are used only in `for` loops as was intended.

More generally, Python provides several special method attributes relating to list behavior. __setitem__ provides a way of defining what should be done when an object is used in the syntactic context of a list assignment, `obj[n] = val`. Some other special method attributes provide less-obvious list functionality, such as the __add__ attribute, which enables objects to respond to the + operator and hence to perform their version of list concatenation. Several other special methods also need to be defined before a class fully emulates a list, but you can achieve complete list emulation by defining the appropriate Python special method attributes. The next section gives an example that goes farther toward implementing a full list emulation class.

17.8   *Giving an object full list capability*

__getitem__ is one of many Python special function attributes that may be defined in a class to permit instances of that class to display special behavior. To see how special method attributes can be carried farther, effectively integrating new abilities into Python in a seamless manner, look at another, more comprehensive example.

When lists are used, it's common for any particular list to contain elements of only one type, such as a list of strings or a list of numbers. Some languages, such as C++, have the ability to enforce this restriction. In large programs, the ability to declare a list as containing a certain type of element can help you track down errors. An attempt to add an element of the wrong type to a typed list results in an error message, potentially identifying a problem at an earlier stage of program development than would otherwise be the case.

Python doesn't have typed lists built in, and most Python coders don't miss them. But if you're concerned about enforcing the homogeneity of a list, special method attributes make it easy to create a class that behaves like a typed list. Here's the beginning of such a class (which makes extensive use of the Python built-in `type` and `isinstance` functions to check the type of objects):

```
class TypedList:
    def __init__(self, example_element, initial_list=[]):
        self.type = type(example_element)                          ◄──── ❶
        if not isinstance(initial_list, list):
            raise TypeError("Second argument of TypedList must "
                            "be a list.")
        for element in initial_list:
            if not isinstance(element, self.type):
                raise TypeError("Attempted to add an element of "
                                "incorrect type to a typed list.")
        self.elements = initial_list[:]
```

The `example_element` argument defines the type that this list can contain by providing an example of the type of element ❶.

The `TypedList` class, as defined here, gives you the ability to make a call of the form

```
x = TypedList ('Hello', ["List", "of", "strings"])
```

The first argument, `'Hello'`, isn't incorporated into the resulting data structure at all. It's used as an example of the type of element the list must contain (strings, in this case). The second argument is an optional list that can be used to give an initial list of values. The `__init__` function for the `TypedList` class checks that any list elements, passed in when a `TypedList` instance is created, are of the same type as the example value given. If there are any type mismatches, an exception is raised.

This version of the `TypedList` class can't be used as a list, because it doesn't respond to the standard methods for setting or accessing list elements. To fix this problem, you need to define the `__setitem__` and `__getitem__` special method attributes. The `__setitem__` method is called automatically by Python any time a statement of the form `TypedListInstance[i]` = `value` is executed, and the `__getitem__` method is called any time the expression `TypedListInstance[i]` is evaluated to return the value in the *i*th slot of `TypedListInstance`. Here's the next version of the `TypedList` class. Because you'll be type-checking a lot of new elements, this function is abstracted out into the new private method `__check`:

```
class TypedList:
    def __init__(self, example_element, initial_list=[]):
        self.type = type(example_element)
```

```
        if not isinstance(initial_list, list):
            raise TypeError("Second argument of TypedList must "
                            "be a list.")
        for element in initial_list:
            self.__check(element)
        self.elements = initial_list[:]
    def __check(self, element):
        if type(element) != self.type:
            raise TypeError("Attempted to add an element of "
                            "incorrect type to a typed list.")
    def __setitem__(self, i, element):
        self.__check(element)
        self.elements[i] = element
    def __getitem__(self, i):
        return self.elements[i]
```

Now instances of the `TypedList` class look more like lists. The following code is valid, for example:

```
>>> x = TypedList("", 5 * [""])
>>> x[2] = "Hello"
>>> x[3] = "There"
>>> print(x[2] + ' ' + x[3])
Hello There
>>> a, b, c, d, e = x
>>> a, b, c, d
('', '', 'Hello', 'There')
```

The accesses of elements of x in the `print` statement are handled by `__getitem__`, which passes them down to the list instance stored in the `TypedList` object. The assignments to x[2] and x[3] are handled by `__setitem__`, which checks that the element being assigned into the list is of the appropriate type and then performs the assignment on the list contained in `self.elements`. The last line uses `__getitem__` to unpack the first five items in x and then pack them into the variables a, b, c, d, and e, respectively. The calls to `__getitem__` and `__setitem__` are made automatically by Python.

Completion of the `TypedList` class, so that `TypedList` objects behave in all respects like list objects, requires more code. The special method attributes `__setitem__` and `__getitem__` should be defined so that `TypedList` instances can handle slice notation as well as single item access. `__add__` should be defined so that list addition (concatenation) can be performed, and `__mul__` should be defined so that list multiplication can be performed. `__len__` should be defined so that calls of `len(TypedListInstance)` are evaluated correctly. `__delitem__` should be defined so that the `TypedList` class can handle `del` statements correctly. Also, an append method should be defined so that elements can be appended to `TypedList` instances by means of the standard list-style `append`, as well as `insert` and `extend` methods.

TRY THIS: IMPLEMENTING LIST SPECIAL METHODS Try implementing the `__len__` and `__delitem__` special methods, as well as an append method.

17.9   *Subclassing from built-in types*

The previous example makes for a good exercise in understanding how to implement a listlike class from scratch, but it's also a lot of work. In practice, if you were planning to implement your own listlike structure along the lines demonstrated here, you might instead consider subclassing the list type or the `UserList` type.

17.9.1   *Subclassing list*

Instead of creating a class for a typed list from scratch, as you did in the previous examples, you can subclass the list type and override all the methods that need to be aware of the allowed type. One big advantage of this approach is that your class has default versions of all list operations because it's a list already. The main thing to keep in mind is that every type in Python is a class, and if you need a variation on the behavior of a built-in type, you may want to consider subclassing that type:

```python
class TypedListList(list):
    def __init__(self, example_element, initial_list=[]):
        self.type = type(example_element)
        if not isinstance(initial_list, list):
            raise TypeError("Second argument of TypedList must "
                                "be a list.")
        for element in initial_list:
            self.__check(element)
        super().__init__(initial_list)

    def __check(self, element):
        if type(element) != self.type:
            raise TypeError("Attempted to add an element of "
                                "incorrect type to a typed list.")

    def __setitem__(self, i, element):
        self.__check(element)
        super().__setitem__(i, element)

>>> x = TypedListList("", 5 * [""])
>>> x[2] = "Hello"
>>> x[3] = "There"
>>> print(x[2] + ' ' + x[3])
Hello There
>>> a, b, c, d, e = x
>>> a, b, c, d
('', '', 'Hello', 'There')
>>> x[:]
['', '', 'Hello', 'There', '']
>>> del x[2]
>>> x[:]
['', '', 'There', '']
>>> x.sort()
>>> x[:]
['', '', '', 'There']
```

Note that all that you need to do in this case is implement a method to check the type of items being added and then tweak __setitem__ to make that check before calling list's regular __setitem__ method. Other methods, such as sort and del, work without any further coding. Overloading a built-in type can save a fair amount of time if you need only a few variations in its behavior, because the bulk of the class can be used unchanged.

17.9.2 Subclassing UserList

If you need a variation on a list (as in the previous examples), there's a third alternative: You can subclass the UserList class, a list wrapper class found in the collections module. UserList was created for earlier versions of Python when subclassing the list type wasn't possible, but it's still useful, particularly for the current situation, because the underlying list is available as the data attribute:

```
from collections import UserList
class TypedUserList(UserList):
    def __init__(self, example_element, initial_list=[]):
        self.type = type(example_element)
        if not isinstance(initial_list, list):
            raise TypeError("Second argument of TypedList must "
                            "be a list.")
        for element in initial_list:
            self.__check(element)
        super().__init__(initial_list)

    def __check(self, element):
        if type(element) != self.type:
            raise TypeError("Attempted to add an element of "
                            "incorrect type to a typed list.")
    def __setitem__(self, i, element):
        self.__check(element)
        self.data[i] = element
    def __getitem__(self, i):
        return self.data[i]

>>> x = TypedUserList("", 5 * [""])
>>> x[2] = "Hello"
>>> x[3] = "There"
>>> print(x[2] + ' ' + x[3])
Hello There
>>> a, b, c, d, e = x
>>> a, b, c, d
('', '', 'Hello', 'There')
>>> x[:]
['', '', 'Hello', 'There', '']
>>> del x[2]
>>> x[:]
['', '', 'There', '']
>>> x.sort()
>>> x[:]
['', '', '', 'There']
```

This example is much the same as subclassing `list`, except that in the implementation of the class, the list of items is available internally as the `data` member. In some situations, having direct access to the underlying data structure can be useful. Also, in addition to `UserList`, there are `UserDict` and `UserString` wrapper classes.

17.10 *When to use special method attributes*

As a rule, it's a good idea to be somewhat cautious with the use of special method attributes. Other programmers who need to work with your code may wonder why one sequence-type object responds correctly to standard indexing notation, whereas another doesn't.

My general guidelines are to use special method attributes in either of two situations:

- If I have a frequently used class in my own code that behaves in some respects like a Python built-in type, I'll define such special method attributes as useful. This situation occurs most often with objects that behave like sequences in one way or another.
- If I have a class that behaves identically or almost identically to a built-in class, I may choose to define all of the appropriate special function attributes or subclass the built-in Python type and distribute the class. An example of the latter solution might be lists implemented as balanced trees so that access is slower but insertion is faster than with standard lists.

These rules aren't hard-and-fast rules. It's often a good idea to define the __str__ special method attribute for a class, for example, so that you can say `print(instance)` in debugging code and get an informative, nice-looking representation of your object printed to the screen.

> **QUICK CHECK: SPECIAL METHOD ATTRIBUTES AND SUBCLASSING EXISTING TYPES** Suppose that you want a dictionary-like type that allows only strings as keys (maybe to make it work like a `shelf` object, as described in chapter 13). What options would you have for creating such a class? What would be the advantages and disadvantages of each option?

Summary

- Python has the tools to do type checking as needed in your code, but by taking advantage of duck typing, you can write more flexible code that doesn't need to be as concerned with type checking.
- Special method attributes and subclassing built-in classes can be used to add listlike behavior to user-created classes.
- Python's use of duck typing, special method attributes, and subclassing makes it possible to construct and combine classes in a variety of ways.

Packages

Modules make reusing small chunks of code easy. The problem comes when the project grows and the code you want to reload outgrows, either physically or logically, what would fit into a single file. If having one giant module file is an unsatisfactory solution, having a host of little unconnected modules isn't much better. The answer to this problem is to combine related modules into a package.

18.1 What is a package?

A *module* is a file containing code. A module defines a group of usually related Python functions or other objects. The name of the module is derived from the name of the file.

When you understand modules, packages are easy, because a package is a directory containing code and possibly further subdirectories. A package contains a group of usually related code files (modules). The name of the package is derived from the name of the main package directory.

Packages are a natural extension of the module concept and are designed to handle very large projects. Just as modules group related functions, classes, and variables, packages group related modules.

18.2 *A first example*

To see how packages might work in practice, consider a design layout for a type of project that by nature is very large: a generalized mathematics package along the lines of Mathematica, Maple, or MATLAB. Maple, for example, consists of thousands of files, and some sort of hierarchical structure is vital to keeping such a project ordered. Call your project as a whole `mathproj`.

You can organize such a project in many ways, but a reasonable design splits the project into two parts: `ui`, consisting of the UI elements, and `comp`, the computational elements. Within `comp`, it may make sense to further segment the computational aspect into `symbolic` (real and complex symbolic computation, such as high school algebra) and `numeric` (real and complex numerical computation, such as numerical integration). Then it may make sense to have a constants.py file in both the `symbolic` and `numeric` parts of the project.

The constants.py file in the numeric part of the project defines pi as

```
pi = 3.141592
```

whereas the constants.py file in the symbolic part of the project defines pi as

```
class PiClass:
    def __str__(self):
        return "PI"
pi = PiClass()
```

This means that a name like `pi` can be used in (and imported from) two different files named constants.py, as shown in figure 18.1.

The symbolic constants.py file defines `pi` as an abstract Python object, the sole instance of the `PiClass` class. As the system is developed, various operations can be implemented in this class, which return symbolic rather than numeric results.

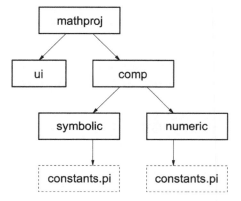

Figure 18.1 **Organizing a math package**

There's a natural mapping from this design structure to a directory structure. The top-level directory of the project, called `mathproj`, contains subdirectories `ui` and `comp`; `comp` in turn contains subdirectories `symbolic` and `numeric`; and each of `symbolic` and `numeric` contains its own `constants.pi` file.

Given this directory structure, and assuming that the root mathproj directory is installed somewhere in the Python search path, Python code both inside and outside the `mathproj` package can access the two variants of `pi` as `mathproj.symbolic.constants.pi` and `mathproj.numeric.constants.pi`. In other words, the Python name for an item in the package is a reflection of the directory pathname to the file containing that item.

That's what packages are all about. They're ways of organizing very large collections of Python code into coherent wholes, by allowing the code to be split among different files and directories and imposing a module/submodule naming scheme based on the directory structure of the package files. Unfortunately, packages aren't this simple in practice because details intrude to make their use more complex than their theory. The practical aspects of packages are the basis for the remainder of this chapter.

18.3 A concrete example

The rest of this chapter uses a running example to illustrate the inner workings of the package mechanism (see figure 18.2). Filenames and paths are shown in plain text to clarify whether I'm talking about a file/directory or the module/package defined by that file/directory. The files you'll be using in your example package are shown in listings 18.1 through 18.6.

Listing 18.1   File mathproj/__init__.py

```
print("Hello from mathproj init")
__all__ = ['comp']
version = 1.03
```

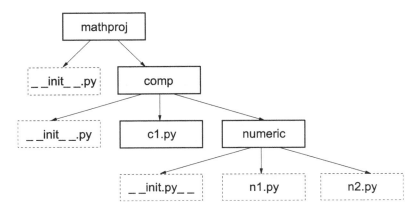

Figure 18.2   Example package

Listing 18.2   File mathproj/comp/__init__.py

```
__all__ = ['c1']
print("Hello from mathproj.comp init")
```

Listing 18.3   File mathproj/comp/c1.py

```
x = 1.00
```

Listing 18.4   File mathproj/comp/numeric/__init__.py

```
print("Hello from numeric init")
```

Listing 18.5   File mathproj/comp/numeric/n1.py

```
from mathproj import version
from mathproj.comp import c1
from mathproj.comp.numeric.n2 import h
def g():
    print("version is", version)
    print(h())
```

Listing 18.6   File mathproj/comp/numeric/n2.py

```
def h():
    return "Called function h in module n2"
```

For the purposes of the examples in this chapter, assume that you've created these files in a mathproj directory that's on the Python search path. (It's sufficient to ensure that the current working directory for Python is the directory containing mathproj when executing these examples.)

> **NOTE**   In most of the examples in this book, it's not necessary to start up a new Python shell for each example. You can usually execute the examples in a Python shell that you've used for previous examples and still get the results shown. *This isn't true for the examples in this chapter,* however, because the Python namespace must be clean (unmodified by previous import statements) for the examples to work properly. If you do run the examples that follow, *please ensure that you run each separate example in its own shell.* In IDLE, this requires exiting and restarting the program, not just closing and reopening its Shell window.

18.3.1   __init__.py files in packages

You'll have noticed that all the directories in your package—mathproj, mathproj/comp, and mathproj/numeric—contain a file called __init__.py. An __init__.py file serves two purposes:

- Python requires that a directory contain an __init__.py file before it can be recognized as a package. This requirement prevents directories containing miscellaneous Python code from being accidentally imported as though they defined a package.

■ The __init__.py file is automatically executed by Python the first time a package or subpackage is loaded. This execution permits whatever package initialization you desire.

The first point is usually more important. For many packages, you won't need to put anything in the package's __init__.py file; just make sure that an empty __init__.py file is present.

18.3.2 *Basic use of the mathproj package*

Before getting into the details of packages, look at accessing items contained in the mathproj package. Start a new Python shell, and do the following:

```
>>> import mathproj
Hello from mathproj init
```

If all goes well, you should get another input prompt and no error messages. Also, the message "Hello from mathproj init" should be printed to the screen by code in the mathproj/__init__.py file. I talk more about __init__.py files soon; for now, all you need to know is that the files run automatically whenever a package is first loaded.

The mathproj/__init__.py file assigns 1.03 to the variable version. version is in the scope of the mathproj package namespace, and after it's created, you can see it via mathproj, even from outside the mathproj/__init__.py file:

```
>>> mathproj.version
1.03
```

In use, packages can look a lot like modules; they can provide access to objects defined within them via attributes. This fact isn't surprising, because packages are a generalization of modules.

18.3.3 *Loading subpackages and submodules*

Now start looking at how the various files defined in the mathproj package interact with one another. To do so, invoke the function g defined in the file mathproj/comp/numeric/n1.py. The first obvious question is whether this module has been loaded. You've already loaded mathproj, but what about its subpackage? To see whether it's known to Python, type

```
>>> mathproj.comp.numeric.n1
Traceback (most recent call last):
  File "<stdin>", line 1, in <module>
AttributeError: module 'mathproj' has no attribute 'comp'
```

In other words, loading the top-level module of a package isn't enough to load all the submodules, which is in keeping with Python's philosophy that it shouldn't do things behind your back. Clarity is more important than conciseness.

This restriction is simple enough to overcome. You import the module of interest and then execute the function g in that module:

```
>>> import mathproj.comp.numeric.n1
Hello from mathproj.comp init
Hello from numeric init
>>> mathproj.comp.numeric.n1.g()
version is 1.03
Called function h in module n2
```

Notice, however, that the lines beginning with Hello are printed out as a side effect of loading mathproj.comp.numeric.n1. These two lines are printed out by print statements in the __init__.py files in mathproj/comp and mathproj/comp/ numeric. In other words, before Python can import mathproj.comp.numeric.n1, it has to import mathproj.comp and then mathproj.comp.numeric. Whenever a package is first imported, its associated __init__.py file is executed, resulting in the Hello lines. To confirm that both mathproj.comp and mathproj.comp.numeric are imported as part of the process of importing mathproj.comp.numeric.n1, you can check to see that mathproj.comp and mathproj.comp.numeric are now known to the Python session:

```
>>> mathproj.comp
<module 'mathproj.comp' from 'mathproj/comp/__init__.py'>
>>> mathproj.comp.numeric
<module 'mathproj.comp.numeric'  from 'mathproj/comp/numeric/__init__.py'>
```

18.3.4 *import statements within packages*

Files within a package don't automatically have access to objects defined in other files in the same package. As in outside modules, you must use import statements to explicitly access objects from other package files. To see how this use of import works in practice, look back at the n1 subpackage. The code contained in n1.py is

```
from mathproj import version
from mathproj.comp import c1
from mathproj.comp.numeric.n2 import h
def g():
    print("version is", version)
    print(h())
```

g makes use of both version from the top-level mathproj package and the function h from the n2 module; hence, the module containing g must import both version and h to make them accessible. You import version as you would in an import statement from outside the mathproj package: by saying from mathproj import version. In this example, you explicitly import h into the code by saying from mathproj.comp.numeric.n2 import h, and this technique works in any file; explicit imports of package files are always allowed. But because n2.py is in the same directory as n1.py, you can also use a relative import by prepending a single dot to the submodule name. In other words, you can say

```
from .n2 import h
```

as the third line in n1.py, and it works fine.

You can add more dots to move up more levels in the package hierarchy, and you can add module names. Instead of writing

```
from mathproj import version
from mathproj.comp import c1
from mathproj.comp.numeric.n2 import h
```

you could have written the imports of n1.py as

```
from ... import version
from ..  import c1
from . n2 import h
```

Relative imports can be handy and quick to type, but be aware that they're *relative* to the module's __name__ property. Therefore, any module being executed as the main module and thus having __main__ as its __name__ can't use relative imports.

18.4 *The __all__ attribute*

If you look back at the various __init__.py files defined in mathproj, you'll notice that some of them define an attribute called __all__. This attribute has to do with execution of statements of the form from ... import *, and it requires explanation.

Generally speaking, you'd hope that if outside code executed the statement from mathproj import *, it would import all nonprivate names from mathproj. In practice, life is more difficult. The primary problem is that some operating systems have an ambiguous definition of case when it comes to filenames. Because objects in packages can be defined by files or directories, this situation leads to ambiguity as to the exact name under which a subpackage might be imported. If you say from mathproj import *, will comp be imported as comp, Comp, or COMP? If you were to rely only on the name as reported by the operating system, the results might be unpredictable.

There's no good solution to this problem, which is an inherent one caused by poor OS design. As the best possible fix, the __all__ attribute was introduced. If present in an __init__.py file, __all__ should give a list of strings, defining those names that are to be imported when a from ... import * is executed on that particular package. If __all__ isn't present, from ... import * on the given package does nothing. Because case in a text file is always meaningful, the names under which objects are imported aren't ambiguous, and if the operating system thinks that comp is the same as COMP, that's its problem.

Fire up Python again, and try the following:

```
>>> from mathproj import *
Hello from mathproj init
Hello from mathproj.comp init
```

The __all__ attribute in mathproj/__init__.py contains a single entry, comp, and the import statement imports only comp. It's easy enough to check whether comp is now known to the Python session:

```
>>> comp
<module 'mathproj.comp' from 'mathproj/comp/__init__.py'>
```

But note that there's no recursive importing of names with a from ... import * statement. The __all__ attribute for the comp package contains c1, but c1 isn't magically loaded by your from mathproj import * statement:

```
>>> c1
Traceback (most recent call last):
  File "<stdin>", line 1, in <module>
NameError: name 'c1' is not defined
```

To insert names from mathproj.comp, you must again do an explicit import:

```
>>> from mathproj.comp import c1
>>> c1
<module 'mathproj.comp.c1' from 'mathproj/comp/c1.py'>
```

18.5 *Proper use of packages*

Most of your packages shouldn't be as structurally complex as these examples imply. The package mechanism allows wide latitude in the complexity and nesting of your package design. It's obvious that very complex packages *can* be built, but it isn't obvious that they *should* be built.

Here are a couple of suggestions that are appropriate in most circumstances:

- Packages shouldn't use deeply nested directory structures. Except for absolutely huge collections of code, there should be no need to do so. For most packages, a single top-level directory is all that's needed. A two-level hierarchy should be able to effectively handle all but a few of the rest. As written in *The Zen of Python*, by Tim Peters (see appendix A), "Flat is better than nested."

- Although you can use the __all__ attribute to hide names from from ... import * by not listing those names, doing so probably is *not* a good idea, because it's inconsistent. If you want to hide names, make them private by prefacing them with an underscore.

QUICK CHECK: PACKAGES Suppose that you're writing a package that takes a URL, retrieves all images on the page pointed to by that URL, resizes them to a standard size, and stores them. Leaving aside the exact details of how each of these functions will be coded, how would you organize those features into a package?

LAB 18: CREATE A PACKAGE In chapter 14, you added error handling to the text cleaning and word frequency counting module that you created in chapter 11. Refactor that code into a package containing one module for the cleaning functions, one for the processing functions, and one for the custom exceptions. Then write a simple main function that uses all three.

Summary

- Packages let you create libraries of code that span multiple files and directories.
- Using packages allows better organization of large collections of code than single modules would allow.
- You should be wary of nesting directories in your packages more than one or two levels deep unless you have a very large and complex library.

Using Python libraries

Python has long proclaimed that one of its key advantages is its "batteries included" philosophy. This means that a stock install of Python comes with a rich standard library that lets you handle a wide variety of situations without the need to install additional libraries. This chapter gives you a high-level survey of some of the contents of the standard library, as well as some suggestions on finding and installing external modules.

19.1 *"Batteries included": The standard library*

In Python, what's considered to be the *library* consists of several components, including built-in data types and constants that can be used without an `import` statement, such as numbers and lists, as well as some built-in functions and exceptions. The largest part of the library is an extensive collection of modules. If you have Python, you also have libraries to manipulate diverse types of data and files, to interact with your operating system, to write servers and clients for many internet protocols, and to develop and debug your code.

What follows is a survey of the high points. Although most of the major modules are mentioned, for the most complete and current information I recommend that you spend time on your own exploring the library reference that's part of the Python documentation. In particular, before you go in search of an external library, be sure to scan through what Python already offers. You may be surprised by what you find.

19.1.1 *Managing various data types*

The standard library naturally contains support for Python's built-in types, which I touch on in this section. In addition, three categories in the standard library deal with various data types: string services, data types, and numeric modules.

String services include the modules in table 19.1 that deal with bytes as well as strings. The three main things these modules deal with are strings and text, sequences of bytes, and Unicode operations.

Table 19.1   String services modules

Module	Description and possible uses
`string`	Compare with string constants, such as `digits` or `whitespace`; format strings (see chapter 6)
`re`	Search and replace text using regular expressions (see chapter 16)
`struct`	Interpret bytes as packed binary data, and read and write structured data to/from files
`difflib`	Use helpers for computing deltas, find differences between strings or sequences, and create patches and diff files
`textwrap`	Wrap and fill text, and format text by breaking lines or adding spaces

The data types category is a diverse collection of modules covering various data types, particularly time, date, and collections, as shown in table 19.2.

Table 19.2   Data types modules

Module	Description and possible uses
`datetime, calendar`	Date, time, and calendar operations
`collections`	Container data types

Table 19.2   Data types modules *(continued)*

Module	Description and possible uses
enum	Allows creation of enumerator classes that bind symbolic names to constant values
array	Efficient arrays of numeric values
sched	Event scheduler
queue	Synchronized queue class
copy	Shallow and deep copy operations
pprint	Data pretty printer
typing	Support for annotating code with hints as to the types of objects, particularly of function parameters and return values

As the name indicates, the numeric and mathematical modules deal with numbers and mathematical operations, and the most common of these modules are listed in table 19.3. These modules have everything you need to create your own numeric types and handle a wide range of math operations.

Table 19.3   Numeric and mathematical modules

Module	Description and possible uses
numbers	Numeric abstract base classes
math, cmath	Mathematical functions for real and complex numbers
decimal	Decimal fixed-point and floating-point arithmetic
statistics	Functions for calculating mathematical statistics
fractions	Rational numbers
random	Generate pseudorandom numbers and choices, and shuffle sequences
itertools	Functions that create iterators for efficient looping
functools	Higher-order functions and operations on callable objects
operator	Standard operators as functions

19.1.2 *Manipulating files and storage*

Another broad category in the standard library covers files, storage, and data persistence and is summarized in table 19.4. This category ranges from modules for file access to modules for data persistence and compression and handling special file formats.

Table 19.4 File and storage modules

Module	Description and possible uses
os.path	Perform common pathname manipulations
pathlib	Deal with pathnames in an object-oriented way
fileinput	Iterate over lines from multiple input streams
filecmp	Compare files and directories
tempfile	Generate temporary files and directories
glob, fnmatch	Use UNIX-style pathname and filename pattern handling
linecache	Gain random access to text lines
shutil	Perform high-level file operations
pickle, shelve	Enable Python object serialization and persistence
sqlite3	Work with a DB-API 2.0 interface for SQLite databases
zlib, gzip, bz2, zipfile, tarfile	Work with archive files and compressions
csv	Read and write CSV files
configparser	Use a configuration file parser; read/write Windows-style configuration .ini files

19.1.3 Accessing operating system services

This category is another broad one, containing modules for dealing with your operating system. As shown in table 19.5, this category includes tools for handling command-line parameters, redirecting file and print output and input, writing to log files, running multiple threads or processes, and loading non-Python (usually, C) libraries for use in Python.

Table 19.5 Operating system modules

Module	Description
os	Miscellaneous operating system interfaces
io	Core tools for working with streams
time	Time access and conversions
optparse	Powerful command-line option parser
logging	Logging facility for Python
getpass	Portable password input
curses	Terminal handling for character-cell displays

Table 19.5 Operating system modules *(continued)*

Module	Description
platform	Access to underlying platform's identifying data
ctypes	Foreign function library for Python
select	Waiting for I/O completion
threading	Higher-level threading interface
multiprocessing	Process-based threading interface
subprocess	Subprocess management

19.1.4 *Using internet protocols and formats*

The internet protocols and formats category is concerned with encoding and decoding the many standard formats used for data exchange on the internet, from MIME and other encodings to JSON and XML. This category also has modules for writing servers and clients for common services, particularly HTTP, and a generic socket server for writing servers for custom services. The most commonly used of these modules are listed in table 19.6.

Table 19.6 Modules supporting internet protocols and formats

Module	Description
socket, ssl	Low-level networking interface and SSL wrapper for socket objects
email	Email and MIME handling package
json	JSON encoder and decoder
mailbox	Manipulate mailboxes in various formats
mimetypes	Map filenames to MIME types
base64, binhex, binascii, quopri, uu	Encode/decode files or streams with various encodings
html.parser, html.entities	Parse HTML and XHTML
xml.parsers.expat, xml.dom, xml.sax, xml.etree.ElementTree	Various parsers and tools for XML
cgi, cgitb	Common Gateway Interface support
wsgiref	WSGI utilities and reference implementation
urllib.request, urllib.parse	Open and parse URLs
ftplib, poplib, imaplib, nntplib, smtplib, telnetlib	Clients for various internet protocols
socketserver	Framework for network servers

Table 19.6 Modules supporting internet protocols and formats

Module	Description
`http.server`	HTTP servers
`xmlrpc.client`, `xmlrpc.server`	XML-RPC client and server

19.1.5 Development and debugging tools and runtime services

Python has several modules to help you debug, test, modify, and otherwise interact with your Python code at runtime. As shown in table 19.7, this category includes two testing tools, profilers, modules to interact with error tracebacks, the interpreter's garbage collection, and so on, as well as modules that let you tweak the importing of other modules.

Table 19.7 Development, debugging, and runtime modules

Module	Description
`pydoc`	Documentation generator and online help system
`doctest`	Test interactive Python examples
`unittest`	Unit testing framework
`test.support`	Utility functions for tests
`pdb`	Python debugger
`profile`, `cProfile`	Python profilers
`timeit`	Measure execution time of small code snippets
`trace`	Trace or track Python statement execution
`sys`	System-specific parameters and functions
`atexit`	Exit handlers
`__future__`	Future statement definitions—features to be added to Python
`gc`	Garbage collector interface
`inspect`	Inspect live objects
`imp`	Access the import internals
`zipimport`	Import modules from zip archives
`modulefinder`	Find modules used by a script

19.2 Moving beyond the standard library

Although Python's "batteries included" philosophy and well-stocked standard library mean that you can do a lot with Python out of the box, there will inevitably come a situation in which you need some functionality that doesn't come with Python. This section surveys your options when you need to do something that isn't in the standard library.

19.3   *Adding more Python libraries*

Finding a Python package or module can be as easy as entering the functionality you're looking for (such as `mp3 tags` and `Python`) in a search engine and then sorting through the results. If you're lucky, you may find the module you need packaged for your OS—with an executable Windows or macOS installer or a package for your Linux distribution.

This technique is one of the easiest ways to add a library to your Python installation, because the installer or your package manager takes care of all the details of adding the module to your system correctly. It can also be the answer for installing more complex libraries, such as scientific libraries with complex build requirements and dependencies.

In general, except for scientific libraries, such prebuilt packages aren't the rule for Python software. Such packages tend to be a bit older, and they offer less flexibility in where and how they're installed.

19.4   *Installing Python libraries using pip and venv*

If you need a third-party module that isn't prepackaged for your platform, you'll have to turn to its source distribution. This fact presents a couple of problems:

- To install the module, you must find and download it.
- Installing even a single Python module correctly can involve a certain amount of hassle in dealing with Python's paths and your system's permissions, which makes a standard installation system helpful.

Python offers `pip` as the current solution to both problems. `pip` tries to find the module in the Python Package index (more about that soon), downloads it and any dependencies, and takes care of the installation. The basic syntax of `pip` is quite simple. To install the popular requests library from the command line, for example, all you have to do is

```
$ python3.6 -m pip install requests
```

Upgrading to the library's latest version requires only the addition of the `--upgrade` switch:

```
$ python3.6 -m pip install --upgrade requests
```

Finally, if you need to specify a particular version of a package, you can append it to the name like this:

```
$ python3.6 -m pip install requests==2.11.1
$ python3.6 -m pip install requests>=2.9
```

19.4.1 *Installing with the –user flag*

On many occasions, you can't or don't want to install a Python package in the main system instance of Python. Maybe you need a bleeding-edge version of the library, but some other application (or the system itself) still uses an older version. Or maybe you don't have access privileges to modify the system's default Python. In cases like those, one answer is to install the library with the --user flag. This flag installs the library in the user's home directory, where it's not accessible by any other users. To install requests for only the local user:

```
$ python3.6 -m pip install --user requests
```

As I mentioned previously, this scheme is particularly useful if you're working on a system on which you don't have sufficient administrator rights to install software, or if you want to install a different version of a module. If your needs go beyond the basic installation methods discussed here, a good place to start is "Installing Python Modules," which you can find in the Python documentation.

19.4.2 *Virtual environments*

You have another, better option if you need to avoid installing libraries in the system Python. This option is called a virtual environment (virtualenv). A *virtual environment* is a self-contained directory structure that contains both an installation of Python and its additional packages. Because the entire Python environment is contained in the virtual environment, the libraries and modules installed there can't conflict with those in the main system or in other virtual environments, allowing different applications to use different versions on both Python and its packages.

Creating and using a virtual environment takes two steps. First, you create the environment:

```
$ python3.6 -m venv test-env
```

This step creates the environment with Python and pip installed in a directory called test-env. Then, when the environment is created, you activate it. On Windows, you do this:

```
> test-env\Scripts\activate.bat
```

On Unix or MacOS systems, you source the activate script:

```
$ source test-env/bin/activate
```

When you've activated the environment, you can use pip to manage packages as earlier, but in the virtual environment pip is a standalone command:

```
$ pip install requests
```

In addition, whatever version of Python you used to create the environment is the default Python for that environment, so you can use just `python` instead of `python3` or `python3.6`.

Virtual environments are very useful for managing projects and their dependencies and are very much a standard practice, particularly for developers working on multiple projects. For more information, look at the "Virtual Environments and Packages" section of the Python tutorial in the Python online documentation.

19.5 PyPI (a.k.a. "The Cheese Shop")

Although `distutils` packages get the job done, there's one catch: You have to find the correct package, which can be a chore. And after you've found a package, it would be nice to have a reasonably reliable source from which to download that package.

To meet this need, various Python package repositories have been made available over the years. Currently, the official (but by no means the only) repository for Python code is the Python Package Index, or PyPI (formerly also known as "The Cheese Shop," after the Monty Python sketch) on the Python website. You can access it from a link on the main page or directly at https://pypi.python.org. PyPI contains more than 6,000 packages for various Python versions, listed by date added and name, but also searchable and broken down by category.

At this writing, a new version of PyPI is in the wings; currently, it's called "The Warehouse." This version is still in testing but promises to provide a much smoother and friendlier search experience.

PyPI is the logical next stop if you can't find the functionality you want with a search of the standard library.

Summary

- Python has a rich standard library that covers more common situations than many other languages, and you should check what's in the standard library carefully before looking for external modules.
- If you do need an external module, prebuilt packages for your operating system are the easiest option, but they're sometimes older and often hard to find.
- The standard way to install from source is to use pip, and the best way to prevent conflicts among multiple projects is to create virtual environments with the venv module.
- Usually, the logical first step in searching for external modules is the Python Package Index (PyPI).

Part 4

Working with data

In this part, you get some practice in using Python, and in particular using it to work with data. Handling data is one of Python's strengths. I start with basic file handling; then I move through reading from and writing to flat files, working with more structured formats such as JSON and Excel, using databases, and using Python to explore data.

These chapters are more project-oriented than the rest of the book and are intended to give you the opportunity to get hands-on experience in using Python to handle data. The chapters and projects in this part can be done in any order or combination that suits your needs.

Basic file wrangling

This chapter deals with the basic operations you can use when you have an ever-increasing collection of files to manage. Those files might be log files, or they might be from a regular data feed, but whatever their source, you can't simply discard them immediately. How do you save them, manage them, and ultimately dispose of them according to a plan, but without manual intervention?

20.1 The problem: The never-ending flow of data files

Many systems generate a continuous series of data files. These files might be the log files from an e-commerce server or a regular process; they might be a nightly feed of product information from a server; they might be automated feeds of items for online advertising;   historical data of stock trades; or they might come from a thousand other sources. They're often flat text files, uncompressed, with raw data that's either an input or a byproduct of other processes. In spite of their humble nature, however, the data they contain has some potential value, so the files can't be discarded at the end of the day—which means that every day, their numbers grow. Over time, files accumulate until dealing with them manually becomes unworkable and until the amount of storage they consume becomes unacceptable.

20.2   *Scenario: The product feed from hell*

A typical situation I've encountered is a daily feed of product data. This data might be coming in from a supplier or going out for online marketing, but the basic aspects are the same.

Consider the example of a product feed coming from a supplier. The feed file comes in once a day, with one row for each item that the business supplies. Each row has fields for the supplier's stock-keeping unit (SKU) number; a brief description of the item; the item's cost, height, width, length, and width; the item's status (in stock or back-ordered, say); and probably several other things, depending on the business.

In addition to this basic info file, you might well be getting others, possibly of related products, more detailed item attributes, or something else. In that case, you end up with several files with the same filenames arriving every day and landing in the same directory for processing.

Now assume that you get three related files every day: item_info.txt, item_attributes.txt, related_items.txt. These three files come in every day and get processed. If processing were the only requirement, you wouldn't have to worry much; you could just let each day's set of files replace the last and be done with it. But what if you can't throw the data away? You may want to keep the raw data in case there's a question about the accuracy of the process and you need to refer to past files. Or you may want to track the changes in the data over time. Whatever the reason, the need to keep the files means that you need to do some processing.

The simplest thing you might do is mark the files with the dates on which they were received and move them to an archive folder. That way, each new set of files can be received, processed, renamed, and moved out of the way so that the process can be repeated with no loss of data.

After a few repetitions, the directory structure might look something like this:

```
working/
    item_info.txt
    item_attributes.txt
    related_items.txt
    archive/
        item_info_2017-09-15.txt
        item_attributes_2017-09-15.txt
        related_items_2017-09-15.txt
        item_info_2016-07-16.txt
        item_attributes_2017-09-16.txt
        related_items_2017-09-16.txt
        item_info_2017-09-17.txt
        item_attributes_2017-09-17.txt
        related_items_2017-09-17.txt
        ...
```

◁──┐ **Main working folder, with current files for processing**

◁──┐ **Subdirectory for archiving processed files**

Think about the steps needed to make this process happen. First, you need to rename the files so that the current date is added to the filename. To do that, you need to get the names of the files you want to rename; then you need to get the stem of the filenames without the extensions. When you have the stem, you need to add a string based on the current date, add the extension back to the end, and then actually change the filename and move it to the archive directory.

> **QUICK CHECK : CONSIDER THE CHOICES** What are your options for handling the tasks I've identified? What modules in the standard library can you think of that will do the job? If you want, you can even stop right now and work out the code to do it. Then compare your solution with the one you develop later.

You can get the names of the files in several ways. If you're sure that the names are always exactly the same and that there aren't many files, you *could* hardcode them into your script. A safer way, however, is to use the `pathlib` module and a path object's `glob` method, as follows:

```
>>> import pathlib
>>> cur_path = pathlib.Path(".")
>>> FILE_PATTERN = "*.txt"
>>> path_list = cur_path.glob(FILE_PATTERN)
>>> print(list(path_list))
[PosixPath('item_attributes.txt'), PosixPath('related_items.txt'),
    PosixPath('item_info.txt')]
```

Now you can step through the paths that match your `FILE_PATTERN` and apply the needed changes. Remember that you need to add the date as part of the name of each file, as well move the renamed files to the archive directory. When you use `pathlib`, the entire operation might look like this.

Listing 20.1 File files_01.py

```
import datetime
import pathlib

FILE_PATTERN = "*.txt"          ◁─┐ Sets the pattern to match files
ARCHIVE = "archive"               └─ and the archive directory
                                ◁── A directory named
                                    "archive" must exist
if __name__ == '__main__':          for this code to run.

    date_string = datetime.date.today().strftime("%Y-%m-%d")    ◁──┐

    cur_path = pathlib.Path(".")                    Uses the date object from the
    paths = cur_path.glob(FILE_PATTERN)             datetime library to create a date
                                                    string based on today's date
    for path in paths:
        new_filename = "{}_{}{}".format(path.stem, date_string, path.suffix)
        new_path = cur_path.joinpath(ARCHIVE, new_filename)
        path.rename(new_path)       ◁──┐ Renames (and moves)
                                        the file as one step
```

Creates a new path from the current path, the archive directory, and the new filename

It's worth noting here that `Path` objects make this operation simpler, because no special parsing is needed to separate the filename stem and suffix. This operation is also simpler than you might expect because the `rename` method can in effect move a file by using a path that includes the new location.

This script is a very simple one and does the job effectively in very few lines of code. In the next sections, you consider how to handle more complex requirements.

> **QUICK CHECK: POTENTIAL PROBLEMS**   Because the preceding solution is very simple, there are likely to be many situations that it won't handle well. What are some potential issues or problems that might arise with the example script? How might you remedy these problems?
>
> Consider the naming convention used for the files, which is based on the year, month and name, in that order. What advantages do you see in that convention? What might be the disadvantages? Can you make any arguments for putting the date string somewhere else in the filename, such as the beginning or the end?

20.3 *More organization*

The solution to storing files described in the previous section works, but it does have some disadvantages. For one thing, as the files accumulate, managing them might become a bit more trouble, because over the course of a year, you'd have 365 sets of related files in the same directory, and you could find the related files only by inspecting their names. If the files arrive more frequently, of course, or if there are more related files in a set, the hassle would be even greater.

To mitigate this problem, you can change the way you archive the files. Instead of changing the filenames to include the dates on which they were received, you can create a separate subdirectory for each set of files and name that subdirectory after the date received. Your directory structure might look like this:

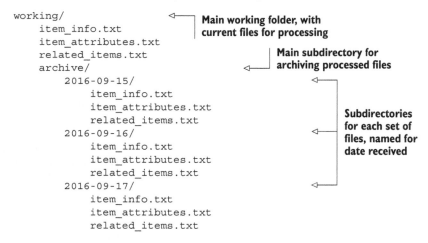

This scheme has the advantage that each set of files is grouped together. No matter how many sets of files you get or how many files you have in a set, it's easy to find all the files of a particular set.

> **TRY THIS: IMPLEMENTATION OF MULTIPLE DIRECTORIES** How would you modify the code that you developed to archive each set of files in subdirectories named according to date received? Feel free to take the time to implement the code and test it.

It turns out that archiving the files by subdirectory isn't much more work than the first solution. The only additional step is to create the subdirectory before renaming the file. This script is one way to perform this step.

Listing 20.2 File files_02.py

```python
import datetime
import pathlib

FILE_PATTERN = "*.txt"
ARCHIVE = "archive"

if __name__ == '__main__':

    date_string = datetime.date.today().strftime("%Y-%m-%d")

    cur_path = pathlib.Path(".")

    new_path = cur_path.joinpath(ARCHIVE, date_string)
    new_path.mkdir()

    paths = cur_path.glob(FILE_PATTERN)

    for path in paths:
        path.rename(new_path.joinpath(path.name))
```

Note that this directory needs to be created only once, before the files are moved into it.

This solution groups related files, which makes managing them as sets somewhat easier.

> **QUICK CHECK: ALTERNATE SOLUTIONS** How might you create a script that does the same thing without using `pathlib`? What libraries and functions would you use?

20.4 Saving storage space: Compression and grooming

So far, you've been concerned mainly with managing the groups of files received. Over time, however, the data files accumulate until the amount of storage they need becomes a concern. When that happens, you have several choices. One option is to get a bigger disk. Particularly if you're on a cloud-based platform, it may be easy and economical to adopt this strategy. Do keep in mind, however, that adding storage doesn't really solve the problem; it merely postpones solving it.

20.4.1 *Compressing files*

If the space that the files are taking up is an issue, the next approach you might consider is compressing them. You have numerous ways to compress a file or set of files, but in general, these methods are similar. In this section, you consider archiving each day's data file to a single zip file. If the files are mainly text files and are fairly large, the savings in storage achieved by compression can be impressive.

For this script, you use the same date string with a `.zip` extension as the name of each zip file. In listing 20.2, you created a new directory in the archive directory and then moved the files into it, which resulted in a directory structure that looks like this:

```
working/          ◁──┐  Main working folder, where current files are processed;
    archive/             these files are archived and removed after processing.
        2016-09-15.zip
        2016-09-16.zip       Zip files, each one containing that day's
        2016-09-17.zip       item_info.txt, attribute_info.text, and
                             related_items.txt
```

Obviously, to use zip files you need to change some of the steps you used previously.

> **TRY THIS: ARCHIVING TO ZIP FILES PSEUDOCODE** Write the pseudocode for a solution that stores data files in zip files. What modules and functions or methods do you intend to use? Try coding your solution to make sure that it works.

One key addition in the new script is an import of the zipfile library and with it, the code to create a new zip file object in the archive directory. After that, you can use the zip file object to write the data files to the new zip file. Finally, because you're no longer actually moving files, you need to remove the original files from the working directory. One solution looks like this.

Listing 20.3 File files_03.py

```python
import datetime
import pathlib
import zipfile              ◁──┐  Imports zipfile
                                  library

FILE_PATTERN = "*.txt"
ARCHIVE = "archive"
                                              Creates the path to the zip
if __name__ == '__main__':                    file in the archive directory

    date_string = datetime.date.today().strftime("%Y-%m-%d")

    cur_path = pathlib.Path(".")
    paths = cur_path.glob(FILE_PATTERN)

    zip_file_path = cur_path.joinpath(ARCHIVE, date_string + ".zip")   ◁──┐
    zip_file = zipfile.ZipFile(str(zip_file_path), "w")        ◁──┐

                    Opens the new zip file object for writing; str()
                    is needed  to convert a Path to a string.
```

```
for path in paths:
    zip_file.write(str(path))
    path.unlink()
```

Writes the current file to the zip file

Removes the current file from the working directory

20.4.2 Grooming files

Compressing data files into zipfile archives can save an impressive amount of space and may be all you need. If you have a lot of files, however, or files that don't compress much (such as JPEG image files), you may still find yourself running short of storage space. You may also find that your data doesn't change much, making it unnecessary to keep an archived copy of every data set in the longer term. That is, although it may be useful to keep every day's data for the past week or month, it may not be worth the storage to keep every data set for much longer. For data older than a few months, it may be acceptable to keep just one set of files per week or even one set per month.

The process of removing files after they reach a certain age is sometimes called *grooming*. Suppose that after several months of receiving a set of data files every day and archiving them in a zip file, you're told that you should retain only one file a week of the files that are more than one month old.

The simplest grooming script removes any files that you no longer need—in this case, all but one file a week for anything older than a month old. In designing this script, it's helpful to know the answers to two questions:

- Because you need to save one file a week, would it be much easier to simply pick the day of the week you want to save?
- How often should you do this grooming: daily, weekly, or once a month? If you decide that grooming should take place daily, it might make sense to combine the grooming with the archiving script. If, on the other hand, you need to groom only once a week or once a month, the two operations should be in separate scripts.

For this example, to keep things clear, you write a separate grooming script that can be run at any interval and that removes all the unneeded files. Further, assume that you've decided to keep only the files received on Tuesdays that are more than one month old. Here is a sample grooming script.

Listing 20.4 File files_04.py

```python
from datetime import datetime, timedelta
import pathlib
import zipfile

FILE_PATTERN = "*.zip"
ARCHIVE = "archive"
ARCHIVE_WEEKDAY = 1
if __name__ == '__main__':
```

```
                      cur_path = pathlib.Path(".")
                      zip_file_path = cur_path.joinpath(ARCHIVE)
```

Gets a datetime object for the current day

path.stem returns the filename without any extension.

```
                      paths = zip_file_path.glob(FILE_PATTERN)
                      current_date = datetime.today()
```

strptime parses a string into a datetime object based on the format string.

```
                      for path in paths:
                          name = path.stem
                          path_date = datetime.strptime(name, "%Y-%m-%d")
```

Subtracting one date from another yields a timedelta object.

```
                          path_timedelta = current_date - path_date
                          if path_timedelta > timedelta(days=30) and path_date.weekday() !=
                      ARCHIVE_WEEKDAY:
                              path.unlink()
```

timedelta(days=30) creates a timedelta object of 30 days; the weekday() method returns an integer for the day of the week, with Monday = 0.

The code shows how Python's datetime and pathlib libraries can be combined to groom files by date with only a few lines of code. Because your archive files have names derived from the dates on which they were received, you can get those file paths by using the glob method, extract the stem, and use strptime to parse it into a datetime object. From there, you can use datetime's timedelta objects and the weekday() method to find a file's age and the day of the week, and then remove (unlink) the files you don't need.

QUICK CHECK: CONSIDER DIFFERENT PARAMETERS   Take some time to consider different grooming options. How would you modify the code in listing 20.4 to keep only one file a month? How would you change it so that files from the previous month and older were groomed to save one a week? (Note: This is *not* the same as older than 30 days!)

Summary

- The pathlib module can greatly simplify file operations such as finding the root and extension, moving and renaming, and matching wildcards.
- As the number and complexity of files increase, automated archiving solutions are vital, and Python offers several easy ways to create them.
- You can dramatically save storage space by compressing and grooming data files.

Processing data files

21

This chapter covers

- Using ETL (extract-transform-load)
- Reading text data files (plain text and CSV)
- Reading spreadsheet files
- Normalizing, cleaning, and sorting data
- Writing data files

Much of the data available is contained in text files. This data can range from unstructured text, such as a corpus of tweets or literary texts, to more structured data in which each row is a record and the fields are delimited by a special character, such as a comma, a tab, or a pipe (|). Text files can be huge; a data set can be spread over tens or even hundreds of files, and the data in it can be incomplete or horribly dirty. With all the variations, it's almost inevitable that you'll need to read and use data from text files. This chapter gives you strategies for using Python to do exactly that.

21.1   *Welcome to ETL*

The need to get data out of files, parse it, turn it into a useful format, and then do something with it has been around for as long as there have been data files. In fact, there is a standard term for the process: extract-transform-load (ETL). The extraction refers to the process of reading a data source and parsing it, if necessary. The transformation can be cleaning and normalizing the data, as well as combining, breaking up, or reorganizing the records it contains. The loading refers to storing the transformed data in a new place, either a different file or a database. This chapter deals with the basics of ETL in Python, starting with text-based data files and storing the transformed data in other files. I look at more structured data files in chapter 22 and storage in databases in chapter 23.

21.2   *Reading text files*

The first part of ETL—the "extract" portion—involves opening a file and reading its contents. This process seems like a simple one, but even at this point there can be issues, such as the file's size. If a file is too large to fit into memory and be manipulated, you need to structure your code to handle smaller segments of the file, possibly operating one line at a time.

21.2.1   *Text encoding: ASCII, Unicode, and others*

Another possible pitfall is in the encoding. This chapter deals with text files, and in fact, much of the data exchanged in the real world is in text files. But the exact nature of *text* can vary from application to application, from person to person, and of course from country to country.

Sometimes, *text* means something in the ASCII encoding, which has 128 characters, only 95 of which are printable. The good news about ASCII encoding is that it's the lowest common denominator of most data exchange. The bad news is that it doesn't begin to handle the complexities of the many alphabets and writing systems of the world. Reading files using ASCII encoding is almost certain to cause trouble and throw errors on character values that it doesn't understand, whether it's a German ü, a Portuguese ç, or something from almost any language other than English.

These errors arise because ASCII is based on 7-bit values, whereas the bytes in a typical file are 8 bits, allowing 256 possible values as opposed to the 128 of a 7-bit value. It's routine to use those additional values to store additional characters—anything from extra punctuation (such as the printer's en dash and em dash) to symbols (such as the trademark, copyright, and degree symbols) to accented versions of alphabetical characters. The problem has always been that if, in reading a text file, you encounter a character in the 128 outside the ASCII range, you have no way of knowing for sure how it was encoded. Is the character value of 214, say, a division symbol, an Ö, or something else? Short of having the code that created the file, you have no way to know.

UNICODE AND UTF-8

One way to mitigate this confusion is Unicode. The Unicode encoding called UTF-8 accepts the basic ASCII characters without any change but also allows an almost unlimited set of other characters and symbols according to the Unicode standard. Because of its flexibility, UTF-8 was used in more 85% of web pages served at the time I wrote this chapter, which means that your best bet for reading text files is to assume UTF-8 encoding. If the files contain only ASCII characters, they'll still be read correctly, but you'll also be covered if other characters are encoded in UTF-8. The good news is that the Python 3 string data type was designed to handle Unicode by default.

Even with Unicode, there'll be occasions when your text contains values that can't be successfully encoded. Fortunately, the `open` function in Python accepts an optional errors parameter that tells it how to deal with encoding errors when reading or writing files. The default option is `'strict'`, which causes an error to be raised whenever an encoding error is encountered. Other useful options are `'ignore'`, which causes the character causing the error to be skipped; `'replace'`, which causes the character to be replaced by a marker character (often, ?); `'backslashreplace'`, which replaces the character with a backslash escape sequence; and `'surrogateescape'`, which translates the offending character to a private Unicode code point on reading and back to the original sequence of bytes on writing. Your particular use case will determine how strict you need to be in handling or resolving encoding issues.

Look at a short example of a file containing an invalid UTF-8 character, and see how the different options handle that character. First, write the file, using bytes and binary mode:

```
>>> open('test.txt', 'wb').write(bytes([65, 66, 67, 255, 192,193]))
```

This code results in a file that contains "ABC" followed by three non-ASCII characters, which may be rendered differently depending on the encoding used. If you use vim to look at the file, you see

```
ABCÿÀÁ
~
```

Now that you have the file, try reading it with the default `'strict'` errors option:

```
>>> x = open('test.txt').read()
Traceback (most recent call last):
  File "<stdin>", line 1, in <module>
  File "/usr/local/lib/python3.6/codecs.py", line 321, in decode
    (result, consumed) = self._buffer_decode(data, self.errors, final)
UnicodeDecodeError: 'utf-8' codec can't decode byte 0xff in position 3:
    invalid start byte
```

The fourth byte, which had a value of 255, isn't a valid UTF-8 character in that position, so the `'strict'` errors setting raises an exception. Now see how the other error options handle the same file, keeping in mind that the last three characters raise an error:

```
>>> open('test.txt', errors='ignore').read()
'ABC'
>>> open('test.txt', errors='replace').read()
'ABC���'
>>> open('test.txt', errors='surrogateescape').read()
'ABC\udcff\udcc0\udcc1'
>>> open('test.txt', errors='backslashreplace').read()
'ABC\\xff\\xc0\\xc1'
>>>
```

If you want any problem characters to disappear, `'ignore'` is the option to use. The `'replace'` option only marks the place occupied by the invalid character, and the other options in different ways attempt to preserve the invalid characters without interpretation.

21.2.2 *Unstructured text*

Unstructured text files are the easiest sort of data to read but the hardest to extract information from. Processing unstructured text can vary enormously, depending on both the nature of the text and what you want to do with it, so any comprehensive discussion of text processing is beyond the scope of this book. A short example, however, can illustrate some of the basic issues and set the stage for a discussion of structured text data files.

One of the simplest issues is deciding what forms a basic logical unit in the file. If you have a corpus of thousands of tweets, the text of *Moby Dick*, or a collection of news stories, you need to be able to break them up into cohesive units. In the case of tweets, each may fit onto a single line, and you can read and process each line of the file fairly simply.

In the case of *Moby Dick* or even a news story, the problem can be trickier. You may not want to treat all of a novel or news item as a single item in many cases. But if that's the case, you need to decide what sort of unit you do want and then come up with a strategy to divide the file accordingly. Perhaps you want to consider the text paragraph by paragraph. In that case, you need to identify how paragraphs are separated in your file and create your code accordingly. If a paragraph is the same as a line in the text file, the job is easy. Often, however, the line breaks in a text file are shorter, and you need to do a bit more work.

Now look at a couple of examples:

```
Call me Ishmael.  Some years ago--never mind how long precisely--
having little or no money in my purse, and nothing particular
to interest me on shore, I thought I would sail about a little
and see the watery part of the world.  It is a way I have
of driving off the spleen and regulating the circulation.
Whenever I find myself growing grim about the mouth;
whenever it is a damp, drizzly November in my soul; whenever I
find myself involuntarily pausing before coffin warehouses,
and bringing up the rear of every funeral I meet;
and especially whenever my hypos get such an upper hand of me,
```

```
that it requires a strong moral principle to prevent me from
deliberately stepping into the street, and methodically knocking
people's hats off--then, I account it high time to get to sea
as soon as I can.  This is my substitute for pistol and ball.
With a philosophical flourish Cato throws himself upon his sword;
I quietly take to the ship.  There is nothing surprising in this.
If they but knew it, almost all men in their degree, some time
or other, cherish very nearly the same feelings towards
the ocean with me.

There now is your insular city of the Manhattoes, belted round by wharves
as Indian isles by coral reefs--commerce surrounds it with her surf.
Right and left, the streets take you waterward.  Its extreme downtown
is the battery, where that noble mole is washed by waves, and cooled
by breezes, which a few hours previous were out of sight of land.
Look at the crowds of water-gazers there.
```

In the sample, which is indeed the beginning of *Moby Dick*, the lines are broken more or less as they might be on the page, and paragraphs are indicated by a single blank line. If you want to deal with each paragraph as a unit, you need to break the text on the blank lines. Fortunately, this task is easy if you use the string split() method. Each newline character in a string can represented by "\n". Naturally, the last line of a paragraph's text ends with a newline, and if the next line is blank, it's immediately followed by a second newline for the blank line:

Reads all of file as a single string

Splits on two newlines together

```
>>> moby_text = open("moby_01.txt").read()
>>> moby_paragraphs = moby_text.split("\n\n")
>>> print(moby_paragraphs[1])
There now is your insular city of the Manhattoes, belted round by wharves
as Indian isles by coral reefs--commerce surrounds it with her surf.
Right and left, the streets take you waterward.  Its extreme downtown
is the battery, where that noble mole is washed by waves, and cooled
by breezes, which a few hours previous were out of sight of land.
Look at the crowds of water-gazers there.
```

Splitting the text into paragraphs is a very simple first step in handling unstructured text. You might also need to do more normalization of the text before processing. Suppose that you want to count the rate of occurrence of every word in a text file. If you just split the file on whitespace, you get a list of words in the file. Counting their occurrences accurately will be hard, however, because *This, this, this.*, and *this,* are not the same. The way to make this code work is to normalize the text by removing the punctuation and making everything the same case before processing. For the example text above, the code for a normalized list of words might look like this:

Reads all of the file as a single string

Makes everything lowercase

```
>>> moby_text = open("moby_01.txt").read()
>>> moby_paragraphs = moby_text.split("\n\n")
>>> moby = moby_paragraphs[1].lower()
```

```
>>> moby = moby.replace (".", "")        ⟵─────┐  Removes
>>> moby = moby.replace (",", "")   ⟵───┐       │  periods
>>> moby_words = moby.split ()       Removes ───┘
>>> print(moby_words)                commas
['there', 'now', 'is', 'your', 'insular', 'city', 'of', 'the', 'manhattoes,',
    'belted', 'round', 'by', 'wharves', 'as', 'indian', 'isles', 'by',
    'coral', 'reefs--commerce', 'surrounds', 'it', 'with', 'her', 'surf',
    'right', 'and', 'left,', 'the', 'streets', 'take', 'you', 'waterward',
    'its', 'extreme', 'downtown', 'is', 'the', 'battery,', 'where', 'that',
    'noble', 'mole', 'is', 'washed', 'by', 'waves,', 'and', 'cooled', 'by',
    'breezes,', 'which', 'a', 'few', 'hours', 'previous', 'were', 'out',
    'of', 'sight', 'of', 'land', 'look', 'at', 'the', 'crowds', 'of',
    'water-gazers', 'there']
```

> **QUICK CHECK: NORMALIZATION**   Look closely at the list of words generated. Do you see any issues with the normalization so far? What other issues do you think you might encounter in a longer section of text? How do you think you might deal with those issues?

21.2.3 *Delimited flat files*

Although reading unstructured text files is easy, the downside is their very lack of structure. It's often much more useful to have some organization in the file to help with picking out individual values. The simplest way is break the file into lines and have one element of information per line. You may have a list of the names of files to be processed, a list of people's names that need to be printed (on name tags, say), or maybe a series of temperature readings from a remote monitor. In such cases, the data parsing is very simple: You read in the line and convert it to the right type, if necessary. Then the file is ready to use.

Most of the time, however, things aren't not quite so simple. Usually, you need to group multiple related bits of information, and you need your code to read them in together. The common way to do this is to put the related pieces of information on the same line, separated by a special character. That way, as you read each line of the file, you can use the special characters to split the file into its different fields and put the values of those fields in variables for later processing.

This file is a simple example of temperature data in delimited format:

```
State|Month Day, Year Code|Avg Daily Max Air Temperature (F)|Record Count for
    Daily Max Air Temp (F)
Illinois|1979/01/01|17.48|994
Illinois|1979/01/02|4.64|994
Illinois|1979/01/03|11.05|994
Illinois|1979/01/04|9.51|994
Illinois|1979/05/15|68.42|994
Illinois|1979/05/16|70.29|994
Illinois|1979/05/17|75.34|994
Illinois|1979/05/18|79.13|994
Illinois|1979/05/19|74.94|994
```

This data is pipe-delimited, meaning that each field in the line is separated by the pipe (|) character, in this case giving you four fields: the state of the observations, the date of the observations, the average high temperature, and the number of stations reporting. Other common delimiters are the tab character and the comma. The comma is perhaps the most common, but the delimiter could be any character you don't expect to occur in the values. (More about that issue next.) Comma delimiters are so common that this format is often called CSV (comma-separated values), and files of this type often have a .csv extension as a hint of their format.

Whatever character is being used as the delimiter, if you know what character it is, you can write your own code in Python to break each line into its fields and return them as a list. In the previous case, you can use the string `split()` method to break a line into a list of values:

```
>>> line = "Illinois|1979/01/01|17.48|994"
>>> print(line.split("|"))
['Illinois', '1979/01/01', '17.48', '994']
```

Note that this technique is very easy to do but leaves all the values as strings, which might not be convenient for later processing.

> **TRY THIS: READ A FILE** Write the code to read a text file (assume temp_data_pipes_00a.txt, as shown in the example), split each line of the file into a list of values, and add that list to a single list of records.
>
> What issues or problems did you encounter in implementing this code? How might you go about converting the last three fields to the correct date, real, and int types?

21.2.4 *The csv module*

If you need to do much processing of delimited data files, you should become familiar with the `csv` module and its options. When I've been asked to name my favorite module in the Python standard library, more than once I've cited the `csv` module—not because it's glamorous (it isn't), but because it has probably saved me more work and kept me from more self-inflicted bugs over my career than any other module.

The `csv` module is a perfect case of Python's "batteries included" philosophy. Although it's perfectly possible, and in many cases not even terribly hard, to roll your own code to read delimited files, it's even easier and much more reliable to use the Python module. The `csv` module has been tested and optimized, and it has features that you probably wouldn't bother to write if you had to do it yourself, but that are truly handy and time-saving when available.

Look at the previous data, and decide how you'd read it by using the `csv` module. The code to parse the data has to do two things: read each line and strip off the trailing newline character, and then break up the line on the pipe character and append that list of values to a list of lines. Your solution to the exercise might look something like this:

```
>>> results = []
>>> for line in open("temp_data_pipes_00a.txt"):
...     fields = line.strip().split("|")
```

```
...         results.append(fields)
...
>>> results
[['State', 'Month Day, Year Code', 'Avg Daily Max Air Temperature (F)',
    'Record Count for Daily Max Air Temp (F)'], ['Illinois', '1979/01/01',
    '17.48', '994'], ['Illinois', '1979/01/02', '4.64', '994'], ['Illinois',
    '1979/01/03', '11.05', '994'], ['Illinois', '1979/01/04', '9.51',
    '994'], ['Illinois', '1979/05/15', '68.42', '994'], ['Illinois', '1979/
    05/16', '70.29', '994'], ['Illinois', '1979/05/17', '75.34', '994'],
    ['Illinois', '1979/05/18', '79.13', '994'], ['Illinois', '1979/05/19',
    '74.94', '994']]
```

To do the same thing with the csv module, the code might be something like this:

```
>>> import csv
>>> results = [fields for fields in
    csv.reader(open("temp_data_pipes_00a.txt", newline=''), delimiter="|")]
>>> results
[['State', 'Month Day, Year Code', 'Avg Daily Max Air Temperature (F)',
    'Record Count for Daily Max Air Temp (F)'], ['Illinois', '1979/01/01',
    '17.48', '994'], ['Illinois', '1979/01/02', '4.64', '994'], ['Illinois',
    '1979/01/03', '11.05', '994'], ['Illinois', '1979/01/04', '9.51',
    '994'], ['Illinois', '1979/05/15', '68.42', '994'], ['Illinois', '1979/
    05/16', '70.29', '994'], ['Illinois', '1979/05/17', '75.34', '994'],
    ['Illinois', '1979/05/18', '79.13', '994'], ['Illinois', '1979/05/19',
    '74.94', '994']]
```

In this simple case, the gain over rolling your own code doesn't seem so great. Still, the code is two lines shorter and a bit clearer, and there's no need to worry about stripping off newline characters. The real advantages come when you want to deal with more challenging cases.

The data in the example is real, but it's actually been simplified and cleaned. The real data from the source is more complex. The real data has more fields, some fields are in quotes while others are not, and the first field is empty. The original is tab-delimited, but for the sake of illustration, I present it as comma-delimited here:

```
"Notes","State","State Code","Month Day, Year","Month Day, Year Code",Avg
    Daily Max Air Temperature (F),Record Count for Daily Max Air Temp
    (F),Min Temp for Daily Max Air Temp (F),Max Temp for Daily Max Air Temp
    (F),Avg Daily Max Heat Index (F),Record Count for Daily Max Heat Index
    (F),Min for Daily Max Heat Index (F),Max for Daily Max Heat Index
    (F),Daily Max Heat Index (F) % Coverage

,"Illinois","17","Jan 01, 1979","1979/01/
    01",17.48,994,6.00,30.50,Missing,0,Missing,Missing,0.00%
,"Illinois","17","Jan 02, 1979","1979/01/02",4.64,994,-
    6.40,15.80,Missing,0,Missing,Missing,0.00%
,"Illinois","17","Jan 03, 1979","1979/01/03",11.05,994,-
    0.70,24.70,Missing,0,Missing,Missing,0.00%
,"Illinois","17","Jan 04, 1979","1979/01/
    04",9.51,994,0.20,27.60,Missing,0,Missing,Missing,0.00%
,"Illinois","17","May 15, 1979","1979/05/
    15",68.42,994,61.00,75.10,Missing,0,Missing,Missing,0.00%
,"Illinois","17","May 16, 1979","1979/05/
    16",70.29,994,63.40,73.50,Missing,0,Missing,Missing,0.00%
```

```
,"Illinois","17","May 17, 1979","1979/05/
    17",75.34,994,64.00,80.50,82.60,2,82.40,82.80,0.20%
,"Illinois","17","May 18, 1979","1979/05/
    18",79.13,994,75.50,82.10,81.42,349,80.20,83.40,35.11%
,"Illinois","17","May 19, 1979","1979/05/
    19",74.94,994,66.90,83.10,82.87,78,81.60,85.20,7.85%
```

Notice that some fields include commas. The convention in that case is to put quotes around a field to indicate that it's not supposed to be parsed for delimiters. It's quite common, as here, to quote only some fields, especially those in which a value might contain the delimiter character. It also happens, as here, that some fields are quoted even if they're not likely to contain the delimiting character.

In a case like this one, your home-grown code becomes cumbersome. Now you can no longer split the line on the delimiting character; you need to be sure that you look only at delimiters that aren't inside quoted strings. Also, you need to remove the quotes around quoted strings, which might occur in any position or not at all. With the csv module, you don't need to change your code at all. In fact, because the comma is the default delimiter, you don't even need to specify it:

```
>>> results2 = [fields for fields in csv.reader(open("temp_data_01.csv",
    newline=''))]
>>> results2
[['Notes', 'State', 'State Code', 'Month Day, Year', 'Month Day, Year Code',
    'Avg Daily Max Air Temperature (F)', 'Record Count for Daily Max Air
    Temp (F)', 'Min Temp for Daily Max Air Temp (F)', 'Max Temp for Daily
    Max Air Temp (F)', 'Avg Daily Min Air Temperature (F)', 'Record Count
    for Daily Min Air Temp (F)', 'Min Temp for Daily Min Air Temp (F)', 'Max
    Temp for Daily Min Air Temp (F)', 'Avg Daily Max Heat Index (F)',
    'Record Count for Daily Max Heat Index (F)', 'Min for Daily Max Heat
    Index (F)', 'Max for Daily Max Heat Index (F)', 'Daily Max Heat Index
    (F) % Coverage'], ['', 'Illinois', '17', 'Jan 01, 1979', '1979/01/01',
    '17.48', '994', '6.00', '30.50', '2.89', '994', '-13.60', '15.80',
    'Missing', '0', 'Missing', 'Missing', '0.00%'], ['', 'Illinois', '17',
    'Jan 02, 1979', '1979/01/02', '4.64', '994', '-6.40', '15.80', '-9.03',
    '994', '-23.60', '6.60', 'Missing', '0', 'Missing', 'Missing', '0.00%'],
    ['', 'Illinois', '17', 'Jan 03, 1979', '1979/01/03', '11.05', '994', '-
    0.70', '24.70', '-2.17', '994', '-18.30', '12.90', 'Missing', '0',
    'Missing', 'Missing', '0.00%'], ['', 'Illinois', '17', 'Jan 04, 1979',
    '1979/01/04', '9.51', '994', '0.20', '27.60', '-0.43', '994', '-16.30',
    '16.30', 'Missing', '0', 'Missing', 'Missing', '0.00%'], ['',
    'Illinois', '17', 'May 15, 1979', '1979/05/15', '68.42', '994', '61.00',
    '75.10', '51.30', '994', '43.30', '57.00', 'Missing', '0', 'Missing',
    'Missing', '0.00%'], ['', 'Illinois', '17', 'May 16, 1979', '1979/05/
    16', '70.29', '994', '63.40', '73.50', '48.09', '994', '41.10', '53.00',
    'Missing', '0', 'Missing', 'Missing', '0.00%'], ['', 'Illinois', '17',
    'May 17, 1979', '1979/05/17', '75.34', '994', '64.00', '80.50', '50.84',
    '994', '44.30', '55.70', '82.60', '2', '82.40', '82.80', '0.20%'], ['',
    'Illinois', '17', 'May 18, 1979', '1979/05/18', '79.13', '994', '75.50',
    '82.10', '55.68', '994', '50.00', '61.10', '81.42', '349', '80.20',
    '83.40', '35.11%'], ['', 'Illinois', '17', 'May 19, 1979', '1979/05/19',
    '74.94', '994', '66.90', '83.10', '58.59', '994', '50.90', '63.20',
    '82.87', '78', '81.60', '85.20', '7.85%']]
```

Notice that the extra quotes have been removed and that any field values with commas have the commas intact inside the fields—all without any more characters in the command.

> **QUICK CHECK: HANDLING QUOTING**   Consider how you'd approach the problems of handling quoted fields and embedded delimiter characters if you didn't have the `csv` library. Which would be easier to handle: the quoting or the embedded delimiters?

21.2.5 *Reading a csv file as a list of dictionaries*

In the preceding examples, you got a row of data back as a list of fields. This result works fine in many cases, but sometimes it may be handy to get the rows back as dictionaries where the field name is the key. For this use case, the `csv` library has a `DictReader`, which can take a list of fields as a parameter or can read them from the first line of the data. If you want to open the data with a `DictReader`, the code would look like this:

```
>>> results = [fields for fields in csv.DictReader(open("temp_data_01.csv",
    newline=''))]
>>> results[0]
OrderedDict([('Notes', ''), ('State', 'Illinois'), ('State Code', '17'),
    ('Month Day, Year', 'Jan 01, 1979'), ('Month Day, Year Code', '1979/01/
    01'), ('Avg Daily Max Air Temperature (F)', '17.48'), ('Record Count for
    Daily Max Air Temp (F)', '994'), ('Min Temp for Daily Max Air Temp (F)',
    '6.00'), ('Max Temp for Daily Max Air Temp (F)', '30.50'), ('Avg Daily
    Min Air Temperature (F)', '2.89'), ('Record Count for Daily Min Air Temp
    (F)', '994'), ('Min Temp for Daily Min Air Temp (F)', '-13.60'), ('Max
    Temp for Daily Min Air Temp (F)', '15.80'), ('Avg Daily Max Heat Index
    (F)', 'Missing'), ('Record Count for Daily Max Heat Index (F)', '0'),
    ('Min for Daily Max Heat Index (F)', 'Missing'), ('Max for Daily Max
    Heat Index (F)', 'Missing'), ('Daily Max Heat Index (F) % Coverage',
    '0.00%')])
```

Note that the `csv.DictReader` returns `OrderedDicts`, so the fields stay in their original order. Although their representation is a little different, the fields still behave like dictionaries:

```
>>> results[0]['State']
'Illinois'
```

If the data is particularly complex, and specific fields need to be manipulated, a `DictReader` can make it much easier to be sure you're getting the right field; it also makes your code somewhat easier to understand. Conversely, if your data set is quite large, you need to keep in mind that `DictReader` can take on the order of twice as long to read the same amount of data.

21.3 *Excel files*

The other common file format that I discuss in this chapter is the Excel file, which is the format that Microsoft Excel uses to store spreadsheets. I include Excel files here because the way you end up treating them is very similar to the way you treat delimited files. In fact, because Excel can both read and write CSV files, the quickest and easiest way to extract data from an Excel spreadsheet file often is to open it in Excel and then save it as a CSV file. This procedure doesn't always make sense, however, particularly if you have a lot of files. In that case, even though you could theoretically automate the process of opening and saving each file in CSV format, it's probably faster to deal with the Excel files directly.

It's beyond the scope of this book to have an in-depth discussion of spreadsheet files, with their options for multiple sheets in the same file, macros, and various formatting options. Instead, in this section I look at an example of reading a simple one-sheet file simply to extract the data from it.

As it happens, Python's standard library doesn't have a module to read or write Excel files. To read that format, you need to install an external module. Fortunately, several modules are available to do the job. For this example, you use one called OpenPyXL, which is available from the Python package repository. You can install it with the following command from a command line:

```
$pip install openpyxl
```

Here's a view of the previous data, but in a spreadsheet:

	A	B	C	D	E	F	G	H	I	J	K	L	M	N	C
1	Notes	State	State Code	Month Day, Year	Month Day, Year Code	Avg Daily I	Record Co	Min Temp	Max Temp	Avg Daily I	Record Co	Min for Da	Max for Da	Daily Max Heat In
2		Illinois	17	Jan 01, 1979	1979/01/01	17.48	994	6	30.5	Missing	0	Missing	Missing	0.00%
3		Illinois	17	Jan 02, 1979	1979/01/02	4.64	994	-6.4	15.8	Missing	0	Missing	Missing	0.00%
4		Illinois	17	Jan 03, 1979	1979/01/03	11.05	994	-0.7	24.7	Missing	0	Missing	Missing	0.00%
5		Illinois	17	Jan 04, 1979	1979/01/04	9.51	994	0.2	27.6	Missing	0	Missing	Missing	0.00%
6		Illinois	17	May 15, 1979	1979/05/15	68.42	994	61	75.1	Missing	0	Missing	Missing	0.00%
7		Illinois	17	May 16, 1979	1979/05/16	70.29	994	63.4	73.5	Missing	0	Missing	Missing	0.00%
8		Illinois	17	May 17, 1979	1979/05/17	75.34	994	64	80.5	82.6	2	82.4	82.8	0.20%
9		Illinois	17	May 18, 1979	1979/05/18	79.13	994	75.5	82.1	81.42	349	80.2	83.4	35.11%
10		Illinois	17	May 19, 1979	1979/05/19	74.94	994	66.9	83.1	82.87	78	81.6	85.2	7.85%
11														
12														

Reading the file is fairly simple, but it's still more work than CSV files require. First, you need to load the workbook; next, you need to get the specific sheet; then you can iterate over the rows; and from there, you extract the values of the cells. Some sample code to read the spreadsheet looks like this:

```
>>> from openpyxl import load_workbook
>>> wb = load_workbook('temp_data_01.xlsx')
>>> results = []
>>> ws = wb.worksheets[0]
>>> for row in ws.iter_rows():
...     results.append([cell.value for cell in row])
...
>>> print(results)
[['Notes', 'State', 'State Code', 'Month Day, Year', 'Month Day, Year Code',
    'Avg Daily Max Air Temperature (F)', 'Record Count for Daily Max Air
    Temp (F)', 'Min Temp for Daily Max Air Temp (F)', 'Max Temp for Daily
```

```
Max Air Temp (F)', 'Avg Daily Max Heat Index (F)', 'Record Count for
Daily Max Heat Index (F)', 'Min for Daily Max Heat Index (F)', 'Max for
Daily Max Heat Index (F)', 'Daily Max Heat Index (F) % Coverage'],
[None, 'Illinois', 17, 'Jan 01, 1979', '1979/01/01', 17.48, 994, 6,
30.5, 'Missing', 0, 'Missing', 'Missing', '0.00%'], [None, 'Illinois',
17, 'Jan 02, 1979', '1979/01/02', 4.64, 994, -6.4, 15.8, 'Missing', 0,
'Missing', 'Missing', '0.00%'], [None, 'Illinois', 17, 'Jan 03, 1979',
'1979/01/03', 11.05, 994, -0.7, 24.7, 'Missing', 0, 'Missing',
'Missing', '0.00%'], [None, 'Illinois', 17, 'Jan 04, 1979', '1979/01/
04', 9.51, 994, 0.2, 27.6, 'Missing', 0, 'Missing', 'Missing', '0.00%'],
[None, 'Illinois', 17, 'May 15, 1979', '1979/05/15', 68.42, 994, 61,
75.1, 'Missing', 0, 'Missing', 'Missing', '0.00%'], [None, 'Illinois',
17, 'May 16, 1979', '1979/05/16', 70.29, 994, 63.4, 73.5, 'Missing', 0,
'Missing', 'Missing', '0.00%'], [None, 'Illinois', 17, 'May 17, 1979',
'1979/05/17', 75.34, 994, 64, 80.5, 82.6, 2, 82.4, 82.8, '0.20%'],
[None, 'Illinois', 17, 'May 18, 1979', '1979/05/18', 79.13, 994, 75.5,
82.1, 81.42, 349, 80.2, 83.4, '35.11%'], [None, 'Illinois', 17, 'May 19,
1979', '1979/05/19', 74.94, 994, 66.9, 83.1, 82.87, 78, 81.6, 85.2,
'7.85%']]
```

This code gets you the same results as the much simpler code did for a csv file. It's not surprising that the code to read a spreadsheet is more complex, because spreadsheets are themselves much more complex objects. You should also be sure that you understand the way that data has been stored in the spreadsheet. If the spreadsheet contains formatting that has some significance, if labels need to be disregarded or handled differently, or if formulas and references need to be processed, you need to dig deeper into how those elements should be processed, and you need to write more-complex code.

Spreadsheets also often have other possible issues. At this writing, it's common for spreadsheets to be limited to around a million rows. Although that limit sounds large, more and more often you'll need to handle data sets that are larger. Also, spreadsheets sometimes automatically apply inconvenient formatting. One company I worked for had part numbers that consisted of a digit and at least one letter followed by some combination of digits and letters. It was possible to get a part number such as 1E20. Most spreadsheets automatically interpret 1E20 as scientific notation and save it as 1.00E+20 (1 times 10 to the 20th power) while leaving 1F20 as a string. For some reason, it's rather difficult to keep this from happening, and particularly with a large data set, the problem won't be detected until farther down the pipeline, if all. For these reasons, I recommend using CSV or delimited files when at all possible. Users usually can save a spreadsheet as CSV, so there's usually no need put up with the extra complexity and formatting hassles that spreadsheets involve.

21.4 *Data cleaning*

One common problem you'll encounter in processing text-based data files is dirty data. By *dirty*, I mean that there are all sorts of surprises in the data, such as null values, values that aren't legal for your encoding, or extra whitespace. The data may also be unsorted or in an order that makes processing difficult. The process of dealing with situations like these is called *data cleaning*.

21.4.1 *Cleaning*

In a very simple example data clean, you might need to process a file that was exported from a spreadsheet or other financial program, and the columns dealing with money may have percentage and currency symbols (such as %, $, £, and ?), as well as extra groupings that use a period or comma. Data from other sources may have other surprises that make processing tricky if they're not caught in advance. Look again at the temperature data you saw previously. The first data line looks like this:

```
[None, 'Illinois', 17, 'Jan 01, 1979', '1979/01/01', 17.48, 994, 6, 30.5,
    2.89, 994, -13.6, 15.8, 'Missing', 0, 'Missing', 'Missing', '0.00%']
```

Some columns, such as 'State' (field 2) and 'Notes' (field 1), are clearly text, and you wouldn't be likely to do much with them. There are also two date fields in different formats, and you might well want to do calculations with the dates, possibly to change the order of the data and to group rows by month or day, or possibly to calculate how far apart in time two rows are.

The rest of the fields seem to be different types of numbers; the temperatures are decimals, and the record counts columns are integers. Notice, however, that the heat index temperatures have a variation: When the value for the 'Max Temp for Daily Max Air Temp (F)' field is below 80, the values for the heat index fields aren't reported, but instead are listed as 'Missing', and the record count is 0. Also note that the 'Daily Max Heat Index (F) % Coverage' field is expressed as a percentage of the number of temperature records that also qualify to have a heat index. Both of these issues will be problematic if you want to do any math calculations on the values in those fields, because both 'Missing' and any number ending with % will be parsed as strings, not numbers.

Cleaning data like this can be done at different steps in the process. Quite often, I prefer to clean the data as it's being read from the file, so I might well replace the 'Missing' with a None value or an empty string as the lines are being processed. You could also leave the 'Missing' strings in place and write your code so that no math operations are performed on a value if it is 'Missing'.

> **TRY THIS: CLEANING DATA**　How would you handle the fields with 'Missing' as possible values for math calculations? Can you write a snippet of code that averages one of those columns?
>
> What would you do with the average column at the end so that you could also report the average coverage? In your opinion, would the solution to this problem be at all linked to the way that the 'Missing' entries were handled?

21.4.2 *Sorting*

As I mentioned earlier, it's often useful to have data in the text file sorted before processing. Sorting the data makes it easier to spot and handle duplicate values, and it can also help bring together related rows for quicker or easier processing. In one case, I received a 20 million–row file of attributes and values, in which arbitrary numbers of them needed to be matched with items from a master SKU list. Sorting the rows by the item ID made gathering each item's attributes much faster. How you do the sorting depends on the size of the data file relative to your available memory and on the complexity of the sort. If all the lines of the file can fit comfortably into available memory, the easiest thing may be to read all of the lines into a list and use the list's sort method:

```
>>> lines = open("datafile").readlines()
>>> lines.sort()
```

You could also use the `sorted()` function, as in `sorted_lines = sorted(lines)`. This function preserves the order of the lines in your original list, which usually is unnecessary. The drawback to using the `sorted()` function is that it creates a new copy of the list. This process takes slightly longer and consumes twice as much memory, which might be a bigger concern.

If the data set is larger than memory and the sort is very simple (just by an easily grabbed field), it may be easier to use an external utility, such as the UNIX `sort` command, to preprocess the data:

```
$ sort data > data.srt
```

In either case, sorting can be done in reverse order and can be keyed by values, not the beginning of the line. For such occasions, you need to study the documentation of the sorting tool you choose to use. A simple example in Python would be to make a sort of lines of text case-insensitive. To do this, you give the `sort` method a key function that makes the element lowercase before making a comparison:

```
>>> lines.sort(key=str.lower)
```

This example uses a `lambda` function to ignore the first five characters of each string:

```
>>> lines.sort(key=lambda x: x[5:])
```

Using key functions to determine the behavior of sorts in Python is very handy, but be aware that the key function is called a lot in the process of sorting, so a complex key function could mean a real performance slowdown, particularly with a large data set.

21.4.3 *Data cleaning issues and pitfalls*

It seems that there are as many types of dirty data as there are sources and use cases for that data. Your data will always have quirks that do everything from making processing less accurate to making it impossible to even load the data. As a result, I can't provide an exhaustive list of the problems you might encounter and how to deal with them, but I can give you some general hints.

- *Beware of whitespace and null characters.* The problem with whitespace characters is that you can't see them, but that doesn't mean that they can't cause troubles. Extra whitespace at the beginning and end of data lines, extra whitespace around individual fields, and tabs instead of spaces (or vice versa) can all make your data loading and processing more troublesome, and these problems aren't always easily apparent. Similarly, text files with null characters (ASCII 0) may seem okay on inspection but break on loading and processing.

- *Beware punctuation.* Punctuation can also be a problem. Extra commas or periods can mess up CSV files and the processing of numeric fields, and unescaped or unmatched quote characters can also confuse things.
- *Break down and debug the steps.* It's easier to debug a problem if each step is separate, which means putting each operation on a separate line, being more verbose, and using more variables. But the work is worth it. For one thing, it makes any exceptions that are raised easier to understand, and it also makes debugging easier, whether with print statements, logging, or the Python debugger. It may also be helpful to save the data after each step and to cut the file size to just a few lines that cause the error.

21.5 Writing data files

The last part of the ETL process may involve saving the transformed data to a database (which I discuss in chapter 22), but often it involves writing the data to files. These files may be used as input for other applications and analysis, either by people or by other applications. Usually, you have a particular file specification listing what fields of data should be included, what they should be named, what format and constraints there should be for each, and so on

21.5.1 CSV and other delimited files

Probably the easiest thing of all is to write your data to CSV files. Because you've already loaded, parsed, cleaned, and transformed the data, you're unlikely to hit any unresolved issues with the data itself. And again, using the csv module from the Python standard library makes your work much easier.

Writing delimited files with the csv module is pretty much the reverse of the read process. Again, you need to specify the delimiter that you want to use, and again, the csv module takes care of any situations in which your delimiting character is included in a field:

```
>>> temperature_data = [['State', 'Month Day, Year Code', 'Avg Daily Max Air
    Temperature (F)', 'Record Count for Daily Max Air Temp (F)'],
    ['Illinois', '1979/01/01', '17.48', '994'], ['Illinois', '1979/01/02',
    '4.64', '994'], ['Illinois', '1979/01/03', '11.05', '994'], ['Illinois',
    '1979/01/04', '9.51', '994'], ['Illinois', '1979/05/15', '68.42',
    '994'], ['Illinois', '1979/05/16', '70.29', '994'], ['Illinois', '1979/
    05/17', '75.34', '994'], ['Illinois', '1979/05/18', '79.13', '994'],
    ['Illinois', '1979/05/19', '74.94', '994']]
>>> csv.writer(open("temp_data_03.csv", "w",
    newline='')).writerows(temperature_data)
```

This code results in the following file:

```
State,"Month Day, Year Code",Avg Daily Max Air Temperature (F),Record Count
    for Daily Max Air Temp (F)
```

```
Illinois,1979/01/01,17.48,994
Illinois,1979/01/02,4.64,994
Illinois,1979/01/03,11.05,994
Illinois,1979/01/04,9.51,994
Illinois,1979/05/15,68.42,994
Illinois,1979/05/16,70.29,994
Illinois,1979/05/17,75.34,994
Illinois,1979/05/18,79.13,994
Illinois,1979/05/19,74.94,994
```

Just as when reading from a CSV file, it's possible to write dictionaries instead of lists if you use a `DictWriter`. If you do use a `DictWriter`, be aware of a couple of points: You must specify the fields names in a list when you create the writer, and you can use the `DictWriter`'s `writeheader` method to write the header at the top of the file. So assume that you have the same data as previously, but in dictionary format:

```
{'State': 'Illinois', 'Month Day, Year Code': '1979/01/01', 'Avg Daily Max
    Air Temperature (F)': '17.48', 'Record Count for Daily Max Air Temp
    (F)': '994'}
```

You can use a `DictWriter` object from the `csv` module to write each row, a dictionary, to the correct fields in the CSV file:

```
>>> fields = ['State', 'Month Day, Year Code', 'Avg Daily Max Air Temperature
    (F)', 'Record Count for Daily Max Air Temp (F)']
>>> dict_writer = csv.DictWriter(open("temp_data_04.csv", "w"),
    fieldnames=fields)
>>> dict_writer.writeheader()
>>> dict_writer.writerows(data)
>>> del dict_writer
```

21.5.2 *Writing Excel files*

Writing spreadsheet files is unsurprisingly similar to reading them. You need to create a workbook, or spreadsheet file; then you need to create a sheet or sheets; and finally, you write the data in the appropriate cells. You could create a new spreadsheet from your CSV data file like this:

```
>>> from openpyxl import Workbook
>>> data_rows = [fields for fields in csv.reader(open("temp_data_01.csv"))]
>>> wb = Workbook()
>>> ws = wb.active
>>> ws.title = "temperature data"
>>> for row in data_rows:
...     ws.append(row)
...
>>> wb.save("temp_data_02.xlsx")
```

It's also possible to add formatting to cells as you write them to the spreadsheet file. For more on how to add formatting, please refer to the `xlswriter` documentation.

21.5.3 *Packaging data files*

If you have several related data files, or if your files are large, it may make sense to package them in a compressed archive. Although various archive formats are in use, the zip file remains popular and almost universally accessible to users on almost every platform. For hints on how to create zip-file packages of your data files, please refer to chapter 20.

> **LAB 21: WEATHER OBSERVATIONS**   The file of weather observations provided here is by month and then by county for the state of Illinois from 1979 to 2011. Write the code to process this file to extract the data for Chicago (Cook County) into a single CSV or spreadsheet file. This process includes replacing the `'Missing'` strings with empty strings and translating the percentage to a decimal. You may also consider what fields are repetitive (and therefore can be omitted or stored elsewhere). The proof that you've got it right occurs when you load the file into a spreadsheet. You can download a solution with the book's source code.

Summary

- ETL (extract-transform-load) is the process of getting data from one format, making sure that it's consistent, and then putting it in a format you can use. ETL is the basic step in most data processing.
- Encoding can be problematic with text files, but Python lets you deal with some encoding problems when you load files.
- Delimited or CSV files are common, and the best way to handle them is with the `csv` module.
- Spreadsheet files can be more complex than CSV files but can be handled much the same way.
- Currency symbols, punctuation, and null characters are among the most common data cleaning issues; be on the watch for them.
- Presorting your data file can make other processing steps faster.

Data over the network

This chapter covers

- Fetching files via FTP/SFTP, SSH/SCP, and HTTPS
- Getting data via APIs
- Structured data file formats: JSON and XML
- Scraping data

You've seen how to deal with text-based data files. In this chapter, you use Python to move data files over the network. In some cases, those files might be text or spreadsheet files, as discussed in chapter 21, but in other cases, they might be in more structured formats and served from REST or SOAP application programming interfaces (APIs). Sometimes, getting the data may mean scraping it from a website. This chapter discusses all of these situations and shows some common use cases.

22.1 Fetching files

Before you can do anything with data files, you have to get them. Sometimes, this process is very easy, such as manually downloading a single zip archive, or maybe the files have been pushed to your machine from somewhere else. Quite often, however, the process is more involved. Maybe a large number of files needs to be retrieved from a remote server, files need to be retrieved regularly, or the retrieval process is sufficiently complex to be a pain to do manually. In any of those cases, you might well want to automate fetching the data files with Python.

First of all, I want to be clear that using a Python script isn't the only way, or always the best way, to retrieve files. The following sidebar offers more explanation of the factors I consider when deciding whether to use a Python script for file retrieval. Assuming that using Python does make sense for your particular use case, however, this section illustrates some common patterns you might employ.

Do I use Python?

Although using Python to retrieve files can work very well, it's not always the best choice. In making a decision, you might want to consider two things.

- *Are simpler options available?* Depending on your operating system and your experience, you may find that simple shell scripts and command-line tools are simpler and easier to configure. If you don't have those tools available or aren't comfortable using them (or the people who will be maintaining them aren't comfortable with them), you may want to consider a Python script.

- *Is the retrieval process complex or tightly coupled with processing?* Although those situations are never desirable, they can occur. My rule these days is that if a shell script requires more than a few lines, or if I have to think hard about how to do something in a shell script, it's probably time to switch to Python.

22.1.1 *Using Python to fetch files from an FTP server*

File Transfer Protocol (FTP) has been around for a very long time, but it's still a simple and easy way to share files when security isn't a huge concern. To access an FTP server in Python, you can use the `ftplib` module from the standard library. The steps to follow are straightforward: create an FTP object, connect to a server, and then log in with a username and password (or, quite commonly, with a username of "anonymous" and an empty password).

To continue working with weather data, you can connect to the National Oceanic and Atmospheric Administration (NOAA) FTP server, as shown here:

```
>>> import ftplib
>>> ftp = ftplib.FTP('tgftp.nws.noaa.gov')
>>> ftp.login()
'230 Login successful.'
```

When you're connected, you can use the `ftp` object to list and change directories:

```
>>> ftp.cwd('data')
'250 Directory successfully changed.'
>>> ftp.nlst()
```

```
['climate', 'fnmoc', 'forecasts', 'hurricane_products', 'ls_SS_services',
    'marine', 'nsd_bbsss.txt', 'nsd_cccc.txt', 'observations', 'products',
    'public_statement', 'raw', 'records', 'summaries', 'tampa',
    'watches_warnings', 'zonecatalog.curr', 'zonecatalog.curr.tar']
```

Then you can fetch, for example, the latest METAR report for Chicago O'Hare International Airport:

```
>>> x = ftp.retrbinary('RETR observations/metar/decoded/KORD.TXT',
    open('KORD.TXT', 'wb').write)
'226 Transfer complete.'
```

You pass the `ftp.retrbinary` method both the path to the file on the remote server and a method to handle that file's data on your end—in this case, the `write` method of a file you open for binary writing with the same name. When you look at KORD.TXT, you see that it contains the downloaded data:

```
CHICAGO O'HARE INTERNATIONAL, IL, United States (KORD) 41-59N 087-55W 200M
Jan 01, 2017 - 09:51 PM EST / 2017.01.02 0251 UTC
Wind: from the E (090 degrees) at 6 MPH (5 KT):0
Visibility: 10 mile(s):0
Sky conditions: mostly cloudy
Temperature: 33.1 F (0.6 C)
Windchill: 28 F (-2 C):1
Dew Point: 21.9 F (-5.6 C)
Relative Humidity: 63%
Pressure (altimeter): 30.14 in. Hg (1020 hPa)
Pressure tendency: 0.01 inches (0.2 hPa) lower than three hours ago
ob: KORD 020251Z 09005KT 10SM SCT150 BKN250 01/M06 A3014 RMK AO2 SLP214
    T00061056 58002
cycle: 3
```

You can also use `ftplib` to connect to servers using TLS encryption by using FTP_TLS instead of FTP:

```
ftp = ftplib.FTPTLS('tgftp.nws.noaa.gov')
```

22.1.2 *Fetching files with SFTP*

If the data requires more security, such as in a corporate context in which business data is being transferred over the network, it's fairly common to use SFTP. SFTP is a full-featured protocol that allows file access, transfer, and management over a Secure Shell (SSH) connection. Even though SFTP stands for SSH File Transfer Protocol and FTP stands for File Transfer Protocol, the two aren't related. SFTP isn't a reimplementation of FTP on SSH, but a fresh design specifically for SSH.

Using SSH-based transfers is attractive both because SSH is already the de facto standard for accessing remote servers and because enabling support for SFTP on a server is fairly easy (and quite often on by default).

Python doesn't have an SFTP/SCP client module in its standard library, but a community-developed library called `paramiko` manages SFTP operations as well as SSH connections. To use `paramiko`, the easiest thing is to install it via `pip`. If the NOAA site mentioned earlier in this chapter were using SFTP (which it doesn't, so this code won't work!), the SFTP equivalent of the code above would be

```
>>> import paramiko
>>> t = paramiko.Transport((hostname, port))
>>> t.connect(username, password)
>>> sftp = paramiko.SFTPClient.from_transport(t)
```

It's also worth noting that although `paramiko` supports running commands on a remote server and receiving its outputs, just like a direct `ssh` session, it doesn't include an `scp` function. This function is rarely something you'll miss; if all you want to do is move a file or two over an `ssh` connection, a command-line `scp` utility usually makes the job easier and simpler.

22.1.3 *Retrieving files over HTTP/HTTPS*

The last common option for retrieving data files that I discuss in this chapter is getting files over an HTTP or HTTPS connection. This option is probably the easiest of all the options; you are in effect retrieving your data from a web server, and support for accessing web servers is very widespread. Again, in this case you may not need to use Python. Various command-line tools retrieve files via HTTP/HTTPS connections and have most of the capabilities you might need. The two most common of these tools are wget and curl. If you have a reason to do the retrieval in your Python code, however, that process isn't much harder. The `requests` library is by far the easiest and most reliable way to access HTTP/HTTPS servers from Python code. Again, `requests` is easiest to install with `pip install requests`.

When you have requests installed, fetching a file is straightforward: import `requests` and use the correct HTTP verb (usually, GET) to connect to the server and return your data.

The following example code fetches the monthly temperature data for Heathrow Airport since 1948—a text file that's served via a web server. If you want to, you can put the URL in your browser, load the page, and then save it. If the page is large or you have a lot of pages to get, however, it's easier to use code like this:

```
>>> import requests
>>> response = requests.get("http://www.metoffice.gov.uk/pub/data/weather/uk/
    climate/stationdata/heathrowdata.txt")
```

The response will have a fair amount of information, including the header returned by the web server, which can be helpful in debugging if things aren't working. The part of the response object you'll most often be interested in, however, is data returned. To retrieve this data, you want to access the response's `text` property, which contains the response body as a string, or the `content` property, which contains the response body as bytes:

```
>>> print(response.text)
Heathrow (London Airport)
Location 507800E 176700N, Lat 51.479 Lon -0.449, 25m amsl
```

```
Estimated data is marked with a * after the value.
Missing data (more than 2 days missing in month) is marked by   ---.
Sunshine data taken from an automatic Kipp & Zonen sensor marked with a #,
    otherwise sunshine data taken from a Campbell Stokes recorder.
   yyyy  mm   tmax    tmin    af    rain    sun
              degC    degC   days    mm    hours
   1948  1    8.9     3.3    ---    85.0    ---
   1948  2    7.9     2.2    ---    26.0    ---
   1948  3    14.2    3.8    ---    14.0    ---
   1948  4    15.4    5.1    ---    35.0    ---
   1948  5    18.1    6.9    ---    57.0    ---
```

Typically, you'd write the response text to a file for later processing, but depending on your needs, you might first do some cleaning or even process directly.

> **TRY THIS: RETRIEVING A FILE** If you're working with the example data file and want to break each line into separate fields, how might you do that? What other processing would you expect to do? Try writing some code to retrieve this file and calculate the average annual rainfall or (for more of a challenge) the average maximum and minimum temperature for each year.

22.2 *Fetching data via an API*

Serving data by way of an API is quite common, following a trend toward decoupling applications into services that communicate via APIs. APIs can work in several ways, but they commonly operate over regular HTTP/HTTPS protocols using the standard HTTP verbs, GET, POST, PUT, and DELETE. Fetching data this way is very similar to retrieving a file, as in section 22.1.3, but the data isn't in a static file. Instead of the application serving static files that contain the data, it queries some other data source and then assembles and serves the data dynamically on request.

Although there's a lot of variation in the ways that an API can be set up, one of the most common is a RESTful (REpresentational State Transfer) interface that operates over the same HTTP/HTTPS protocols as the web. There are endless variations on how an API might work, but commonly, data is fetched by using a GET request, which is what your web browser uses to request a web page. When you're fetching via a GET request, the parameters to select the data you want are often appended to the URL in a query string.

If you want to get the current weather on Mars from the Curiosity rover, use http://mng.bz/g6UY as your URL.[1] The ?format=json is a query string parameter that specifies that the information be returned in JSON, which I discuss in section 22.3.1. If you want the Martian weather for a specific Martian day, or sol, of its mission—say, the 155th sol—use the URL http://mng.bz/4e0r. If you want to get the weather on Mars for a range of Earth dates, such as the month of October 2012, use http://mng.bz/83WO. Notice that the elements of the query string are separated by ampersands (&).

---

[1] The site (ingenology.com) has been reliable in the past, but is down at the time of this writing and its future is uncertain.

When you know the URL to use, you can use the requests library to fetch data from an API and either process it on the fly or save it to a file for later processing. The simplest way to do this is exactly like retrieving a file:

```
>>> import requests
>>> response = requests.get("http://marsweather.ingenology.com/v1/latest/
    ?format=json")
>>> response.text
'{"report": {"terrestrial_date": "2017-01-08", "sol": 1573, "ls": 295.0,
    "min_temp": -74.0, "min_temp_fahrenheit": -101.2, "max_temp": -2.0,
    "max_temp_fahrenheit": 28.4, "pressure": 872.0, "pressure_string":
    "Higher", "abs_humidity": null, "wind_speed": null, "wind_direction": "-
    -", "atmo_opacity": "Sunny", "season": "Month 10", "sunrise": "2017-01-
    08T12:29:00Z", "sunset": "2017-01-09T00:45:00Z"}}'
>>> response = requests.get("http://marsweather.ingenology.com/v1/archive/
    ?sol=155&format=json")
>>> response.text
'{"count": 1, "next": null, "previous": null, "results":
    [{"terrestrial_date": "2013-01-18", "sol": 155, "ls": 243.7, "min_temp":
    -64.45, "min_temp_fahrenheit": -84.01, "max_temp": 2.15,
    "max_temp_fahrenheit": 35.87, "pressure": 9.175, "pressure_string":
    "Higher", "abs_humidity": null, "wind_speed": 2.0, "wind_direction":
    null, "atmo_opacity": null, "season": "Month 9", "sunrise": null,
    "sunset": null}]}'
```

Keep in mind that you should escape spaces and most punctuation in your query parameters, because those elements aren't allowed in URLs even though many browsers automatically do the escaping on URLs.

For a final example, suppose that you want to grab the crime data for Chicago between noon and 1 PM on Jan. 10, 2017. The way that the API works, you specify a date range with the query string parameters of `$where date=between <start datetime>` and `<end datetime>`, where the start and end datetimes are quoted in ISO format. So the URL for getting that one hour of Chicago crime data would be https://data.cityofchicago.org/resource/6zsd-86xi.json?$where=date between '2015-01-10T12:00:00' and '2015-01-10T13:00:00'.

In the example, several characters aren't welcome in URLs, such as the quote characters and the spaces. This is another situation in which the requests library makes good on its aim of making things easier for the user, because before it sends the URL, it takes care of quoting it properly. The URL that the request actually sends is https://data.cityofchicago.org/resource/6zsd-86xi.json?$where=date%20between%20%222015-01-10T12:00:00%22%20and%20%222015-01-10T14:00:00%22'.

Note that all of the single-quote characters have been quoted with %22 and all of the spaces with %20 without your even needing to think about it.

> **TRY THIS: ACCESSING AN API** Write some code to fetch some data from the city of Chicago website. Look at the fields mentioned in the results, and see whether you can select records based on another field in combination with the date range.

22.3 Structured data formats

Although APIs sometimes serve plain text, it's much more common for data served from APIs to be served in a structured file format. The two most common file formats are JSON and XML. Both of these formats are built on plain text but structure their contents so that they're more flexible and able to store more complex information.

22.3.1 JSON data

JSON, which stands for JavaScript Object Notation, dates to 1999. It consists of only two structures: key-value pairs, called *structures*, that are very similar to Python dictionaries; and ordered lists of values, called *arrays*, that are very much like Python lists.

Keys can be only strings in double quotes, and values can be strings in double quotes, numbers, true, false, null, arrays, or objects. These elements make JSON a lightweight way to represent most data in a way that's easily transmitted over the network and also fairly easy for humans to read. JSON is so common that most languages have features to translate JSON to and from native data types. In the case of Python, that feature is the `json` module, which became part of the standard library with version 2.6. The original externally maintained version of the module is available as `simplejson`, which is still available. In Python 3, however, it's far more common to use the standard library version.

The data you retrieved from the Mars rover and the city of Chicago APIs in section 22.2 is in JSON format. To send JSON across the network, the JSON object needs to be serialized— that is, transformed into a sequence of bytes. So although the batch of data you retrieved from the Mars rover and Chicago APIs looks like JSON, in fact it's just a byte string representation of a JSON object. To transform that byte string into a real JSON object and translate it into a Python dictionary, you need to use the JSON `loads()` function. If you want to get the Mars weather report, for example, you can do that just as you did previously, but this time you'll convert it to a Python dictionary:

```
>>> import json
>>> import requests
>>> response = requests.get("http://marsweather.ingenology.com/v1/latest/
      ?format=json")
>>> weather = json.loads(response.text)
>>> weather
{'report': {'terrestrial_date': '2017-01-10', 'sol': 1575, 'ls': 296.0,
    'min_temp': -58.0, 'min_temp_fahrenheit': -72.4, 'max_temp': 0.0,
    'max_temp_fahrenheit': None, 'pressure': 860.0, 'pressure_string':
    'Higher', 'abs_humidity': None, 'wind_speed': None, 'wind_direction': '-
    -', 'atmo_opacity': 'Sunny', 'season': 'Month 10', 'sunrise': '2017-01-
    10T12:30:00Z', 'sunset': '2017-01-11T00:46:00Z'}}
>>> weather['report']['sol']
1575
```

Note that the call to `json.loads()` is what takes the string representation of the JSON object and transforms, or loads, it into a Python dictionary. Also, a `json.load()` function will read from any filelike object that supports a read method.

If you look at a dictionary's representation as earlier, it can be very hard to make sense of what's going on. Improved formatting, also called *pretty printing*, can make data structures much easier to understand. Use the Python `prettyprint` module to see what's in the example dictionary:

```
>>> from pprint import pprint as pp
>>> pp(weather)
{'report': {'abs_humidity': None,
            'atmo_opacity': 'Sunny',
            'ls': 296.0,
            'max_temp': 0.0,
            'max_temp_fahrenheit': None,
            'min_temp': -58.0,
            'min_temp_fahrenheit': -72.4,
            'pressure': 860.0,
            'pressure_string': 'Higher',
            'season': 'Month 10',
            'sol': 1575,
            'sunrise': '2017-01-10T12:30:00Z',
            'sunset': '2017-01-11T00:46:00Z',
            'terrestrial_date': '2017-01-10',
            'wind_direction': '--',
            'wind_speed': None}}
```

Both load functions can be configured to control how to parse and decode the original JSON to Python objects, but the default translation is listed in table 22.1.

Table 22.1   JSON to Python default decoding

JSON	Python
object	dict
array	list
string	str
number (int)	int
number (real)	float
true	True
false	False
null	None

Fetching JSON with the requests library

In this section, you used the requests library to retrieve the JSON formatted data and then used the `json.loads()` method to parse it into a Python object. This technique works fine, but because the requests library is used so often for exactly this

(continued)

purpose, the library provides a shortcut: The response object actually has a `json()` method that does that conversion for you. So in the example, instead of

```
>>> weather = json.loads(response.text)
```

you could have used

```
>>> weather = response.json()
```

The result is the same, but the code is simpler, more readable, and more Pythonic.

If you want to write JSON to a file or serialize it to a string, the reverse of `load()` and `loads()` is `dump()` and `dumps()`. `json.dump()` takes a file object with a `write()` method as a parameter, and `json.dumps()` returns a string. In both cases, the encoding to a JSON formatted string can be highly customized, but the default is still based on table 22.1. So if you want to write your Martian weather report to a JSON file, you could do this:

```
>>> outfile = open("mars_data_01.json", "w")
>>> json.dump(weather, outfile)
>>> outfile.close()
>>> json.dumps(weather)
'{"report": {"terrestrial_date": "2017-01-11", "sol": 1576, "ls": 296.0,
    "min_temp": -72.0, "min_temp_fahrenheit": -97.6, "max_temp": -1.0,
    "max_temp_fahrenheit": 30.2, "pressure": 869.0, "pressure_string":
    "Higher", "abs_humidity": null, "wind_speed": null, "wind_direction": "-
    -", "atmo_opacity": "Sunny", "season": "Month 10", "sunrise": "2017-01-
    11T12:31:00Z", "sunset": "2017-01-12T00:46:00Z"}}'
```

As you can see, the entire object has been encoded as a single string. Here again, it might be handy to format the string in a more readable way, just as you did by using the `pprint` module. To do so easily, use the `indent` parameter with the `dump` or `dumps` function:

```
>>> print(json.dumps(weather, indent=2))
{
  "report": {
    "terrestrial_date": "2017-01-10",
    "sol": 1575,
    "ls": 296.0,
    "min_temp": -58.0,
    "min_temp_fahrenheit": -72.4,
    "max_temp": 0.0,
    "max_temp_fahrenheit": null,
    "pressure": 860.0,
    "pressure_string": "Higher",
    "abs_humidity": null,
    "wind_speed": null,
    "wind_direction": "--",
    "atmo_opacity": "Sunny",
    "season": "Month 10",
```

```
    "sunrise": "2017-01-10T12:30:00Z",
    "sunset": "2017-01-11T00:46:00Z"
  }
}
```

You should be aware, however, that if you use repeated calls to `json.dump()` to write a series of objects to a file, the result is a *series* of legal JSON-formatted objects, but the contents of the file *as a whole* is *not* a legal JSON-formatted object, and attempting to read and parse the entire file by using a single call to `json.load()` will fail. If you have more than one object that you'd like to encode as a single JSON object, you need to put all those objects into a list (or, better still, an object) and then encode that item to the file.

If you have two or more days' worth of Martian weather data that you want to store as JSON, you have to make a choice. You could use `json.dump()` once for each object, which would result in a file containing JSON-formatted objects. If you assume that `weather_list` is a list of weather-report objects, the code might look like this:

```
>>> outfile = open("mars_data.json", "w")
>>> for report in weather_list:
...     json.dump(weather, outfile)
>>> outfile.close()
```

If you do this, then you need to load each line as a separate JSON-formatted object:

```
>>> for line in open("mars_data.json"):
...     weather_list.append(json.loads(line))
```

As an alternative, you could put the list into a single JSON object. Because there's a possible vulnerability with top-level arrays in JSON, the recommended way is to put the array in a dictionary:

```
>>> outfile = open("mars_data.json", "w")
>>> weather_obj = {"reports": weather_list, "count": 2}
>>> json.dump(weather, outfile)
>>> outfile.close()
```

With this approach, you can use one operation to load the JSON-formatted object from the file:

```
>>> with open("mars_data.json") as infile:
>>> weather_obj = json.load(infile)
```

The second approach is fine if the size of your JSON files is manageable, but it may be less than ideal for very large files, because handling errors may be a bit harder and you may run out of memory.

> **TRY THIS: SAVING SOME JSON CRIME DATA** Modify the code you wrote in section 22.2 to fetch the Chicago crime data. Then convert the fetched data from a JSON-formatted string to a Python object. Next, see whether you can save the crime events as a series of separate JSON objects in one file and as one JSON object in another file. Then see what code is needed to load each file.

22.3.2 *XML data*

XML (eXtensible Markup Language) has been around since the end of the 20th century. XML uses an angle-bracket tag notation similar to HTML, and elements are nested within other elements to form a tree structure. XML was intended to be readable by both machines and humans, but XML is often so verbose and complex that it's very difficult for people to understand. Nevertheless, because XML is an established standard, it's quite common to find data in XML format. And although XML is machine-readable, it's very likely that you'll want to translate it into something a bit easier to deal with.

Take a look at some XML data, in this case the XML version of weather data for Chicago:

```
<dwml xmlns:xsd="http://www.w3.org/2001/XMLSchema" xmlns:xsi="http://
    www.w3.org/2001/XMLSchema-instance" version="1.0"
    xsi:noNamespaceSchemaLocation="http://www.nws.noaa.gov/forecasts/xml/
    DWMLgen/schema/DWML.xsd">
  <head>
    <product srsName="WGS 1984" concise-name="glance" operational-
    mode="official">
      <title>
NOAA's National Weather Service Forecast at a Glance
      </title>
      <field>meteorological</field>
      <category>forecast</category>
      <creation-date refresh-frequency="PT1H">2017-01-08T02:52:41Z</creation-
      date>
    </product>
    <source>
      <more-information>http://www.nws.noaa.gov/forecasts/xml/</more-
      information>
      <production-center>
Meteorological Development Laboratory
<sub-center>Product Generation Branch</sub-center>
      </production-center>
      <disclaimer>http://www.nws.noaa.gov/disclaimer.html</disclaimer>
      <credit>http://www.weather.gov/</credit>
      <credit-logo>http://www.weather.gov/images/xml_logo.gif</credit-logo>
      <feedback>http://www.weather.gov/feedback.php</feedback>
    </source>
  </head>
  <data>
    <location>
      <location-key>point1</location-key>
      <point latitude="41.78" longitude="-88.65"/>
    </location>
    …
  </data>
</dwml>
```

This example is just the first section of the document, with most of the data omitted. Even so, it illustrates some of the issues you typically find in XML data. In particular, you can see the verbose nature of the protocol, with the tags in some cases taking more space than the value contained in them. This sample also shows the nested or tree structure common in XML, as well as the common use of a sizeable header of metadata before the actual data begins. On a spectrum from simple to complex for data files, you could think of CSV or delimited files as being at the simple end and XML at the complex end.

Finally, this file illustrates another feature of XML that makes pulling data a bit more of a challenge. XML supports the use of attributes to store data as well as the text values within the tags. So if you look at the point element at the bottom of this sample, you see that the `point` element doesn't have a text value. That element has just latitude and longitude values within the `<point>` tag itself:

```
<point latitude="41.78" longitude="-88.65"/>
```

This code is certainly legal XML, and it works for storing the data, but it would also be possible (likely, even) for the same data to be stored as

```
<point>
    <latitude>41.78</ latitude >
    <longitude>-88.65</longitude>
</point>
```

You really don't know which way any given bit of data will be handled without carefully inspecting the data or studying a specification document.

This kind of complexity can make simple data extraction from XML more of a challenge. You have several ways to handle XML. The Python standard library comes with modules that parse and handle XML data, but none of them is particularly convenient for simple data extraction.

For simple data extraction, the handiest utility I've found is a library called `xmltodict`, which parses your XML data and returns a dictionary that reflects the tree. In fact, behind the scenes it uses the standard library's expat XML parser, parses your XML document into a tree, and uses that tree to create the dictionary. As a result, `xmltodict` can handle whatever the parser can, and it's also able to take a dictionary and "unparse" it to XML if necessary, making it a very handy tool. Over several years of use, I found this solution to be up to all my XML handling needs. To get `xmltodict`, you can again use `pip install xmltodict`.

To convert the XML to a dictionary, you can import `xmltodict` and use the `parse` method on an XML formatted string:

```
>>> import xmltodict
>>> data = xmltodict.parse(open("observations_01.xml").read())
```

In this case, for compactness, pass the contents of the file directly to the `parse` method. After being parsed, this data object is an ordered dictionary with the same values it would have if it had been loaded from this JSON:

```
{
    "dwml": {
        "@xmlns:xsd": "http://www.w3.org/2001/XMLSchema",
```

```
        "@xmlns:xsi": "http://www.w3.org/2001/XMLSchema-instance",
        "@version": "1.0",
        "@xsi:noNamespaceSchemaLocation": "http://www.nws.noaa.gov/forecasts/
xml/DWMLgen/schema/DWML.xsd",
        "head": {
            "product": {
                "@srsName": "WGS 1984",
                "@concise-name": "glance",
                "@operational-mode": "official",
                "title": "NOAA's National Weather Service Forecast at a Glance",
                "field": "meteorological",
                "category": "forecast",
                "creation-date": {
                    "@refresh-frequency": "PT1H",
                    "#text": "2017-01-08T02:52:41Z"
                }
            },
            "source": {
                "more-information": "http://www.nws.noaa.gov/forecasts/xml/",
                "production-center": {
                    "sub-center": "Product Generation Branch",
                    "#text": "Meteorological Development Laboratory"
                },
                "disclaimer": "http://www.nws.noaa.gov/disclaimer.html",
                "credit": "http://www.weather.gov/",
                "credit-logo": "http://www.weather.gov/images/xml_logo.gif",
                "feedback": "http://www.weather.gov/feedback.php"
            }
        },
        "data": {
            "location": {
                "location-key": "point1",
                "point": {
                    "@latitude": "41.78",
                    "@longitude": "-88.65"
                }
            }
        }
    }
}
```

Notice that the attributes have been pulled out of the tags, but with an @ prepended to indicate that they were originally attributes of their parent tag. If an XML node has both a text value and a nested element in it, notice that the key for the text value is "#text", as in the "sub-center" element under "production-center".

Earlier, I said that the result of parsing is an *ordered dictionary* (officially, an OrderedDict), so if you print it, the code looks like this:

```
OrderedDict([('dwml', OrderedDict([('@xmlns:xsd', 'http://www.w3.org/2001/
    XMLSchema'), ('@xmlns:xsi', 'http://www.w3.org/2001/XMLSchema-
    instance'), ('@version', '1.0'), ('@xsi:noNamespaceSchemaLocation',
    'http://www.nws.noaa.gov/forecasts/xml/DWMLgen/schema/DWML.xsd'),
    ('head', OrderedDict([('product', OrderedDict([('@srsName', 'WGS 1984'),
    ('@concise-name', 'glance'), ('@operational-mode', 'official'),
    ('title', "NOAA's National Weather Service Forecast at a Glance"),
```

```
('field', 'meteorological'), ('category', 'forecast'), ('creation-date',
OrderedDict([('@refresh-frequency', 'PT1H'), ('#text', '2017-01-
08T02:52:41Z')])])])), ('source', OrderedDict([('more-information',
'http://www.nws.noaa.gov/forecasts/xml/'), ('production-center',
OrderedDict([('sub-center', 'Product Generation Branch'), ('#text',
'Meteorological Development Laboratory')])), ('disclaimer', 'http://
www.nws.noaa.gov/disclaimer.html'), ('credit', 'http://www.weather.gov/
'), ('credit-logo', 'http://www.weather.gov/images/xml_logo.gif'),
('feedback', 'http://www.weather.gov/feedback.php')])])]), ('data',
OrderedDict([('location', OrderedDict([('location-key', 'point1'),
('point', OrderedDict([('@latitude', '41.78'), ('@longitude', '-
88.65')])])), ('#text', '…')])])])]
```

Even though the representation of an `OrderedDict`, with its lists of tuples, looks rather strange, it behaves exactly the same way as a normal `dict` except that it promises to maintain the order of elements, which is useful in this case.

If an element is repeated, it becomes a list. In a further section of the full version of the file shown previously the following element occurs (some elements omitted from this sample):

```
<time-layout >
    <start-valid-time period-name="Monday">2017-01-09T07:00:00-06:00</start-
    valid-time>
    <end-valid-time>2017-01-09T19:00:00-06:00</end-valid-time>
    <start-valid-time period-name="Tuesday">2017-01-10T07:00:00-06:00</start-
    valid-time>
    <end-valid-time>2017-01-10T19:00:00-06:00</end-valid-time>
    <start-valid-time period-name="Wednesday">2017-01-11T07:00:00-06:00</
    start-valid-time>
    <end-valid-time>2017-01-11T19:00:00-06:00</end-valid-time>
</time-layout >
```

Note that two elements—"start-valid-time" and "end-valid-time"—repeat in alternation. These two repeating elements are each translated to a list in the dictionary, keeping each set of elements in their proper order:

```
"time-layout":
    {
        "start-valid-time": [
            {
                "@period-name": "Monday",
                "#text": "2017-01-09T07:00:00-06:00"
            },
            {
                "@period-name": "Tuesday",
                "#text": "2017-01-10T07:00:00-06:00"
            },
            {
                "@period-name": "Wednesday",
                "#text": "2017-01-11T07:00:00-06:00"
            }
        ],
        "end-valid-time": [
            "2017-01-09T19:00:00-06:00",
```

```
                    "2017-01-10T19:00:00-06:00",
                    "2017-01-11T19:00:00-06:00"
              ]
       },
```

Because dictionaries and lists, even nested dictionaries and lists, are fairly easy to deal with in Python, using `xmltodict` is an effective way to handle most XML. In fact, I've used it for the past several years in production on a variety of XML documents and never had a problem.

> **TRY THIS: FETCHING AND PARSING XML** Write the code to pull the Chicago XML weather forecast from http://mng.bz/103V. Then use `xmltodict` to parse the XML into a Python dictionary and extract tomorrow's forecast maximum temperature. Hint: To match up time layouts and values, compare the layout-key value of the first time-layout section and the time-layout attribute of the temperature element of the parameters element.

22.4   *Scraping web data*

In some cases, the data is on a website but for whatever reason isn't available anywhere else. In those situations, it may make sense to collect the data from the web pages themselves through a process called *crawling* or *scraping*.

Before saying anything more about scraping, let me make a disclaimer: Scraping or crawling websites that you don't own or control is at best a legal grey area, with a host of inconclusive and contradictory considerations involving things such as the terms of use of the site, the way in which the site is accessed, and the use to which the scraped data is put. Unless you have control of the site you want to scrape, the answer to the question "Is it legal for me to scrape this site?" usually is "It depends."

If you do decide to scrape a production website, you also need to be sensitive to the load you're putting on the site. Although an established, high-traffic site might well be able to handle anything you can throw at it, a smaller, less-active site might be brought to a standstill by a series of continuous requests. At the very least, you need to be careful that your scraping doesn't turn into an inadvertent denial-of-service attack.

Conversely, I've worked in situations in which it was actually easier to scrape our own website to get some needed data than it was to go through corporate channels. Although scraping web data has its place, it's too complex for full treatment here. In this section, I present a very simple example to give you a general idea of the basic method and follow up with suggestions to pursue in more complex cases.

Scraping a website consists of two parts: fetching the web page and extracting the data from it. Fetching the page can be done via requests and is fairly simple.

Consider the code of a very simple web page with only a little content and no CSS or JavaScript, as this one.

Listing 22.1   File test.html

```
<!DOCTYPE HTML PUBLIC "-//IETF//DTD HTML//EN">
<html> <head>
```

```
<title>Title</title>
</head>

<body>
<h1>Heading 1</h1>

This is plan text, and is boring
<span class="special">this is special</span>

Here is a <a href="http://bitbucket.dev.null">link</a>

<hr>
<address>Ann Address, Somewhere, AState 00000
</address>
</body> </html>
```

Suppose that you're interested in only a couple of kinds of data from this page: anything in an element with a class name of "special" and any links. You can process the file by searching for the strings 'class="special"' and "<a href" and then write code to pick out the data from there, but even using regular expressions, this process will be tedious, bug-prone, and hard to maintain. It's much easier to use a library that knows how to parse HTML, such as Beautiful Soup. If you want to try the following code and experiment with parsing HTML pages, you can use pip install bs4.

When you have Beautiful Soup installed, parsing a page of HTML is simple. For this example, assume that you've already retrieved the web page (presumably, using the requests library), so you'll just parse the HTML.

The first step is to load the text and create a Beautiful Soup parser:

```
>>> import bs4
>>> html = open("test.html").read()
>>> bs = bs4.BeautifulSoup(html, "html.parser")
```

This code is all it takes to parse the HTML into the parser object bs. A Beautiful Soup parser object has a lot of cool tricks, and if you're working with HTML at all, it's really worth your time to experiment a bit and get a feel for what it can do for you. For this example, you look at only two things: extracting content by HTML tag and getting data by CSS class.

First, find the link. The HTML tag for a link is <a> (Beautiful Soup by default converts all tags to lowercase), so to find all link tags, you can use the "a" as a parameter and call the bs object itself:

```
>>> a_list = bs("a")
>>> print(a_list)
[<a href="http://bitbucket.dev.null">link</a>]
```

Now you have a list of all (one in this case) of the HTML link tags. If that list is all you get, that's not so bad, but in fact, the elements returned in the list are also parser objects and can do the rest of the work of getting the link and text for you:

```
>>> a_item = a_list[0]
>>> a_item.text
```

```
'link'
>>> a_item["href"]
'http://bitbucket.dev.null'
```

The other feature you're looking for is anything with a CSS class of `"special"`, which you can extract by using the parser's `select` method as follows:

```
>>> special_list = bs.select(".special")
>>> print(special_list)
[<span class="special">this is special</span>]
>>> special_item = special_list[0]
>>> special_item.text
'this is special'
>>> special_item["class"]
['special']
```

Because the items returned by the tag or by the `select` method are themselves parser objects, you can nest them, which allows you to extract just about anything from HTML or even XML.

> **TRY THIS: PARSING HTML**   Given the file forecast.html (which you can find in the code on this book's website), write a script using Beautiful Soup that extracts the data and saves it as a CSV file, shown here.

Listing 22.2   File forecast.html

```html
<html>
  <body>
    <div class="row row-forecast">
        <div class="grid col-25 forecast-label"><b>Tonight</b></div>
        <div class="grid col-75 forecast-text">A slight chance of showers and
    thunderstorms before 10pm. Mostly cloudy, with a low around 66. West
    southwest wind around 9 mph. Chance of precipitation is 20%. New
    rainfall amounts between a tenth and quarter of an inch possible.</div>
    </div>
    <div class="row row-forecast">
        <div class="grid col-25 forecast-label"><b>Friday</b></div>
        <div class="grid col-75 forecast-text">Partly sunny. High near 77,
    with temperatures falling to around 75 in the afternoon. Northwest wind
    7 to 12 mph, with gusts as high as 18 mph.</div>
    </div>
    <div class="row row-forecast">
        <div class="grid col-25 forecast-label"><b>Friday Night</b></div>
        <div class="grid col-75 forecast-text">Mostly cloudy, with a low
    around 63. North wind 7 to 10 mph.</div>
    </div>
    <div class="row row-forecast">
        <div class="grid col-25 forecast-label"><b>Saturday</b></div>
        <div class="grid col-75 forecast-text">Mostly sunny, with a high near
    73. North wind around 10 mph.</div>
    </div>
    <div class="row row-forecast">
```

```
        <div class="grid col-25 forecast-label"><b>Saturday Night</b></div>
        <div class="grid col-75 forecast-text">Partly cloudy, with a low
    around 63. North wind 5 to 10 mph.</div>
    </div>
    <div class="row row-forecast">
        <div class="grid col-25 forecast-label"><b>Sunday</b></div>
        <div class="grid col-75 forecast-text">Mostly sunny, with a high near
    73.</div>
    </div>
    <div class="row row-forecast">
        <div class="grid col-25 forecast-label"><b>Sunday Night</b></div>
        <div class="grid col-75 forecast-text">Mostly cloudy, with a low
    around 64.</div>
    </div>
    <div class="row row-forecast">
        <div class="grid col-25 forecast-label"><b>Monday</b></div>
        <div class="grid col-75 forecast-text">Mostly sunny, with a high near
    74.</div>
    </div>
    <div class="row row-forecast">
        <div class="grid col-25 forecast-label"><b>Monday Night</b></div>
        <div class="grid col-75 forecast-text">Mostly clear, with a low
    around 65.</div>
    </div>
    <div class="row row-forecast">
        <div class="grid col-25 forecast-label"><b>Tuesday</b></div>
        <div class="grid col-75 forecast-text">Sunny, with a high near 75.</
    div>
    </div>
    <div class="row row-forecast">
        <div class="grid col-25 forecast-label"><b>Tuesday Night</b></div>
        <div class="grid col-75 forecast-text">Mostly clear, with a low
    around 65.</div>
    </div>
    <div class="row row-forecast">
        <div class="grid col-25 forecast-label"><b>Wednesday</b></div>
        <div class="grid col-75 forecast-text">Sunny, with a high near 77.</
    div>
    </div>
    <div class="row row-forecast">
        <div class="grid col-25 forecast-label"><b>Wednesday Night</b></div>
        <div class="grid col-75 forecast-text">Mostly clear, with a low
    around 67.</div>
    </div>
    <div class="row row-forecast">
        <div class="grid col-25 forecast-label"><b>Thursday</b></div>
        <div class="grid col-75 forecast-text">A chance of rain showers after
    1pm. Mostly sunny, with a high near 81. Chance of precipitation is
    30%.</div>
    </div>
  </body>
</html>
```

LAB 22: TRACK CURIOSITY'S WEATHER Use the API described in section 22.2 to gather a weather history of *Curiosity*'s stay on Mars for a month. Hint: You can specify Martian days (sols) by adding ?sol=*sol_number* to the end of the archive query, like this:

http://marsweather.ingenology.com/v1/archive/?sol=155

Transform the data so that you can load it into a spreadsheet and graph it. For a version of this project, see the book's source code.

Summary

- Using a Python script may not be the best choice for fetching files. Be sure to consider the options.
- Using the `requests` module is your best bet for fetching files by using HTTP/HTTPS and Python.
- Fetching files from an API is very similar to fetching static files.
- Parameters for API requests often need to be quoted and added as a query string to the request URL.
- JSON-formatted strings are quite common for data served from APIs, and XML is also used.
- Scraping sites that you don't control may not be legal or ethical and requires consideration not to overload the server.

Saving data

This chapter covers

- Storing data in relational databases
- Using the Python DB-API
- Accessing databases through an Object Relational Mapper (ORM)
- Understanding NoSQL databases and how they differ from relational databases

When you have data and have it cleaned, it's likely that you'll want to store it. You'll not only want to store it, but also be able to get at it in the future with as little hassle as possible. The need to store and retrieve significant amounts of data usually calls for some sort of database. Relational databases such as PostgreSQL, MySQL, and SQL Server have been established favorites for data storage for decades, and they can still be great options for many use cases. In recent years, NoSQL databases, including MongoDB and Redis, have found favor and can be very useful for a variety of use cases. A detailed discussion of databases would take several books, so in this chapter I look at some scenarios to show how you can access both SQL and NoSQL databases with Python.

319

23.1   *Relational databases*

Relational databases have long been a standard for storing and manipulating data. They're a mature technology and a ubiquitous one. Python can connect with a number relational databases, but I don't have the time or the inclination to go through the specifics of each one in this book. Instead, because Python handles databases in a mostly consistent way, I illustrate the basics with one of them—sqlite3—and then discuss some differences and considerations in choosing and using a relational database for data storages.

23.1.1   *The Python Database API*

As I mention, Python handles SQL database access very similarly across several database implementations because of PEP-249 (www.python.org/dev/peps/pep-0249/), which specifies some common practices for connecting to SQL databases. Commonly called the Database API or DB-API, it was created to encourage "code that is generally more portable across databases, and a broader reach of database connectivity." Thanks to the DB-API, the examples of SQLite that you see in this chapter are quite similar to what you'd use for PostgreSQL, MySQL, or several other databases.

23.2   *SQLite: Using the sqlite3 database*

Although Python has modules for many databases, in the following examples I look at sqlite3. Although it's not suited for large, high-traffic applications, sqlite3 has two advantages:

- Because it's part of the standard library, it can be used anywhere you need a database without worrying about adding dependencies.
- sqlite3 stores all of its records in a local file, so it doesn't need both a client and server, which would be the case for PostgreSQL, MySQL, and other larger databases.

These features make sqlite3 a handy option for both smaller applications and quick prototypes.

To use a sqlite3 database, the first thing you need is a `Connection` object. Getting a `Connection` object requires only calling the `connect` function with the name of file that will be used to store the data:

```
>>> import sqlite3
>>> conn = sqlite3.connect("datafile.db")
```

It's also possible to hold the data in memory by using `":memory:"` as the filename. For storing Python integers, strings, and floats, nothing more is needed. If you want sqlite3 to automatically convert query results for some columns into other types, it's useful to include the `detect_types` parameter set to `sqlite3.PARSE_DECLTYPES |sqlite3.PARSE_COLNAMES`, which directs the `Connection` object to parse the name and types of columns in queries and attempts to match them with converters you've already defined.

The second step is creating a `Cursor` object from the connection:

```
>>> cursor = conn.cursor()
>>> cursor
<sqlite3.Cursor object at 0xb7a12980>
```

At this point, you're able to make queries against the database. In the current situation, because the database has no tables or records yet, you first need to create a table and insert a couple of records:

```
>>> cursor.execute("create table people (id integer primary key, name text,
    count integer)")
>>> cursor.execute("insert into people (name, count) values ('Bob', 1)")
>>> cursor.execute("insert into people (name, count) values (?, ?)",
...                ("Jill", 15))
>>> conn.commit()
```

The last `insert` query illustrates the preferred way to make a query with variables. Rather than constructing the query string, it's more secure to use a ? for each variable and then pass the variables as a tuple parameter to the `execute` method. The advantage is that you don't need to worry about incorrectly escaping a value; sqlite3 takes care of it for you.

You can also use variable names prefixed with : in the query and pass in a corresponding dictionary with the values to be inserted:

```
>>> cursor.execute("insert into people (name, count) values (:username, \
                   :usercount)", {"username": "Joe", "usercount": 10})
```

After a table is populated, you can query the data by using SQL commands, again using either ? for variable binding or names and dictionaries:

```
>>> result = cursor.execute("select * from people")
>>> print(result.fetchall())
[('Bob', 1), ('Jill', 15), ('Joe', 10)]
>>> result = cursor.execute("select * from people where name like :name",
...                         {"name": "bob"})
>>> print(result.fetchall())
[('Bob', 1)]
>>> cursor.execute("update people set count=? where name=?", (20, "Jill"))
>>> result = cursor.execute("select * from people")
>>> print(result.fetchall())
[('Bob', 1), ('Jill', 20), ('Joe', 10)]
```

In addition to the `fetchall` method, the `fetchone` method gets one row of the result, and `fetchmany` returns an arbitrary number of rows. For convenience, it's also possible to iterate over a cursor object's rows similarly to iterating over a file:

```
>>> result = cursor.execute("select * from people")
>>> for row in result:
...     print(row)
...
('Bob', 1)
```

```
('Jill', 20)
('Joe', 10)
```

Finally, by default, sqlite3 doesn't immediately commit transactions. This fact means that you have the option of rolling back a transaction if it fails, but it also means that you need to use the `Connection` object's `commit` method to ensure that any changes made have been saved. Doing so before you close a connection to a database is a particularly good idea because the `close` method doesn't automatically commit any active transactions:

```
>>> cursor.execute("update people set count=? where name=?", (20, "Jill"))
>>> conn.commit()
>>> conn.close()
```

Table 23.1 gives an overview of the most common operations on an sqlite3 database.

Table 23.1   Common sqlite3 database operations

Operation	sqlite3 command
Create a connection to a database.	`conn = sqlite3.connect(filename)`
Create a cursor for a connection.	`Cursor = conn.cursor()`
Execute a query with the cursor.	`cursor.execute(query)`

Return the results of a query.	`cursor.fetchall(), cursor.fetchmany(num_rows),`
	`cursor.fetchone()`
	`for row in cursor:`
	`    ....`

Commit a transaction to a database.	`conn.commit()`
Close a connection.	`conn.close()`

These operations usually are all you need to manipulate an sqlite3 database. Of course, several options let you control their precise behavior; see the Python documentation for more information.

> **TRY THIS: CREATING AND MODIFYING TABLES**   Using sqlite3, write the code that creates a database table for the Illinois weather data you loaded from a flat file in section 21.2. Suppose that you have similar data for more states and want to store more information about the states themselves. How could you modify your database to use a related table to store the state information?

23.3   *Using MySQL, PostgreSQL, and other relational databases*

As I mentioned earlier in this chapter, several other SQL databases have client libraries that follow the DB-API. As a result, accessing those databases in Python is quite similar, but there are a couple of differences to look out for:

- Unlike SQLite, those databases require a database server that the client connects to and that may or may not be on a different machine, so the connection requires more parameters—usually including host, account name, and password.
- The way in which parameters are interpolated into queries, such as `"select * from test where name like :name"`, could use a different format—something like `?`, `%s 5(name)s`.

These changes aren't huge, but they tend to keep code from being completely portable across different databases.

23.4 *Making database handling easier with an ORM*

There are a few problems with the DB-API database client libraries mentioned earlier in this chapter and their requirement to write raw SQL:

- Different SQL databases have implemented SQL in subtly different ways, so the same SQL statements won't always work if you move from one database to another, as you might want to do if, say, you do local development against sqlite3 and then want to use MySQL or PostgreSQL in production. Also, as mentioned earlier, the different implementations have different ways of doing things like passing parameters into queries.
- The second drawback is the need to use raw SQL statements. Including SQL statements in your code can make your code more difficult to maintain, particularly if you have a lot of them. In that case, some of the statements will be boilerplate and routine; others will be complex and tricky; and all of them need to be tested, which can get cumbersome.
- The need to write SQL means that you need to think in at least two languages: Python and a specific SQL variant. In plenty of cases, it's worth these hassles to use raw SQL, but in many other cases, it isn't.

Given those issues, people wanted a way to handle databases in Python that was easier to manage and didn't require anything more than writing regular Python code. The solution is an Object Relational Mapper (ORM), which converts, or maps, relational database types and structures to objects in Python. Two of the most common ORMs in the Python world are the Django ORM and SQLAlchemy, although of course there are many others. The Django ORM is rather tightly integrated with the Django web framework and usually isn't used outside it. Because I'm not delving into Django in this book, I won't discuss the Django ORM other than to note that it's the default choice for Django applications and a good one, with fully developed tools and generous community support.

23.4.1 *SQLAlchemy*

SQLAlchemy is the other big-name ORM in the Python space. SQLAlchemy's goal is to automate redundant database tasks and provide Python object-based interfaces to the data while still allowing the developer control of the database and access to the underlying SQL. In this section, I look at some basic examples of storing data into a relational database and then retrieving it with SQLAlchemy.

You can install SQLAlchemy in your environment with `pip`:

```
> pip install sqlalchemy
```

> **NOTE** In working with SQLAlchemy and its related tools from this point, it will be more convenient to have two shell windows open in the same virtual environment: one for Python and one for your system's command line.

SQLAlchemy offers several ways to interact with database and its tables. Although an ORM lets you write SQL statements if you want or need to, the strength of an ORM is doing what the name suggests: mapping the relational database tables and columns to Python objects.

Use SQLAlchemy to replicate what you did in section 23.2: Create a table, add three rows, query the table, and update one row. You need to do a bit more setup to use the ORM, but in larger projects, this effort is more than worth it.

First, you need to import the components you need to connect to the database and map a table to Python objects. From the base `sqlalchemy` package, you need the `create_engine` and `select` methods and the `MetaData` and `Table` classes. But because you need to specify the schema information when you create the `table` object, you also need to import the `Column` class and the classes for the data type of each column—in this case, `Integer` and `String`. From the `sqlalchemy.orm` sub-package, you also need the `sessionmaker` function:

```
>>> from sqlalchemy import create_engine, select, MetaData, Table, Column,
     Integer, String
>>> from sqlalchemy.orm import sessionmaker
```

Now you can think about connecting to the database:

```
>>> dbPath = 'datafile2.db'
>>> engine = create_engine('sqlite:///%s' % dbPath)
>>> metadata = MetaData(engine)
>>> people  = Table('people', metadata,
...                  Column('id', Integer, primary_key=True),
...                  Column('name', String),
...                  Column('count', Integer),
...                 )
>>> Session = sessionmaker(bind=engine)
>>> session = Session()
>>> metadata.create_all(engine)
```

To create and connect, you need to create a database engine appropriate for your database; then you need a `MetaData` object, which is a container for managing tables and their schemas. Create a `Table` object called `data`, giving the table's name in the database, the `MetaData` object you just created, and the column you want to create, as well as their data types. Finally, you use the `sessionmaker` function to create a

Session class for your engine and use that class to instantiate a session object. At this point, you're connected to the database, and the last step is to use the create_all method to create the table.

When the table is created, the next step is inserting some records. Again, you have many options for doing this in SQLAlchemy, but you'll be fairly explicit in this example. Create an insert object, which you then execute:

```
>>> people_ins = people.insert().values(name='Bob', count=1)
>>> str(people_ins)
'INSERT INTO people (name, count) VALUES (?, ?)'
>>> session.execute(people_ins)
<sqlalchemy.engine.result.ResultProxy object at 0x7f126c6dd438>
>>> session.commit()
```

Here, you use the insert() method to create an insert object, also specifying the fields and values you want to insert. people_ins is the insert object, and you use the str() function to show that behind the scenes, you created the correct SQL command. Then you use the session object's execute method to perform the insertion and the commit method to commit it to the database:

```
>>> session.execute(people_ins, [
...     {'name': 'Jill', 'count':15},
...     {'name': 'Joe', 'count':10}
... ])
<sqlalchemy.engine.result.ResultProxy object at 0x7f126c6dd908>
>>> session.commit()
>>> result = session.execute(select([people]))
>>> for row in result:
...     print(row)
...
(1, 'Bob', 1)
(2, 'Jill', 15)
(3, 'Joe', 10)
```

You can streamline things a bit and perform multiple inserts by passing in a list of dictionaries of the field names and values for each insert:

```
>>> result = session.execute(select([people]).where(people.c.name == 'Jill'))
>>> for row in result:
...     print(row)
...
(2, 'Jill', 15)
```

You can also use the select() method with a where() method to find a particular record. In the example, you're looking for any records in which the name column equals 'Jill'. Note that the where expression uses people.c.name, with the c indicating that name is a column in the people table:

```
>>> result = session.execute(people.update().values(count=20).where
...     (people.c.name == 'Jill'))
>>> session.commit()
>>> result = session.execute(select([people]).where(people.c.name == 'Jill'))
```

```
>>> for row in result:
...     print(row)
...
(2, 'Jill', 20)
>>>
```

Finally, you can combine an `update()` method with the `where()` method to update just one row.

MAPPING TABLE OBJECTS TO CLASSES

So far, you've used table objects directly, but it's also possible to use SQLAlchemy to map a table directly to a class. This technique has the advantage that the columns are mapped directly to class attributes. For illustration, make a class `People`:

```
>>> from sqlalchemy.ext.declarative import declarative_base
>>> Base = declarative_base()
>>> class People(Base):
...     __tablename__ = "people"
...     id = Column(Integer, primary_key=True)
...     name = Column(String)
...     count = Column(Integer)
...
>>> results = session.query(People).filter_by(name='Jill')
>>> for person in results:
...     print(person.id, person.name, person.count)
...
2 Jill 20
```

Inserts can be done just by creating an instance of the mapped class and adding it to the session:

```
>>> new_person = People(name='Jane', count=5)
>>> session.add(new_person)
>>> session.commit()
>>>
>>> results = session.query(People).all()
>>> for person in results:
...     print(person.id, person.name, person.count)
...
1 Bob 1
2 Jill 20
3 Joe 10
4 Jane 5
```

Updates are also fairly straightforward. You retrieve the record you want to update, change the values on the mapped instance, and then add the updated record to the session to be written back to the database:

```
>>> jill = session.query(People).filter_by(name='Jill').first()
>>> jill.name
'Jill'
>>> jill.count = 22
```

```
>>> session.add(jill)
>>> session.commit()
>>> results = session.query(People).all()
>>> for person in results:
...     print(person.id, person.name, person.count)
...
1 Bob 1
2 Jill 22
3 Joe 10
4 Jane 5
```

Deleting is similar to updating; you fetch the record to be deleted and then use the session's `delete()` method to delete it:

```
>>> jane = session.query(People).filter_by(name='Jane').first()
>>> session.delete(jane)
>>> session.commit()
>>> jane = session.query(People).filter_by(name='Jane').first()
>>> print(jane)
None
```

Using SQLAlchemy does take a bit more setup than just using raw SQL, but it also has some real benefits. For one thing, using the ORM means that you don't need to worry about any subtle differences in the SQL supported by different databases. The example works equally well with sqlite3, MySQL, and PostgreSQL without making any changes in the code other than giving the string to the create engine and making sure that the correct database driver is available.

Another advantage is that the interaction with the data can happen through Python objects, which may be more accessible to coders who lack SQL experience. Instead of constructing SQL statements, they can use Python objects and their methods.

> **TRY THIS: USING AN ORM** Using the database from earlier, write an SQLAlchemy class to map to the data table, and use it to read the records from the table.

23.4.2 *Using Alembic for database schema changes*

In the course of developing code that uses a relational database it's quite common, if not universal, to have to change the structure or schema of the database after you've started work. Fields need to be added, or their types need to be changed, and so on. It's possible, of course, to manually make the changes to both the database tables and to the code for the ORM that accesses them, but that approach has some drawbacks. For one thing, such changes are difficult to roll back if you need to, and it's hard to keep track of the configuration of the database that goes with a particular version of your code.

The solution is to use a database migration tool to help you make the changes and track them. Migrations are written as code and should include code both to apply the needed changes and to reverse them. Then the changes can be tracked and applied or reversed in the correct sequence. As a result, you can reliably upgrade or downgrade your database to any of the states it was in over the course of development.

As an example, this section looks briefly at Alembic, a popular lightweight migration tool for SQLAlchemy. To start, switch to the system command-line window in your project directory, install Alembic, and create a generic environment by using `alemic init`:

```
> pip install alembic
> alembic init alembic
```

This code creates the file structure you need to use Alembic for data migrations. There's an alembic.ini file that you need to edit in at least one place. The `sqlalchemy.url` line needs to be updated to match your current situation:

```
sqlalchemy.url = driver://user:pass@localhost/dbname
```

Change the line to

```
sqlalchemy.url = sqlite:///datafile.db
```

Because you're using a local sqlite file, you don't need a username or password.

The next step is creating a revision by using Alembic's revision command:

```
> alembic revision -m "create an address table"
Generating /home/naomi/qpb_testing/alembic/versions/
    384ead9efdfd_create_a_test_address_table.py ... done
```

This code creates a revision script, 384ead9efdfd_create_a_test_address_table.py, in the alembic/versions directory. This file looks like this:

```
"""create an address table

Revision ID: 384ead9efdfd
Revises:
Create Date: 2017-07-26 21:03:29.042762

"""
from alembic import op
import sqlalchemy as sa


# revision identifiers, used by Alembic.
revision = '384ead9efdfd'
down_revision = None
branch_labels = None
depends_on = None


def upgrade():
    pass


def downgrade():
    pass
```

You can see that the file contains the revision ID and date in the header. It also contains a `down_revision` variable to guide the rollback of each version. If you make a second revision, its `down_revision` variable should contain this revision's ID.

To perform the revision, update the revision script to supply both the code describing how to perform the revision in the `upgrade()` method and the code to reverse it in the `downgrade()` method:

```
def upgrade():
    op.create_table(
        'address',
        sa.Column('id', sa.Integer, primary_key=True),
        sa.Column('address', sa.String(50), nullable=False),
        sa.Column('city', sa.String(50), nullable=False),
        sa.Column('state', sa.String(20), nullable=False),
    )

def downgrade():
    op.drop_table('address')
```

When this code is created, you can apply the upgrade. But first, switch back to the Python shell window to see what tables you have in your database:

```
>>> print(engine.table_names())
['people']
```

As you might expect, you have only the one table you created earlier. Now you can run Alembic's `upgrade` command to apply the upgrade and add a new table. Switch over to your system command line, and run

```
> alembic upgrade head
INFO  [alembic.runtime.migration] Context impl SQLiteImpl.
INFO  [alembic.runtime.migration] Will assume non-transactional DDL.
INFO  [alembic.runtime.migration] Running upgrade  -> 384ead9efdfd, create an
    address table
```

If you pop back to Python and check, you see that the database has two additional tables:

```
>>> engine.table_names()
['alembic_version', 'people', 'address']
```

The first new table, `'alembic version'`, is created by Alembic to help track which version your database is currently on (for reference for future upgrades and downgrades). The second new table, `'address'`, is the table you added through your upgrade and is ready to use.

If you want to roll back the state of the database to what it was before, all you need to do is run Alembic's `downgrade` command in the system window. You give the downgrade command `-1` to tell Alembic that you want to downgrade by one version:

```
> alembic downgrade -1
INFO  [alembic.runtime.migration] Context impl SQLiteImpl.
```

```
INFO  [alembic.runtime.migration] Will assume non-transactional DDL.
INFO  [alembic.runtime.migration] Running downgrade 384ead9efdfd -> , create
    an address table
```

Now if you check in your Python session, you'll be back to where you started except that the version tracking table remains:

```
>>> engine.table_names()
['alembic_version', 'people']
```

If you want to, of course, you can run the upgrade again to put the table back, add further revisions, make upgrades, and so on.

> **TRY THIS: MODIFYING A DATABASE WITH ALEMBIC**   Experiment with creating an Alembic upgrade that adds a state table to your database, with columns for ID, state name, and abbreviation. Upgrade and downgrade. What other changes would be needed if you were going to use the state table along with the existing data table?

23.5   *NoSQL databases*

In spite of their longstanding popularity, relational databases aren't the only ways to think about storing data. Although relational databases are all about normalizing data within related tables, other approaches look at data differently. Quite commonly, these types of databases are referred to as *NoSQL* databases, because they usually don't adhere to the row/column/table structure that SQL was created to describe.

Rather than handle data as collections of rows, columns, and tables, NoSQL databases can look at the data they store as key-value pairs, as indexed documents, and even as graphs. Many NoSQL databases are available, all with somewhat different ways of handling data. In general, they're less likely to be strictly normalized, which can make retrieving information faster and easier. As examples, in this chapter I look at using Python to access two common NoSQL databases: Redis and MongoDB. What follows barely scratches the surface of what you can do with NoSQL databases and Python, but it should give you a basic idea of the possibilities. If you're already familiar with Redis or MongoDB, you'll see a little of how the Python client libraries work, and if you're new to NoSQL databases, you'll at least get an idea of how databases like these work.

23.6   *key:value stores with Redis*

Redis is an in-memory networked key:value store. Because the values are in memory, lookups can be quite fast, and the fact that it's designed to be accessed over the network makes it useful in a variety of situations. Redis is commonly used for caching, as a message broker, and for quick lookups of information. In fact, the name (which comes from Remote Dictionary Server) is an excellent way to think of it; it behaves much like a Python dictionary translated to a network service.

The following example gives you an idea of how Redis works with Python. If you're familiar with the Redis command-line interface or have used a Redis client for another language, these short examples should get you well on your way to using Redis with Python. If Redis is new to you, the following gives you an idea of how it works; you can explore more at https://redis.io.

Although several Python clients are available for Redis, at this writing the way to go (according to the Redis website) is one called redis-py. You can install it with `pip install redis`.

Running a Redis server

To experiment, you need to have a Redis server running. Although you could use cloud-based Redis services, for experimentation your best choices are using a Docker instance or installing a server on a machine.

If you have Docker installed, using the Redis Docker instance is probably the quickest and easiest way to get a server up and running. You should be able to launch a Redis instance from the command line with a command like `> docker run -p 6379:6379 redis`.

On Linux systems, it should be fairly easy to install Redis by using the system package manager, and on Mac systems, `brew install redis` should work. On Windows systems, you should check the https://redis.io website or search online for the current options for running Redis on Windows. When Redis is installed, you may need to look online for instructions to make sure that the Redis server is running.

When you get a server running, the following are examples of simple Redis interactions with Python. First, you need to import the Redis library and create a Redis connection object:

```
>>> import redis
>>> r = redis.Redis(host='localhost', port=6379)
```

You can use several connection options when creating a Redis connection, including the host, port, and password or SSH certificate. If the server is running on localhost on the default port of 6379, no options are needed. When you have the connection, you can use it to access the key:value store.

One of the first things you might do is use the `keys()` method to get a list of the keys in the database, which returns a list of keys currently stored (if any). Then you can set some keys of different types and try some ways to retrieve their values:

```
>>> r.keys()
[]
>>> r.set('a_key', 'my value')
True
>>> r.keys()
[b'a_key']
>>> v = r.get('a_key')
>>> v
b'my value'
```

```
>>> r.incr('counter')
1
>>> r.get('counter')
b'1'
>>> r.incr('counter')
2
>>> r.get('counter')
b'2'
```

These examples show how you can get a list of the keys in the Redis database, how to set a key with a value, and how to set a key with a `counter` variable and increment it.

These examples deal with storing arrays or lists:

```
>>> r.rpush("words", "one")
1
>>> r.rpush("words", "two")
2
>>> r.lrange("words", 0, -1)
[b'one', b'two']
>>> r.rpush("words", "three")
3
>>> r.lrange("words", 0, -1)
[b'one', b'two', b'three']
>>> r.llen("words")
3
>>> r.lpush("words", "zero")
4
>>> r.lrange("words", 0, -1)
[b'zero', b'one', b'two', b'three']
>>> r.lrange("words", 2, 2)
[b'two']
>>> r.lindex("words", 1)
b'one'
>>> r.lindex("words", 2)
b'two'
```

When you start the key, `"words"` isn't in the database, but the act of adding or pushing a value to the end (from the right, the `r` in `rpush`) creates the key, makes an empty list as its value, and then appends the value `'one'`. Using `rpush` again adds another word to the end. To retrieve the values in the list, you can use the `lrange()` function, giving the key and both a starting index and an ending index, with `-1` indicating the end of the list.

Also note that you can add to the beginning, or left side, of the list with `lpush()`. You can use `lindex()` to retrieve a single value in the same way as `lranger()`, except that you give it the index of the value you want.

EXPIRATION OF VALUES

One feature of Redis that makes it particularly useful for caching is the ability to set an expiration for a key-value pair. After that time has elapsed, the key and value are removed. This technique is particularly useful for using Redis as a cache. You can set the timeout value in seconds when you set the value for a key:

```
>>> r.setex("timed", "10 seconds", 10)
True
>>> r.pttl("timed")
7165
>>> r.pttl("timed")
5208
>>> r.pttl("timed")
1542
>>> r.pttl("timed")
>>>
```

In this case, you set the expiration of `"timed"` to 10 seconds. Then, as you use the `pttl()` method, you can see the time remaining before expiration in milliseconds. When the value expires, both the key and value are automatically removed from the database. This feature and the fine-grained control of it that Redis offers are really useful. For simple caches, you may not need to write much more code to have your problem solved.

It's worth noting that Redis holds its data in memory, so keep in mind that the data isn't persistent; if the server crashes, some data is likely to be lost. To mitigate the possibility of data loss, Redis has options to manage persistence—everything from writing every change to disk as it occurs to making periodic snapshots at predetermined times to not saving to disk at all. You can also use the Python client's `save()` and `bgsave()` methods to programmatically force a snapshot to be saved, either blocking until the save is complete with `save()` or saving in the background in the case of `bgsave()`.

In this chapter, I've only touched on a small part of what Redis can do, as well as its data types and the ways it can manipulate them. If you're interested in finding out more, several sources of documentation are available online, including at https://redislabs.com and https://redis-py.readthedocs.io.

> **QUICK CHECK: USES OF KEY:VALUE STORES**   What sorts of data and applications would benefit most from a key:value store like Redis?

23.7   *Documents in MongoDB*

Another popular NoSQL database is MongoDB, which is sometimes called a document-based database because it isn't organized in rows and columns but instead stores documents. MongoDB is designed to scale across many nodes in multiple clusters while potentially handling billions of documents. In the case of MongoDB, a document is stored in a format called BSON (Binary JSON), so a document consists of key-value pairs and looks like a JSON object or Python dictionary. The following examples give you a taste of how you can use Python to interact with MongoDB collections and documents, but a word of warning is appropriate. In situations requiring scale and distribution of data, high insert rates, complex and unstable schemas, and so on, MongoDB is an excellent choice. However, MongoDB isn't the best choice in many situations, so be sure to investigate your needs and options thoroughly before choosing.

> ### Running a MongoDB server
>
> As with Redis, if you want to experiment with MongoDB, you need to have access to a MongoDB server. Numerous cloud-hosted Mongo services are available, but again, if you're just experimenting, you'll probably be better off running a Docker instance or installing on a server you own.
>
> As is the case with Redis, the easiest solution is to run a Docker instance. All you need to do if you have Docker is enter > `docker run -p 27017:27017 mongo` at the command line. On a Linux system, your package manager should do the job, and the Mac's `brew install mongodb` will do it. On Windows systems, check on www.mongodb.com for the Windows version and installation instructions. As with Redis, search online for any instructions on how to configure and start the server.

As is the case with Redis, several Python client libraries connect to MongoDB databases. To give you an idea of how they work, look at pymongo. The first step in using pymongo is installing it, which you can do with pip:

```
> pip install pymongo
```

When you have pymongo installed, you can connect to a MongoDB server by creating an instance of MongoClient and specifying the usual connection details:

```
>>> from pymongo import MongoClient
>>> mongo = MongoClient(host='localhost', port=27017)
```

host='localhost' and port=27017 are defaults and don't need to be specified.

MongoDB is organized in terms of a database which contains collections, each of which can contain documents. Databases and collections don't need to be created before you try to access them, however. If they don't exist, they're created as you insert into them, or they simply return no results if you try to retrieve records from them.

To test the client, make a sample document, which can be a Python dictionary:

```
>>> import datetime
>>> a_document = {'name': 'Jane',
...                'age': 34,
...                'interests': ['Python', 'databases', 'statistics'],
...                'date_added': datetime.datetime.now()
... }
>>> db = mongo.my_data
>>> collection = db.docs
>>> collection.find_one()
>>> db.collection_names()
[]
```

Selects a database (which hasn't been created yet)

Selects a collection in the database (also not yet created)

Searches for first item; doesn't throw exception even though neither collection nor database exists yet

Here, you connect to a database and a collection of documents. In this case, they don't exist, but they'll be created as you access them. Note that no exceptions were raised even though the database and collection didn't exist. When you asked for a list of the collections, however, you got an empty list because nothing has been stored in your collection. To store a document, use the collection's `insert()` method, which returns the document's unique `ObjectId` if the operation is successful:

```
>>> collection.insert(a_document)
ObjectId('59701cc4f5ef0516e1da0dec')          ◄──┐ Unique ObjectId
>>> db.collection_names()
['docs']
```

Now that you've stored a document in the `docs` collection, it shows up when you ask for the collection names in your database. When the document is stored in the collection, you can query for it, update it, replace it, and delete it:

```
                                                        Retrieves first record
>>> collection.find_one()                       ◄──────┐
{'_id': ObjectId('59701cc4f5ef0516e1da0dec'), 'name': 'Jane', 'age': 34,
    'interests': ['Python', 'databases', 'statistics'], 'date_added':
    datetime.datetime(2017, 7, 19, 21, 59, 32, 752000)}
>>> from bson.objectid import ObjectId
>>> collection.find_one({"_id":ObjectId('59701cc4f5ef0516e1da0dec')})    ◄──┐
{'_id': ObjectId('59701cc4f5ef0516e1da0dec'), 'name': 'Jane',
    'age': 34, 'interests': ['Python', 'databases',          Retrieves record
    'statistics'], 'date_added': datetime.datetime(2017,     matching specification—
    7, 19, 21, 59, 32, 752000)}                              in this case, ObjectId
>>> collection.update_one({"_id":ObjectId('59701cc4f5ef0516e1da0dec')},
      {"$set": {"name":"Ann"}})
<pymongo.results.UpdateResult object at 0x7f4ebd601d38>
>>> collection.find_one({"_id":ObjectId('59701cc4f5ef0516e1da0dec')})
{'_id': ObjectId('59701cc4f5ef0516e1da0dec'), 'name': 'Ann', 'age': 34,
    'interests': ['Python', 'databases', 'statistics'], 'date_added':
    datetime.datetime(2017, 7, 19, 21, 59, 32, 752000)}
>>> collection.replace_one({"_id":ObjectId('59701cc4f5ef0516e1da0dec')},
      {"name":"Ann"})
<pymongo.results.UpdateResult object at 0x7f4ebd601750>         Replaces
>>> collection.find_one({"_id":ObjectId('59701cc4f5ef0516e1da0dec')})  record with
{'_id': ObjectId('59701cc4f5ef0516e1da0dec'), 'name': 'Ann'}   new object
>>> collection.delete_one({"_id":ObjectId('59701cc4f5ef0516e1da0dec')})  ◄──
<pymongo.results.DeleteResult object at 0x7f4ebd601d80>
>>> collection.find_one()                                      Deletes record
                                                               matching specification
```

Updates record according to contents of $set object points to the `update_one` line.

First, notice that MongoDB matches according to dictionaries of the fields and their values to match. Dictionaries are also used to indicate operators, such as `$lt` (less than) and `$gt` (greater than), as well as commands such as `$set` for the update. The other thing to notice is that even though the record has been deleted and the collection is now empty, it still exists unless it's specifically dropped:

```
>>> db.collection_names()
['docs']
>>> collection.drop()
>>> db.collection_names()
[]
```

MongoDB can do many other things, of course. In addition to operating on one record, versions of the same commands cover multiple records, such as `find_many` and `update_many`. MongoDB also supports indexing to improve performances and has several methods to group, count, and aggregate data, as well as a built in map-reduce method.

> **QUICK CHECK: USES OF MONGODB** Thinking back over the various data samples you've seen so far and other types of data in your experience, which do you think would be well suited to being stored in a database like MongoDB? Would others clearly not be suited, and if so, why not?

> **LAB 23: CREATE A DATABASE** Choose one of the datasets I've discussed in the past few chapters, and decide which type of database would be best for storing that data. Create that database, and write the code to load the data into it. Then choose the two most common and/or likely types of search criteria, and write the code to retrieve both single and multiple matching records.

Summary

- Python has a Database API (DB-API) that provides a generally consistent interface for clients of several relational databases.
- Using an Object Relational Mapper (ORM) can make database code even more standard across databases.
- Using an ORM also lets you access relational databases through Python code and objects rather than SQL queries.
- Tools such as Alembic work with ORMs to use code to make reversible changes to a relational database schema.
- Key:value stores such as Redis provide quick in-memory data access.
- MongoDB provides scalability without the strict structure of relational databases.

Exploring data

Over the past few chapters, I've dealt with some aspects of using Python to get and clean data. Now it's time to look at a few of the things that Python can help you do to manipulate and explore data.

24.1 Python tools for data exploration

In this chapter, we'll look at some common Python tools for data exploration: Jupyter notebook, pandas, and matplotlib. I can only touch briefly on a few features of these tools, but the aim is to give you an idea of what is possible and some initial tools to use in exploring data with Python.

24.1.1 *Python's advantages for exploring data*

Python has become one of the leading languages for data science and continues to grow in that area. As I've mentioned, however, Python isn't always the fastest language in terms of raw performance. Conversely, some data-crunching libraries, such as NumPy, are largely written in C and heavily optimized to the point that speed isn't an issue. In addition, considerations such as readability and accessibility often outweigh pure speed; minimizing the amount of developer time needed is often more important. Python is readable and accessible, and both on its own and in combination with tools developed in the Python community, it's an enormously powerful tool for manipulating and exploring data.

24.1.2 *Python can be better than a spreadsheet*

Spreadsheets have been the tools of choice for ad-hoc data manipulation for decades. People who are skilled with spreadsheets can make them do truly impressive tricks: spreadsheets can combine different but related data sets, pivot tables, use lookup tables to link data sets, and much more. But although people everywhere get a vast amount of work done with them every day, spreadsheets do have limitations, and Python can help you go beyond those limitations.

One limitation that I've already alluded to is the fact that most spreadsheet software has a row limit—currently, about 1 million rows, which isn't enough for many data sets. Another limitation is the central metaphor of the spreadsheet itself. Spreadsheets are two-dimensional grids, rows and columns, or at best stacks of grids, which limits the ways you can manipulate and think about complex data.

With Python, you can code your way around the limitations of spreadsheets and manipulate data the way you want. You can combine Python data structures such as lists, tuples, sets, and dictionaries in endlessly flexible ways, or you can create your own classes to package both data and behavior exactly the way you need.

24.2 *Jupyter notebook*

Probably one of the most compelling tools for exploring data with Python doesn't augment what the language itself does, but changes the way you use the language to interact with your data. Jupyter notebook is a web application that allows you to create and share documents that contain live code, equations, visualizations, and explanatory text. Although several other languages are now supported, it originated in connection with IPython, an alternative shell for Python developed by the scientific community.

What makes Jupyter such a convenient and powerful tool is the fact that you interact with it in a web browser. It lets you combine text and code, as well as modify and execute your code interactively. You can not only run and modify code in chunks, but also save and share the notebooks with others.

The best way to get a feel for what Jupyter notebook can do is start playing with it. It's fairly easy to run a Jupyter process locally on your machine, or you can access online versions. For some options, see the sidebar on ways to run Jupyter.

> **Ways to run Jupyter**
>
> *Jupyter online:* Accessing online instances of Jupyter is one of the easiest ways to get started. Currently, Project Jupyter, the community behind Jupyter, hosts free notebooks at https://jupyter.org/try. You can also find demo notebooks and kernels for other languages. At this writing, you can also access free notebooks on Microsoft's Azure platform at https://notebooks.azure.com, and many other ways are available.
>
> *Jupyter locally:* Although using an online instance is quite convenient, it's not very much work to set up your own instance of Jupyter on your computer. Usually for local versions, you point your browser to localhost:8888.
>
> If you use Docker, you have several containers to choose among. To run the data science notebook container, use something like this:
>
> ```
> docker run -it --rm -p 8888:8888 jupyter/datascience-notebook
> ```
>
> If you'd rather run directly on your system, it's easy to install and run Jupyter in a virtualenv.
>
> *macOS and Linux systems:* First, open a command window, and enter the following commands:
>
> ```
> > python3 -m venv jupyter
> > cd jupyter
> > source bin/activate
> > pip install jupyter
> > jupyter-notebook
> ```
>
> *Windows systems:*
>
> ```
> > python3 -m venv jupyter
> > cd jupyter
> > Scripts/bin/activate
> > pip install jupyter
> > Scripts/jupyter-notebook
> ```
>
> The last command should run the Jupyter notebook web app and open a browser window pointing at it.

24.2.1 Starting a kernel

When you have Jupyter installed, running, and open in your browser, you need to start a Python kernel. One nice thing about Jupyter is that it lets you run multiple kernels at the same time. You can run kernels for different versions of Python and for other languages such as R, Julia, and even Ruby.

Figure 24.1   Starting a Python kernel

Starting a kernel is easy. Just click the new button and select Python 3 (figure 24.1).

24.2.2   *Executing code in a cell*

When you have a kernel running, you can start entering and running Python code. Right away, you'll notice a few differences from the ordinary Python command shell. You won't get the >>> prompt that you see in the standard Python shell, and pressing Enter just adds new lines in the cell. To execute the code in a cell, illustrated in figure 24.2, choose Cell > Run Cells, click the Run button immediately to the left of the down arrow on the button bar, or use the key combination Alt-Enter. After you use Jupyter notebook a little bit, it's quite likely that the Alt-Enter key combination will become quite natural to you.

You can test how it works by entering some code or an expression into the first cell of your new notebook and then pressing Alt-Enter.

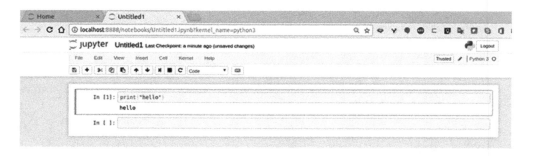

Figure 24.2   Executing code in a notebook cell

As you can see, any output is shown immediately below the cell, and a new cell is created and ready for your next input. Also note that each cell that's executed is numbered in the order in which it's executed.

TRY THIS: USING JUPYTER NOTEBOOK   Enter some code in the notebook and experiment with running it. Check out the Edit, Cell, and Kernel menus to see what options are there. When you have a little code running, use the Kernel menu to restart the kernel, repeat your steps, and then use the Cell menu to rerun the code in all of the cells.

24.3   Python and pandas

In the course of exploring and manipulating data, you perform quite a few common operations, such as loading data into a list or dictionary, cleaning data, and filtering data. Most of these operations are repeated often, have to be done in standard patterns, and are simple and often tedious. If you think that this combination is a strong reason to automate those tasks you're not alone. One of the now-standard tools for handling data in Python—pandas—was created to automate the boring heavy lifting of handling data sets.

24.3.1   Why you might want to use pandas

pandas was created to make manipulating and analyzing tablular or relational data easy by providing a standard framework for holding the data, with convenient tools for frequent operations. As a result, it's almost more of an extension to Python than a library, and it changes the way you can interact with data. The plus side is that after you grok how pandas work, you can do some impressive things and save a lot of time. It does take time to learn how to get the most from pandas, however. As with many tools, if you use pandas for what it was designed for, it excels. The simple examples I show you in the following sections should give you a rough idea whether pandas is a tool that's suited for your use cases.

24.3.2   Installing pandas

pandas is easy to install with `pip`. It's often used along with matplotlib for plotting, so you can install both tools from the command line of your Jupyter virtual environment with this code:

```
> pip install pandas matplotlib
```

From a cell in a Jupyter notebook, you can use

```
In [ ]: !pip install pandas matplotlib
```

If you use pandas, life will be easier if you use the following three lines:

```
%matplotlib inline
import pandas as pd
import numpy as np
```

The first line is a Jupyter "magic" function that enables matplotlib to plot data in the cell where your code is (which is very useful). The second line imports pandas with the alias of pd, which is both easier to type and common among pandas users; the last line also imports numpy. Although pandas depends quite a bit on numpy, you won't use it explicitly in the following examples, but it's reasonable to get into the habit of importing it anyway.

24.3.3 *Data frames*

One basic structure that you get with pandas is a data frame. A *data frame* is a two-dimensional grid, rather similar to a relational database table except in memory. Creating a data frame is easy; you give it some data. To keep things absolutely simple, give it a 3 x 3 grid of numbers as the first example. In Python, such a grid is a list of lists:

```
grid = [[1,2,3], [4,5,6], [7,8,9]]
print(grid)

[[1, 2, 3], [4, 5, 6], [7, 8, 9]]
```

Sadly, in Python the grid won't look like a grid unless you make some additional effort. So see what you can do with the same grid as a pandas data frame:

```
import pandas as pd
df = pd.DataFrame(grid)
print(df)

   0  1  2
0  1  2  3
1  4  5  6
2  7  8  9
```

That code is fairly straightforward; all you needed to do was turn your grid into a data frame. You've gained a more gridlike display, and now you have both row and column numbers. It's often rather bothersome to keep track of what column number is what, of course, so give your columns names:

```
df = pd.DataFrame(grid, columns=["one", "two", "three"] )
print(df)

   one  two  three
0    1    2      3
1    4    5      6
2    7    8      9
```

You may wonder whether naming the columns has any benefit, but the column names can be put to use with another pandas trick: the ability to select columns by name. If you want the contents only of column "two", for example, you can get it very simply:

```
print(df["two"])
0    2
1    5
2    8
Name: two, dtype: int64
```

Here, you've already saved time in comparison to Python. To get only column two of your grid, you'd need to use a list comprehension while also remembering to use a zero-based index (and you still wouldn't get the nice output):

```
print([x[1] for x in grid])
[2, 5, 8]
```

You can loop over data frame column values just as easily as the list you got by using a comprehension:

```
for x in df["two"]:
    print(x)
2
5
8
```

That's not bad for a start, but by using a list of columns in double brackets, you can do better, getting a subset of the data frame that's another data frame. Instead of getting the middle column, get the first and last columns of your data frame as another data frame:

```
edges = df[["one", "three"]]
print(edges)
   one  three
0   1      3
1   4      6
2   7      9
```

A data frame also has several methods that apply the same operation and argument to every item in the frame. If you want to add two to every item in the data frame's edges, you could use the add() method:

```
print(edges.add(2))
   one  three
0   3      5
1   6      8
2   9     11
```

Here again, it's possible to get the same result by using list comprehensions and/or nested loops, but those techniques aren't as convenient. It's pretty easy to see how such functionality can make life easier, particularly for someone who's more interested in the information that the data contains than in the process of manipulating it.

24.4 Data cleaning

In earlier chapters, I discussed a few ways to use Python to clean data. Now that I've added pandas to the mix, I'll show you examples of how to use its functionality to clean data. As I present the following operations, I also refer to ways that the same operation might be done in plain Python, both to illustrate how using pandas is different and to show why pandas isn't right for every use case (or user, for that matter).

24.4.1 *Loading and saving data with pandas*

pandas has an impressive collection of methods to load data from different sources. It supports several file formats (including fixed-width and delimited text files, spreadsheets, JSON, XML, and HTML), but it's also possible to read from SQL databases, Google BiqQuery, HDF, and even clipboard data. You should be aware that many of these operations aren't actually part of pandas itself; pandas relies on having other libraries installed to handle those operations, such as SQLAlchemy for reading from SQL databases. This distinction matters mostly if something goes wrong; quite often, the problem that needs to be fixed is outside pandas, and you're left to deal with the underlying library.

Reading a JSON file with the read_json() method is simple:

```
mars = pd.read_json("mars_data_01.json")
```

This code gives you a data frame like this:

```
                            report
abs_humidity                  None
atmo_opacity                 Sunny
ls                             296
max_temp                        -1
max_temp_fahrenheit           30.2
min_temp                       -72
min_temp_fahrenheit          -97.6
pressure                       869
pressure_string             Higher
season                    Month 10
sol                           1576
sunrise       2017-01-11T12:31:00Z
sunset        2017-01-12T00:46:00Z
terrestrial_date        2017-01-11
wind_direction                  --
wind_speed                    None
```

For another example of how simple reading data into pandas is, load some data from the CSV file of temperature data from chapter 21 and from the JSON file of Mars weather data used in chapter 22. In the first case, use the read_csv() method:

Note that the \ at the end of the header line is an indication that the table is too long to be printed on one line and more columns are printed below.

```
temp = pd.read_csv("temp_data_01.csv")
```

		4	5	6	7	8	9	10	11	12	14 \
0	1979/01/01	17.48	994	6.0	30.5	2.89	994	-13.6	15.8	NaN	0
1	1979/01/02	4.64	994	-6.4	15.8	-9.03	994	-23.6	6.6	NaN	0
2	1979/01/03	11.05	994	-0.7	24.7	-2.17	994	-18.3	12.9	NaN	0
3	1979/01/04	9.51	994	0.2	27.6	-0.43	994	-16.3	16.3	NaN	0
4	1979/05/15	68.42	994	61.0	75.1	51.30	994	43.3	57.0	NaN	0
5	1979/05/16	70.29	994	63.4	73.5	48.09	994	41.1	53.0	NaN	0
6	1979/05/17	75.34	994	64.0	80.5	50.84	994	44.3	55.7	82.60	2

```
7   1979/05/18   79.13   994   75.5   82.1   55.68   994   50.0   61.1   81.42   349
8   1979/05/19   74.94   994   66.9   83.1   58.59   994   50.9   63.2   82.87    78

        15      16      17
0      NaN     NaN   0.0000
1      NaN     NaN   0.0000
2      NaN     NaN   0.0000
3      NaN     NaN   0.0000
4      NaN     NaN   0.0000
5      NaN     NaN   0.0000
6     82.4    82.8   0.0020
7     80.2    83.4   0.3511
8     81.6    85.2   0.0785
```

Clearly, loading the file in a single step is appealing, and you can see that pandas had no issues loading the file. You can also see that the empty first column has been translated into NaN (not a number). You do still have the same issue with 'Missing' for some values, and in fact it might make sense to have those 'Missing' values converted to NaN:

```
temp = pd.read_csv("temp_data_01.csv", na_values=['Missing'])
```

The addition of the na_values parameter controls what values will be translated to NaN on load. In this case, you added the string 'Missing' so that the row of the data frame was translated from

```
NaN   Illinois   17   Jan 01, 1979   1979/01/01   17.48   994   6.0   30.5   2.89994
      -13.6   15.8   Missing   0   Missing   Missing   0.00%
```

to

```
NaN   Illinois   17   Jan 01, 1979   1979/01/01   17.48   994   6.0   30.5   2.89994
      -13.6   15.8   NaN0   NaN   NaN   0.00%
```

This technique can be particularly useful if you have one of those data files in which, for whatever reason, "no data" is indicated in a variety of ways: NA, N/A, ?, -, and so on. To handle a case like that, you can inspect the data to find out what's used and then reload it, using the na_values parameter to standardize all those variations as NaN.

SAVING DATA

If you want to save the contents of a data frame, a pandas data frame has a similarly broad collection of methods. If you take your simple grid data frame, you can write it in several ways. This line

```
df.to_csv("df_out.csv", index=False)
```

⟵ **Setting index to False means that the row indexes will not be written.**

writes a file that looks like this:

```
one,two,three
1,2,3
4,5,6
7,8,9
```

Similarly, you can transform a data grid to a JSON object or write it to a file:

> **Supplying a file path as an argument writes the JSON to that file rather than returning it.**

```
df.to_json()
'{"one":{"0":1,"1":4,"2":7},"two":{"0":2,"1":5,"2":8},"three":{"0":3,"1":6,"2
    ":9}}'
```

24.4.2 *Data cleaning with a data frame*

Converting a particular set of values to NaN on load is a very simple bit of data cleaning that pandas makes trivial. Going beyond that, data frames support several operations that can make data cleaning less of a chore. To see how this works, reopen the temperature CSV file, but this time, instead of using the headers to name the columns, use the range() function with the names parameter to give them numbers, which will make referring to them easier. You also may recall from an earlier example that the first field of every line—the "Notes" field—is empty and loaded with NaN values. Although you could ignore this column, it would be even easier if you didn't have it. You can use the range() function again, this time starting from 1, to tell pandas to load all columns except the first one. But if you know that all of your values are from Illinois and you don't care about the long-form date field, you could start from 4 to make things much more manageable:

> **Setting header=0 turns off reading the header for column labels.**

```
temp = pd.read_csv("temp_data_01.csv", na_values=['Missing'], header=0,
    names=range(18), usecols=range(4,18))
print(temp)

            4      5    6     7     8      9    10     11    12     13    14  \
0  1979/01/01  17.48  994   6.0  30.5   2.89  994  -13.6  15.8    NaN     0
1  1979/01/02   4.64  994  -6.4  15.8  -9.03  994  -23.6   6.6    NaN     0
2  1979/01/03  11.05  994  -0.7  24.7  -2.17  994  -18.3  12.9    NaN     0
3  1979/01/04   9.51  994   0.2  27.6  -0.43  994  -16.3  16.3    NaN     0
4  1979/05/15  68.42  994  61.0  75.1  51.30  994   43.3  57.0    NaN     0
5  1979/05/16  70.29  994  63.4  73.5  48.09  994   41.1  53.0    NaN     0
6  1979/05/17  75.34  994  64.0  80.5  50.84  994   44.3  55.7  82.60     2
7  1979/05/18  79.13  994  75.5  82.1  55.68  994   50.0  61.1  81.42   349
8  1979/05/19  74.94  994  66.9  83.1  58.59  994   50.9  63.2  82.87    78

     15    16      17
0   NaN   NaN   0.00%
1   NaN   NaN   0.00%
2   NaN   NaN   0.00%
3   NaN   NaN   0.00%
4   NaN   NaN   0.00%
5   NaN   NaN   0.00%
6  82.4  82.8   0.20%
7  80.2  83.4  35.11%
8  81.6  85.2   7.85%
```

Now you have a data frame that has only the columns you might want to work with. But you still have an issue: the last column, which lists the percentage of coverage for the heat index, is still a string ending with a percentage sign rather than an actual percentage. This problem is apparent if you look at the first row's value for column 17:

```
temp[17][0]
'0.00%'
```

To fix this problem, you need to do two things: Remove the `%` from the end of the value and then cast the value from string to a number. Optionally, if you want to represent the resulting percentage as a fraction, you need to divide it by 100. The first bit is simple because pandas lets you use a single command to repeat an operation on a column:

```
temp[17] = temp[17].str.strip("%")
temp[17][0]
'0.00'
```

This code takes the column and calls a string `strip()` operation on it to remove the trailing `%`. Now when you look at the first value in the column (or any of the other values), you see that the offending percentage sign is gone. It's also worth noting that you could have used other operations, such as `replace("%", "")`, to achieve the same result.

The second operation is to convert the string to a numeric value. Again, pandas lets you perform this operation with one command:

```
temp[17] = pd.to_numeric(temp[17])
temp[17][0]
0.0
```

Now the values in column 17 are numeric, and if you want to, you can use the `div()` method to finish the job of turning those values into fractions:

```
temp[17] = temp[17].div(100)
temp[17]

0    0.0000
1    0.0000
2    0.0000
3    0.0000
4    0.0000
5    0.0000
6    0.0020
7    0.3511
8    0.0785
Name: 17, dtype: float64
```

In fact, it would be possible to achieve the same result in a single line by chaining the three operations together:

```
temp[17] = pd.to_numeric(temp[17].str.strip("%")).div(100)
```

This example is very simple, but it gives you an idea of the convenience that pandas can bring to cleaning your data. pandas has a wide variety of operations for transforming data, as well as the ability to use custom functions, so it would be hard to think of a scenario in which you couldn't streamline data cleaning with pandas.

Although the number of options is almost overwhelming, a wide variety of tutorials and videos is available, and the documentation at http://pandas.pydata.org is excellent.

> **TRY THIS: CLEANING DATA WITH AND WITHOUT PANDAS** Experiment with the operations. When the final column has been converted to a fraction, can you think of a way to convert it back to a string with the trailing percentage sign?
>
> By contrast, load the same data into a plain Python list by using the `csv` module, and apply the same changes by using plain Python.

24.5 *Data aggregation and manipulation*

The preceding examples probably gave you some idea of the many options pandas gives you for performing fairly complex operations on your data with only a few commands. As you might expect, this level of functionality is also available for aggregating data. In this section, I walk through a few simple examples of aggregating data to illustrate some of the many possibilities. Although many options are available, I focus on merging data frames, performing simple data aggregation, and grouping and filtering.

24.5.1 *Merging data frames*

Quite often in the course of handling data, you need to relate two data sets. Suppose that you have one file containing the number of sales calls made per month by members of a sales team, and in another file, you have the dollar amounts of the sales in each of their territories:

```
calls = pd.read_csv("sales_calls.csv")
print(calls)

    Team member  Territory  Month  Calls
0         Jorge          3      1    107
1         Jorge          3      2     88
2         Jorge          3      3     84
3         Jorge          3      4    113
4           Ana          1      1     91
5           Ana          1      2    129
6           Ana          1      3     96
7           Ana          1      4    128
8           Ali          2      1    120
9           Ali          2      2     85
10          Ali          2      3     87
11          Ali          2      4     87

revenue = pd.read_csv("sales_revenue.csv")
print(revenue)

   Territory  Month  Amount
0          1      1   54228
1          1      2   61640
2          1      3   43491
```

```
3        1     4     52173
4        2     1     36061
5        2     2     44957
6        2     3     35058
7        2     4     33855
8        3     1     50876
9        3     2     57682
10       3     3     53689
11       3     4     49173
```

Clearly, it would be very useful to link revenue and team-member activity. These two files are very simple, yet merging them with plain Python isn't entirely trivial. pandas has a function to merge two data frames:

```
calls_revenue = pd.merge(calls, revenue, on=['Territory', 'Month'])
```

The `merge` function creates a new data frame by joining the two frames on the columns specified in the column field. The `merge` function works similarly to a relational-database join, giving you a table that combines the columns from the two files:

```
print(calls_revenue)
    Team member   Territory   Month   Calls   Amount
0         Jorge           3       1     107    50876
1         Jorge           3       2      88    57682
2         Jorge           3       3      84    53689
3         Jorge           3       4     113    49173
4           Ana           1       1      91    54228
5           Ana           1       2     129    61640
6           Ana           1       3      96    43491
7           Ana           1       4     128    52173
8           Ali           2       1     120    36061
9           Ali           2       2      85    44957
10          Ali           2       3      87    35058
11          Ali           2       4      87    33855
```

In this case, you have a one-to-one correspondence between the rows in the two fields, but the `merge` function can also do one-to-many and many-to-many joins, as well as right and left joins.

> **QUICK CHECK: MERGING DATA SETS** How would you go about merging to data sets like the ones in the Python example?

24.5.2 Selecting data

It can also be useful to select or filter the rows in a data frame based on some condition. In the example sales data, you may want to look only at territory 3, which is also easy:

```
print(calls_revenue[calls_revenue.Territory==3])

    Team member   Territory   Month   Calls   Amount
0         Jorge           3       1     107    50876
1         Jorge           3       2      88    57682
2         Jorge           3       3      84    53689
3         Jorge           3       4     113    49173
```

In this example, you select only rows in which the territory is equal to 3 but using exactly that expression, `revenue.Territory==3`, as the index for the data frame. From the point of view of plain Python, such use is nonsense and illegal, but for a pandas data frame, it works and makes for a much more concise expression.

More complex expressions are also allowed, of course. If you want to select only rows in which the amount per call is greater than 500, you could use this expression instead:

```
print(calls_revenue[calls_revenue.Amount/calls_revenue.Calls>500])
```

	Team member	Territory	Month	Calls	Amount
1	Jorge	3	2	88	57682
2	Jorge	3	3	84	53689
4	Ana	1	1	91	54228
9	Ali	2	2	85	44957

Even better, you could calculate and add that column to your data frame by using a similar operation:

```
calls_revenue['Call_Amount'] = calls_revenue.Amount/calls_revenue.Calls
print(calls_revenue)
```

	Team member	Territory	Month	Calls	Amount	Call_Amount
0	Jorge	3	1	107	50876	475.476636
1	Jorge	3	2	88	57682	655.477273
2	Jorge	3	3	84	53689	639.154762
3	Jorge	3	4	113	49173	435.159292
4	Ana	1	1	91	54228	595.912088
5	Ana	1	2	129	61640	477.829457
6	Ana	1	3	96	43491	453.031250
7	Ana	1	4	128	52173	407.601562
8	Ali	2	1	120	36061	300.508333
9	Ali	2	2	85	44957	528.905882
10	Ali	2	3	87	35058	402.965517
11	Ali	2	4	87	33855	389.137931

Again, note that pandas's built-in logic replaces a more cumbersome structure in plain Python.

QUICK CHECK: SELECTING IN PYTHON What Python code structure would you use to select only rows meeting certain conditions?

24.5.3 *Grouping and aggregation*

As you might expect, pandas has plenty of tools to summarize and aggregate data as well. In particular, getting the sum, mean, median, minimum, and maximum values from a column uses clearly named column methods:

```
print(calls_revenue.Calls.sum())
print(calls_revenue.Calls.mean())
print(calls_revenue.Calls.median())
print(calls_revenue.Calls.max())
print(calls_revenue.Calls.min())
```

```
1215
101.25
93.5
129
84
```

If, for example, you want to get all of the rows in which the amount per call is above the median, you can combine this trick with the selection operation:

```
print(calls_revenue.Call_Amount.median())
print(calls_revenue[calls_revenue.Call_Amount >=
    calls_revenue.Call_Amount.median()])
```

```
464.2539427570093
   Team member  Territory  Month  Calls  Amount  Call_Amount
0        Jorge          3      1    107   50876   475.476636
1        Jorge          3      2     88   57682   655.477273
2        Jorge          3      3     84   53689   639.154762
4          Ana          1      1     91   54228   595.912088
5          Ana          1      2    129   61640   477.829457
9          Ali          2      2     85   44957   528.905882
```

In addition to being able to pick out summary values, it's often useful to group the data based on other columns. In this simple example, you can use the groupby method to group your data. You may want to know the total calls and amounts by month or by territory, for example. In those cases, use those fields with the data frame's groupby method:

```
print(calls_revenue[['Month', 'Calls', 'Amount']].groupby(['Month']).sum())
```

```
       Calls  Amount
Month
1        318  141165
2        302  164279
3        267  132238
4        328  135201
```

```
print(calls_revenue[['Territory', 'Calls',
    'Amount']].groupby(['Territory']).sum())
```

```
           Calls  Amount
Territory
1            444  211532
2            379  149931
3            392  211420
```

In each case, you select the columns that you want to aggregate, group them by the values in one of those columns, and (in this case) sum the values for each group. You could also use any of the other methods mentioned earlier in this chapter.

Again, all these examples are simple, but they illustrate a few of the options you have for manipulating and selecting data with pandas. If these ideas resonate with your needs, you can learn more by studying the pandas documentation at http://pandas.pydata.org.

TRY THIS: GROUPING AND AGGREGATING   Experiment with pandas and the data in previous examples. Can you get the calls and amounts by both team member and month?

24.6   *Plotting data*

Another very attractive feature of pandas is the ability to plot the data in a data frame very easily. Although you have many options for plotting data in Python and Jupyter notebook, pandas can use matplotlib directly from a data frame. You may recall that when you started your Jupyter session, one of the first commands you gave was the Jupyter "magic" command to enable matplotlib for inline plotting:

```
%matplotlib inline
```

Because you have the ability to plot, see how you might plot some data (figure 24.3). To continue with the sales example, if you want to plot the quarter's mean sales by territory, you can get a graph right in your notebook just by adding `.plot.bar()`:

```
calls_revenue[['Territory', 'Calls']].groupby(['Territory']).sum().plot.bar()
```

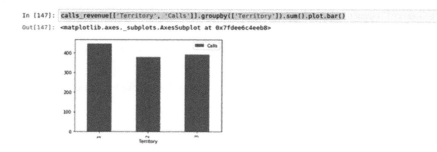

Figure 24.3   Bar plot of a pandas data frame in Jupyter notebook

Other options are available. `plot()` alone or `.plot.line()` creates a line graph, `.plot.pie()` creates a pie chart, and so on.

Thanks to the combination of pandas and matplotlib, plotting data in a Jupyter notebook is quite easy. I should also note that although such plotting is easy, there are many things that it doesn't do extremely well.

TRY THIS: PLOTTING   Plot a line graph of the monthly average amount per call.

24.7   *Why you might not want to use pandas*

The preceding examples illustrate only a tiny fraction of the tools pandas can offer you in cleaning, exploring, and manipulating data. As I mentioned at the beginning of this chapter, pandas is an excellent tool set that excels in what it was designed to do. That doesn't mean, however, that pandas is the tool for all situations or for all people.

There are reasons why you might elect to use plain old Python (or some other tool) instead. For one thing, as I mention earlier, learning to fully use pandas is in some ways like learning another language, which may not be something you have the time or inclination for. Also, pandas may not be ideal in all production situations, particularly with very large data sets that don't require much in the way of math operations or with data that isn't easy to put into the formats that work best with pandas. Munging large collections of product information, for example, probably wouldn't benefit so much from pandas; neither would basic processing of a stream of transactions.

The point is that you should choose your tools thoughtfully based on the problems at hand. In many cases, pandas will truly make your life easier as you work with data, but in other cases, plain old Python may be your best bet.

Summary

- Python offers many benefits for data handling, including the ability to handle very large data sets and the flexibility to handle data in ways that match your needs.
- Jupyter notebook is a useful way to access Python via a web browser, which also makes improved presentation easier.
- pandas is a tool that makes many common data-handling operations much easier, including cleaning, combining, and summarizing data.
- pandas also makes simple plotting much easier.

Case study

In this case study, you walk through using Python to fetch some data, clean it, and then graph it. This project may be a short one, but it combines several features of the language I've discussed, and it gives you a chance to a see a project worked through from beginning to end. At almost every step, I briefly call out alternatives and enhancements that you can make.

Global temperature change is the topic of much discussion, but those discussions are based on a global scale. Suppose that you want to know what the temperatures have been doing near where you are. One way of finding out is to get historical data for your location, process that data, and plot it to see exactly what's been happening.

Getting the case study code

The following case study was done by using a Jupyter notebook, as explained in chapter 24. If you're using Jupyter, you can find the notebook I used (with this text and code) in the source code downloads as `Case Study.ipynb`. You can also execute the code in a standard Python shell, and a version that supports that shell is in the source code as `Case Study.py`.

Fortunately, several sources of historical weather data are freely available. I'm going to walk you through using data from the Global Historical Climatology Network, which has data from around the world. You may find other sources, which may have different data formats, but the steps and the processes I discuss here should be generally applicable to any data set.

Downloading the data

The first step will be to get the data. An archive of daily historical weather data at https://www1.ncdc.noaa.gov/pub/data/ghcn/daily/ has a wide array of data. The first step is to figure out which files you want and exactly where they are; then you

download them. When you have the data, you can move on to processing and ultimately displaying your results.

   To download the files, which are accessible via HTTPS, you need the `requests`
library. You can get `requests` with `pip install requests` at the command
prompt. When you have `requests`, your first step is to fetch the readme.txt file,
which can guide you as to the formats and location of the data files you want:

```
# import requests

import requests
# get readme.txt file

r = requests.get('https://www1.ncdc.noaa.gov/pub/data/ghcn/daily/readme.txt')
readme = r.text.
```

When you look at the readme file, you should see something like this:

```
print(readme)
README FILE FOR DAILY GLOBAL HISTORICAL CLIMATOLOGY NETWORK (GHCN-DAILY)
Version 3.22

-------------------------------------------------------------------------
How to cite:

Note that the GHCN-Daily dataset itself now has a DOI (Digital Object Identifier)
so it may be relevant to cite both the methods/overview journal article as well
as the specific version of the dataset used.

The journal article describing GHCN-Daily is:
Menne, M.J., I. Durre, R.S. Vose, B.E. Gleason, and T.G. Houston, 2012:  An
    overview
of the Global Historical Climatology Network-Daily Database.  Journal of
    Atmospheric
and Oceanic Technology, 29, 897-910, doi:10.1175/JTECH-D-11-00103.1.

To acknowledge the specific version of the dataset used, please cite:
Menne, M.J., I. Durre, B. Korzeniewski, S. McNeal, K. Thomas, X. Yin, S.
    Anthony, R. Ray,
R.S. Vose, B.E.Gleason, and T.G. Houston, 2012: Global Historical Climatology
    Network -
Daily (GHCN-Daily), Version 3. [indicate subset used following decimal,
e.g. Version 3.12].
NOAA National Climatic Data Center. http://doi.org/10.7289/V5D21VHZ [access
    date].
```

In particular, you're interested in section II, which lists the contents:

```
II. CONTENTS OF ftp://ftp.ncdc.noaa.gov/pub/data/ghcn/daily

all:               Directory with ".dly" files for all of GHCN-Daily
gsn:               Directory with ".dly" files for the GCOS Surface Network
                   (GSN)
```

```
hcn:                    Directory with ".dly" files for U.S. HCN
by_year:                Directory with GHCN Daily files parsed into yearly
                        subsets with observation times where available. See the
                /by_year/readme.txt and
                /by_year/ghcn-daily-by_year-format.rtf
                files for further information
grid:                   Directory with the GHCN-Daily gridded dataset known
                        as HadGHCND
papers:                 Directory with pdf versions of journal articles relevant
                        to the GHCN-Daily dataset
figures:                Directory containing figures that summarize the inventory
                        of GHCN-Daily station records

ghcnd-all.tar.gz:  TAR file of the GZIP-compressed files in the "all"
    directory
ghcnd-gsn.tar.gz:  TAR file of the GZIP-compressed "gsn" directory
ghcnd-hcn.tar.gz:  TAR file of the GZIP-compressed "hcn" directory

ghcnd-countries.txt:  List of country codes (FIPS) and names
ghcnd-inventory.txt:  File listing the periods of record for each station and

                      element
ghcnd-stations.txt:   List of stations and their metadata (e.g., coordinates)
ghcnd-states.txt:     List of U.S. state and Canadian Province codes
                      used in ghcnd-stations.txt
ghcnd-version.txt:    File that specifies the current version of GHCN Daily

readme.txt:           This file
status.txt:           Notes on the current status of GHCN-Daily
```

As you look at the files available, you see that ghcnd-inventory.txt has a listing of the recording periods for each station, which will help you find a good data set; and ghcnd-stations.txt lists the stations, which should help you find the station closest to your location, so you'll grab those two files first:

```
II. CONTENTS OF ftp://ftp.ncdc.noaa.gov/pub/data/ghcn/daily

all:                Directory with ".dly" files for all of GHCN-Daily
gsn:                Directory with ".dly" files for the GCOS Surface
    Network
                    (GSN)
hcn:                Directory with ".dly" files for U.S. HCN
by_year:            Directory with GHCN Daily files parsed into yearly
                    subsets with observation times where available.  See
    the
                /by_year/readme.txt and
                /by_year/ghcn-daily-by_year-format.rtf
                files for further information
grid:                   Directory with the GHCN-Daily gridded dataset known
                        as HadGHCND
papers:                 Directory with pdf versions of journal articles relevant
                        to the GHCN-Daily dataset
figures:                Directory containing figures that summarize the inventory
                        of GHCN-Daily station records
```

```
ghcnd-all.tar.gz:   TAR file of the GZIP-compressed files in the "all"
                    directory
ghcnd-gsn.tar.gz:   TAR file of the GZIP-compressed "gsn" directory
ghcnd-hcn.tar.gz:   TAR file of the GZIP-compressed "hcn" directory

ghcnd-countries.txt:  List of country codes (FIPS) and names
ghcnd-inventory.txt:  File listing the periods of record for each station and
                      element
ghcnd-stations.txt:   List of stations and their metadata (e.g., coordinates)
ghcnd-states.txt:     List of U.S. state and Canadian Province codes
                      used in ghcnd-stations.txt
ghcnd-version.txt:    File that specifies the current version of GHCN Daily

readme.txt:           This file
status.txt:           Notes on the current status of GHCN-Daily

# get inventory and stations files

r = requests.get('https://www1.ncdc.noaa.gov/pub/data/ghcn/daily/ghcnd-
    inventory.txt')
inventory_txt = r.text
r = requests.get('https://www1.ncdc.noaa.gov/pub/data/ghcn/daily/ghcnd-
    stations.txt')
stations_txt = r.text
```

When you have those files, you can save them to your local disk so that you won't need to download them again if you need to go back to the original data:

```
# save both the inventory and stations files to disk, in case we need them

with open("inventory.txt", "w") as inventory_file:
    inventory_file.write(inventory_txt)

with open("stations.txt", "w") as stations_file:
    stations_file.write(stations_txt)
```

Start by looking at the inventory file. Here's what the first 137 characters show you:

```
print(inventory_txt[:137])
ACW00011604  17.1167  -61.7833 TMAX 1949 1949
ACW00011604  17.1167  -61.7833 TMIN 1949 1949
ACW00011604  17.1167  -61.7833 PRCP 1949 1949
```
If we look at section VII of the readme.txt file we can see that the format
    of the inventory file is:
VII. FORMAT OF "ghcnd-inventory.txt"

```
------------------------------
Variable   Columns   Type
------------------------------

ID              1-11   Character
LATITUDE       13-20   Real
LONGITUDE      22-30   Real
ELEMENT        32-35   Character
FIRSTYEAR      37-40   Integer
LASTYEAR       42-45   Integer
------------------------------
```

These variables have the following definitions:

```
ID          is the station identification code. Please see "ghcnd-stations.txt"
            for a complete list of stations and their metadata.

LATITUDE    is the latitude of the station (in decimal degrees).

LONGITUDE   is the longitude of the station (in decimal degrees).

ELEMENT     is the element type. See section III for a definition of elements.

FIRSTYEAR   is the first year of unflagged data for the given element.

LASTYEAR    is the last year of unflagged data for the given element.
```

From this description, you can tell that the inventory list has most of the information you need to find the station you want to look at. You can use the latitude and longitude to find the stations closest to you; then you can use the FIRSTYEAR and LAST-YEAR fields to find a station with records covering a long span of time.

The only question remaining is what the ELEMENT field is; for that, the file suggests that you look at section III. In section III (which I look at in more detail later), you find the following description of the main elements:

```
ELEMENT     is the element type. There are five core elements as well as a
            number of addition elements.

    The five core elements are:

            PRCP = Precipitation (tenths of mm)
            SNOW = Snowfall (mm)
            SNWD = Snow depth (mm)
            TMAX = Maximum temperature (tenths of degrees C)
            TMIN = Minimum temperature (tenths of degrees C)
```

For purposes of this example, you're interested in the TMAX and TMIN elements, which are maximum and minimum temperatures in tenths of degrees Celsius.

Parsing the inventory data

The readme.txt file tells you what you've got in the inventory file so that you can parse the data into a more usable format. You could just store the parsed inventory data as a list of lists or list of tuples, but it takes only a little more effort to use `namedtuple` from the collections library to create a custom class with the attributes named:

```
# parse to named tuples

# use namedtuple to create a custom Inventory class
from collections import namedtuple
Inventory = namedtuple("Inventory", ['station', 'latitude', 'longitude',
    'element', 'start', 'end'])
```

Using the `Inventory` class you created is very straightforward; you simply create each instance from the appropriate values, which in this case are a parsed row of inventory data.

The parsing involves two steps. First, you need to pick out slices of a line according to the field sizes specified. As you look at the field descriptions in the readme file, it's also clear that there's an extra space between files, which you need to consider in coming up with any approach to parsing. In this case, because you're specifying each slice, the extra spaces are ignored. In addition, because the sizes of the STATION and ELEMENT fields exactly correspond to the values stored in them, you shouldn't need to worry about stripping excess spaces from them.

The second thing that would be nice to do is convert the latitude and longitude values to floats and the start and end years to ints. You could do this at a later stage of data cleaning, and in fact, if the data is inconsistent and doesn't have values that convert correctly in every row, you might want to wait. But in this case, the data lets you handle these conversions in the parsing step, so do it now:

```
# parse inventory lines and convert some values to floats and ints

inventory = [Inventory(x[0:11], float(x[12:20]), float(x[21:30]), x[31:35],
    int(x[36:40]), int(x[41:45]))
        for x in inventory_txt.split("\n") if x.startswith("US")]

for line in inventory[:5]:
    print(line)
Inventory(station='US009052008', latitude=43.7333, longitude=-96.6333,
    element='TMAX', start=2008, end=2016)
Inventory(station='US009052008', latitude=43.7333, longitude=-96.6333,
    element='TMIN', start=2008, end=2016)
Inventory(station='US009052008', latitude=43.7333, longitude=-96.6333,
    element='PRCP', start=2008, end=2016)
Inventory(station='US009052008', latitude=43.7333, longitude=-96.6333,
    element='SNWD', start=2009, end=2016)
Inventory(station='US10RMHS145', latitude=40.5268, longitude=-105.1113,
    element='PRCP', start=2004, end=2004)
```

Selecting a station based on latitude and longitude

Now that the inventory is loaded, you can use the latitude and longitude to find the stations closest to your location and then pick the one with the longest run of temperatures based on start and end years. At even the first line of the data, you can see two things to worry about:

- There are various element types, but you're concerned only with TMIN and TMAX, for minimum and maximum temperature.
- None of the first inventory entries you see covers more than a few years. If you're going to be looking for an historical perspective, you want to find a much longer run of temperature data.

To pick out what you need quickly, we can use a list comprehension to make a sublist of only the station inventory items in which the element is TMIN or TMAX. The other thing that you care about is getting a station with a long run of data, so while you're creating this sublist, also make sure that the start year is before 1920 and that the end year is at least 2015. That way, you're looking only at stations with at least 95 years' worth of data:

```
inventory_temps = [x for x in inventory if x.element in ['TMIN', 'TMAX']
                   and x.end >= 2015 and x.start < 1920]
inventory_temps[:5]
```

```
[Inventory(station='USC00010252', latitude=31.3072, longitude=-86.5225,
     element='TMAX', start=1912, end=2017),
 Inventory(station='USC00010252', latitude=31.3072, longitude=-86.5225,
     element='TMIN', start=1912, end=2017),
 Inventory(station='USC00010583', latitude=30.8839, longitude=-87.7853,
     element='TMAX', start=1915, end=2017),
 Inventory(station='USC00010583', latitude=30.8839, longitude=-87.7853,
     element='TMIN', start=1915, end=2017),
 Inventory(station='USC00012758', latitude=31.445, longitude=-86.9533,
     element='TMAX', start=1890, end=2017)]
```

Looking at the first five records in your new list, you see that you're in better shape. Now you have only temperature records, and the start and end years show that you have longer runs.

That leaves the problem of selecting the station nearest your location. To do that, compare the latitude and longitude of the station inventories with those of your location. There are various ways to get the latitude and longitude of any place, but probably the easiest way is to use an online mapping application or online search. (When I do that for the Chicago Loop, I get a latitude of 41.882 and a longitude of -87.629.)

Because you're interested in the stations closest to your location, that interest implies sorting based on how close the latitude and longitude of the stations are to those of your location. Sorting a list is easy enough, and sorting by latitude and longitude isn't too hard. But how do you sort by the distance from your latitude and longitude?

The answer is to define a key function for your sort that gets the difference between your latitude and the station's latitude, and the difference between your longitude and the station's longitude, and combines them into one number. The only other thing to remember is that you'll want to add the absolute value of the differences before you combine them to avoid having a high negative difference combined with an equally high positive difference that would fool your sort:

```
# Downtown Chicago, obtained via online map
latitude, longitude = 41.882, -87.629

inventory_temps.sort(key=lambda x:  abs(latitude-x.latitude) + abs(longitude-
    x.longitude))

inventory_temps[:20]
Out[24]:
[Inventory(station='USC00110338', latitude=41.7806, longitude=-88.3092,
     element='TMAX', start=1893, end=2017),
 Inventory(station='USC00110338', latitude=41.7806, longitude=-88.3092,
     element='TMIN', start=1893, end=2017),
```

```
Inventory(station='USC00112736', latitude=42.0628, longitude=-88.2861,
    element='TMAX', start=1897, end=2017),
Inventory(station='USC00112736', latitude=42.0628, longitude=-88.2861,
    element='TMIN', start=1897, end=2017),
Inventory(station='USC00476922', latitude=42.7022, longitude=-87.7861,
    element='TMAX', start=1896, end=2017),
Inventory(station='USC00476922', latitude=42.7022, longitude=-87.7861,
    element='TMIN', start=1896, end=2017),
Inventory(station='USC00124837', latitude=41.6117, longitude=-86.7297,
    element='TMAX', start=1897, end=2017),
Inventory(station='USC00124837', latitude=41.6117, longitude=-86.7297,
    element='TMIN', start=1897, end=2017),
Inventory(station='USC00119021', latitude=40.7928, longitude=-87.7556,
    element='TMAX', start=1893, end=2017),
Inventory(station='USC00119021', latitude=40.7928, longitude=-87.7556,
    element='TMIN', start=1894, end=2017),
Inventory(station='USC00115825', latitude=41.3708, longitude=-88.4336,
    element='TMAX', start=1912, end=2017),
Inventory(station='USC00115825', latitude=41.3708, longitude=-88.4336,
    element='TMIN', start=1912, end=2017),
Inventory(station='USC00115326', latitude=42.2636, longitude=-88.6078,
    element='TMAX', start=1893, end=2017),
Inventory(station='USC00115326', latitude=42.2636, longitude=-88.6078,
    element='TMIN', start=1893, end=2017),
Inventory(station='USC00200710', latitude=42.1244, longitude=-86.4267,
    element='TMAX', start=1893, end=2017),
Inventory(station='USC00200710', latitude=42.1244, longitude=-86.4267,
    element='TMIN', start=1893, end=2017),
Inventory(station='USC00114198', latitude=40.4664, longitude=-87.685,
    element='TMAX', start=1902, end=2017),
Inventory(station='USC00114198', latitude=40.4664, longitude=-87.685,
    element='TMIN', start=1902, end=2017),
Inventory(station='USW00014848', latitude=41.7072, longitude=-86.3164,
    element='TMAX', start=1893, end=2017),
Inventory(station='USW00014848', latitude=41.7072, longitude=-86.3164,
    element='TMIN', start=1893, end=2017)]
```

Selecting a station and getting the station metadata

As you look at the top 20 entries in your newly sorted list, it seems that the first station, USC00110338, is a good fit. It's got both TMIN and TMAX and one of the longer series, starting in 1893 and running up through 2017, for more than 120 years' worth of data. So save that station into your station variable and quickly parse the station data you've already grabbed to pick up a little more information about the station.

Back in the readme file, you find the following information about the station data:

```
IV. FORMAT OF "ghcnd-stations.txt"

------------------------------
Variable    Columns    Type
------------------------------
ID              1-11    Character
LATITUDE       13-20    Real
LONGITUDE      22-30    Real
ELEVATION      32-37    Real
```

```
STATE          39-40   Character
NAME           42-71   Character
GSN FLAG       73-75   Character
HCN/CRN FLAG 77-79    Character
WMO ID         81-85   Character
-----------------------------
```

These variables have the following definitions:

ID   is the station identification code. Note that the first two
            characters denote the FIPS country code, the third character
            is a network code that identifies the station numbering system
            used, and the remaining eight characters contain the actual
            station ID.

            See "ghcnd-countries.txt" for a complete list of country codes.
            See "ghcnd-states.txt" for a list of state/province/territory
            codes.

            The network code has the following five values:

            0 = unspecified (station identified by up to eight
            alphanumeric characters)
        1 = Community Collaborative Rain, Hail,and Snow (CoCoRaHS)
            based identification number. To ensure consistency with
            with GHCN Daily, all numbers in the original CoCoRaHS IDs
            have been left-filled to make them all four digits long.
            In addition, the characters "-" and "_" have been removed
            to ensure that the IDs do not exceed 11 characters when
            preceded by "US1". For example, the CoCoRaHS ID
            "AZ-MR-156" becomes "US1AZMR0156" in GHCN-Daily
        C = U.S. Cooperative Network identification number (last six
            characters of the GHCN-Daily ID)
        E = Identification number used in the ECA&D non-blended
            dataset
        M = World Meteorological Organization ID (last five
            characters of the GHCN-Daily ID)
        N = Identification number used in data supplied by a
            National Meteorological or Hydrological Center
        R = U.S. Interagency Remote Automatic Weather Station (RAWS)
            identifier
        S = U.S. Natural Resources Conservation Service SNOwpack
            TELemtry (SNOTEL) station identifier
            W = WBAN identification number (last five characters of the
            GHCN-Daily ID)

LATITUDE   is latitude of the station (in decimal degrees).

LONGITUDE   is the longitude of the station (in decimal degrees).

ELEVATION   is the elevation of the station (in meters, missing = -999.9).

STATE   is the U.S. postal code for the state (for U.S. stations only).

NAME   is the name of the station.

GSN FLAG   is a flag that indicates whether the station is part of the GCOS
             Surface Network (GSN). The flag is assigned by cross-referencing
             the number in the WMOID field with the official list of GSN
             stations. There are two possible values:

             Blank = non-GSN station or WMO Station number not available
             GSN   = GSN station

HCN/   is a flag that indicates whether the station is part of the U.S.
CRN FLAG   Historical Climatology Network (HCN). There are three possible
             values:

             Blank = Not a member of the U.S. Historical Climatology
                 or U.S. Climate Reference Networks
             HCN   = U.S. Historical Climatology Network station
             CRN   = U.S. Climate Reference Network or U.S. Regional Climate
                 Network Station

WMO ID   is the World Meteorological Organization (WMO) number for the
             station. If the station has no WMO number (or one has not yet
             been matched to this station), then the field is blank.

Although you might care more about the metadata fields for more serious research, right now you want to match the start and end year from the inventory records to the rest of the station metadata in the station file.

You have several ways to sift through the stations file to find the one station that matches the station ID you selected. You could create a `for` loop to go through each line and break out when you find it; you could split the data into lines and then sort and use a binary search, and so on. Depending on the nature and amount of data you have, one approach or another might be appropriate. In this case, because you have the data loaded already, and it's not too large, use a list comprehension to return a list with its single element being the station you're looking for:

```
station_id = 'USC00110338'

# parse stations
Station = namedtuple("Station", ['station_id', 'latitude', 'longitude',
    'elevation', 'state', 'name', 'start', 'end'])

stations = [(x[0:11], float(x[12:20]), float(x[21:30]), float(x[31:37]),
    x[38:40].strip(), x[41:71].strip())
          for x in stations_txt.split("\n") if x.startswith(station_id)]

station = Station(*stations[0] + (inventory_temps[0].start,
    inventory_temps[0].end))
print(station)
Station(station_id='USC00110338', latitude=41.7806, longitude=-88.3092,
    elevation=201.2, state='IL', name='AURORA', start=1893, end=2017)
```

At this point, you've identified that you want weather data from the station at Aurora, Illinois, which is the nearest station to downtown Chicago with more than a century's worth of temperature data.

Fetching and parsing the actual weather data

With the station identified, the next step is fetching the actual weather data for that station and parsing it. The process is quite similar to what you did in the preceding section.

Fetching the data

First, fetch the data file and save it, in case you need to go back to it:

```
# fetch daily records for selected station

r = requests.get('https://www1.ncdc.noaa.gov/pub/data/ghcn/daily/all/
    {}.dly'.format(station.station_id))
weather = r.text

# save into a text file, so we won't need to fetch again

with open('weather_{}.txt'.format(station), "w") as weather_file:
    weather_file.write(weather)

# read from saved daily file if needed (only used if we want to start the
    process over without downloadng the file)

with open('weather_{}.txt'.format(station)) as weather_file:
    weather = weather_file.read()

print(weather[:540])
USC00110338189301TMAX  -11  6  -44  6 -139  6  -83  6 -100  6  -83  6  -72  6
     -83  6  -33  6 -178  6 -150  6 -128  6 -172  6 -200  6 -189  6 -150  6 -
     106  6  -61  6  -94  6  -33  6  -33  6  -33  6  -33  6    6  6  -33  6
     -78  6  -33  6   44  6  -89 I6  -22  6    6  6
USC00110338189301TMIN  -50  6 -139  6 -250  6 -144  6 -178  6 -228  6 -144  6
    -222  6 -178  6 -250  6 -200  6 -206  6 -267  6 -272  6 -294  6 -294  6
    -311  6 -200  6 -233  6 -178  6 -156  6  -89  6 -200  6 -194  6 -194  6
    -178  6 -200  6  -33 I6 -156  6 -139  6 -167  6
```

Parsing the weather data

Again, now that you have the data, you can see it's quite a bit more complex than the station and inventory data. Clearly, it's time to head back to the readme.txt file and section III, which is the description of a weather data file. You have a lot of options, so filter them down to the ones that concern you, and leave out the other element types as well as the whole system of flags specifying the source, quality, and type of the values:

```
III. FORMAT OF DATA FILES (".dly" FILES)

Each ".dly" file contains data for one station.  The name of the file
corresponds to a station's identification code.  For example,
    "USC00026481.dly"
contains the data for the station with the identification code USC00026481).
```

Each record in a file contains one month of daily data. The variables on each
line include the following:

```
------------------------------
Variable   Columns   Type
------------------------------
ID              1-11   Character
YEAR           12-15   Integer
MONTH          16-17   Integer
ELEMENT        18-21   Character
VALUE1         22-26   Integer
MFLAG1         27-27   Character
QFLAG1         28-28   Character
SFLAG1         29-29   Character
VALUE2         30-34   Integer
MFLAG2         35-35   Character
QFLAG2         36-36   Character
SFLAG2         37-37   Character
    .            .       .
    .            .       .
    .            .       .
VALUE31      262-266   Integer
MFLAG31      267-267   Character
QFLAG31      268-268   Character
SFLAG31      269-269   Character
------------------------------
```

These variables have the following definitions:

ID   is the station identification code. Please see "ghcnd-stations.txt"
            for a complete list of stations and their metadata.

YEAR   is the year of the record.

MONTH   is the month of the record.

ELEMENT   is the element type.   There are five core elements as well as a
            number of addition elements.

    The five core elements are:

            PRCP = Precipitation (tenths of mm)
            SNOW = Snowfall (mm)
            SNWD = Snow depth (mm)
            TMAX = Maximum temperature (tenths of degrees C)
            TMIN = Minimum temperature (tenths of degrees C)

...

VALUE1   is the value on the first day of the month (missing = -9999).

MFLAG1   is the measurement flag for the first day of the month.

QFLAG1   is the quality flag for the first day of the month.

```
SFLAG1      is the source flag for the first day of the month.

VALUE2      is the value on the second day of the month

MFLAG2      is the measurement flag for the second day of the month.

QFLAG2      is the quality flag for the second day of the month.

SFLAG2      is the source flag for the second day of the month.
```

... and so on through the 31st day of the month. Note: If the month has less than 31 days, then the remaining variables are set to missing (e.g., for April, VALUE31 = -9999, MFLAG31 = blank, QFLAG31 = blank, SFLAG31 = blank).

The key points you care about right now are that the station ID is the 11 characters of a row, the year is the next 4, the month the next 2, and the element the next 4 after that. After that, there are 31 slots for daily data, with each slot consisting of 5 characters for the temperature, expressed in tenths of a degree Celsius, and 3 characters of flags. As I mentioned earlier, you can disregard the flags for this exercise. You can also see that missing values for the temperatures are coded with -9999 if that day isn't in the month, so for a typical February, for example, the 29th, 30th, and 31st values would be -9999.

As you process your data in this exercise, you're looking to get overall trends, so you don't need to worry much about individual days. Instead, find average values for the month. You can save the maximum, minimum, and mean values for the entire month and use those.

This means that to process each line of weather data, you need to:

- Split the line into its separate fields, and ignore or discard the flags for each daily value.
- Remove the values with -9999, and convert the year and month into ints and the temperature values into floats, keeping in mind that the temperature readings are in tenths of degrees centigrade.
- Calculate the average value, and pick out the high and low values.

To accomplish all these tasks, you can take a couple of approaches. You could do several passes over the data, splitting into fields, discarding the placeholders, converting strings to numbers, and finally calculating the summary values. Or you can write a function that performs all of these operations on a single line and do everything in one pass. Both approaches can be valid. In this case, take the latter approach and create a parse_line function to perform all of your data transformations:

```
def parse_line(line):
    """ parses line of weather data
        removes values of -9999 (missing value)
    """

    # return None if line is empty
    if not line:
        return None
```

```
# split out first 4 fields and string containing temperature values
record, temperature_string = (line[:11], int(line[11:15]),
 int(line[15:17]), line[17:21]), line[21:]

# raise exception if the temperature string is too short
if len(temperature_string) < 248:
    raise ValueError("String not long enough - {}
 {}".format(temperature_string, str(line)))

# use a list comprehension on the temperature_string to extract and
 convert the
values = [float(temperature_string[i:i + 5])/10 for i in range(0, 248, 8)
          if not temperature_string[i:i + 5].startswith("-9999")]

# get the number of values, the max and min, and calculate average
count = len(values)
tmax = round(max(values), 1)
tmin = round(min(values), 1)
mean = round(sum(values)/count, 1)

# add the temperature summary values to the record fields extracted
 earlier and return
return record + (tmax, tmin, mean, count)
```

If you test this function with the first line of your raw weather data, you get the following result:

```
parse_line(weather[:270])
Out[115]:
('USC00110338', 1893, 1, 'TMAX', 4.4, -20.0, -7.8, 31)
```

So it looks like you have a function that will work to parse your data. If that function works, you can parse the weather data and either store it or continue with your processing:

```
# process all weather data

# list comprehension, will not parse empty lines
weather_data = [parse_line(x) for x in weather.split("\n") if x]

len(weather_data)

weather_data[:10]

[('USC00110338', 1893, 1, 'TMAX', 4.4, -20.0, -7.8, 31),
 ('USC00110338', 1893, 1, 'TMIN', -3.3, -31.1, -19.2, 31),
 ('USC00110338', 1893, 1, 'PRCP', 8.9, 0.0, 1.1, 31),
 ('USC00110338', 1893, 1, 'SNOW', 10.2, 0.0, 1.0, 31),
 ('USC00110338', 1893, 1, 'WT16', 0.1, 0.1, 0.1, 2),
 ('USC00110338', 1893, 1, 'WT18', 0.1, 0.1, 0.1, 11),
 ('USC00110338', 1893, 2, 'TMAX', 5.6, -17.2, -0.9, 27),
 ('USC00110338', 1893, 2, 'TMIN', 0.6, -26.1, -11.7, 27),
 ('USC00110338', 1893, 2, 'PRCP', 15.0, 0.0, 2.0, 28),
 ('USC00110338', 1893, 2, 'SNOW', 12.7, 0.0, 0.6, 28)]
```

Now you have all the weather records, not just the temperature records, parsed and in your list.

Saving the weather data in a database (optional)

At this point, you can save all of the weather records (and the station records and inventory records as well, if you want) in a database. Doing so lets you come back in later sessions and use the same data without having to go to the hassle of fetching and parsing the data again.

As an example, the following code is how you could save the weather data in a sqlite3 database:

```
import sqlite3

conn = sqlite3.connect("weather_data.db")
cursor = conn.cursor()

# create weather table

create_weather = """CREATE TABLE "weather" (
    "id" text NOT NULL,
    "year" integer NOT NULL,
    "month" integer NOT NULL,
    "element" text NOT NULL,
    "max" real,
    "min" real,
    "mean" real,
    "count" integer)"""
cursor.execute(create_weather)
conn.commit()

# store parsed weather data in database

for record in weather_data:
    cursor.execute("""insert into weather (id, year, month, element, max,
    min, mean, count) values (?,?,?,?,?,?,?,?) """,
                        record)

conn.commit()
```

When you have the data stored, you could retrieve it from the database with code like the following, which fetches only the TMAX records:

```
cursor.execute("""select * from weather where element='TMAX' order by year,
    month""")
tmax_data = cursor.fetchall()
tmax_data[:5]

[('USC00110338', 1893, 1, 'TMAX', 4.4, -20.0, -7.8, 31),
 ('USC00110338', 1893, 2, 'TMAX', 5.6, -17.2, -0.9, 27),
 ('USC00110338', 1893, 3, 'TMAX', 20.6, -7.2, 5.6, 30),
 ('USC00110338', 1893, 4, 'TMAX', 28.9, 3.3, 13.5, 30),
 ('USC00110338', 1893, 5, 'TMAX', 30.6, 7.2, 19.2, 31)]
```

Selecting and graphing data

Because you're concerned only with temperature, you need to select just the temperature records. You can do that quickly enough by using a couple of list comprehensions to pick out a list for TMAX and one for TMIN. Or you could use the features of pandas, which you'll be using for graphing the date, to filter out the records you don't want. Because you're more concerned with pure Python than with pandas, take the first approach:

```
tmax_data = [x for x in weather_data if x[3] == 'TMAX']
tmin_data = [x for x in weather_data if x[3] == 'TMIN']
tmin_data[:5]
```

```
[('USC00110338', 1893, 1, 'TMIN', -3.3, -31.1, -19.2, 31),
 ('USC00110338', 1893, 2, 'TMIN', 0.6, -26.1, -11.7, 27),
 ('USC00110338', 1893, 3, 'TMIN', 3.3, -13.3, -4.6, 31),
 ('USC00110338', 1893, 4, 'TMIN', 12.2, -5.6, 2.2, 30),
 ('USC00110338', 1893, 5, 'TMIN', 14.4, -0.6, 5.7, 31)]
```

Using pandas to graph your data

At this point, you have your data cleaned and ready to graph. To make the graphing easier, you can use pandas and matplotlib, as described in chapter 24. To do this, you need to have a Jupyter server running and have pandas and matplotlib installed. To make sure that they're installed from within your Jupyter notebook, use the following command:

```
# Install pandas and matplotlib using pip
! pip3.6 install pandas matplotlib

import pandas as pd
%matplotlib inline
```

When pandas and matplotlib are installed, you can load pandas and create data frames for your TMAX and TMIN data:

```
tmax_df = pd.DataFrame(tmax_data, columns=['Station', 'Year', 'Month',
    'Element', 'Max', 'Min', 'Mean', 'Days'])
tmin_df = pd.DataFrame(tmin_data, columns=['Station', 'Year', 'Month',
    'Element', 'Max', 'Min', 'Mean', 'Days'])
```

You could plot the monthly values, but 123 years times 12 months of data is almost 1,500 data points, and the cycle of seasons also makes picking out patterns difficult.

Instead, it probably makes more sense to average the high, low, and mean monthly values into yearly values and plot those values. You could do this in Python, but because you already have your data loaded in a pandas data frame, you can use that to group by year and get the mean values:

```
# select Year, Min, Max, Mean columns, group by year, average and line plot

tmin_df[['Year','Min', 'Mean', 'Max']].groupby('Year').mean().plot(
    kind='line', figsize=(16, 4))
```

This result has a fair amount of variation, but it does seem to indicate that the minimum temperature has been on the rise for the past 20 years.

Note that if you wanted to get the same graph without using Jupyter notebook and matplotlib, you could use still use pandas, but you'd write to a CSV or Microsoft Excel file, using the data frame's `to_csv` or `to_excel` method. Then you could load the resulting file into a spreadsheet and graph from there.

appendix A
A guide to Python's documentation

The best and most current reference for Python is the documentation that comes with Python itself. With that in mind, it's more useful to explore the ways you can access that documentation than to print pages of edited documentation.

The standard bundle of documentation has several sections, including instructions on documenting, distributing, installing, and extending Python on various platforms, and is the logical starting point when you're looking for answers to questions about Python. The two main areas of the Python documentation that are likely to be the most useful are the *Library Reference* and the *Language Reference*. The *Library Reference* is absolutely essential because it has explanations of both the built-in data types and every module included with Python. The *Language Reference* is the explanation of how the core of Python works, and it contains the official word on the core of the language, explaining the workings of data types, statements, and so on. The "What's New" section is also worth reading, particularly when a new version of Python is released, because it summarizes all of the changes in the new version.

A.1   Accessing Python documentation on the web

For many people, the most convenient way to access the Python documentation is to go to www.python.org and browse the documentation collection there. Although doing so requires a connection to the web, it has the advantage that the content is always the most current. Given that for many projects, it's often useful to search the web for other documentation and information, having a browser tab permanently open and pointing to the online Python documentation is an easy way to have a Python reference at your fingertips.

A.1.1   *Browsing Python documentation on your computer*

Many distributions of Python include the full documentation by default. In some Linux distributions, the documentation is a separate package that you need to install separately. In most cases, however, full documentation is already on your computer and easily accessible.

ACCESSING HELP IN THE INTERACTIVE SHELL OR AT A COMMAND LINE

In chapter 2, you saw how to use the `help` command in the interactive interpreter to access online help for any Python module or object:

```
>>> help(int)
Help on int object:

class int(object)
 |   int(x[, base]) -> integer
 |
 |   Convert a string or number to an integer, if possible.  A floating
 |   point argument will be truncated towards zero (this does not include a
 |   string representation of a floating point number!)  When converting a
 |   string, use the optional base.  It is an error to supply a base when
 |   converting a non-string.
 |
 |   Methods defined here:
... (continues with a list of methods for an int)
```

What's happening is that the interpreter is calling the `pydoc` module to generate the documentation. You can also use the `pydoc` module to search the Python documentation from a command line. On a Linux or macOS system, to get the same output in a terminal window, you need only type `pydoc int` at the prompt; to exit, type q. In a Windows command window, unless you've set your search path to include the Python Lib directory, you need to type the entire path—probably something like `C:\Users \<user>\AppData\Local\Programs\Python\Python36\Lib\pydoc.py    int`, where <user> is your Windows username.

GENERATING HTML HELP PAGES WITH PYDOC

If you want a sleeker look to the documentation that `pydoc` generates for a Python object or module, you can have the output written to an HTML file, which you can view in any browser. To do this, add the –w option to the `pydoc` command, which on Windows would then be `C:\Users\<user>\AppData\Local\Programs\Python \Python36\Lib\pydoc.py -w int`. In this case, in which you're looking up documentation on the `int` object, `pydoc` creates a file named int.html in the current directory, and you can open and view it in a browser from there. Figure A.1 shows what int.html looks like in a browser.

If for some reason you want only a limited number pages of documentation available, this method works well. But in most cases, it's probably better to use `pydoc` to serve more complete documentation, as discussed in the next section.

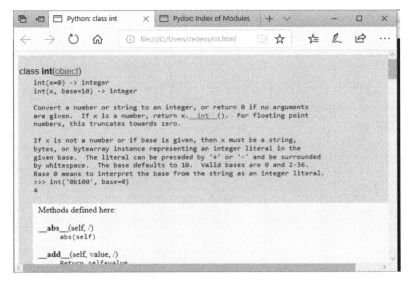

Figure A.1   int.html as generated by `pydoc`

USING PYDOC AS A DOCUMENTATION SERVER

In addition to being able to generate text and HTML documentation on any Python object, the `pydoc` module can be used as a server to serve web-based docs. You can run `pydoc` with -p and a port number to open a server on that port. Then you can enter the "b" command to open a browser and access the documentation of all the modules available, as shown in figure A.2.

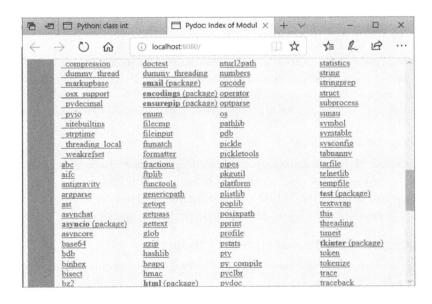

**Figure A.2
A partial view of
the module
documentation
served by** `pydoc`

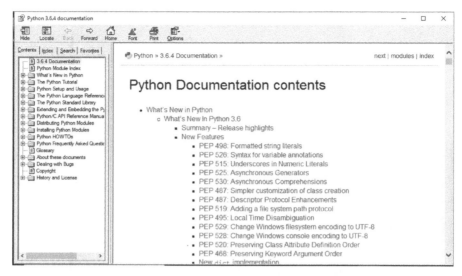

Figure A.3   If you're comfortable with using Window Help files, this file may be all the documentation you'll ever need.

A bonus in using `pydoc` to serve documentation is that it also scans the current directory and extracts documentation from the docstrings of any modules it finds, even if they aren't part of the standard library. This makes it useful for accessing the documentation of any Python modules. There's one caveat, however. To extract the documentation from a module, `pydoc` must import it, which means that it will execute any code at the module's top level. Thus, scripts that aren't written to be imported without side effects (as discussed in chapter 11) will be run, so use this feature with care.

USING THE WINDOWS HELP FILE

On Windows systems, the standard Python 3 package includes complete Python documentation as Windows Help files. You can find these files in the Doc folder inside the folder where Python was installed; usually, they're in the Python 3 program group on the program menu. When you open the main manuals file, it looks something like figure A.3.

A.1.2   Downloading documentation

If you want the Python documentation on a computer but don't necessarily want or need to be running Python, you can also download the complete documentation from www.python.org in PDF, HTML, or text format, which is convenient if you want to be able to access the docs from an e-book reader or similar device.

A.2   Best practices: How to become a Pythonista

Every programming language develops its own traditions and culture, and Python is a strong example. Most experienced Python programmers (*Pythonistas*, as they're sometimes called) care a great deal about writing Python in a way that matches the style and best practices of Python. This type of code is commonly called *Pythonic* code and is valued highly, as opposed to Python code that looks like Java, C, or JavaScript.

The question that coders new to Python face is how they learn to write Pythonic code. Although getting a feel for the language and its style takes a little time and effort, the rest of this appendix gives you some suggestions on how to start.

A.2.1 Ten tips for becoming a Pythonista

The tips in this section are ones that I share with intermediate Python classes and are my suggestions for leveling up your Python skills. I'm not saying that everyone absolutely agrees with me, but from what I've seen over the years, these tips will put you soundly on the path to being a true Pythonista:

- *Consider the Zen of Python.* The Zen of Python, or PEP 20, sums up the design philosophy underlying Python as a language and is commonly invoked in discussions of what makes scripts more Pythonic. In particular, "Beautiful is better than ugly" and "Simple is better than complex" should guide your coding. I've included the Zen of Python at the end of this appendix; you can always find it by typing `import this` at a Python shell prompt.

- *Follow PEP 8.* PEP 8 is the official Python style guide, which is also included later in this appendix. PEP 8 offers good advice on everything from code formatting and variable naming to the use of the language. If you want to write Pythonic code, become familiar with PEP 8.

- *Be familiar with the docs.* Python has a rich, well-maintained collection of documentation, and you should refer to it often. The most useful documents probably are the standard library documentation, but the tutorials and how-to files are also rich veins of information on using the language effectively.

- *Write as little code as you can as much as you can.* Although this advice might apply to many languages, it fits Python particularly well. What I mean is that you should strive to make your programs as short and as simple as possible (but no shorter and no simpler) and that you should practice that style of coding as much as you can.

- *Read as much code as you can.* From the beginning, the Python community has been aware that reading code is more important than writing code. Read as much Python code as you can, and if possible, discuss the code that you read with others.

- *Use the built-in data structures over all else.* You should turn first to Python's built-in structures before writing your own classes to hold data. Python's various data types can be combined with nearly unlimited flexibility and have the advantage of years of debugging and optimization. Take advantage of them.

- *Dwell on generators and comprehensions.* Coders who are new to Python almost always fail to appreciate how much list and dictionary comprehensions and generator expressions are part of Pythonic coding. Look at examples in the Python code that you read, and practice them. You won't be a Pythonista until you can write a list comprehension almost without thinking.

- *Use the standard library.* When the built-ins fail you, look next to the standard library. The elements in the standard library are the famed "batteries included" of Python. They've stood the test of time and have been optimized and documented better than almost any other Python code. Use them if you can.

- *Write as few classes as you can.* Write your own classes only if you must. Experienced Pythonistas tend to be very economical with classes, knowing that designing good classes isn't trivial and that any classes they create are also classes that they have to test and debug.

- *Be wary of frameworks.* Frameworks can be attractive, particularly to coders new to the language, because they offer so many powerful shortcuts. You should use frameworks when they're helpful, of course, but be aware of their downsides. You may spend more time learning the quirks of an un-Pythonic framework than learning Python itself, or you may find yourself adapting what you do to the framework rather than the other way around.

A.3   PEP 8—Style guide for Python code

This section contains a slightly edited excerpt from PEP (Python Enhancement Proposal) 8. Written by Guido van Rossum and Barry Warsaw, PEP 8 is the closest thing Python has to a style manual. Some more-specific sections have been omitted, but the main points are covered. You should make your code conform to PEP 8 as much as possible; your Python style will be the better for it.

You can access the full text of PEP 8 and all of the other PEPs issued in the history of Python by going to the documentation section of www.python.org and looking for the PEP index. The PEPs are excellent sources for the history and lore of Python as well as explanations of current issues and future plans.

A.3.1   Introduction

This document gives coding conventions for the Python code comprising the standard library in the main Python distribution. Please see the companion informational PEP describing style guidelines for the C code in the C implementation of Python.[1] This document was adapted from Guido's original Python Style Guide essay, with some additions from Barry's style guide.[2] Where there's conflict, Guido's style rules for the purposes of this PEP. This PEP may still be incomplete (in fact, it may never be finished <wink>).

A FOOLISH CONSISTENCY IS THE HOBGOBLIN OF LITTLE MINDS

One of Guido's key insights is that code is read much more often than it's written. The guidelines provided here are intended to improve the readability of code and make it

---

[1] PEP 7, Style Guide for C Code, van Rossum, https://www.python.org/dev/peps/pep-0007/.
[2] Barry's GNU Mailman style guide, http://barry.warsaw.us/software/STYLEGUIDE.txt. The URL is empty although it is presented in the PEP 8 style guide.

consistent across the wide spectrum of Python code. As PEP 20[3] says, "Readability counts."

A style guide is about consistency. Consistency with this style guide is important. Consistency within a project is more important. Consistency within one module or function is most important.

But most important, know when to be inconsistent—sometimes the style guide just doesn't apply. When in doubt, use your best judgment. Look at other examples and decide what looks best. And don't hesitate to ask!

Here are two good reasons to break a particular rule:

- When applying the rule would make the code less readable, even for someone who is used to reading code that follows the rules
- To be consistent with surrounding code that also breaks it (maybe for historic reasons), although this is also an opportunity to clean up someone else's mess (in true XP style)

A.3.2 Code layout

INDENTATION

Use four spaces per indentation level.

For really old code that you don't want to mess up, you can continue to use eight-space tabs.

TABS OR SPACES?

Never mix tabs and spaces.

The most popular way of indenting Python is with spaces only. The second most popular way is with tabs only. Code indented with a mixture of tabs and spaces should be converted to using spaces exclusively. When you invoke the Python command-line interpreter with the -t option, it issues warnings about code that illegally mixes tabs and spaces. When you use -tt, these warnings become errors. These options are highly recommended!

For new projects, spaces only are strongly recommended over tabs. Most editors have features that make this easy to do.

MAXIMUM LINE LENGTH

Limit all lines to a maximum of 79 characters.

Many devices are still around that are limited to 80-character lines; plus, limiting windows to 80 characters makes it possible to have several windows side by side. The default wrapping on such devices disrupts the visual structure of the code, making it more difficult to understand. Therefore, please limit all lines to a maximum of 79 characters. For flowing long blocks of text (docstrings or comments), limiting the length to 72 characters is recommended.

The preferred way of wrapping long lines is by using Python's implied line continuation inside parentheses, brackets, and braces. If necessary, you can add an extra pair

---

[3] PEP 20, The Zen of Python, www.python.org/dev/peps/pep-0020/.

of parentheses around an expression, but sometimes using a backslash looks better. Make sure to indent the continued line appropriately. The preferred place to break around a binary operator is *after* the operator, not before it. Here are some examples:

```
class Rectangle(Blob):
    def __init__(self, width, height,
                     color='black', emphasis=None, highlight=0):
        if width == 0 and height == 0 and \
           color == 'red' and emphasis == 'strong' or \
           highlight > 100:
            raise ValueError("sorry, you lose")
        if width == 0 and height == 0 and (color == 'red' or
                                           emphasis is None):
            raise ValueError("I don't think so -- values are %s, %s" %
                                (width, height))
        Blob.__init__(self, width, height,
                      color, emphasis, highlight)
```

BLANK LINES

Separate top-level function and class definitions with two blank lines.

Method definitions inside a class are separated by a single blank line.

Extra blank lines may be used (sparingly) to separate groups of related functions. Blank lines may be omitted between a bunch of related one-liners (for example, a set of dummy implementations).

Use blank lines in functions, sparingly, to indicate logical sections.

Python accepts the Control-L (^L) form feed character as whitespace. Many tools treat these characters as page separators, so you may use them to separate pages of related sections of your file.

IMPORTS

Imports should usually be on separate lines, for example:

```
import os
import sys
```

Don't put them together like this:

```
import sys, os
```

It's okay to say this, though:

```
from subprocess import Popen, PIPE
```

Imports are always put at the top of the file, just after any module comments and docstrings and before module globals and constants.

Imports should be grouped in the following order:

1 Standard library imports
2 Related third-party imports
3 Local application/library–specific imports

Put a blank line between each group of imports.

Put any relevant __all__ specification after the imports.

Relative imports for intra-package imports are highly discouraged. Always use the absolute package path for all imports. Even now that PEP 328[4] is fully implemented in Python 2.5, its style of explicit relative imports is actively discouraged; absolute imports are more portable and usually more readable.

When importing a class from a class-containing module, it's usually okay to spell them

```
from myclass import MyClass
from foo.bar.yourclass import YourClass
```

If this spelling causes local name clashes, then spell them

```
import myclass
import foo.bar.yourclass
and use myclass.MyClass and foo.bar.yourclass.YourClass.
```

WHITESPACE IN EXPRESSIONS AND STATEMENTS

Pet peeves—avoid extraneous whitespace in the following situations:

- Immediately inside parentheses, brackets, or braces
  Yes:
  ```
  spam(ham[1], {eggs: 2})
  ```
  No:
  ```
  spam( ham[ 1 ], { eggs: 2 } )
  ```

- Immediately before a comma, semicolon, or colon
  Yes:
  ```
  if x == 4: print x, y; x, y = y, x
  ```
  No:
  ```
  if x == 4 : print x , y ; x , y = y , x
  ```

- Immediately before the open parenthesis that starts the argument list of a function call
  Yes:
  ```
  spam(1)
  ```
  No:
  ```
  spam (1)
  ```

- Immediately before the open parenthesis that starts an indexing or slicing
  Yes:
  ```
  dict['key'] = list[index]
  ```
  No:
  ```
  dict ['key'] = list [index]
  ```

---

[4] PEP 328, Imports: Multi-Line and Absolute/Relative, www.python.org/dev/peps/pep-0328/.

- More than one space around an assignment (or other) operator to align it with another

    Yes:

    ```
    x = 1
    y = 2
    long_variable = 3
    ```

    No:

    ```
    x             = 1
    y             = 2
    long_variable = 3
    ```

OTHER RECOMMENDATIONS

Always surround these binary operators with a single space on either side: assignment (=), augmented assignment (+=, -=, and so on), comparisons (==, <, >, !=, <>, <=, >=, in, not in, is, is not), and Booleans (and, or, not).

Use spaces around arithmetic operators.

Yes:

```
i = i + 1
submitted += 1

x = x * 2 - 1
hypot2 = x * x + y * y
c = (a + b) * (a - b)
```

No:

```
i=i+1
submitted +=1
x = x*2 - 1
hypot2 = x*x + y*y
c = (a+b) * (a-b)
```

Don't use spaces around the = sign when used to indicate a keyword argument or a default parameter value.

Yes:

```
def complex(real, imag=0.0):
    return magic(r=real, i=imag)
```

No:

```
def complex(real, imag = 0.0):
    return magic(r = real, i = imag)
```

Compound statements (multiple statements on the same line) are generally discouraged.

Yes:

```
if foo == 'blah':
    do_blah_thing()
do_one()
```

```
do_two()
do_three()
```

Rather not:

```
if foo == 'blah': do_blah_thing()
do_one(); do_two(); do_three()
```

While sometimes it's okay to put an `if/for/while` with a small body on the same line, never do this for multiclause statements. Also avoid folding such long lines!

Rather not:

```
if foo == 'blah': do_blah_thing()
for x in lst: total += x
    while t < 10: t = delay()
```

Definitely not:

```
if foo == 'blah': do_blah_thing()
else: do_non_blah_thing()
try: something()
finally: cleanup()
do_one(); do_two(); do_three(long, argument,
                              list, like, this)
if foo == 'blah': one(); two(); three()
```

A.4   Comments

Comments that contradict the code are worse than no comments. Always make a priority of keeping the comments up to date when the code changes!

Comments should be complete sentences. If a comment is a phrase or sentence, its first word should be capitalized, unless it's an identifier that begins with a lowercase letter (never alter the case of identifiers!).

If a comment is short, the period at the end can be omitted. Block comments generally consist of one or more paragraphs built out of complete sentences, and each sentence should end in a period.

You should use two spaces after a sentence-ending period.

When writing English, Strunk and White apply.

Python coders from non-English-speaking countries: please write your comments in English, unless you are 120% sure that the code will never be read by people who don't speak your language.

BLOCK COMMENTS

Block comments generally apply to some (or all) code that follows them and are indented to the same level as that code. Each line of a block comment starts with a # and a single space (unless it is indented text inside the comment).

Paragraphs inside a block comment are separated by a line containing a single # .

INLINE COMMENTS

Use inline comments sparingly.

An inline comment is a comment on the same line as a statement. Inline comments should be separated by at least two spaces from the statement. They should start with a # and a single space.

Inline comments are unnecessary and in fact distracting if they state the obvious. Don't do this:

```
x = x + 1                   # Increment x
```

But sometimes, this is useful:

```
x = x + 1                   # Compensate for border
```

DOCUMENTATION STRINGS

Conventions for writing good documentation strings (aka docstrings) are immortalized in PEP 257.[5]

Write docstrings for all public modules, functions, classes, and methods. Docstrings are not necessary for nonpublic methods, but you should have a comment that describes what the method does. This comment should appear after the def line.

PEP 257 describes good docstring conventions. Note that, most importantly, the """ that ends a multiline docstring should be on a line by itself and preferably preceded by a blank line, for example:

```
"""Return a foobang
Optional plotz says to frobnicate the bizbaz first.

"""
```

For one-liner docstrings, it's okay to keep the closing """ on the same line.

VERSION BOOKKEEPING

If you have to have Subversion, CVS, or RCS crud in your source file, do it as follows:

```
__version__ = "$Revision: 68852 $"      # $Source$
```

These lines should be included after the module's docstring, before any other code, separated by a blank line above and below.

A.4.1 Naming conventions

The naming conventions of Python's library are a bit of a mess, so we'll never get this completely consistent. Nevertheless, here are the currently recommended naming standards. New modules and packages (including third-party frameworks) should be written to these standards, but where an existing library has a different style, internal consistency is preferred.

DESCRIPTIVE: NAMING STYLES

There are many different naming styles. It helps to be able to recognize what naming style is being used, independent of what it's used for.

---

[5] PEP 257, Docstring Conventions, Goodger, van Rossum, www.python.org/dev/peps/pep-0257/.

The following naming styles are commonly distinguished:

- b (single lowercase letter)
- B (single uppercase letter)
- lowercase
- lower_case_with_underscores
- UPPERCASE
- UPPER_CASE_WITH_UNDERSCORES
- CapitalizedWords (or CapWords, or CamelCase—so named because of the bumpy look of its letters[6]). This is also sometimes known as StudlyCaps.
  Note: When using abbreviations in CapWords, capitalize all the letters of the abbreviation. Thus `HTTPServerError` is better than `HttpServerError`.
- mixedCase (differs from CapitalizedWords by initial lowercase character!)
- Capitalized_Words_With_Underscores (ugly!)

There's also the style of using a short unique prefix to group related names together. This is seldom used in Python, but I mention it for completeness. For example, the `os.stat()` function returns a tuple whose items traditionally have names like `st_mode`, `st_size`, `st_mtime`, and so on. (This is done to emphasize the correspondence with the fields of the POSIX system call struct, which helps programmers familiar with that.)

The X11 library uses a leading X for all its public functions. In Python, this style is generally deemed unnecessary because attribute and method names are prefixed with an object, and function names are prefixed with a module name.

In addition, the following special forms using leading or trailing underscores are recognized (these can generally be combined with any case convention):

- _single_leading_underscore
  Weak "internal use" indicator. For example, `from M import *` does not import objects whose name starts with an underscore.
- single_trailing_underscore_
  Used by convention to avoid conflicts with Python keyword. For example, `tkinter.Toplevel(master, class_='ClassName')`.
- __double_leading_underscore
  When naming a class attribute, it invokes name mangling (inside class `FooBar`, `__boo` becomes `_FooBar__boo`; see below).
- __double_leading_and_trailing_underscore__
  "Magic" objects or attributes that live in user-controlled namespaces. For example, `__init__`, `__import__` or `__file__`. Never invent such names; use them only as documented.

---

[6] For a complete description, see www.wikipedia.com/wiki/CamelCase.

- Names to avoid

    Never use the characters *l* (lowercase letter el), *O* (uppercase letter oh), or *I* (uppercase letter eye) as single-character variable names.

    In some fonts, these characters are indistinguishable from the numerals 1 (one) and 0 (zero). When tempted to use *l*, use *L* instead.

- Package and module names

    Modules should have short, all-lowercase names. Underscores can be used in a module name if it improves readability. Python packages should also have short, all-lowercase names, although the use of underscores is discouraged.

    Since module names are mapped to filenames, and some file systems are case-insensitive and truncate long names, it's important that module names be fairly short—this won't be a problem on UNIX, but it may be a problem when the code is transported to older Mac or Windows versions or DOS.

    When an extension module written in C or C++ has an accompanying Python module that provides a higher-level (for example, more object-oriented) interface, the C/C++ module has a leading underscore (for example, `_socket`).

- Class names

    Almost without exception, class names use the CapWords convention. Classes for internal use have a leading underscore in addition.

- Exception names

    Because exceptions should be classes, the class-naming convention applies here. However, you should use the suffix `Error` on your exception names (if the exception actually is an error).

- Global variable names

    (Let's hope that these variables are meant for use inside one module only.) The conventions are about the same as those for functions.

    Modules that are designed for use via `from M import *` should use the `__all__` mechanism to prevent exporting globals or use the older convention of prefixing such globals with an underscore (which you might want to do to indicate these globals are module nonpublic).

- Function names

    Function names should be lowercase, with words separated by underscores as necessary to improve readability.

    mixedCase is allowed only in contexts where that's already the prevailing style (for example, threading.py), to retain backward compatibility.

- Function and method arguments

    Always use `self` for the first argument to instance methods.

    Always use `cls` for the first argument to class methods.

If a function argument's name clashes with a reserved keyword, it's generally better to append a single trailing underscore than to use an abbreviation or spelling corruption. Thus, `print_` is better than `prnt`. (Perhaps better is to avoid such clashes by using a synonym.)

- Method names and instance variables

  Use the function-naming rules: lowercase with words separated by underscores as necessary to improve readability.

  Use one leading underscore only for nonpublic methods and instance variables.

  To avoid name clashes with subclasses, use two leading underscores to invoke Python's name-mangling rules.

  Python mangles these names with the class name: if class `Foo` has an attribute named `__a`, it cannot be accessed by `Foo.__a`. (An insistent user could still gain access by calling `Foo._Foo__a`.) Generally, double leading underscores should be used only to avoid name conflicts with attributes in classes designed to be subclassed.

  Note: there is some controversy about the use of `__`names (see below).

- Constants

  Constants are usually declared on a module level and written in all capital letters with underscores separating words. Examples include `MAX_OVERFLOW` and `TOTAL`.

- Designing for inheritance

  Always decide whether a class's methods and instance variables (collectively called attributes) should be public or nonpublic. If in doubt, choose nonpublic; it's easier to make it public later than to make a public attribute nonpublic.

  Public attributes are those that you expect unrelated clients of your class to use, with your commitment to avoid backward-incompatible changes. Nonpublic attributes are those that are not intended to be used by third parties; you make no guarantees that nonpublic attributes won't change or even be removed.

  We don't use the term *private* here, since no attribute is really private in Python (without a generally unnecessary amount of work).

  Another category of attributes includes those that are part of the subclass API (often called *protected* in other languages). Some classes are designed to be inherited from, either to extend or modify aspects of the class's behavior. When designing such a class, take care to make explicit decisions about which attributes are public, which are part of the subclass API, and which are truly only to be used by your base class.

With this in mind, here are the Pythonic guidelines:

- Public attributes should have no leading underscores.

- If your public attribute name collides with a reserved keyword, append a single trailing underscore to your attribute name. This is preferable to an abbreviation or corrupted spelling. (However, notwithstanding this rule, `cls` is the preferred spelling for any variable or argument that's known to be a class, especially the first argument to a class method.)

  Note 1: See the argument name recommendation above for class methods.

- For simple public data attributes, it's best to expose just the attribute name, without complicated accessor/mutator methods. Keep in mind that Python provides an easy path to future enhancement, should you find that a simple data attribute needs to grow functional behavior. In that case, use properties to hide functional implementation behind simple data attribute access syntax.

  Note 1: Properties work only on new-style classes.

  Note 2: Try to keep the functional behavior side-effect free, although side effects such as caching are generally fine.

  Note 3: Avoid using properties for computationally expensive operations; the attribute notation makes the caller believe that access is (relatively) cheap.

- If your class is intended to be subclassed, and you have attributes that you don't want subclasses to use, consider naming them with double leading underscores and no trailing underscores. This invokes Python's name-mangling algorithm, where the name of the class is mangled into the attribute name. This helps avoid attribute name collisions should subclasses inadvertently contain attributes with the same name.

  Note 1: Only the simple class name is used in the mangled name, so if a subclass chooses both the same class name and attribute name, you can still get name collisions.

  Note 2: Name mangling can make certain uses, such as debugging and `__getattr__()`, less convenient. However the name-mangling algorithm is well documented and easy to perform manually.

  Note 3: Not everyone likes name mangling. Try to balance the need to avoid accidental name clashes with potential use by advanced callers.

A.4.2   *Programming recommendations*

You should write code in a way that does not disadvantage other implementations of Python (PyPy, Jython, IronPython, Pyrex, Psyco, and such).

For example, don't rely on CPython's efficient implementation of in-place string concatenation for statements in the form `a+=b` or `a=a+b`. Those statements run more slowly in Jython. In performance-sensitive parts of the library, you should use the `''.join()` form instead. This will ensure that concatenation occurs in linear time across various implementations.

Comparisons to singletons like `None` should always be done with `is` or `is not`, never the equality operators.

Also, beware of writing `if x` when you really mean `if x is not None`, for example, when testing whether a variable or argument that defaults to `None` was set to some other value. The other value might have a type (such as a container) that could be false in a Boolean context!

Use class-based exceptions.

String exceptions in new code are forbidden, because this language feature has been removed in Python 2.6.

Modules or packages should define their own domain-specific base exception class, which should be subclassed from the built-in `Exception` class. Always include a class docstring, for example:

```
class MessageError(Exception):
    """Base class for errors in the email package."""
```

Class-naming conventions apply here, although you should add the suffix `Error` to your exception classes if the exception is an error. Non-error exceptions need no special suffix.

When raising an exception, use `raise ValueError('message')` instead of the older form `raise ValueError, 'message'`.

The paren-using form is preferred because when the exception arguments are long or include string formatting, you don't need to use line continuation characters thanks to the containing parentheses. The older form has been removed in Python 3.

When catching exceptions, mention specific exceptions whenever possible instead of using a bare `except:` clause. For example, use

```
try:
    import platform_specific_module
except ImportError:
    platform_specific_module = None
```

A bare `except:` clause will catch `SystemExit` and `KeyboardInterrupt` exceptions, making it harder to interrupt a program with Control-C, and can disguise other problems. If you want to catch all exceptions that signal program errors, use `except Exception:`.

A good rule of thumb is to limit use of bare `except` clauses to two cases:

- If the exception handler will be printing out or logging the traceback; at least the user will be aware that an error has occurred.
- If the code needs to do some cleanup work but then lets the exception propagate upward with `raise`, then `try...finally` is a better way to handle this case.

In addition, for all `try/except` clauses, limit the `try` clause to the absolute minimum amount of code necessary. Again, this avoids masking bugs.

Yes:

```
try:
    value = collection[key]
except KeyError:
```

```
        return key_not_found(key)
else:
    return handle_value(value)
```

No:

```
try:              # Too broad!
    return handle_value(collection[key])
except KeyError:
    return key_not_found(key)
```

Will also catch KeyError
raised by handle_value()

Use string methods instead of the string module.

String methods are always much faster and share the same API with Unicode strings. Override this rule if backward compatibility with Python versions older than 2.0 is required.

Use `''.startswith()` and `''.endswith()` instead of string slicing to check for prefixes or suffixes.

`startswith()` and `endswith()` are cleaner and less error prone.

Yes:

```
if foo.startswith('bar'):
```

No:

```
if foo[:3] == 'bar':
```

The exception is if your code must work with Python 1.5.2 (but let's hope not!).

Object type comparisons should always use `isinstance()` instead of comparing types directly.

Yes:

```
if isinstance(obj, int):
```

No:

```
if type(obj) is type(1):
```

When checking to see if an object is a string, keep in mind that it might be a Unicode string too! In Python 2.3, `str` and `unicode` have a common base class, `basestring`, so you can do the following:

```
if isinstance(obj, basestring):
```

In Python 2.2, the `types` module has the `StringTypes` type defined for that purpose, for example:

```
from types import StringTypes
if isinstance(obj, StringTypes):
```

In Python 2.0 and 2.1, you should do the following:

```
from types import StringType, UnicodeType
if isinstance(obj, StringType) or \
   isinstance(obj, UnicodeType) :
```

For sequences (strings, lists, tuples), use the fact that empty sequences are false.

Yes:

```
if not seq:        if seq:
```

No:

```
if len(seq)        if not len(seq)
```

Don't write string literals that rely on significant trailing whitespace. Such trailing whitespace is visually indistinguishable, and some editors (or more recently, reindent.py) will trim them.

Don't compare Boolean values to `True` or `False` using ==.

Yes:

```
if greeting:
```

No:

```
if greeting == True:
```

Worse:

```
if greeting is True:
```

Copyright—this document has been placed in the public domain.

A.4.3 *Other guides for Python style*

Although PEP 8 remains the most influential style guide for Python, you have other options. In general, these guides don't contradict PEP 8, but they offer wider examples and fuller reasoning about how to make your code Pythonic. One good choice is *The Elements of Python Style*, freely available at https://github.com/amontalenti/elements-of-python-style/blob/master/README.md. Another useful guide is The Hitchhiker's Guide to Python, by Kenneth Reitz and Tanya Schlusser, also freely available at http://docs.python-guide.org/en/latest/.

As the language and programmers' skills continue to evolve, there will certainly be other guides, and I encourage you to take advantage of new guides as they're produced, but only after starting with PEP 8.

A.5 *The Zen of Python*

The following document is PEP 20, also referred to as "The Zen of Python," a slightly tongue-in-cheek statement of the philosophy of Python. In addition to being included in the Python documentation, the Zen of Python is an Easter egg in the Python interpreter. Type `import this` at the interactive prompt to see it.

Longtime Pythoneer Tim Peters succinctly channels the BDFL's (Benevolent Dictator for Life) guiding principles for Python's design into 20 aphorisms, only 19 of which have been written down.

The Zen of Python

Beautiful is better than ugly.

Explicit is better than implicit.

Simple is better than complex.

Complex is better than complicated.

Flat is better than nested.

Sparse is better than dense.

Readability counts.

Special cases aren't special enough to break the rules.

Although practicality beats purity.

Errors should never pass silently.

Unless explicitly silenced.

In the face of ambiguity, refuse the temptation to guess.

There should be one—and preferably only one—obvious way to do it.

Although that way may not be obvious at first unless you're Dutch.

Now is better than never.

Although never is often better than *right* now.

If the implementation is hard to explain, it's a bad idea.

If the implementation is easy to explain, it may be a good idea.

Namespaces are one honking great idea—let's do more of those!

appendix B
Exercise answers

B.1 Chapter 4

TRY THIS: VARIABLES AND EXPRESSIONS In the Python shell, create some variables. What happens when you try to put spaces, dashes, or other non-alphanumeric characters in the variable name? Play around with a few complex expressions, such as x = 2 + 4 * 5 – 6 / 3. Use parentheses to group the numbers in different ways, and see how that changes the result compared with the original ungrouped expression.

```
>>> x = 3
>>> y = 3.14
>>> y
3.14
>>> x
3
>>> big var = 12
  File "<stdin>", line 1
    big var = 12
            ^
SyntaxError: invalid syntax
>>> big-var
Traceback (most recent call last):
  File "<stdin>", line 1, in <module>
NameError: name 'big' is not defined
>>> big&var
Traceback (most recent call last):
  File "<stdin>", line 1, in <module>
NameError: name 'big' is not defined
>>> x = 2 + 4 * 5 - 6 /3
>>> x
20.0
>>> x = (2 + 4) * 5 - 6 /3
>>> x
28.0
```

```
>>> x = (2 + 4) * (5 - 6) /3
>>> x
-2.0
```

TRY THIS: MANIPULATING STRINGS AND NUMBERS   In the Python shell, create some string and number variables (integers, floats, *and* complex numbers). Experiment a bit with what happens when you do operations with them, including across types. Can you multiply a string by an integer, for example, or by a float or complex number? Also, load the math module and try out a few of the functions; then load the cmath module and do the same. What happens if you try to use one of those functions on an integer or float after loading the cmath module? How might you get the math module functions back?

```
>>> i = 3
>>> f = 3.14
>>> c = 3j2
  File "<stdin>", line 1
    c = 3j2
          ^
SyntaxError: invalid syntax
>>> c = 3J2
  File "<stdin>", line 1
    c = 3J2
          ^
SyntaxError: invalid syntax
>>> c = 3 + 2j
>>> c
(3+2j)
>>> s = 'hello'
>>> s * f
Traceback (most recent call last):
  File "<stdin>", line 1, in <module>
TypeError: can't multiply sequence by non-int of type 'float'
>>> s * i
'hellohellohello'
>>> s * c
Traceback (most recent call last):
  File "<stdin>", line 1, in <module>
TypeError: can't multiply sequence by non-int of type 'complex'
>>> c * i
(9+6j)
>>> c * f
(9.42+6.28j)
>>> from math import sqrt
>>> sqrt(16)
4.0
>>> from cmath import sqrt
>>> sqrt(16)
(4+0j)
```

To reconnect the first sqrt to your current namespace, you can reimport it. Note that this code doesn't reload the file:

```
>>> from math import sqrt
>>> sqrt(4)
2.0
```

TRY THIS: GETTING INPUT   Experiment with the input() function to get string and integer input. Using code similar to the code above, what is the effect of not using int() around the call to input() for integer input? Can you modify that code to accept a float, such as 28.5? What happens if you deliberately enter the "wrong" type of value, such as a float where an int is expected or a string where a number is expected, and vice versa?

```
>>> x = input("int?")
int?3
>>> x
'3'
>>> y = float(input("float?"))
float?3.5
>>> y
3.5
>>> z = int(input("int?"))
int?3.5
Traceback (most recent call last):
  File "<stdin>", line 1, in <module>
ValueError: invalid literal for int() with base 10: '3.5'
```

QUICK CHECK : PYTHONIC STYLE   Which of the following variable and function names do you think are *not* good Pythonic style, and why?: bar(, varName, VERYLONGVARNAME, foobar, longvarname, foo_bar(), really_very _long_var_name

bar(: Not good, not legal, includes symbol
varName: Not good, mixed case
VERYLONGVARNAME: Not good, long, all caps, hard to read
foobar: Good
longvarname: Good, although underscores to separate words would be better
foo_bar(): Good
really_very_long_var_name: Long, but good if all of the words are needed, perhaps to distinguish among similar variables

B.2   Chapter 5

QUICK CHECK: LEN()   What would len() return for each of the following: [0]; []; [[1, 3, [4, 5], 6], 7]?

len([0]) - 1
len([]) - 0
len([[1, 3, [4, 5], 6], 7 s]) - 2
([1, 3, [4, 5], 6] is a list and a single item in the list before the second item, 7.

TRY THIS: LIST SLICES AND INDEXES Using what you know about the `len()` function and list slices, how would you combine the two to get the second half of a list when you don't know what size it is? Experiment in the Python shell to confirm that your solution works.

```
>>> my_list = [1, 2, 3, 4, 5, 6]
>>> last_half = my_list[len(my_list)//2:]
>>> last_half
[4, 5, 6]
```

`len(my_list) // 2` is the halfway point; slice from there to the end.

TRY THIS: MODIFYING LISTS Suppose that you have a list 10 items long. How might you move the last three items from the end of the list to the beginning, keeping them in the same order?

```
>>> my_list = my_list[-3:] + my_list[:-3]
>>> my_list
[4, 5, 6, 1, 2, 3]
```

TRY THIS: SORTING LISTS Suppose that you have a list in which each element is in turn a list: `[[1, 2, 3], [2, 1, 3], [4, 0, 1]]`. If you want to sort this list by the second element in each list, so that the result is `[[4, 0, 1], [2, 1, 3], [1, 2, 3]]`, what function would you write to pass as the key value to the `sort()` method?

```
>>> the_list =  [[1, 2, 3], [2, 1, 3], [4, 0, 1]]
>>> the_list.sort(key=lambda x: x[1])
>>> the_list
[[4, 0, 1], [2, 1, 3], [1, 2, 3]]
```

or

```
>>> the_list =  [[1, 2, 3], [2, 1, 3], [4, 0, 1]]
>>> the_list.sort(key=lambda x: x[1])
>>> the_list
[[4, 0, 1], [2, 1, 3], [1, 2, 3]]
```

QUICK CHECK: LIST OPERATIONS What is the result of `len([[1,2]] * 3)`?

3

What are two differences between using the `in` operator and a list's `index()` method?

- index gives position; in gives a true/false answer.
- index gives an error if an element isn't in the list.

Which of the following raises an exception? `min(["a",  "b",  "c"])`; `max([1, 2, "three"])`; `[1, 2, 3].count("one")`

`max([1, 2, "three"])`: Strings and ints can't be compared, so it's impossible to get a max value.

TRY THIS: LIST OPERATIONS If you have a list x, write the code to safely remove an item if and only if that value is in the list.

```
if element in x:
    x.remove(element)
```

Modify that code to remove the element only if the item occurs in the list more than once.

```
if x.count(element) > 1:
    x.remove(element)
```

Note: This code removes only the first occurrence of element.

TRY THIS: LIST COPIES Suppose that you have the following list: x = [[1, 2, 3], [4, 5, 6], [7, 8, 9]]. What code could you use to get a copy y of that list in which you could change its elements *without* the side effect of changing the contents of x?

```
import copy
copy_x = copy.deepcopy(x)
```

QUICK CHECK: TUPLES Explain why the following operations aren't legal for the tuple x = (1, 2, 3, 4):

```
x.append(1)
x[1] = "hello"
del x[2]
```

All of these operations change the object in place, and tuples can't be changed.

If you had a tuple x = (3, 1, 4, 2), how might you end up with x sorted?

```
x = sorted(x)
```

QUICK CHECK: SETS If you were to construct a set from the following list, how many elements would it have?: [1, 2, 5, 1, 0, 2, 3, 1, 1, (1, 2, 3)]

Six unique elements: 1, 2, 5, 0, 3, and the tuple (1, 2, 3)

LAB 5: EXAMINING A LIST In this lab, the task is to read a set of temperature data (in fact, the monthly high temperatures at Heathrow Airport for 1948–2016) from a file and then find some basic information: the highest and lowest temperatures, the mean (average) temperature, and the median temperature (the temperature in the middle if all of the temperatures are sorted).

The temperature data is in the file lab_05.txt in the source code directory for this chapter. Because I've not yet discussed reading files, the code to read the files into a list is here:

```
with open('lab_05.txt') as infile:
    for row in infile:
        temperatures.append(float(row.strip()))
```

As mentioned, you should find the highest and lowest temperature, the average, and the median. You'll probably want to use `min()`, `max()`, `sum()`, `len()`, and `sort()`.

```
max_temp = max(temperatures)
min_temp = min(temperatures)
mean_temp = sum(temperatures)/len(temperatures)
# we'll need to sort to get the median temp
temperatures.sort()
median_temp = temperatures[len(temperatures)//2]
print("max = {}".format(max_temp))
print("min = {}".format(min_temp))
print("mean = {}".format(mean_temp))
print("median = {}".format(median_temp))

max = 28.2
min = 0.8
mean = 14.848309178743966
median = 14.7
```

Bonus: Determine how many unique temperatures are in the list.

```
unique_temps = len(set(temperatures))

print("number of temps - {}".format(len(temperatures)))
print("number of temps - {}".format(unique_temps))
number of temps - 828
number of unique temps - 217
```

B.3   Chapter 6

QUICK CHECK: SPLIT AND JOIN How could you use `split` and join to change all of the whitespace in string x to dashes (such as `"this is a test"` to `"this-is-a-test"`)?

```
>>> x = "this is a test"
>>> "-".join(x.split())
'this-is-a-test'
```

QUICK CHECK: STRINGS TO NUMBERS Which of the following will not be converted to numbers, and why?

1 `int('a1')`
2 `int('12G', 16)`
3 `float("12345678901234567890")`
4 `int("12*2")`

Only #3 `float("12345678901234567890")` converts; all the others have a character that wouldn't be allowed for conversion to an int.

QUICK CHECK: STRIP If the string x equals `"(name, date), \n"`, which of the following returns a string containing `"name, date"` ?

1 `x.rstrip("),")`
2 `x.strip("),\n")`

3 `x.strip("\n)(,")`

3 `x.strip("\n)(,")` will remove the newline as well as the comma and parentheses.

QUICK CHECK: STRING SEARCHING   If you want to see whether a line ends with the string `"rejected"`, what string method would you use? Are there any other ways you could get the same result?

`endswith('rejected')`

You could also do `line[:-8] == rejected`, but that wouldn't be as clear or Pythonic.

QUICK CHECK: MODIFYING STRINGS   What would be a quick way to change all punctuation in a string to spaces?

```
>>> punct = str.maketrans("!.,:;-?", "        ")
>>> x = "This is text, with: punctuation! Right?"
>>> x.translate(punct)
'This is text  with  punctuation  Right '
```

TRY THIS: STRING OPERATIONS   Suppose that you have a list of strings in which some (but not necessarily all) of the strings begin and end with the double quote character:

`x = ['"abc"', 'def', '"ghi"', '"klm"', 'nop']`

What code would you use on each element to remove just the double quotes?

```
>>> for item in x:
...     print(item.strip('"'))
...
abc
def
ghi
klm
nop
```

What code could you use to find the position of the *last p* in *Mississippi*? When you've found its position, what code would you use to remove just that letter?

```
>>> state = "Mississippi"
>>> pos = state.rfind("p")

>>> state = state[:pos] + state[pos+1:]
>>> print(state)

Mississipi
```

QUICK CHECK: THE FORMAT() METHOD   What will be in x when the following snippets of code are executed?

```
x = "{1:{0}}".format(3, 4)
'   4'

x = "{0:$>5}".format(3)
'$$$$3'
```

```
x = "{a:{b}}".format(a=1, b=5)
'    1'

x = "{a:{b}}:{0:$>5}".format(3, 4, a=1, b=5, c=10)
'    1:$$$$3'
```

QUICK CHECK: FORMATTING STRINGS WITH %   What would be in the variable x after the following snippets of code have executed?

```
x = "%.2f" % 1.1111
x will contain '1.11'
x = "%(a).2f" % {'a':1.1111}
x will contain '1.11'
x = "%(a).08f" % {'a':1.1111}
x will contain '1.11110000'
```

QUICK CHECK: BYTES   For which of the following kinds of data would you want to use a string? For which could you use bytes?

(1) Data file storing binary data

Bytes. Because the data is binary, you're more concerned with the contents as numbers rather than text. Therefore, it would make sense to use bytes.

(2) Text in a language with accented characters

String. Python 3 strings are Unicode, so they can handle accented characters.

(3) Text with only uppercase and lowercase roman characters

String. Strings should be used for all text in Python 3.

(4) A series of integers no larger than 255

Bytes. A byte is an integer no larger than 255, so the bytes type is perfect for storing integers like this.

LAB 6: PREPROCESSING TEXT   In processing raw text, it's quite often necessary to clean and normalize the text before doing anything else. If you want to find the frequency of words in text, for example, you can make the job easier if, before you start counting, you make sure that everything is lowercase (or uppercase, if you prefer) and that all punctuation has been removed. It can also make things easier to break the text into a series of words.

In this lab, the task is to read an excerpt of the first chapter of *Moby Dick*, make sure that everything is one case, remove all punctuation, and write the words one per line to a second file. Again, because I haven't yet covered reading and writing files, the code for those operations is supplied below.

Your task is to come up with the code to replace the commented lines in the sample below:

```
with open("moby_01.txt") as infile, open("moby_01_clean.txt", "w") as
    outfile:
    for line in infile:
        # make all one case
        # remove punctuation
```

```
              # split into words
              # write all words for line
              outfile.write(cleaned_words)
punct = str.maketrans("",   "",  "!.,:;-?")

with open("moby_01.txt") as infile, open("moby_01_clean.txt", "w") as
   outfile:
      for line in infile:
          # make all one case
          cleaned_line = line.lower()

          # remove punctuation
          cleaned_line = cleaned_line.translate(punct)

          # split into words
          words = cleaned_line.split()
          cleaned_words = "\n".join(words)
          # write all words for line
          outfile.write(cleaned_words)
```

B.4   Chapter 7

TRY THIS: CREATE A DICTIONARY   Write the code to ask the user for three names and three ages. After the names and ages are entered, ask the user for one of the names, and print the correct age.

```
>>> name_age = {}
>>> for i in range(3):
...      name = input("Name? ")
...      age = int(input("Age? "))
...      name_age[name] = age

>>> name_choice = input("Name to find? ")
>>> print(name_age[name_choice])

Name? Tom
Age? 33
Name? Talita
Age? 28
Name? Rania
Age? 35
Name to find? Talita
28
```

QUICK CHECK: DICTIONARY OPERATIONS   Assume that you have a dictionary x = {'a':1, 'b':2, 'c':3, 'd':4} and a dictionary y = {'a':6, 'e':5, 'f':6}. What would be the contents of x after the following snippets of code have executed?

```
del x['d']
z = x.setdefault('g', 7)
x.update(y)

>>> x = {'a':1, 'b':2, 'c':3, 'd':4}
>>> y = {'a':6, 'e':5, 'f':6}
```

```
>>> del x['d']
>>> print(x)
{'a': 1, 'b': 2, 'c': 3}
>>> z = x.setdefault('g', 7)
>>> print(x)
{'a': 1, 'b': 2, 'c': 3, 'g': 7}
>>> x.update(y)
>>> print(x)
{'a': 6, 'b': 2, 'c': 3, 'g': 7, 'e': 5, 'f': 6}
```

QUICK CHECK: WHAT CAN BE A KEY? Decide which of the following expressions can be a dictionary key: 1; 'bob'; ('tom', [1, 2, 3]); ["filename"]; "filename"; ("filename", "extension")

1: Yes.

'bob': Yes.

('tom', [1, 2, 3]): No; it contains a list, which isn't hashable.

["filename"]: No; it's a list, which isn't hashable.

"filename": Yes.

("filename", "extension"): Yes; it's a tuple.

TRY THIS: USING DICTIONARIES Suppose that you're writing a program that works like a spreadsheet. How might you use a dictionary to store the contents of a sheet? Write some sample code to both store a value and retrieve a value in a particular cell. What might be some drawbacks to this approach?

You could use tuples of row, column values as keys to store the values in a dictionary. One drawback would be that the keys wouldn't be sorted, so you'd have to manage that situation as you grabbed the keys/values to render as a spreadsheet.

```
>>> sheet = {}
>>> sheet[('A', 1)] = 100
>>> sheet[('B', 1)] = 1000

>>> print(sheet[('A', 1)])
100
```

LAB 7: WORD COUNTING In Lab 6, you took the text of the first chapter of *Moby Dick*, normalized the case, removed punctuation, and wrote the separated words to a file. In this lab, you read that file, use a dictionary to count the number of times each word occurs, and report the most common and least common words.

Use this code to read the words from the file into a list called moby_words:

```
moby_words = []
    for word in infile:
        if word.strip():
            moby_words.append(word.strip())

moby_words = []
with open('moby_01_clean.txt') as infile:
```

```
        for word in infile:
            if word.strip():
                moby_words.append(word.strip())

word_count = {}
for word in moby_words:
    count = word_count.setdefault(word, 0)
    count += 1
    word_count[word] += 1

word_list = list(word_count.items())
word_list.sort(key=lambda x: x[1])
print("Most common words:")
for word in reversed(word_list[-5:]):
    print(word)
print("\nLeast common words:")
for word in word_list[:5]:
    print(word)

Most common words:
('the', 14)
('and', 9)
('i', 9)
('of', 8)
('is', 7)

Least common words:
('see', 1)
('growing', 1)
('soul', 1)
('having', 1)
('regulating', 1)
```

B.5   Chapter 8

TRY THIS: LOOPING AND IF STATEMENTS   Suppose that you have a list x = [1, 3, 5, 0, -1, 3, -2], and you need to remove all negative numbers from that list. Write the code to do this.

```
x = [1, 3, 5, 0, -1, 3, -2]
for i in x:
    if i < 0:
        x.remove(i)
print(x)

[1, 3, 5, 0, 3]
```

How would you count the total number of negative numbers in a list y = [[1, -1, 0], [2, 5, -9], [-2, -3, 0]]?

```
count = 0
y = [[1, -1, 0], [2, 5, -9], [-2, -3, 0]]
for row in y:
    for col in row:
        if col < 0:
            count += 1
```

```
print(count)
```

4

What code would you use to print "very low" if the value of x is below -5, "low" if it's from -4 up to 0, "neutral" if it's equal to 0, "high" if it's greater than 0 up to 4, and "very high" if it's greater than 5?

```
if x < -5:
    print("very low")
elif x <= 0:
    print("low")
elif x <= 5:
    print("high")
else:
    print("very high")
```

TRY THIS: COMPREHENSIONS What list comprehension would you use to process the list x so that all negative values are removed?

```
x = [1, 3, 5, 0, -1, 3, -2]
new_x = [i for i in x if i >= 0]
print(new_x)
[1, 3, 5, 0, 3]
```

Create a generator that returns only odd numbers from 1 to 100. (Hint: A number is odd if there's a remainder when it's divided by 2; use % 2 to do this.)

```
odd_100 = (x for x in range(100) if x % 2)
for i in odd_100:
    print(i))
```

Write the code to create a dictionary of the numbers and their cubes from 11 through 15.

```
cubes = {x: x**3 for x in range(11, 16)}
print(cubes)
{11: 1331, 12: 1728, 13: 2197, 14: 2744, 15: 3375}
```

QUICK CHECK: BOOLEANS AND TRUTHINESS Decide whether the following statements are true or false: 1, 0, -1, [0], 1 and 0, 1 > 0 or []

1 ->: True.
0 ->: False.
-1: True.
[0]: True; it's a list containing one item.
1 and 0: False.
1 > 0 or []: True.

LAB: REFACTOR WORD_COUNT Rewrite the word-count program in section 8.7 to make it shorter. You may want to look at the string and list operations already discussed, as well as think about different ways to organize the code.

You may also want to make the program smarter so that only alphabetic strings (not symbols or punctuation) count as words.

Listing B.1   File: word_count_refactored.py

```
# File: word_count_refactored.py
""" Reads a file and returns the number of lines, words,
    and characters - similar to the UNIX wc utility
"""

# initialze counts
line_count = 0
word_count = 0
char_count = 0

# open the file
with  open('word_count.tst') as infile:
    for line in infile:
        line_count += 1
        char_count += len(line)
        words = line.split()
        word_count += len(words)

# print the answers using the format() method
print("File has {0} lines, {1} words, {2} characters".format(line_count,
                                        word_count, char_count))
```

B.6   *Chapter 9*

QUICK CHECK: FUNCTIONS AND PARAMETERS   How would you write a function that could take any number of unnamed arguments and print their values in reverse order?

```
def my_funct(*params):
    for i in reversed(params):
        print(i)

my_funct(1,2,3,4)
```

What do you need to do to create a procedure or void function—that is, a function with no return value?

Either don't return a value (use a bare return) or don't use a return statement at all.

What happens if you capture the return value of a function with a variable?

The only result is that you can use that value, whatever it might be.

QUICK CHECK: MUTABLE FUNCTION PARAMETERS   What would be the result of changing a list or dictionary that was passed into a function as a parameter value? Which operations would be likely to create changes that would be visible outside the function? What steps might you take to minimize that risk?

The changes would persist for future uses of the default parameter. Operations such as adding and deleting elements, as well as changing the value of an element, are particularly likely to be problems. To minimize the risk, it's better not to use mutable types as default parameters.

TRY THIS: GLOBAL VS LOCAL VARIABLES   Assuming that x = 5, what will be the value of x after funct_1() below executes? After funct_2()?

```
def funct_1():
    x = 3
def funct_2():
    global x
    x = 2
```

After calling funct_1(), x will be unchanged; after funct_2(), the value in the global x will be 2.

QUICK CHECK: GENERATOR FUNCTIONS   What would you need to modify in the code for the function four() above to make it work for any number? What would you need to add to allow the starting point to also be set?

```
>>> def four(limit):
...     x = 0
...     while x < limit:
...         print("in generator, x =", x)
...         yield x
...         x += 1
...
>>> for i in four(4):
...     print(i)
```

To specify the start:

```
>>> def four(start, limit):
...     x = start
...     while x < limit:
...         print("in generator, x =", x)
...         yield x
...         x += 1
...
>>> for i in four(1, 4):
...     print(i)
```

TRY THIS: DECORATORS   How would you modify the code for the decorator function above to remove unneeded messages and enclose the return value of wrapped function in "<html>" and "</html>" so that myfunction ("hello") would return "<html>hello<html>"?

This exercise is a hard one, because to define a function that changes the return value, you need to add an inner wrapper function to call the original function and add to the return value.

```
def decorate(func):
    def wrapper_func(*args):
```

```
        def inner_wrapper(*args):
                return_value = func(*args)
                return "<html>{}<html>".format(return_value)

        return inner_wrapper(*args)
    return wrapper_func

@decorate
def myfunction(parameter):
    return parameter

print(myfunction("Test"))

<html>Test<html>
```

LAB 9: USEFUL FUNCTIONS Looking back at chapters 6 and 7, refactor the code into functions for cleaning and processing the data. The goal should be that most of the logic is moved into functions. Use your own judgment as to the types of functions and parameters, but keep in mind that functions should do just one thing and that they shouldn't have any side effects that carry over outside the function.

```
punct = str.maketrans("",   "", "!.,:;-?")

def clean_line(line):
    """changes case and removes punctuation"""
    # make all one case
    cleaned_line = line.lower()

    # remove punctuation
    cleaned_line = cleaned_line.translate(punct)
    return cleaned_line


def get_words(line):
    """splits line into words, and rejoins with newlines"""
    words = line.split()
    return "\n".join(words) + "\n"


with open("moby_01.txt") as infile, open("moby_01_clean.txt", "w")
  as outfile:
    for line in infile:
        cleaned_line = clean_line(line)

        cleaned_words = get_words(cleaned_line)

        # write all words for line
        outfile.write(cleaned_words)

def count_words(words):
    """takes list of cleaned words, returns count dictionary"""
    word_count = {}
    for word in moby_words:
```

```
        count = word_count.setdefault(word, 0)
        word_count[word] += 1
    return word_count


def word_stats(word_count):
    """Takes word count dictionary and returns top and bottom five
    entries"""
    word_list = list(word_count.items())
    word_list.sort(key=lambda x: x[1])
    least_common = word_list[:5]
    most_common = word_list[-1:-6:-1]
    return most_common, least_common

moby_words = []
with open('moby_01_clean.txt') as infile:
    for word in infile:
        if word.strip():
            moby_words.append(word.strip())


word_count = count_words(moby_words)

most, least = word_stats(word_count)
print("Most common words:")
for word in most:
    print(word)
print("\nLeast common words:")
for word in least:
    print(word)
```

B.7   Chapter 10

QUICK CHECK: MODULES Suppose that you have a module called new_math that contains a function called new_divide. What are the ways that you might import and then use that function? What are the pros and cons of each way?

```
import new_math
new_math.new_divide(...)
```

This solution is often preferred because there won't be a clash between any identifiers in new_module and the importing namespace. This solution is less convenient to type, however.

```
from new_math import new_divide
new_divide(...)
```

This version is more convenient to use but increases the chance of name clashes between identifiers in the module and the importing namespace.

Suppose that the new_math module contains a function call _helper_math(). How will the underscore character affect the way that _helper_math() is imported?

It won't be imported if you use from new_math import *

QUICK CHECK: NAMESPACES AND SCOPE   Consider a variable width that's in the module `make_window.py`. In which of the following contexts is width in scope?

(A) With the module itself
(B) Inside the `resize()` function in the module
(C) Within the script that imported the `make_window.py` module

A and B but not C

LAB 10: CREATE A MODULE   Package the functions that you created at the end of chapter 9 as a standalone module. Although you can include code to run the module as the main program, the goal should be for the functions to be completely usable from another script.

(no answer)

B.8   Chapter 11

TRY THIS: MAKING A SCRIPT EXECUTABLE   Experiment with executing scripts on your platform. Also try to redirect input and output into and out of your scripts.

(no answer)

QUICK CHECK: PROGRAMS AND MODULES What issue is the use of if `__name__` == `"__main__"`: meant to prevent, and how does it do that? Can you think of any other way to prevent this issue?

When Python loads a module, all of its code is executed. By using the pattern above, you can have certain code run only if it's being executed as the main script file.

LAB 11: CREATING A PROGRAM   In chapter 8, you created a version of the UNIX `wc` utility to count the lines, words, and characters in a file. Now that you have more tools at your disposal, refactor that program to make it work more like the original. In particular, it should have options to show only lines (`-l`), only words (`-w`), and only characters (`-c`). If none of those options is given, all three stats are displayed, but if any of them is present, only the specified stats are shown.

For an extra challenge, look at the man page for `wc` on a Linux/UNIX system, and add the `-L` to show the longest line length. Feel free to try to implement the complete behavior as listed in the man page, and test it against your system's `wc` utility.

```
# File: word_count_program.py
""" Reads a file and returns the number of lines, words,
    and characters - similar to the UNIX wc utility
"""
import sys
```

```
def main():
    # initialze counts
    line_count = 0
    word_count = 0
    char_count = 0

    option = None
    params = sys.argv[1:]
    if len(params) > 1:
        # if more than one param, pop the first one as the option
        option = params.pop(0).lower().strip()
    filename = params[0]     # open the file
    with  open(filename) as infile:
        for line in infile:
            line_count += 1
            char_count += len(line)
            words = line.split()
            word_count += len(words)

    if option == "-c":
        print("File has {} characters".format(char_count))
    elif option == "-w":
        print("File has {} words".format(word_count))
    elif option == "-l":
        print("File has {} lines".format(line_count))
    else:
        # print the answers using the format() method
        print("File has {0} lines, {1} words, {2}
characters".format(line_count,
            word_count, char_count))

if __name__ == '__main__':
    main()
```

B.9   Chapter 12

QUICK CHECK: MANIPULATING PATHS How would you use the os module's functions to take a path to a file called test.log and create a new file path in the same directory for a file called test.log.old? How would you do the same thing by using the pathlib module?

```
import os.path
old_path = os.path.abspath('test.log')
print(old_path)
new_path = '{}.{}'.format(old_path, "old")
print(new_path)

import pathlib
path = pathlib.Path('test.log')
abs_path = path.resolve()
print(abs_path)
new_path = str(abs_path) + ".old"
print(new_path)
```

What path would you get if you created a pathlib `Path` object from `os`
`.pardir`? Try it to find out.

```
test_path = pathlib.Path(os.pardir)
print(test_path)
test_path.resolve()
```

```
..
PosixPath('/home/naomi/Documents/QPB3E/qpbe3e')
```

LAB 12: MORE FILE OPERATIONS   How might you calculate the total size of all
files ending with .txt that aren't symlinks in a directory? If your first answer
was using `os.path`, also try it with `pathlib`, and vice versa.

```
import pathlib
cur_path = pathlib.Path(".")

size = 0
for text_path in cur_path.glob("*.txt"):
    if not text_path.is_symlink():
        size += text_path.stat().st_size

print(size)
```

Write some code that builds off your solution above to move the same .txt
files in the question above to a new directory called backup in the same
directory.

```
import pathlib
cur_path = pathlib.Path(".")
new_path = cur_path.joinpath("backup")

size = 0
for text_path in cur_path.glob("*.txt"):
    if not text_path.is_symlink():
        size += text_path.stat().st_size
        text_path.rename(new_path.joinpath(text_path.name))

print(size)
```

B.10   Chapter 13

QUICK CHECK: What is the significance of adding a `"b"` to the file open mode
string?

It makes the file open in binary mode, reading and writing bytes, not characters.

Suppose that you want to open a file named myfile.txt and write some additional data at the end of it. What command would you use to open myfile.txt?
What command would you use to reopen the file to read from the beginning?

```
open("myfile.txt", "a")
open("myfile.txt")
```

TRY THIS: REDIRECTING INPUT AND OUTPUT   Write some code to use the `mio.py` module above to capture all of the print output of a script to a file named myfile.txt, reset the standard output to the screen, and print that file to screen.

```
# mio_test.py

import mio

def main():
    mio.capture_output("myfile.txt")
    print("hello")
    print(1 + 3)
    mio.restore_output()

    mio.print_file("myfile.txt")


if __name__ == '__main__':
    main()

output will be sent to file: myfile.txt
restore to normal by calling 'mio.restore_output()'
standard output has been restored back to normal
hello
4
```

QUICK CHECK: STRUCT   What use cases can you think of in which the `struct` module would be useful for either reading or writing binary data?

- You're trying to read/write from a binary-format application file or image file.
- You're reading from some external interface, such as a thermometer or accelerometer, and you want to save the raw data exactly as it was transmitted.

QUICK CHECK: PICKLES   Think about why a pickle would or wouldn't be a good solution for the following use cases:

(A) Saving some state variables from one run to the next
(B) Keeping a high-score list for a game
(C) Storing usernames and passwords
(D) Storing a large dictionary of English terms

A and B would be reasonable, although pickles aren't secure.

C and D wouldn't be good; the lack of security would be a big problem for C, and for D, there'd be a need to load the entire pickle into memory.

QUICK CHECK: SHELVE   Using a `shelf` object looks very much like using a dictionary. In what ways is using a `shelf` object different? What disadvantages would you expect there to be in using a `shelf` object?

The key difference is that the objects are stored on disk, not in memory. With very large amounts of data, particularly with lots of inserts and/or deletes, you'd expect disk access to make things slow.

LAB: FINAL FIXES TO WC If you look at the man page for the wc utility, you see that two command-line options do very similar things. -c makes the utility count the bytes in the file, and -m makes it count characters (which in the case of some Unicode characters can be two or more bytes long). In addition, if a file is given, it should read from and process that file, but if no file is given, it should read from and process stdin.

Rewrite your version of the wc utility to implement both the distinction between bytes and characters and the ability to read from files and standard input.

```python
# File: word_count_program_stdin.py
""" Reads a file and returns the number of lines, words,
    and characters - similar to the UNIX wc utility
"""
import sys


def main():
    # initialze counts
    line_count = 0
    word_count = 0
    char_count = 0
    filename = None

    option = None
    if len(sys.argv) > 1:
        params = sys.argv[1:]
        if params[0].startswith("-"):
        # if more than one param, pop the first one as the option
            option = params.pop(0).lower().strip()
        if params:
            filename = params[0]     # open the file
    file_mode = "r"
    if option == "-c":
        file_mode = "rb"
    if filename:
        infile =  open(filename, file_mode)
    else:
        infile = sys.stdin
    with infile:
        for line in infile:
            line_count += 1
            char_count += len(line)
            words = line.split()
            word_count += len(words)

    if option in ("-c", "-m"):
        print("File has {} characters".format(char_count))
    elif option == "-w":
        print("File has {} words".format(word_count))
    elif option == "-l":
        print("File has {} lines".format(line_count))
```

```
    else:
        # print the answers using the format() method
        print("File has {0} lines, {1} words, {2}
characters".format(line_count, word_count, char_count))

if __name__ == '__main__':
    main()
```

B.11   Chapter 14

TRY THIS: CATCHING EXCEPTIONS   Write some code that gets two numbers from the user and divides the first number by the second. Check for and catch the exception that occurs if the second number is zero (ZeroDivisionError).

```
# the code of your program should do the following
x = int(input("Please enter an integer: "))
y = int(input("Please enter another integer: "))

try:
    z = x / y
except ZeroDivisionError as e:
    print("Can't divide by zero.")

Please enter an integer: 1
Please enter another integer: 0
Can't divide by zero.
```

QUICK CHECK: EXCEPTIONS AS CLASSES   If MyError inherits from Exception, what will be the difference between except Exception as e and except MyError as e?

The first catches any exception that inherits from Exception (most of them), whereas the second catches only MyError exceptions.

TRY THIS: THE ASSERT STATEMENT   Write a simple program that gets a number from the user and then uses the assert statement to raise an exception if the number is zero. Test to make sure that the assert fires and then turn it off, using one of the methods mentioned above.

```
x = int(input("Please enter a non-zero integer: "))

assert x != 0, "Integer can not be zero."

Please enter a non-zero integer: 0
-----------------------------------------------------------------
AssertionError                         Traceback (most recent call last)
<ipython-input-222-9f7a09820a1c> in <module>()
      2 x = int(input("Please enter a non-zero integer: "))
      3
----> 4 assert x != 0, "Integer can not be zero."

AssertionError: Integer can not be zero.
```

QUICK CHECK: EXCEPTIONS Do Python exceptions force a program to halt?

No. If exceptions are caught and handled correctly, the program won't need to halt.

Suppose that you want accessing a dictionary x to always return None if a key doesn't exist in the dictionary (that is, if a KeyError exception is raised). What code would you use to achieve that goal?

```
try:
    x = my_dict[some_key]
except KeyError as e:
    x = None
```

TRY THIS: EXCEPTIONS What code would you use to create a custom Value-TooLarge exception and raise that exception if the variable x is over 1000?

```
class ValueTooLarge(Exception):
    pass

x = 1001
if x > 1000:
    raise ValueTooLarge()
```

QUICK CHECK: CONTEXT MANAGERS Assume that you're using a context manager in a script that reads and/or writes several files. Which of the following approaches do you think would be best?

(A) Put the entire script in a block managed by a with statement.
(B) Use one with statement for all file reads and another for all file writes.
(C) Use a with statement each time you read a file or write a file (that is, for each line).
(D) Use a with statement for each file that you read or write.

LAB 14: CUSTOM EXCEPTIONS Think about the module you wrote in chapter 9 to count word frequencies. What errors might reasonably occur in those functions? Rewrite the code to handle those exception conditions appropriately.

```
class EmptyStringError(Exception):
    pass
def clean_line(line):
    """changes case and removes punctuation"""

    # raise exception if line is empty
    if not line.strip():
        raise EmptyStringError()
    # make all one case
    cleaned_line = line.lower()

    # remove punctuation
    cleaned_line = cleaned_line.translate(punct)
    return cleaned_line
```

```
def count_words(words):
    """takes list of cleaned words, returns count dictionary"""
    word_count = {}
    for word in words:
        try:
            count = word_count.setdefault(word, 0)
        except TypeError:
            #if 'word' is not hashable, skip to next word.
            pass
        word_count[word] += 1
    return word_count

def word_stats(word_count):
    """Takes word count dictionary and returns top and bottom five
    entries"""
    word_list = list(word_count.items())
    word_list.sort(key=lambda x: x[1])
    try:
        least_common = word_list[:5]
        most_common = word_list[-1:-6:-1]
    except IndexError as e:
        # if list is empty or too short, just return list
        least_common = word_list
        most_common = list(reversed(word_list))

    return most_common, least_common
```

B.12   Chapter 15

TRY THIS: INSTANCE VARIABLES   What code would you use to create a Rectangle class?

```
class Rectangle:
    def __init__(self):
        self.height = 1
        self.width = 2
```

TRY THIS: INSTANCE VARIABLES AND METHODS   Update the code for a Rectangle class so that you can set the dimensions when an instance is created, just as for the Circle class above. Also add an area() method.

```
class Rectangle:
    def __init__(self, width, height):
        self.height = height
        self.width = width

    def area(self):
        return self.height * self.width
```

TRY THIS: CLASS METHODS   Write a class method that's similar to total_area() but returns the total circumference of all circles.

```
class Circle:
    pi = 3.14159
    all_circles = []
```

```
    def __init__(self, radius):
        self.radius = radius
        self.__class__.all_circles.append(self)

    def area(self):
        return self.radius * self.radius * Circle.pi

    def circumference(self):
        return 2 * self.radius * Circle.pi

    @classmethod
    def total_circumference(cls):
        """class method to total the circumference of all Circles """
        total = 0
        for c in cls.all_circles:
            total = total + c.circumference()
        return total
```

TRY THIS: INHERITANCE Rewrite the code for a `Rectangle` class to inherit from `Shape`. Because squares and rectangles are related, would it make sense to inherit one from the other? If so, which would be the base class, and which would inherit?

```
class Shape:
    def __init__(self, x, y):
        self.x = x
        self.y = y

class Rectangle(Shape):
    def __init__(self, x, y):
        super().__init__(x, y)
```

It probably would make sense to inherit. Because squares are special kinds of rectangles, `Square` should inherit from the `Rectangle` class.

If `Square` was specialized so that it had only one dimension x, you would write

```
def area(self):
    return self.x * self.x
```

How would you write the code to add an `area()` method for the `Square` class? Should the `area()` method be moved into the base `Shape` class and inherited by `Circle`, `Square`, and `Rectangle`? What issues would that change cause?

It makes sense to put the `area()` method in a `Rectangle` class that `Square` inherits from, but putting it in `Shape` wouldn't be very helpful, because different types of shapes have their own rules for calculating area. Every shape would be overriding the base `area()` method anyway.

TRY THIS: PRIVATE INSTANCE VARIABLES Modify the `Rectangle` class's code to make the dimension variables private. What restriction will this change impose on using the class?

The dimension variables will no longer be accessible outside the class via `.x` and `.y`.

```
class Rectangle():
    def __init__(self, x, y):
        self.__x = x
        self.__y = y
```

TRY THIS: PROPERTIES Update the dimensions of the `Rectangle` class to be properties with getters and setters that don't allow negative sizes.

```
class Rectangle():
    def __init__(self, x, y):
        self.__x = x
        self.__y = y

    @property
    def x(self):
        return self.__x

    @x.setter
    def x(self, new_x):
        if new_x >= 0:
            self.__x = new_x

    @property
    def y(self):
        return self.__y

    @y.setter
    def y(self, new_y):
        if new_y >= 0:
            self.__y = new_y

my_rect = Rectangle(1,2)
print(my_rect.x, my_rect.y)
my_rect.x = 4
my_rect.y = 5
print(my_rect.x, my_rect.y)


1 2
4 5
```

LAB 15: HTML CLASSES In this lab, you create classes to represent an HTML document. To keep things simple, assume that each element can contain only text and one subelement. So the `<html>` element contains only a `<body>` element, and the `<body>` element contains (optional) text and a `<p>` element, which contains only text.

The key feature to implement is the `__str__()` method, which in turn calls its subelement's `__str__()` method so that the entire document is returned when the `str()` function is called on an `<html>` element. You can assume that any text comes before the subelement.

Following is example output from using the classes:

```
para = p(text="this is some body text")
doc_body = body(text="This is the body", subelement=para)
doc = html(subelement=doc_body)
print(doc)

<html>
<body>
This is the body
<p>
this is some body text
</p>
</body>
</html>
```

Answer:

```
class element:
    def __init__(self, text=None, subelement=None):
        self.subelement = subelement
        self.text = text

    def __str__(self):
        value = "<{}>\n".format(self.__class__.__name__)
        if self.text:
            value += "{}\n".format(self.text)
        if self.subelement:
            value += str(self.subelement)
        value += "</{}>\n".format(self.__class__.__name__)
        return value

class html(element):
    def __init__(self, text=None, subelement=None):
        super().__init__(text, subelement)
    def __str__(self):
        return super().__str__()

class body(element):
    def __init__(self, text=None, subelement=None):
        return super().__init__(text, subelement)
    def __str__(self):
        return super().__str__()

class p(element):
    def __init__(self, text=None, subelement=None):
        super().__init__(text, subelement)
    def __str__(self):
        return super().__str__()


para = p(text="this is some body text")
doc_body = body(text="This is the body", subelement=para)
doc = html(subelement=doc_body)
print(doc)
```

B.13   Chapter 16

QUICK CHECK: SPECIAL CHARACTERS IN REGULAR EXPRESSIONS   What regular expression would you use to match strings that represent the numbers -5 through 5?

`r"-{0,1}[0-5]"` matches strings that represent the numbers -5 through 5.

What regular expression would you use to match a hexadecimal digit? Assume that the allowed hexadecimal digits are 1, 2, 3, 4, 5, 6, 7, 8, 9, 0, A, a, B, b, C, c, D, d, E, e, F, and f.

`r"[0-9A-Fa-f]"`

TRY THIS: EXTRACTING MATCHED TEXT   Making international calls usually requires a plus sign (+) and the country code. Assuming that the country code is two digits, how would you modify the code above to extract the plus sign and the country code as part of the number? (Again, not all numbers have a country code.) How would you make the code handle country codes of one to three digits?

```
re.match(r": (?P<phone>(\+\d{2}-)?(\d\d\d-)?\d\d\d-\d\d\d\d)", ":
    +01-111-222-3333")
```

or

```
re.match(r": (?P<phone>(\+\d{2}-)?(\d{3}-)?\d{3}-\d{4})", ":
    +01-111-222-3333")
```

For one- to three-digit country codes:

```
re.match(r": (?P<phone>(\+\d{1,3}-)?(\d{3}-)?\d{3}-\d{4})", ":
    +011-111-222-3333")
```

TRY THIS: REPLACING TEXT   In the checkpoint above, you extended a phone-number regular expression to also recognize a country code. How would you use a function to make any numbers that didn't have a country code now have +1 (the country code for the United States and Canada)?

```
def add_code(match_obj):
    return("+1 "+match_obj.group('phone'))

re.sub(r"(?P<phone>(\d{3}-)?\d{3}-\d{4})", add_code, "111-222-3333")
```

LAB 16: PHONE NUMBER NORMALIZER   In the United States and Canada, phone numbers consist of 10 digits, usually separated into a 3-digit area code, a 3-digit exchange code, and a 4-digit station code. As mentioned above, phone numbers may or may not be preceded by +1, the country code. In practice, there are many ways of formatting a phone number, such as (NNN) NNN-NNNN, NNN-NNN-NNNN, NNN NNN-NNNN, NNN.NNN.NNNN, and NNN NNN NNNN. Also, the country code may not be present, may not have a plus sign, and is usually (not always) separated from the number by a space or dash. Whew!

In this lab, the task is to create a phone number normalizer that takes any of the formats mentioned above and returns a normalized phone number 1-NNN-NNN-NNNN.

The following are all possible phone numbers:

+1 223-456-7890	1-223-456-7890	+1 223 456-7890
(223) 456-7890	1 223 456 7890	223.456.7890

Bonus: The first digit of the area code and the exchange code can be only 2–9, and the second digit of an area code can't be 9. Use this information to validate the input and return the message "invalid phone number" if the number is invalid.

```
test_numbers = ["+1 223-456-7890",
                "1-223-456-7890",
                "+1 223 456-7890",
                "(223) 456-7890",
                "1 223 456 7890",
                "223.456.7890",
                "1-989-111-2222"]


def return_number(match_obj):

    # validate number raise ValueError if not valid
    if not re.match(r"[2-9][0-8]\d", match_obj.group("area") ):
        raise ValueError("invalid phone number area code
{}".format(match_obj.group("area")))
    if not re.match(r"[2-9]\d\d", match_obj.group("exch") ):
        raise ValueError("invalid phone number exchange
{}".format(match_obj.group("exch")))

    return("{}-{}-{}-{}".format(country, match_obj.group('area'),
                               match_obj.group('exch'),
    match_obj.group('number')))

    country = match_obj.group("country")
    if not country:
        country = "1"

regexp = re.compile(r"\+?(?P<country>\d{1,3})?[- .]?\(?(?P<area>\
    d{3})\)?[- .]?(?P<exch>(\d{3}))[- .](?P<number>\d{4})")
for number in test_numbers:
    print(regexp.sub(return_number, number))
```

B.14 *Chapter 17*

QUICK CHECK: TYPES Suppose that you want to make sure that object x is a list before you try appending to it. What code would you use? What would be the difference between using type() and isinstance()? Would this be the LBYL (look before you leap) or EAFP (easier to ask forgiveness than permission) style of programming? What other options might you have besides checking the type explicitly?

```
x = []
if isinstance(x, list):
    print("is list")
```

Using type would get only lists, not anything that subclasses lists. Either way, it's LBYL programming.

You might also wrap the append in a try... except block and catch TypeError exceptions, which would be more EAFP.

QUICK CHECK: __GETITEM__ The example use of __getitem__ above is very limited and won't work correctly in many situations. What are some cases in which the implementation above will fail or work incorrectly?

This implementation will not work if you try to access an item directly by index; neither can you move backward.

TRY THIS: IMPLEMENTING LIST SPECIAL METHODS Try implementing the __len__ and __delitem__ special methods listed earlier, as well as an append method. The implementation is in bold in the code.

```
class TypedList:
    def __init__(self, example_element, initial_list=[]):
        self.type = type(example_element)
        if not isinstance(initial_list, list):
            raise TypeError("Second argument of TypedList must "
                            "be a list.")
        for element in initial_list:
            self.__check(element)
        self.elements = initial_list[:]
    def __check(self, element):
        if type(element) != self.type:
            raise TypeError("Attempted to add an element of "
                            "incorrect type to a typed list.")
    def __setitem__(self, i, element):
        self.__check(element)
        self.elements[i] = element
    def __getitem__(self, i):
        return self.elements[i]

    # added methods
    def __delitem__(self, i):
        del self.elements[i]
    def __len__(self):
        return len(self.elements)
    def append(self, element):
        self.__check(element)
        self.elements.append(element)

x = TypedList(1, [1,2,3])
print(len(x))
x.append(1)
del x[2]
```

QUICK CHECK: SPECIAL METHOD ATTRIBUTES AND SUBCLASSING EXISTING TYPES Suppose that you want a dictionary like type that allows only strings as keys (maybe to make it work like a `shelf` object, as described in Chapter 13). What options would you have for creating such a class? What would be the advantages and disadvantages of each option?

You could use the same approach as you did for `TypedList` and inherit from the `UserDict` class. You could also inherit directly from `dict`, or you could implement all of the `dict` functionality yourself.

Implementing everything yourself provides the most control but is the most work and most prone to bugs. If the changes you need to make are small (in this case, just checking the type before adding a key), it might make the most sense to inherit directly from `dict`. On the other hand, inheriting from `UserDict` is probably safest, because the internal `dict` object will continue to be a regular `dict`, which is a highly optimized and mature implementation.

B.15 Chapter 18

QUICK CHECK: PACKAGES Suppose that you're writing a package that takes a URL, retrieves all images on the page pointed to by that URL, resizes them to a standard size, and stores them. Leaving aside the exact details of how each of these functions will be coded, how would you organize those features into a package?

The package will be performing three types of actions: fetching a page and parsing the HTML for image URLs, fetching the images, and resizing the images. For this reason, you might consider having three modules to keep the actions separate:

```
picture_fetch/
    __init__.py
    find.py
    fetch.py
    resize.py
```

LAB 18: CREATE A PACKAGE In chapter 14, you added error handling to the text cleaning and word frequency counting module you created in chapter 11. Refactor that code into a package containing one module for the cleaning functions, one for the processing functions, and one for the custom exceptions. Then write a simple main function that uses all three modules.

```
word_count
    __init__.py
    exceptions.py
    cleaning.py
    counter.py
```

B.16 Chapter 20

QUICK CHECK: CONSIDER THE CHOICES Take a moment to consider your options for handling the tasks identified above. What modules in the standard library can you think of that will do the job? If you want to, you can even stop right now, work out the code to do it, and compare your solution with the one you'll develop in the next section.

From the standard library, use `datetime` for managing the dates/times of the files, and either `os.path` and `os` or `pathlib` for renaming and archiving the files.

QUICK CHECK: POTENTIAL PROBLEMS   Because the previous solution is very simple, there are likely to be many situations that it won't handle well. What are some potential issues or problems that might arise with the script above? How might you remedy these problems?

Multiple files during the same day would be a problem, for one thing. If you have lots of files, navigating the archive directory will become increasingly difficult.

Consider the naming convention used for the files, which is based on the year, month and name, in that order. What advantages do you see in that convention? What might be the disadvantages? Can you make any arguments for putting the date string somewhere else in the filename, such as the beginning or the end?

Using year-month-day date formats makes a text-based sort of the files sort by date as well. Putting the date at the end of the filename but before the extension makes it more difficult to parse the date element visually.

TRY THIS: IMPLEMENTATION OF MULTIPLE DIRECTORIES   Using the code you developed in the section above as a starting point, how would you modify it to implement archiving each set of files in subdirectories named according to the date received? Feel free to take the time to implement the code and test it.

```
import datetime
import pathlib

FILE_PATTERN = "*.txt"
ARCHIVE = "archive"

if __name__ == '__main__':

    date_string = datetime.date.today().strftime("%Y-%m-%d")

    cur_path = pathlib.Path(".")

    new_path = cur_path.joinpath(ARCHIVE, date_string)
    new_path.mkdir()

    paths = cur_path.glob(FILE_PATTERN)

    for path in paths:
        path.rename(new_path.joinpath(path.name))
```

QUICK CHECK: ALTERNATE SOLUTIONS How might you create a script that does the same thing without using `pathlib`? What libraries and functions would you use?

You'd use the `os.path` and `os` libraries—specifically, `os.path.join()`, `os.mkdir()`, and `os.rename()`.

TRY THIS: ARCHIVING TO ZIP FILES PSEUDOCODE Take a moment to write the pseudocode for a solution that stores data files in zip files as shown above. What modules and functions or methods do you intend to use? Try coding your solution to make sure that it works.

Pseudocode:

```
create path for zip file
create empty zipfile
for each file
    write into zipfile
    remove original file
```

(See the next section for sample code that does this.)

QUICK CHECK: CONSIDER DIFFERENT PARAMETERS Take some time to consider different grooming options. How would you modify the code in the previous Try This to keep only one file a month? How would you change the code so that files from the previous month and older are groomed to save one a week? (Note: This is *not* the same as older than 30 days!)

You could use something similar to the code above but also check the month of the file against the current month.

B.17 Chapter 21

QUICK CHECK: NORMALIZATION Look closely at the list of words generated above. Do you see any issues with the normalization so far? What other issues do you think you might encounter with a longer section of text? How do you think you might deal with those issues?

Double hyphens for em dashes, hyphenation for line breaks and otherwise, and any other punctuation marks would all be potential problems.

Enhancing the word cleaning module you created in chapter 18 would be a good way to cover most of the issues.

TRY THIS: READ A FILE Write the code to read a text file (assume that it's the file temp_data_00a.txt as shown in the example above), split each line of the file into a list of values, and add that list to a single list of records.

(no answer)

What issues or problems did you encounter in implementing this solution? How might you go about converting the last three fields to the correct date, real, and int types?

You could use a list comprehension to explicitly convert those fields.

QUICK CHECK: HANDLING QUOTING   Consider how you'd approach the problems of handling quoted fields and embedded delimiter characters if you didn't have the csv library. Which is easier to handle: the quoting or the embedded delimiters?

Without using the csv module, you'd have to check whether a field began and ended with the quote characters and then strip() them off.

To handle embedded delimiters without using the csv library, you'd have to isolate the quoted fields and treat them differently; then you'd split the rest of the fields by using the delimiter.

TRY THIS: CLEANING DATA   How would you handle the fields with 'Missing' as a possible value for math calculations? Can you write a snippet of code that averages one of those columns?

```
clean_field = [float(x[13]) for x in data_rows if x[13] != 'Missing']
average = sum(clean_field)/len(clean_field)
```

What would you do with the average column at the end so that you could also report the average coverage? In your opinion, would the solution to this problem be at all linked to the way that the 'Missing' entries were handled?

```
coverage_values = [float(x[-1].strip("%"))/100]
```

It may not be done at the same time as the 'Missing' values are handled.

LAB: WEATHER OBSERVATIONS   The file of weather observations provided here is by month and then by county for the state of Illinois from 1979 to 2011. Write the code to process this file and extract the data for Chicago (Cook County) into a single CSV or spreadsheet file. This code includes replacing the 'Missing' strings with empty strings and translating the percentage to a decimal. You may also consider what fields are repetitive and can be omitted or stored elsewhere. The proof that you've got it right occurs when you load the file into a spreadsheet. You can download a solution with the book's source code.

B.18   *Chapter 22*

TRY THIS: RETRIEVING A FILE   If you're working with the data file above and want to break each line into separate fields, how might you do that? What other processing would you expect to do? Try writing some code to retrieve this file and calculate the average annual rainfall or, for more of a challenge, the average maximum and minimum temperature for each year.

```
import requests
response = requests.get("http://www.metoffice.gov.uk/pub/data/weather
    /uk/climate/stationdata/heathrowdata.txt")

data = response.text
data_rows = []
```

```
rainfall = []
for row in data.split("\r\n")[7:]:
    fields = [x for x in row.split(" ") if x]
    data_rows.append(fields)
    rainfall.append(float(fields[5]))

print("Average rainfall = {} mm".format(sum(rainfall)/len(rainfall)))

Average rainfall = 50.43794749403351 mm
```

TRY THIS: ACCESSING AN API Write some code to fetch some data from the city of Chicago site used above. Look at the fields mentioned in the results, and see whether you can select on records based on another field in combination with the date range.

```
import requests
response = requests.get("https://data.cityofchicago.org/resource/
    6zsd-86xi.json?$where=date between '2015-01-10T12:00:00' and
    '2015-01-10T13:00:00'&arrest=true")

print(response.text)
```

TRY THIS: SAVING SOME JSON CRIME DATA Modify the code you wrote to fetch Chicago crime data in section 22.2 to convert the fetched data from a JSON-formatted string to a Python object. See whether you can save the crime events both as a series of separate JSON objects in one file and as one JSON object in another file. Then see what code is needed to load each file.

```
import json
import requests

response = requests.get("https://data.cityofchicago.org/resource/
    6zsd-86xi.json?$where=date between '2015-01-10T12:00:00' and
    '2015-01-10T13:00:00'&arrest=true")

crime_data = json.loads(response.text)

with open("crime_all.json", "w") as outfile:
    json.dump(crime_data, outfile)

with open("crime_series.json", "w") as outfile:
    for record in crime_data:
        json.dump(record, outfile)
        outfile.write("\n")

with open("crime_all.json") as infile:
    crime_data_2 = json.load(infile)

crime_data_3 = []
with open("crime_series.json") as infile:
    for line in infile:
        crime_data_3 = json.loads(line)
```

TRY THIS: FETCHING AND PARSING XML Write the code to pull the Chicago XML weather forecast from http://mng.bz/103V. Then use xmltodict to parse the XML into a Python dictionary and extract tomorrow's forecast maximum temperature. Hint: To match up time layouts and values, compare the layout-key value of the first time-layout section and the time-layout attribute of the temperature element of the parameters element.

```
import requests
import xmltodict

response = requests.get("https://graphical.weather.gov/xml/SOAP_server/
    ndfdXMLclient.php?whichClient=NDFDgen&lat=41.87&lon=+-87.65&
    product=glance")

parsed_dict = xmltodict.parse(response.text)
layout_key = parsed_dict['dwml']['data']['time-layout'][0]['layout-key']
forecast_temp =
    parsed_dict['dwml']['data']['parameters']['temperature'][0]['value'][0]
print(layout_key)
print(forecast_temp)
```

TRY THIS: PARSING HTML   Given the file forecast.html (which you can find with the code on this book's website), write a script using Beautiful Soup that extracts the data and saves it as a CSV file.

```
import csv
import bs4

def read_html(filename):
    with open(filename) as html_file:
        html = html_file.read()
        return html


def parse_html(html):
    bs = bs4.BeautifulSoup(html, "html.parser")
    labels = [x.text for x in bs.select(".forecast-label")]
    forecasts = [x.text for x in bs.select(".forecast-text")]

    return list(zip(labels, forecasts))

def write_to_csv(data, outfilename):
    csv.writer(open(outfilename, "w")).writerows(data)

if __name__ == '__main__':
    html = read_html("forecast.html")
    values = parse_html(html)
    write_to_csv(values, "forecast.csv")
    print(values)
```

LAB 22: TRACK CURIOSITY'S WEATHER   Use the application programming interface (API) described in section 22.2 of chapter 22 to gather a weather history of *Curiosity*'s stay on Mars for a month. Hint: You can specify Martian days (sols) by adding ?sol=*sol_number* to the end of the archive query like this:

http://marsweather.ingenology.com/v1/archive/?sol=155

Transform the data so that you can load it into a spreadsheet and graph it. For a version of this project, see the book's source code.

```
import json
import csv
import requests

for sol in range(1830, 1863):
    response = requests.get("http://marsweather.ingenology.com/v1/
      archive/?sol={}&format=json".format(sol))
    result = json.loads(response.text)
    if not result['count']:
        continue
    weather = result['results'][0]
    print(weather)
    csv.DictWriter(open("mars_weather.csv", "a"),
  list(weather.keys())).writerow(weather)
```

B.19 Chapter 23

TRY THIS: CREATING AND MODIFYING TABLES   Using sqlite3, write the code that creates a database table for the Illinois weather data you loaded from a flat file in section 21.2 of chapter 21. Suppose that you have similar data for more states and want to store more information about the states themselves. How could you modify your database to use a related table to store the state information?

```
import sqlite3
conn = sqlite3.connect("datafile.db")

cursor = conn.cursor()

cursor.execute("""create table weather (id integer primary key,
   state text, state_code text,
             year_text text, year_code text, avg_max_temp real,
   max_temp_count integer,
             max_temp_low real, max_temp_high real,
             avg_min_temp real, min_temp_count integer,
             min_temp_low real, min_temp_high real,
             heat_index real, heat_index_count integer,
             heat_index_low real, heat_index_high real,
             heat_index_coverage text)
             """)
conn.commit()
```

You could add a state table and store only each state's ID field in the weather database.

TRY THIS: USING AN ORM   Using the database from section 22.3, write a SQLAlchemy class to map to the data table and use it to read the records from the table.

```
from sqlalchemy import create_engine, select, MetaData, Table, Column,
   Integer, String, Float
from sqlalchemy.orm import sessionmaker
```

```
dbPath = 'datafile.db'
engine = create_engine('sqlite:///%s' % dbPath)
metadata = MetaData(engine)
weather = Table('weather', metadata,
                Column('id', Integer, primary_key=True),
                Column("state", String),
                Column("state_code", String),
                Column("year_text", String ),
                Column("year_code", String),
                Column("avg_max_temp", Float),
                Column("max_temp_count", Integer),
                Column("max_temp_low", Float),
                Column("max_temp_high", Float),
                Column("avg_min_temp", Float),
                Column("min_temp_count", Integer),
                Column("min_temp_low", Float),
                Column("min_temp_high", Float),
                Column("heat_index", Float),
                Column("heat_index_count", Integer),
                Column("heat_index_low", Float),
                Column("heat_index_high", Float),
                Column("heat_index_coverage", String)
                )
Session = sessionmaker(bind=engine)
session = Session()
result = session.execute(select([weather]))
for row in result:
    print(row)
```

TRY THIS: MODIFYING A DATABASE WITH ALEMBIC   Experiment with creating an a\Alembic upgrade that adds a state table to your database, with columns for ID, state name, and abbreviation. Upgrade and downgrade. What other changes would be necessary if you were going to use the state table along with the existing data table?

(no answer)

QUICK CHECK : USES OF KEY:VALUE STORES   What sorts of data and applications would benefit most from a key:value store like Redis?

- Quick lookup of data
- Caching

QUICK CHECK: USES OF MONGODB   Thinking back over the various data samples you've seen so far and other types of data in your experience, can you come up with any data that you think would be well suited to being stored in a database such as MongoDB? Would others clearly *not* be suited, and if so, why not?

Data that comes in large and/or more loosely organized chunks is suited to MongoDB, such as the contents of a web page or document.

Data with a specific structure is better suited to relational data. The weather data you've seen is a good example.

LAB 23: CREATE A DATABASE Choose one of the datasets discussed in the past few chapters, and decide which type of database would be best to store that data. Create that database, and write the code to load the data into it. Then choose the two most common and/or likely types of search criteria, and write the code to retrieve both single and multiple matching records.

(no answer)

B.20 *Chapter 24*

TRY THIS: USING JUPYTER NOTEBOOK Enter some code in the notebook, and experiment with running it. Check out the Edit, Cell, and Kernel menus to see what options are there. When you have a little code running, use the Kernel menu to restart the kernel, repeat your steps, and then use the cell menu to rerun the code in all of the cells.

(no answer)

TRY THIS: CLEANING DATA WITH AND WITHOUT PANDAS Experiment with the operations mentioned above. When the final column has been converted to a fraction, can you think of a way to convert it back to a string with the trailing percentage sign?

By contrast, load the same data into a plain Python list by using the `csv` module, and apply the same changes by using plain Python.

QUICK CHECK: MERGING DATA SETS How would you go about actually merging to data sets like the above in Python?

If you're sure that you have exactly the same number of items in each set and that the items are in the right order, you could use the `zip()` function. Otherwise, you could create a dictionary, with the keys being something common between the two data sets, and then append the date by key from both sets.

QUICK CHECK: SELECTING IN PYTHON What Python code structure would you use to select only rows that meet certain conditions?

You'd probably use a list comprehension:

```
selected = [x for x in old_list if <x meets selection criteria>]
```

TRY THIS: GROUPING AND AGGREGATING Experiment with pandas and the data above. Can you get the calls and amounts by both team member and month?

```
calls_revenue[['Team member','Month', 'Calls', 'Amount']]
    .groupby(['Team member','Month']).sum())
```

TRY THIS: PLOTTING Plot a line graph of the monthly average amount per call.

```
%matplotlib inline
import pandas as pd
import numpy as np
```

```
# see text for these
calls = pd.read_csv("sales_calls.csv")
revenue = pd.read_csv("sales_revenue.csv")
calls_revenue = pd.merge(calls, revenue, on=['Territory', 'Month'])
calls_revenue['Call_Amount'] = calls_revenue.Amount/calls_revenue.Calls

# plot
calls_revenue[['Month', 'Call_Amount']].groupby(['Month']).mean().plot()
```

index

MORE TITLES FROM MANNING

Deep Learning with Python
by François Chollet

  ISBN: 9781617294433
  384 pages
  $49.99
  November 2017

Machine Learning with TensorFlow
by Nishant Shukla

  ISBN: 9781617293870
  272 pages
  $44.99
  January 2018

Grokking Algorithms
An illustrated guide for programmers
and other curious people
by Aditya Y. Bhargava

  ISBN: 9781617292231
  375 pages
  $44.99
  May 2016

For ordering information go to www.manning.com